OPTIONS TRADING:

THE HIDDEN REALITY

RI$K DOCTOR GUIDE
TO POSITION ADJUSTMENT AND HEDGING

Charles M. Cottle

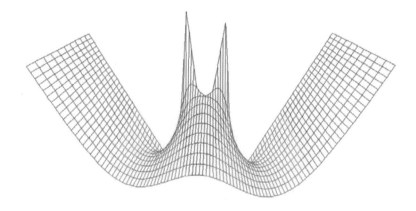

- **OPTIONS: PERCEPTION AND DECEPTION**
  and
- **COULDA WOULDA SHOULDA**
  revised and expanded

www.RiskDoctor.com

www.RiskIllustrated.com

Chicago

Published by RiskDoctor, Inc.

Library of Congress Cataloging-in-Publication Data
Cottle, Charles M.
Adapted from:
Options: Perception and Deception
Position Dissection, Risk Analysis and Defensive Trading Strategies / Charles M. Cottle
    p. cm.
ISBN 1-55738-907-1   ©1996
1. Options (Finance) 2. Risk Management 1. Title
HG6024.A3C68 1996
332.63'228__dc20   96-11870
and
Coulda Woulda Shoulda ©2001

Printed in the United States of America

First Edition: January 2006

To Sarah, JoJo, Austin and Mom

Thanks again to Scott Snyder, Shelly Brown, Brian Schaer for the
OptionVantage Software Graphics, Allan Wolff, Adam Frank,
Tharma Rajenthiran, Ravindra Ramlakhan, Victor Brancale,
Rudi Prenzlin, Roger Kilgore, PJ Scardino, Morgan Parker,
Carl Knox and Sarah Williams the angel
who revived the Appendix and Chapter 10.

Extra Special thanks to Yehudah Grundman of
The Kabbalah Centre International,
for his support and guidance.

P R A I S E

"Having attended many options seminars I can honestly say that The Ri$k Doctor Webinars have been revolutionary to my options education. Unlike many other so called "options gurus" you do not try to attract people by promising them astronomical returns in fact you almost say the opposite...which is that if I am not prepared to put in the work to educate myself about the pitfalls in options trading it can be a very expensive mistake and I should better forget about trading options altogether. This was the first time I had heard anyone say this to me.

The bottom line is that as an ex-market maker and trader you have practiced what you preach......unlike many people out there who have never traded but are more than happy to sell people courses on how to trade. .The way you examine, dissect and manage your risk in your trades has given my trading a significant edge. The weekly Webinars provide a great interactive platform to discuss and review new and old trades directly with you every week! I only wish I had found out about you sooner. In the past I have paid a lot more money to learn a lot less than what you have taught me."

THANK YOU!

Tharma   London, England

"When I think back to my first discussion with Charles in 2001, I like to think that I had "Bambi Legs" as an options trader. I had worked as a clerk on an options floor, attended the expensive seminars, and had a decent grasp of the fundamentals. I had also gone nowhere in 2 years of trading my account and was getting frustrated. What followed for the next several years was a robust education in defining my trading self. From understanding the synthetic relationships inherent in options positions, to managing myself as a trader, Charles was critical in my development. The biggest takeaway for me to this day lies in the fact that Charles was the first teacher or coach who didn't set me up for failure by giving me unrealistic profit expectations. New traders need to define themselves, their risk tolerance, and what strategies mesh with those characteristics. If you've got baseless profit expectations, you'll never find these critical attributes. Charles always had me think about my positions and adjustments constantly in the present by asking: "If I had no position on right now, what would I want."

Having a professional in my corner like Charles gave me the confidence to truly discover my trading personality and potential. I don't think I'd be trading for a hedge fund had I not worked with Charles. Don't find yourself asking Coulda Woulda Shoulda!"

Justin   California

"My goal this past year was to master and gain a deeper understanding of options. I am a practicing physician and a trader. It was a stroke of luck to come across the Ri$k Doctor, Charles Cottle, a true genius of options. RD's approach to options brings to mind a series of analogies and similarities to the field of medicine as follows.

As a medical doctor uses the CAT Scan or MRI to view potential human disease at the tissue or submicroscopic level, the Risk Doctor's laser-like perception sees below the surface of an option strategy and reveals its true nature.

"Primum non nocere" (first do no harm) is one of the most important dictums taught about patient management. Similarly, in his Webinars, the Ri$k Doctor teaches traders to first see and limit downside risks, while developing profitable option strategies, with and without an underlying stock or contract. He does this by teaching his followers to "card up" simple and complex options positions and then to use a variety of synthetic tools to see the true nature and position risks before entering a trade. Floor traders, whom RD has also instructed, sometimes use these very same valuable tools.

Lastly, as a surgeon shows how to handle complications, so the RD teaches how to adjust to changing conditions in the real market on an ongoing basis.

In the ongoing RD3 Webinar series, the Ri$k Doctor teaches by example, following the market real-time on a day-by-day basis and then posting his adjustments for each strategy as the market moves. He ultimately throws his followers into the fray and challenges each of them to construct an option strategy and make adjustments on their own that are appropriate for the perpetually changing market. In this unique scenario, his students have the opportunity of experiencing an almost real-live market trading experience, of putting their egos and emotions on the line, and then of learning from mistakes and oversights without risking hard-earned money. It's as real as can be!

For those who are serious about perfecting their option trading skills, RD's Webinar series is like an exciting roller-coaster ride through the ups and downs of the options markets. I do not know of any other place that offers such a *unique market ride*.

It is a sensational training experience!"

Murph, MD   New Jersey

P R E F A C E

WHY ANOTHER OPTIONS BOOK?

Dear Fellow Trader / Investor / Hedger,

I wrote this book so that you will come to understand that options are either for you or they are not. For those beginners who understand basic options material, this is a good starting point. For those readers who are having problems trading options, this book will help you to determine where the problems lie, and whether you may be successful with options, or whether you should stay away from them.

My mom, dad and most of my relatives don't trade options because options are not for them. I have a cousin who trades options. He came to work for me when he left college. I am going to teach you the same way that I taught him. By learning how to avoid the pot holes and surviving long enough to put together a personal game plan, he has gone on to be one of the most exceptional options traders that the industry has ever known. Experience in the markets will teach you more than I will, just as it taught my cousin and thousands of other people who I have shared this content with over the last 25 years. It starts here and it can end here too, without losing a nickel because you will be able to answer the question, "Are options for me?"

There is a lot of material in this book from my first book, "Options: Perception and Deception" (OPD), which was geared towards professional Market Makers who provide liquidity to the markets by bidding and offering every strike and month. My second book, "Coulda Woulda Shoulda" (CWS) kept a lot of OPD, but added content necessary for retail investors because it was given to clients of an electronic brokerage firm which I co-founded. "CWS meets OPD" merges the information in each of those books, because retail type traders, are now hungry for Market Maker techniques, and are much more sophisticated than industry leaders (exchanges and brokerage houses) give them credit for.

Most of the people reading this book know something about puts and calls. To be able to trade puts and calls profitably, one needs a full grasp of the concepts. The market takes no prisoners. It simply deletes those who do not have enough knowledge and/or are hesitant to make decisions.

You may be wondering how this book is different from other books on options trading. The essence of my educational work is to demonstrate where investors contradict themselves. People who do not yet fully understand options do this a great deal. On the one hand they are intrigued by a strategy, but on the other when they are shown its synthetic alternative (which is the exact same thing), they are not interested at all. The synthetic equivalent seems to be totally different. Here is one of my favorite questions:

Exercise: What amount of money is the most that one can lose with the following position?

QQQQ is trading at 37.30,
The 36 call is going for 1.70 and
The 39 put is going for 1.90.

A trader buys ten of each. Obviously, this is a good position if there is a large move in either direction but what is the worst-case scenario? Owning ten calls at 1.70 and ten puts at 1.90 is 3.60 ten times making a total investment of $3600 (10 x (1.70 + 1.90) x 100 shares).

Most people, given 60 seconds to solve this problem, figure the answer to be $3600, the limited risk amount invested. This is incorrect. The answer is only $600 (10 x .60) x 100 shares. The proof and full explanation is in Chapter 1, following Exhibit 1–10.

After learning market maker methods of trading, and grasping the concepts (confusing at first, but it gets easier with practice), it will be possible to answer this question in less than 5 seconds. Such clarity can make a huge difference in one's trading.

Today's free resources available on the Internet aid retail customers in competing with professional traders. Therefore, methods to monitor and control convoluted positions, with dozens of strikes, have been removed from this version, since retail investors have little need for such measures. That is not to say that I have decided what the reader should and should not know. I have selected topics that help to clarify concepts that have made a difference in the careers of many professional traders. I share my blunders, I think, even more than my triumphs. Most books, I would imagine, talk about all the great ways to make money but a lot of things have to go right in order for that to happen. This book is more about what *can* happen and is different because it provides realistic examples about what goes through the mind of the individual that has the trade on. It relates how the market's emotive powers influence what the trader perceives to be opportunities, based on the pricing available at any given time over the life of the position carried. All sorts of alternative ways to achieve objectives are explored in order to help round out the reader's understanding and find ways to get out of or massage a position. Unique illustrations help to sort out the confusing information that accompanies an options position.

The reader should have the following prerequisite knowledge: the understanding of basic option strategies, i.e. what a call is, what a put is, the definitions of in-, at- and out-of-the-money options, along with strike, premium, time value, volatility, exercise, assignment, expiration, intrinsic and extrinsic value and other common options terms. Familiarity with some of the common strategies will also be useful, like a bull and bear spread, butterfly, strangle, straddle, back spread and ratio spread. Most of this information is readily available, but some is better than others.

A lot of people say that options trading is akin to gambling. (There is even options trading at spread betting firms in England.) I would have to agree up to a point. There is, of course, no house stacking the odds against anybody although the human condition is an obstacle in itself. A trader should get to know his or her trading self long before charging full speed ahead. Options trading is not like the normal process of investing, although it is done in an investment account and with all sorts of investment information available to help in the decision making process. This fact in itself gives a trader better odds than any casino.

Undoubtedly, people can make large amounts of money by buying cheap out-of-the-money calls while enjoying limited risk. That is true but they will probably lose their wagers most of the time just because odds are against the options going in-the-money most of the time. Options are a wasting asset and will expire in a relatively short period of time. There are better ways to play the options game. A little amount of education can go a long way in ensuring long term profitability and help to avoid becoming a statistic.

My grandfather used to buy stocks and put the certificates in a safe for thirty years and then see how they were doing. Those were investments. The same can be done with options but only for days, weeks or months, but it is usually wiser to keep abreast of the position and be prepared for a trade adjustment.

Traditionally bear markets have been bad for the brokerage business, to say the least, but options can be a trader's best friend in a bear market and when the world gets on board with what these products can do, look out!

As the NASD[1] says, "Options are not suitable for everyone". I agree, but not enough people who they are suitable for are using them yet. I believe that options are for almost all stockholders. Why? Because a long stock position acts almost exactly the same as a long call and a short put at the same strike. Keeping this in mind, and the fact that markets decline on occasion, people should be thinking what could be done about the short put aspect of their long stock positions. They could

---

[1] **NASD**

National Association of Securities Dealers

cover (buy back) that put until things calm down, or perhaps buy a different put above or below it, or two for each one. The same people should always be considering position protection in addition to enhancement, because even without a bear market stocks can plummet.

In short, I recommend that options be used to provide protection, and for those with a taste for gambling, a limited amount of risk can be taken with carefully defined parameters, providing that the investor fully understands his potential loss.

Highlights of what "The Hidden Reality" has that CWS did not.
Chapter 1 – More clarification and Color Illustrations
Chapter 3 – 2D and 3D Graphs of the Greeks from OPD
Chapter 4 – Graphic Illustrations for Gamma Scalping
Chapter 5 – Graphs of the Greeks for Verticals and More on Legging Spreads
Chapter 6 – 2D and 3D Graphs of the Greeks for Butterflies, Butterfly Dissection, Skip-Strike-Flies
Chapter 7 – Graphics and Dissection of Diagonals, Double Diagonals, Straddle Strangle Swaps and Double Calendars
Chapter 9 – Hybrid Hedge (Adapted from Slingshot Article)
Chapter 10 – OPD's Skew Library Chapter
Appendix for Chapter 2's Option Metamorphosis showing all dissections.

TODAY'S OPTION TRADING LANDSCAPE

Oh, you are still reading? You are determined, and that is a good sign. Please be prepared to work hard, be patient and make sure that you understand options to the fullest extent possible. If you are not prepared to make this commitment, then stay away from options. You may be lucky for a while, but not long term. Why? because there is a lot of hype out there. Your email inbox is probably full of it -- How you can make unbelievable returns. Guess what? It is unbelievable because it is not true. The best options traders make about 100% a year consistently. That is about 6% per month after commissions. A realistic goal should be about 2-3% per month. By learning the Market Maker Paradigm, as taught in this book and in my live interactive webinars (web based seminars), you will be able to scrutinize what is right and wrong about all those advisory recommendations.

Option trading is on its way to becoming a household word. The players that are still around have learned from the school of hard knocks that mistakes can be avoided if they trade with tried and true rules. Most of the two-dozen 'textbook' option plays and strategies are totally inappropriate for most people, and even the remaining few investors who have used them. There are, however, a handful of strategies that are suitable for even the most sophisticated options strategist.

  Today's Market Makers are basically machines. I have helped professional market maker software vendors design their systems to automatically adjust all the quotes in the options chain with each tick in the underlying market (stock and futures, etc.). In these systems, for every options trade that a market maker's auto-quoting software performs, there follows an instantaneous, offsetting delta hedge with the underlying instrument. Appropriate market quote widths vary according to the risk associated with each trade, i.e. the bid / ask spread width is narrower for a vertical spread (bull or bear debit or credit spread) than for a single option spread and even narrower for a butterfly or condor (where there is a smaller sensitivity to moves in the underlying). This has leveled the playing field, and powerful trading tools are now available to flatten the few year learning curve down to a few months.

  Volume levels have been picking up and are going to explode into the stratosphere. This will translate into more liquidity, tighter markets and better customer fills[2]. The bid/ask spreads are getting narrower as market makers on competing exchanges fight for order flow (the edge[3]). As technology continues to progress, option spread trading will become more and more prevalent and they will become even easier and cheaper to transact than they are today. This will, in turn, allow for even more players and more liquidity.

  The approach of this text will be to stretch the reader's mind in order to allow him or her to handle any situation that can confront the investor while trading options. At the end of the day, perhaps 99% of all customers will find one or two spread strategies, to put on or leg into, that will be their bread and butter positions.

  I would venture to guess that not many speculators have ridden a call or the shares of Yahoo (NASDAQ:YHOO) from almost nothing to $250 a share. Perhaps there are some lucky souls that have ridden Yahoo from $250 back down to $11 and change, with naked puts or a short stock position. There is really no way of telling how many day traders / speculators there are that can ride a play for that kind of a move. Most of the players would have been ecstatic to take 50 points out of one of those moves in the shares. Still others would have been jumping up and down to take even $10. Still, a lot of traders would have taken their profits with less than 5 points.

---

[2] **Fill**

Term used to describe the fact that an order has been executed. A fill includes the time, quantity and price of a given instrument.

[3] **Edge**

Term used for the potential profit margin afforded to market makers by having a bid price below and an ask price above a theoretical value.

   Given the mentality of quick profit in the world of volatile high-tech stocks, the feature of 'unlimited profit potential' long naked calls or puts is only worth employing when the options are cheap to buy and even then it is a long shot to win. Without getting too technical, at the moment, when markets are volatile, demand for options keeps options' premiums (implied volatility) high. In many cases, the prices are really on the moon, making them too expensive to buy. On the other hand, margin requirements make shorting naked options quite a challenge to many. What can one then do? In a word: Spread. Spreads make it simple to take advantage of almost any type of market action.

   In order to be profitable using options it is vital to conserve capital long enough for the market to start contributing funds to one's account in the way of profits. Good luck is a nice thing to have but a sound approach begins by identifying the factors that cause losses. Once learned, options become easy to deploy without any mysteries of where the money goes to and comes from. Everything is quantifiable as long as one understands how to measure it.

All the Best,

Charles

C O N T E N T S

C H A P T E R 1

Picking Up Where The Rest Leave Off Synthetics   1

The Nature of a Position   2
Story: Covered-Write   2
Another Word about Covered Writes   3
Locks   5
Synthesis: Using a Conversion/Reversal (C/R)   5
Conversion/Reversal Value Equations   6
Put-Call Parity   9
Position Dissection - Lesson I   11
Net Call Contracts and Net Put Contracts   12
Common Locks Carded Up   13
Tools for Dissection   14
Synthetic Alternatives   19
10 Examples of Long 10*45/50/55 Butterflies   21
The Risk Profiles   21
Other Risk Profiles   27

C H A P T E R 2

A Just Cause for Adjustments   29

Trading Barrage   29
An Argument for Box Dissection   32
Adjustment Alternatives   37
Managing the Beast   38
Adjustment Costing   42
Rule the Beast   43
Option Metamorphosis   44

C H A P T E R 3

Nuts and Bolts of Options   47

Profit and Loss (P&L) Scenarios   47
Glancing Greek to Greek   50
Implied Volatility   51
Risk   52
Neutrality Depends on One's Perception   54
Delta   55
Gamma   59

Relatively Gamma   63
Theta   65
Vega or Omega   69
Rho   74
Dividends   74
Exercise Nuances Involving Equities with Dividends   77
Nuances of Different Styles of Contracts   77
Exercise Nuances as they Relate to Interest Income or Expense   78
To Exercise or Not To Exercise?   79
Renting Options   80
Pin Risk   86
After Expiration News Event   87
Do Not Forgot to Exercise   89
Renting Stock Options   89
Cost of Doing Business   90
A Final Word   91

C H A P T E R   4

Strangles And Straddles   92

Reasons for Buying and Selling Premium   92
Reasons for Shorting Premium   95
Pontification: Shorting Naked Premium   96
Properties of Strangles and Straddles   97
Gamma Scalping   100
Dynamic Gamma Scalping   110
Spread Scalping   111
Break-Even Analysis   111
Missing the Hedge   113

C H A P T E R   5

Verticals (Bull and Bear Spreads) & Collars   115

Speculative Considerations When Using Verticals   116
Premium: Time and Implied Volatility Effects   117
Premium Perspective   120
Pricing and the Greeks   122
Hedging By Collaring Long Underlying Into a Vertical   125
Rolling/Adjusting Speculative Trades Using Verticals   127
Legging Options in a Click   131
Adjusting the Leg Size   135
Volatility Trading   135
Pricing of Ratios   140
Defensive Flattening of Ratio Spreads   142

Assessing Risk in Ratio Spreads and Backspreads
  Through Ratio Analysis 143
Unbelievable Moves 145
Conclusion 147

C H A P T E R   6

Wingspreads **148**

Butterfly Structure 148
Iron Wingspreads 153
The Greeks of a Butterfly 154
        -Delta 154
        -Gamma 156
        -Vega 156
        -Theta 160
Comparing the Pricing of Butterflies 160
Using Butterflies to Speculate Directionally Can be a Challenge 162
Time Out for a Quick Lesson 163
Options Matrix 166
Condors and Stretched-Out Condors 167
Embedded Butterflies in Wide Butterflies 169
Wingspread Dissection in Practice 170
Skip-Strike-Flies 175
Ratioed Verticals/Unbalanced Butterflies 177
Why Market Makers use Dissection 178
Conclusion 179

C H A P T E R   7

Multi Expiration Spreads **180**

Jelly Rolls 181
Jelly Roller 183
Calendar Spreads: Briefly 184
Time Spread Value 185
Time Spread Price Arc as a Pricing Tool 186
Warning: Don't be a Sucker 187
Diagonals 188
Exercise/ Assignment 190
Double Diagonals, Straddle-Strangle-Swaps,
        Calendarized Wing Spreads 190
Double Time Spreads or Strangle Swaps 194
Conclusion 195

C H A P T E R 8

Market Makers Insights   196

The Edge   197
Fair Value Equations Including Banking   198
Interest Rate Exposure   199
Banking: The Concepts of Borrowing and Lending   200
Short Stock Inventory Problems and Squeezes   201
Equity (Stock) Reversal (Without Dividend)   202
Implied Interest Rate on an Equity
        Conversion/Reversal (No Dividend)   204
Interest Rate Setting in Your Options Pricing Tool   205
Equity Conversion/ Reversal (With Dividend)   207
Jelly Roll: Equities   208
OEX Conversion/ Reversal   208
OEX Synthetic Futures and Theoretical Values   209
The OEX Early Exercise   210
Boxes   212
European-Style Boxes   213
Implied Interest Rate on a Box Trade   213
The Equity Box   214
Exercising and the Money   215
Explanation of Residual Price   217
Stocks Involved in Tender offers   217
        1. Deal Date   218
        2. The Pro Rata Factor   218
        3. Borrowing Shares   219
The Chiron Tender Offer   220
Other Tid-Bits   223
Tax Games   223
Interdepartmental Games   224
Bad Creditor Borrowing Games   224
Conclusion   225

C H A P T E R 9   226

Hybrid Hedging   226

Suitability Issues   227
Time Requirements   227
Capital Allocation   228
Actual Structure   228
Wingspread Dissection   229

Example Pre-Trade Confirmation 232
Closer to Delta Neutral Anyone? 233
How About a Play in Either Direction? 235
Comparison of Ratios 235
Conclusion 236

C H A P T E R   1 0 **237**

You Can Live With or Without Skew **237**
Where Does the Skew Come From? 237
Skew Shapes 238
Modeling the Skew 241
The Day the Skew was Born (For the Author) 243
Skew Library 246
    -Reversal 247
    -Long Box 250
    -Long At-the-Money Call 253
    -Long Out-of-the-Money Put 256
    -Long At-the-Money Straddle 259
    -Short At-the-Money Strangle 262
    -Bull Spread 265
    -Bear Spread 268
    -At-the-Money Butterfly 271
    -Stretched-Out Condor 274
    -Call Ratio Spread 277
    -Put Ratio Spread 280
    -Call Back Spread 283
    -Put Back Spread 286
    -Risk Conversion 289
    -Risk Reversal 292
    -Short Semi-Future 295
    -Call Batwings 298
    -Put Batwings 301
    -Batman Spreads 304
Conclusion 307

C H A P T E R   1 1

Option Dialogue **308**

Getting Started 309
Pulling the Trigger 315
Conclusion 349

E P I L O G U E   **350**

A P P E N D I X : O P T I O N S   M E T A M O R P H O S I S   **352**

G L O S S A R Y   **363**

I N D E X   **406**

C H A P T E R

1

PICKING UP WHERE THE REST LEAVE OFF:

SYNTHETICS

When talking about options, we are talking about alternatives. By studying alternatives and the relationships between various option configurations, it is possible to gain considerable insight into feasible trading strategies and the amount of risk involved in each. A position may be looked at in many different ways. There is the raw (actual) position consisting of the exact options that contribute to an overall strategy. For every raw position there are a number of alternative positions called synthetic positions (synthetics). A synthetic position has the same risk profile as its raw position and achieves the same objectives. Once the reader fully grasps the concept of synthetics, it can be used to assess risk with a great deal more perception. We will explore the concept of position dissection, that is, positions that are broken down into useful components or spreads, so that we may understand how these items impact the overall position in terms of quantifiable risk. This will aid decision-making in building strategies and making position adjustments to the original position (which is crucial for ongoing success in the options arena).

Following an introduction to synthetics, the basic mechanics of locked[1] positions called conversions, reversals, boxes and put-call parity are explained. With these tools the reader will be able to fully comprehend the discussion on position dissection. These tools reveal a whole new way to see and capture opportunity.

One could argue that this is much more than a retail investor needs to know about options in order to trade them. Is it better to know more or less about something that can make or lose money? Here is what

---

[1] **Lock**

Locked positions usually refer to conversions, reverse conversions, boxes, and jelly rolls. It seems as though they cannot lose money, but they can. The factors that can affect *locks* vary between products. If the options were European style with futures-style margining, a lock would truly be bullet proof.

Adam, one reader of the book said, "In essence, the CWS book offers the reader the ability to understand the actual risks of positions more clearly and how to alter positions on the fly. Yes, this will help prevent major losses from risks that you may not have been aware existed. Beyond that, this knowledge also helps you build better positions that more closely match your market opinion from the start AND, as your market opinion changes, you can choose from more alternatives to adjust your positions. Often these adjustments can be made for far less money then simply "removing" yourself from the position entirely – and that adds to your overall efficiency as a trader. In other words, the book offers lower risk and greater profits."

THE NATURE OF A POSITION

There are three main reasons that traders lose money. First, they simply have a wrong opinion of the market in a game where money is made and lost based on opinions. Second, traders lose their discipline and the patience to follow their own rules. They may have a pattern of riding losing trades, coupled with taking profits too soon on winning trades. A third reason can be explained by an insufficient understanding of the nature of a position's risk and where opportunities present themselves to optimize the position as the underlying fluctuates over time. Position dissection allows one to discern those opportunities with greater clarity. Basically, as time passes and the underlying fluctuates, real or synthetic components of the total position reach a point where they are not worth having any longer.

Consider this brief true story that demonstrates where risk has not been correctly assessed:

Story: Covered-Write: A trader once came up to me on the floor of the exchange and asked, "What do you think about selling the 90 calls at about 9.00, and buying the stock here at about 96.00, one to one (one call for each 1oo[2] (100) shares)?" His reasoning was that if the stock stayed at current levels,

---

[2] **1oo Shares**

The "oo" format as in "10oo", for example, is used so that the reader can think of the quantity of underlying shares in terms of units that options can exercise into. Therefore 10oo stands for either 10 units or 1,000 shares of stock (most stock options represent 100 shares of the stock). The "10" refers simply to the number of contracts worth of underlying. On some foreign exchanges, one stock option represents 50 shares, so 1oo = 50 shares. To maintain consistency throughout the book, the quantity of underlying will be expressed as if it were an option contract equivalent, that is "10 underlying contracts" will be expressed as "10oo" meaning either 1000 shares of U.S. stock, 10 futures contracts (one futures contract is delivered upon exercise of a futures option), or 150 shares in the case of a 3 for 2 stock split where the option's contract specification has been altered.

traded higher or at least stayed above 90 he would have a profit of about 3.00 ($300) for each one to one spread. That assumption is correct but I then asked him, "Hold that thought to the side for a moment and instead consider, as an alternative, selling the same quantity of 90 puts at 3.00 naked[3]?" He was quick to answer, "No, never, I would hate to be naked short puts!" I then showed him that the two trades are virtually identical. Being naked short puts is very suitable for certain investors in certain circumstances but it seemed reasonable to assume that the trade was not for this particular person. **End**

Had the trader in the example known that a covered write was like a short put he would have realized that he himself would not do the trade. This is where synthetics come in. It would have been a suitable trade had the trader been willing to be short naked puts and had the financial resources to cover the trade. However, this trader did not know, that for all intents and purposes, a covered write[4] *IS* a short put. A complete consciousness of the consequences of a position beforehand is essential. No matter how the position is viewed (including synthetically), the trader should be happy with it, know approximately how long he wants to remain in the trade, and know how he will handle it under profit and loss scenarios. It is also important to be aware of the 'reason' one is in a trade and only remain in the trade if that 'reason' remains valid.

ANOTHER WORD ABOUT COVERED WRITES

The above covered write example describes this extremely popular strategy (most common in the equity market). The covered write consists of long an underlying instrument and short a call. The package emulates or is synthetically a short put.

---

[3] **Naked**

A short naked position has open-ended exposure, that is, with undefinable, unlimited risk. However, short naked put exposure is limited to the strike price minus the premium collected.

[4] **Exception for Covered Write vs. Short Put**

A short put differs from a covered write when a stock is involved in a merger, buyout, or special dividend. In such a case, a person short the put would not participate in some benefits that a shareholder would. In a partial tender offer, where part of the purchase is with stock and part is with cash or other instruments, there can be a wide disparity between the synthetic relationships (see "*Stocks* Involved in Tender Offers" in Chapter 8). Briefly, it would be more profitable to have the covered write in the case of a partial tender offer than a short put.

Out-of-the-money calls are usually written during a given expiration month against[5] each 1oo shares of stock to enhance the investor's rate of return. The premium collected is an enhancement if the call expires worthless and the stock is the same price or higher. It is also an enhancement if the call is assigned (exercised) when in-the-money because the writer's total proceeds on the sale of his or her shares is the strike price plus the premium collected and that had to have been greater than the available stock price at the time of the call sale. It would not turn out to be an enhancement if the call expired worthless while the stock declined an even greater amount than the premium collected.

This is why covered writes are not suitable for everyone. There are risks to the downside. It can suit long-term retirement account investments as well as widows, orphans and other *trust-funders* very well, that is, shareholders who never intend to sell their stock. Position dissection will help here as well, because as the strategy is working out profitably, the cheap out-of-the-money put that the covered write is equivalent to, will reach a point when it is not worth it any longer to remain short it. That is the time to roll the call to collect a greater worthwhile premium to optimize the income enhancement process that covered writes intend to be.

It was a very popular strategy during the bull market of the 1980s, but unfortunately brokers were putting the wrong kind of clients into the covered writes. It is not prudent for some investors to initiate long stock/short call positions as a spread. If a broker had asked these same people whether they would have liked to sell puts naked, they may well have hung up on them. These positions added fuel to the 1987 crash because they created more positions that had to be liquidated or required new hedges, which helped to create selling pressure and panic.

A covered write offers a limited amount of protection and is inadequate in a severe market decline. The sad truth is that many of the brokers themselves were shocked when they realized just how inadequate these so-called hedges were. I would not call a covered write a "hedge", although it can be a reasonable strategy for some people.

It is important to understand the nature of risk and the synthetic properties that are inherent in options. People too often look at how much they can win and not often enough at what they can lose. This approach has made many people rich, but it is unfortunately only a matter of time before the market eventually ruins those who carry positions that they were not prepared to deal with under different

---

[5] **Against**

Against is synonymous with *versus,* meaning "offset" or "hedged". If I have long deltas with one set of contracts and short deltas to offset them using other contracts, it is said that the first set of contracts are "against" the second set.

scenarios. Traders often suffer from tunnel vision and lose sight of the fact that they hold a position on a security that they never wanted. It is usually too late to act by the time that they realize this.

LOCKS

Synthetics are most useful to arbitrageurs who look for opportunities to purchase one instrument cheaper than they sell another or to purchase a combination of instruments that emulate and/or offset their initial purchase, with the intent of profiting from a mispriced relationship. Some arbitrages or "arbs" involve straightforward strategies while others, such as those that involve interest and dividend streams, may be somewhat complicated and non-transparent[6].

To make the best possible use of synthetics and dissection as tools for trading derivatives, one has to have an understanding of the properties pertaining to locked positions or locks. Lock is a term used to describe a position that has locked in a profit or a loss and theoretically cannot lose any money from that point forward.   Spreads that are commonly referred to as locks are conversions/reversals, boxes, and jelly rolls. Boxes and jelly rolls are a combination of the conversion/reversal. This explanation of locked positions will therefore concentrate on the conversion/reversal.   Since a conversion is the exact opposite of a reversal, the spread will sometimes be referred to as a conversion/reversal (C/R) when it is not specifically one or the other.

SYNTHESIS: USING A CONVERSION/REVERSAL (C/R)

#1, There is a 90% chance that you will never trade a conversion or a reversal or, for that matter, a box or a jelly roll.

#2, Having the C/R consciousness will greatly enhance insight and help one's options trading.

#3, The next eight pages only prove the point about synthetics and give one confidence that dissection is the key to understand options.

A conversion is a spread consisting of long underlying, long put, and short call with the same strike at the same expiration ($+ u + p - c$). A reversal is the opposite or counter-party spread, consisting of short

---

[6] **Non-transparent**

A nontransparent value is one that has other income or expenses associated with it and is not clearly visible, e.g., if you buy stock today and hold it for one year, the cost is greater than the purchase price today because you are either forgoing the interest (implicit interest) on the money you paid or you have to borrow money to buy it with and pay interest on that. Of course, if you receive dividends, your cost is reduced by that amount.

underlying, short put, and long call $(-u - p + c)$. Notice that a reversal is the reverse of a conversion. This means that if two parties trade this spread with each other, one would end up with the conversion and the other with the reversal. If the trade is executed at 'fair value', there will be no profit or loss. The object for a market maker is to trade into the conversion or the reversal at better than fair value, locking in a favorable value, for a profit.

CONVERSION / REVERSAL VALUE EQUATIONS

To set the stage, Market Makers come to work to get "Edge".

Analogy: The Edge as Defined by Airport Banks: A tourist lands at Heathrow Airport in London and needs to buy the local currency, British Pounds (BP). The currency exchange banks provide buy and sell prices. They also charge a commission for the transaction (adding insult to injury). For example, the price to buy one BP is $2.00 and $1.80 to sell one. Therefore, you could say that one BP is fair valued[7] at about 1.90, which is the average between the buy and sell prices. As travelers exchange their money back and forth, the bank is buying on the bid and selling on the ask price all day long and is making as much as $.10 (edge) on each transaction. If they develop a sizable position one way or another, they pass the position on to the currency traders who then hedge it by getting a price in the foreign exchange market, which is much tighter.

The buy-sell pricing mechanism for banks is the same as the bid-ask spread for options market makers. This is how traders hope to make their profit. Every market maker in the world would be ecstatic to get a trade with that much profit ($.10), because by the time the banks lay their risk off to the floor of the exchange in the futures pit on the Chicago Mercantile Exchange (CME), the bid-ask[8] has narrowed to 1.9000 bid, ask 1.9001 where the edge has been cut down to ($.0001). **End**

The conversion/reversal price should have a value similar to a forward contract's (OTC futures contract) value because it represents

---

[7] **Fair Valued**

If the price were in terms of BP then the buy, sell and fair prices would be .5000, .5555 and .5263 which is what you get when you divide 1/2.00, 1/1.80 and 1/1.90, respectively.

[8] **Bid-Ask**

Keep in mind that one futures contract represents BP62,500 and that the average airport transaction is probably under $100. This more or less equalizes the edge on a per transaction basis. However, it depends on the total volume traded to determine which entity receives the greater profit.

interest or interest minus the present value of the dividend flow until expiration. It can be positive or negative (+/−) and is expressed as a debit (paying out funds) or a credit (receiving payment). In other words, the C/R is a spread where the *strike* and **c**all are traded (a strike is not traded but upon exercise the underlying is traded at the strike's price) against or versus (**vs.**) the **u**nderlying and **p**ut. The price is equal to either a small debit (paid) or a small credit (received).

C/R = $(k + c)$ vs. $(u + p)$
where:
k is the strike price
c is the call price
u is the underlying price (stock, futures, bond, currency or index)
p is the put price.

The conversion/reversal price is equal to the difference between $(k + c)$ and $(u + p)$. Again, the k value, though not actually traded, is the price at which the underlying will eventually be transacted upon exercise. It is therefore accounted for in the computation of the spread price.

	Buy	Sell
The conversion *price* is:	$(u + p)$ −	$(k + c)$
	Buy	Sell
The reversal *price* is:	$(k + c)$ −	$(u + p)$

Suppose that in this example the C/R is theoretically worth zero (and it would be if the amount of quarterly dividend was equal to the cost of carry until expiration). The conversion $+ u + p − c = 0$, and the reversal $− u − p + c = 0$. Each is considered to be flat[9] by many traders. It is a break-even situation when the market maker (who competes to buy on the *bid* and sell at the *ask* price) for example, transacts all sides of the trade at fair value. If $(k + c)$ and $(u + p)$ are not equal, then a profit or loss is made. If either side of the equation is sold for a higher price than the other is bought, then the trader has locked in a profit. The following two examples illustrate profitable trades. Each generates a .25 credit (received) on the three-legged transaction, that is, a profit. The option prices in the examples are different for the reversal than they are for the conversion only for the purpose of illustrating these profitable endeavors.

---

[9] **Flat**

Conversions and reversals are not always flat with respect to the Greeks or any other exposure (see Chapter 8). C/Rs are really flat only if the option contract is designed with futures-style margining, and the underlying is a future. With futures-style margining, a fraction of the full amount of the purchase or sale price of the options can be margined with U.S. Treasury bills instead of using cash. Interest would not be a factor because there is no cash flow. In this example, the dividend, although not specified, happens to be equal to the present cost of carry so that for today: $k + c = u + p$.

If they were the same then one of the trades would have had to have been done for a .25 debit (paid), that is a loss.

For the following examples, assume that the theoretical values $(TV)^{10}$ for the 100 strike options at the stock price of 101.00 are 2.00 for the call and 1.00 for the put.

Reversal example:

The c is bought at 1.85 when the market is 1.85 (bid) – 2.15 (ask)
The u is sold (shorted) at 101.00
The p is sold (shorted) at 1.10 when the market is .90 – 1.10

Consider that the k is bought at 100.00 (because it will be traded at 100 at expiration). It represents the stock's purchase price at expiration because the trader will either exercise the 100 call if it is in the money or be assigned on the 100 put if, on the other hand, it is in the money. So:

k + c	versus	u + p
100 + 1.85 paid	and	101.00 + 1.10 received
101.85 debit	against	102.10 credit
	Net Result: .25 credit	

Therefore, the net result is a reversal that has been executed for a .25 credit (received). Since k and c were bought for a cheaper price than u and p were sold for, the reversal was traded for a profit.

Conversion example:

The c is sold/shorted at 2.15 when the market is 1.85 (bid) – 2.15 (ask)
The u is bought at 101.00
The p is bought at .90 when the market is .90 – 1.10

Consider that the k is sold at 100.00 (because it will be traded at 100 at expiration). Again, it represents the stock's sale price at expiration because the trader will either be assigned on the call if it is in-the-money (ITM), or exercise the put if it is in-the-money. So:

k + c	versus	u + p
100 + 2.15 received	and	101.00 + .90 paid
102.15 credit	against	101.90 debit
	Net Result: .25 credit	

---

[10] **Theoretical Value**

An estimated price of a call or put derived from a mathematical model, such as the Black-Scholes or binomial or Whaley models.

Therefore, the net result is a conversion that has been executed for a .25 credit (received). Since u and p were bought for a cheaper price than k and c were sold for, the conversion, in this opposite example, was traded into for a profit.

At this point, there is very little to worry about for a while but by the time expiration approaches, pin risk[11] may become a problem and perhaps there will be an opportunity for an early exercise depending on where the stock is trading at the time. Details on these factors and more are discussed in Chapter 3.

PUT-CALL PARITY

Put-call parity is a term used in option pricing models to describe the relationship between puts and calls. If you have the call or put price you could derive the other by using the C/R equation. Position dissection uses it to prove that a dissected position has the same risk profile as the original raw position. To show you a simple way to demonstrate the put-call parity, I will use the fair values from the last example for a conversion $(+ u + p - c)$. The call price is 2.00, the put price is 1.00, and the underlying is 101.00. More scientific approaches can be found in other options books that emphasize the mathematical equations[12]. Here is a simple way to understand that this conversion basically does not make or lose anything by expiration, irrespective of where the underlying settles, at the closing bell, owing to the put-call parity.

By performing "what-if" analyses (taking values at expiration), it can be determined that the position breaks even at all levels. Begin by checking, for example, at 101.00 (the current stock price), 100.00 (the strike price), 102, and then twice the strike price at 200.00 and half the strike price at 50.00. What will be the theoretical value and P&L, at expiration, at each of these price levels for the three instruments traded? What is their sum? If the sum is zero, then it simply means that there is no profit or loss, proving that the position was indeed, flat.

In Exhibit 1–1, the theoretical value at each of the test levels is shown. If the option is in the money, it is worth the intrinsic value, which is the difference between the strike and the underlying price. If

---

[11] **Pin Risk**

The risk to a trader who is short an option that, at expiration, the underlying stock price is equal to (or "pinned to") the short option's strike price. If this happens, he will not know whether he will be assigned on his short option. The risk is that the trader doesn't know if he will have no stock position, a short stock position (if he was short a *call*), or a long stock position (if he was short a put) on the Monday following expiration and thus be subject to an adverse price move in the stock.

[12] **Mathematical Equations**

Option Pricing and Investment Strategies by Richard M. Bookstaber, 3rd ed. pp. 28–29.

the option is out of the money, it is worthless. Remember that the underlying was bought at 101.00, the 100 put was bought at a fair value of 1.00, and the 100 call was sold at a fair value of 2.00.

The trade in Exhibit 1–1 will be worth zero at expiration. It follows that if either spread in the previous reversal and conversion examples was executed for a .25 credit, there would be a .25 profit. Notice also that the mnemonic, CUP can be used to remember this type of what-if example. How full will your CUP be after the trade?

E X H I B I T   1 – 1

+u at 101 / + 100p at 1 / – 100c at 2 (The slashes "/" represent position separators).

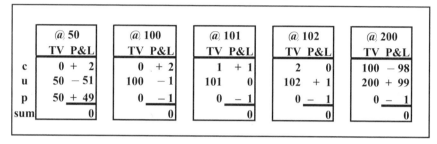

In reality, there is no need to trade out of a lock because it will all go away at expiration[13], unless the underlying causes the strike to be at-the-money creating a pin risk situation. Consider the calculations in Exhibit 1–2. Unlike the last example, this assumes an exercise of the in-the-money option. At expiration there is an exercise (X). The trader delivers the stock, manifesting a trade, at k (at the strike price: 100.00).

E X H I B I T   1 – 2

Exercise to Deliver the Underlying Stock at a Sales Price of 100

+u at 101 / +100p at 1 / – 100c at 2 / –k at 100

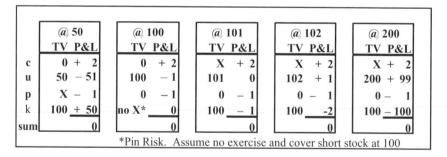

*Pin Risk. Assume no exercise and cover short stock at 100

[13] **Automatic Exercise**

Options .25 ITM are automatically exercised. Don't forget otherwise.

The premium of the exercised option is kept or retained for a short option and lost or forfeited for a long option. Notice that the end result is again zero, which proves that this particular conversion was flat.

POSITION DISSECTION – LESSON I

Position dissection (taking out synthetics) works under the premise that locked positions such as conversions, reversals, and boxes can be removed from the position because they are basically flat and can be used as filters to uncover and detect different aspects about a position that may not at first be apparent. Dissection allows the user to alter his or her perception of a position in order to have more information about how to proceed with a trade and measure risk.

Begin by carding up the position, which simply means to write it down. The origin of the word carding comes from the trading floors where many traders still use position cards to keep track of their positions. Some proprietary fully automated electronic systems have screens formatted to look like the old trading cards

There are numerous ways to card up trades and account for position changes, but the format used in this book will be easy to follow and consistent. All positions will be displayed in a **T-Account**[14] format shown in Exhibit 1–3. "Raw" refers to the actual position. "Net" refers to the position after dissection or synthesis.

E X H I B I T   1 – 3

T-Account Format for Displaying Positions

Net Calls	Raw Calls	Underlying (U) (+/-)	Raw Puts	Net Puts
(nc)	(rc)		(rp)	(np)
long|short	long|short		long|short	long|short
(+)|(-)	(+)|(-)		(+)|(-)	(+)|(-)
		Strike 1		
		Strike 2 *		
		Strike 3		
		etc.		
ncc	net call contracts		net put contracts	npc
(+/-)	(+/-)		(+/-)	(+/-)

* It is counterintuitive to list greater strikes in descending order but this has been the traditional way. Some systems allow one to rearrange the sorting so that the highest strikes are listed at the top and descend downward to the lowest strike.

[14] **T-Account**

Old fashioned method of bookkeeping displaying debits and credits.

Whichever carding method style best for the individual is fine as long as it is methodical and consistent. It is strongly recommended, however, that in the beginning trades be written down and the synthesis performed by hand even though most traders have access to computers. This promotes understanding and makes it easier to memorize the position.

NET CALL CONTRACTS AND NET PUT CONTRACTS

When the market makes a large move in either direction it is very important to know the number of net call contracts (*ncc*) and net put contracts (*npc*) in your position. Why?

If one has net short contracts, then one needs to know the *minimum* number of contracts to buy to shift from unlimited risk to limited risk.

If one has net long contracts, then one needs to know the *maximum* one can sell for taking profits and at the same time not exceeding the number that would shift the position from unlimited gain potential to an unlimited risk position.

Underlying stock or futures positions are included in the count. Net calls are the sum of all the calls, plus any underlying contracts (**add** underlying amount if long the underlying or **subtract** if short the underlying). Net puts are the sum of all the puts, minus any underlying contracts (**subtract** underlying amount if long the underlying or **add** if short the underlying). In other words, while a market crashes a trader wants to know the net amount of puts, including protection of long underlying, that he or she will have to trade to stop the bleeding. When deep in-the-money (ITM) options trade at parity, they may turn into underlying either through exercise or assignment. Put parity options move one to one opposite the underlying, while call parity options move directly with the underlying, one to one.

Take a look at Exhibit 1-4. A position of short one thousand "-10oo" underlying gains as much as long ten "+10" parity puts does (once far enough ITM) so that is why the net put contracts sum is positive ten "+10". Also, a position of short one thousand "-10oo" shares of underlying loses as much as a position of short ten "-10" parity calls does (once far enough ITM) so that is why the net call contracts sum is positive "+10" (+20 Oct 50c and $-10u$).

Net contracts should be tallied at the bottom of each **T-Account** at *each and every* dissection stage. This is the first of the checks and balances for possible errors in dissecting positions. If the net contracts from one stage to the next differ, an error has occurred and it must be found before continuing. Without this special check, an error in judgment could lead to false conclusions about the risk in a given position. It is therefore compulsory to check net contracts following each stage of the dissection.

E X H I B I T   1 – 4

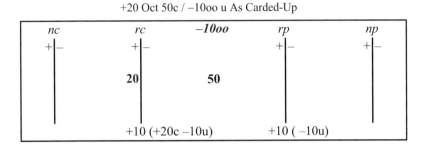

+20 Oct 50c / –10oo u As Carded-Up

COMMON LOCKS CARDED UP

In Exhibit 1–5, section A, one can see that a conversion (top) is the exact opposite of a reversal (bottom). Sometimes the spread is referred to by one name: conversion/reversal. Section B shows a long box (top) and short box (bottom). Section C shows a long jelly roll (top) and short jelly roll (bottom). The top jelly roll is regarded as long because it is long time (long the further dated combo[15] and short the near term). The opposite is true for the short jelly roll.

E X H I B I T   1 – 5

Position Configurations

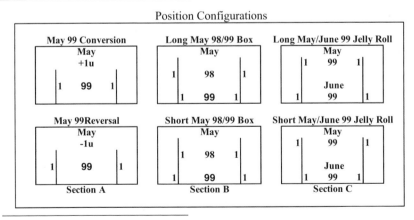

---

[15] **Combo**

Trading jargon for a combination. Usually refers to a same strike call and put "combo" where one is long and the other is short, creating synthetic underlying and is often another term for synthetic stock. The amount of long options and short options nets out to zero. Buying a combo is buying synthetic stock; selling a combo is selling synthetic stock. For example, long a 60 combo is long 1*60 call and short 1*60 *put*. Another type of combo can consist of options at two different strikes in which case it would not be synthetic stock.

An examination of the use of a simple conversion or reverse conversion (reversal) to "synthesize out" a different position shows you something about the risk that may not have been perceived before the dissection process.

Once the properties of put-call parity are understood, it will be easy to understand that long a call is equal to long underlying and long a put of the same strike ($+c = +u+p$).

If	$+c = +u+p$	then;	$-c = -u-p$
and	$+p = +c-u$	and	$-p = -c+u$
and	$+u = +c-p$	and	$-u = -c+p$

Therefore, a conversion $= +u+p-c = 0$ and
a reversal $= -u-p+c = 0$.

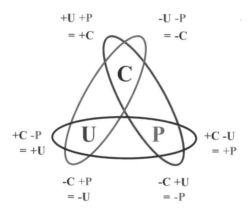

$$+U\ +P$$
$$=\ +C$$

$$-U\ -P$$
$$=\ -C$$

C

$$+C\ -P$$
$$=\ +U$$

U   P

$$+C\ -U$$
$$=\ +P$$

$$-C\ +P$$
$$=\ -U$$

$$-C\ +U$$
$$=\ -P$$

Any of the individual components, **C, U** or **P** by itself can be emulated by the other two components, with the plus sign for long and the minus sign for short the conversion/reversal. For example, as illustrated above, the blue **C** on its own equals the **U** and the **P** grouped together in a blue oval. Specifically, when the **+U** and the **+P** are both long (+) it equals a long **+C** (displayed to the upper left of the big blue **C**) and when the **-U** and **-P** are both short (-) they equal a short **-C** (displayed to the upper right of the big blue **C**).   The red **P** corresponds to what is in the red oval and the purple **U** corresponds to what is in the purple oval.

TOOLS FOR DISSECTION

There are five tools that can be used for position dissection. Only two will be introduced in this chapter; the SynTool, which sets aside Conversions/Reversals and the BoxTool, which sets aside Boxes.

SynTool ∫   **BoxTool** ☐

Although introduced below, the remaining three will be presented when appropriate; the WingTool that sets aside Butterflies, Condors, Irons, etc., the TimeTool that sets aside Calendar spreads and the JellyRoller that sets aside Jelly Rolls.

WingTool ω   TimeTool T   JellyRoller J

SynTool: Using the SynTool is basically taking out a conversion or a reversal at a single strike which removes the cloudiness that the underlying causes. Everyone should remain cognizant that C/Rs and boxes have some additional, contract-specific risks. These risks should not be ignored because they are still alive, even though they represent a lower priority than the risk that the trader wishes to focus on. The position can be likened to a bunch of fires that need to be contained and then later, put out. Once it has been established where the biggest fire is and it has been contained, lesser fires can be attended to. The trader develops a hierarchy of risks, including C/Rs and boxes, so that the focus remains on the imminent danger, the most risky aspect of his position. The trader may not be able to attend to lower priorities, but at least he or she will be in control of the major risk of the position. One can remove C/Rs from the position with an *imaginary* trade by using a 3-piece SynTool (one for the **C**, one for the **U** and one for the **P**). It may seem strange to do this, especially if there is no complete C/R in the position. When a position is synthesized, the intent is to view that position differently and thereby gain a new awareness for future adjustments. The awareness comes from turning some calls into puts at the same strike, and at another strike turning the puts into calls. Any long underlying $(+ u)$ is turned into a long combo_meaning $(+ c - p)$ usually and any $(- u)$ is turned into a short combo $(- c + p)$. The underlying does not always have to be changed into a combo. Sometimes a $(+ c)$ may be turned into a $(+ u + p)$, or a $(+ p)$ into a $(+ c - u)$ depending on the situation.

To be used properly, the SynTool (ç) must be used in a group of three (imaginary trades) for much the same reason that in accounting there is an offsetting credit for every debit. If a bookkeeper posts a debit, a credit has to be posted somewhere or the books are out of balance. If one part of the 3-piece SynTool is missing, the position will be out of balance and not synthetic to the raw position. This will result in a misperception of the position for risk assessment.

The SynTool acts as a template which can be overlaid on an existing position to reveal a less ambiguous (synthetic) position. To demonstrate the point about the Covered Write mentioned earlier, let's apply the SynTool to the position enquired about. The proposed position was to buy **10o** underlying stock at 96.00 and write (short or sell) **10** of the 90 calls at 9.00. By overlaying an imaginary trade (Exhibit 1-6), in this case a 90 reversal, 10 times, that liquidates the stock and calls and initiates a shorting of 10 of the 90 puts, leaving **10** naked short puts. We now would pay primary attention to the Short Puts and virtually ignore the ~~Long Underlying~~ and ~~Short Call.~~ It is easier to deal with one simple (synthetic) contract than the (actual) spread. Its price is absolute. There are no calculations. It is right in front of us all the time.

E X H I B I T   1 – 6

Embedded Conversion Set Aside by SynTool Dissection of Imaginary Reversal

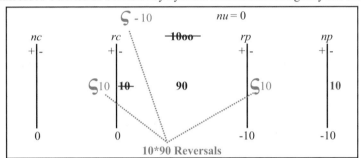

10*90 Reversals

There is only one way to use the SynTool in this particular example but in other positions with several strikes, it can be used at any strike, or used in reverse, yielding many synthetic versions of the trade. It is up to the trader to decide how the position is best viewed. One possibility is a way that shows a trading opportunity, for example the elements that are two expensive to be long or too cheap to be short given the remaining time and replacement candidates. This choice will vary among traders according to styles, current, market opinion, profit objectives, risk threshold, and experience. Irrespective of how the position is viewed, it is the same as its synthetic versions. The way the trader views his or her position depends on the time in the expiration cycle, the price level of the underlying, the implied volatilities, the implied volatility skew[16] shape, and the trader's market objectives.

---

[16] **Implied Volatility Skew**

The implied volatility skew shape, which is often called the skew or the smile, refers to the graph of implied volatility levels plotted against each strike for a given month. *Volatility skew*, or just "skew", arises when the implied volatilities of options in one month on one stock are not equal across the different *strike* prices. For example, there is skew in XYZ April options when the 80 strike has an implied volatility of 45%, the 90 strike has an implied volatility of 47%, and the 100 strike has an *implied volatility* of 50%. If the implied volatilities of options in one month on one stock ARE equal across the different strike prices, the skew is said to be "flat". You should be aware of volatility skew because it can dramatically change the risk of your position when the price of the stock begins to move.

Example: Answer this question: What would the trader want the market to do if he or she had the following position Long 20 Oct 50 calls (at-the-money) and short 10oo underlying (+20 Oct 50c / −10oo$u$)? In live appearances, a show of hands, results in differing opinions. When dissected all the opinions become one: the market needs to move either way fast.

First, the trader cards up the position, as shown in Exhibit 1–4, then dissects it, as shown in Exhibit 1–7, to help with the risk assessment.

E X H I B I T   1 – 7

+10 Synthetic Straddles

After Dissecting Out 10 Reversals by an Imaginary Trade of 10 Conversions

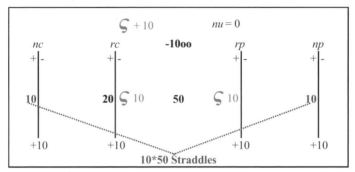

By overlaying the SynTool template, a locked strategy, in this case a conversion, as an imaginary trade, 10 long straddles can be seen. If 10 actual conversions were traded subsequently, the resulting position would in fact, become 10 long straddles. If the conversion dissection is applied (the imaginary opposite or counter conversion trade) it removes the embedded reversal from the position. For risk control, the straddles become the first priority and the reversal becomes the second.

To prove that there is a reversal embedded in the position, notice the original raw position, long 20 Oct 50 calls and short 10oo underlying (+20 Oct 50c -10oo$u$), but this time, say the trader sells *10 straddles in an actual trade* (actual trades are italicized in Exhibit 1–8). The resulting position is 10 reversals at the 50 strike (10*50 Reversals)[17].

It does not matter whether a set of three SynTools are used first or for that matter a set of four BoxTools, as long as each is a complete set and the proper longs and shorts are adhered to.

BoxTool: Using the BoxTool is basically taking out a conversion at one strike and a reversal at the other, without the underlying positions

---

[17] *

The asterisk is used to separate Quantity from Strike throughout the book.

that would offset each other. Once one of these locked positions is removed from the position, we can then see a new position. The C/R and box positions are referred to as zero-sum spreads, meaning they are basically flat. Remember the exercise from the "Preface".

E X H I B I T   1 – 8

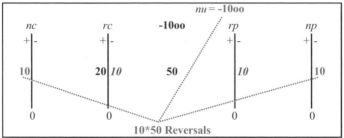

10*50 Reversals as a Result of Selling 10 Actual Straddles

Exercise: What amount of money is the most one can lose with 10*36 Calls bought at 1.70 and 10*39 Puts bought at 1.90, making a total investment of $3600 (10 x (1.70 + 1.90) x 100 shares)? Why is the answer only $600?

Exhibit 1–9 shows the conventional approach to demonstrating the expiration value of a box and it is difficult to understand merging hockey-stick graphs in order to assess risk. Imagine the confusion when positions with more strikes and different ratios are introduced. Learning the dissection methods presented in this book will be a little unusual at first, but can soon become second nature, with a little practice.

E X H I B I T   1 – 9

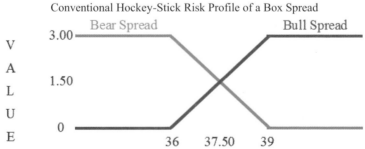

Conventional Hockey-Stick Risk Profile of a Box Spread

To demonstrate the answer, alter the view of the Raw Position (see Exhibit 1–10): 10*36C/39P Guts Strangles going for 3.60 by applying 10 Short 3.00 Boxes using the BoxTool (+10 36/39 Boxes are embedded in the position).the position).

One can much more easily answer a new question, and this time get it right: What amount of money is the most one can lose with 10*36

Puts bought at .40 and 10*39 Calls bought at .20, making a total investment of $600 (10 x (.40 + .20) x 100 shares)?

The minimum value for this position is not "zero" as human nature forces us to believe. Rather it is $3000 (10x 3.00 x 100 shares). The 3.00 Box will hold that value all the way to expiration.

E X H I B I T   1 – 1 0

10*36C/39P Guts Strangles is Synthetically Equivalent to 10*36P/39C Strangles

Because it Contains 10 Embedded 36/39 Box Spreads

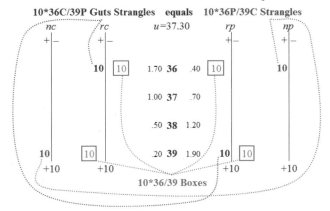

SYNTHETIC ALTERNATIVES

This area includes many of the typical theoretical "hockey-stick" graphs (risk profiles) presented in the pamphlets put out by exchanges, banks, and brokerage houses, and in other books on options, as well as on many web sites. A good one can be found at The Options Institute (www.theocc.com). If you are still challenged by the basics, stop reading and come back to this point when you are ready. This book will be patiently waiting. Rather than reinvent the wheel, the following hockey stick graphs in this chapter are provided as a reference for the synthetics that apply to them. The vertical-axis represents the potential profit and loss as the underlying price changes along the horizontal-axis. The horizontal dashed line in each profile represents the break-even level. There is profit in the region above and loss in the region below the line. It should be made clear that when discussing a position, like long a 50 call it can refer to the risk profile of one of two positions: a long 50 call (+50c), or a spread combination of long underlying and a long 50 put (+ u / +50p). Both positions are virtually identical and have the same risk profile.

There are many ways to skin a butterfly and 10 examples will be demonstrated here. But why now? Why discuss advanced strategies here at this early of a stage before understanding perhaps a lot more first?

So many people, when first introduced to options, go off half-cocked and ready to fire, but what they do is set fire to their wealth. Perhaps this preview will keep the fires contained.

Examine **Long** 10*50 butterfly[18] or +10***45/50/55** butterfly, meaning that the position is +1*45 / −2*50 / +1*55 butterfly, 10 times. Details of whether it is a *call* butterfly or *put* butterfly or *iron*[19] butterfly are not specified because they all have the same basic expiration butterfly risk profile as shown in Exhibit 1–11.

This, 'long the wings', butterfly risk profile can result from an infinite amount of contract combinations. What follows is a list of 10 examples of long "the wings" 45/**50**/55 butterfly, 10 times.

E X H I B I T   1 – 1 1

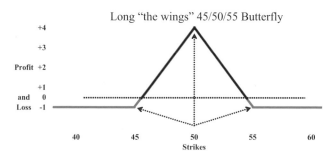

In each case the 45s and 55s (the wings) are long while the 50s (the body) are short. The first 4 are the most common and are usually executed as 2 vertical[20] spreads. The next 3 positions could have started off as long stock and later been hedged off with a married put[21]. Further trades would then have resulted in the long butterflies. The last 3 are example positions that could have started off with bullish long calls (in bold italics) and subsequently turned into bearish long puts by shorting

---

[18] **Butterfly Risk Profile**

The various butterfly risk profiles (call, put, and iron), though slightly different due to exercise and other market nuances, are for all intents and purposes the same.

[19] **'Long the Wings' Iron Butterfly**

Commonly referred to as a "Short" Iron owing to the fact that its value is a credit, money received but the wings are long and the body is short. Any butterfly that is 'long the wings' or outer strikes aims to profit when the underlying remains close to the middle strike.

[20] **Vertical Spreads**

A bull spread and a bear spread

[21] **Married Put**

A long put that goes with long stock creates a hedge. The whole package emulates a long call (see long call diagram on p.19).

the stock (also in bold italics). Again, further trades would then have resulted in the long butterflies.

10 Examples of Long "the wings" 10*45/50/55 Butterflies

1.	+10*45c /	−20*50c	/ +10*55c		Call Butterfly
2.	+10*45p /	−20*50p	/ +10*55p		Put Butterfly
3.	+10*45p /	−10*50p / −10*50c	/ +10*55c		Iron Butterfly
4.	+10*45c /	−10*50c / −10*50p	/ +10*55p		Gut Iron Butterfly
5.	+10*45p /	−20*50c	/ +10*55c	/ *+10oo*u*	Call Butterfly using *Syn 45c*
6.	+10*45p /	−20*50c	/ +10*55p	/ *+20oo*u*	Put Butterfly using *Syn 50p*
7.	+10*45c /	−20*50c	/ +10*55p	/ *+10oo*u*	Call Butterfly using *Syn 55c*
8.	+10*45c /	−20*50p	/ +10*55p	/ *−10oo*u*	Put Butterfly using *Syn 45p*
9.	+10*45c /	−20*50p	/ +10*55c	/ *−20oo*u*	Call Butterfly using *Syn 50c*
10.	+10*45p /	−20*50p	/ +10*55c	/ *−10oo*u*	Put Butterfly using *Syn 55p*

The following is a compilation of common expiration risk profiles, and associated synthetics (alternative configurations[22]) in parenthesis. NOTE: a credit (position generating cash proceeds) is **NOT** better than a debit (position generating a cash payout). Often a credit increases overtime when it intuitively seems that time decay will make it decrease.

THE RISK PROFILES

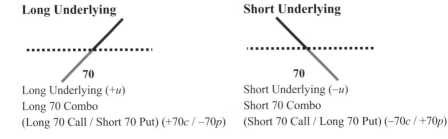

Long Underlying

70
Long Underlying (+u)
Long 70 Combo
(Long 70 Call / Short 70 Put) (+70c / −70p)

Short Underlying

70
Short Underlying (−u)
Short 70 Combo
(Short 70 Call / Long 70 Put) (−70c / +70p)

---

[22] **Common Alternative Configurations**

Examples involving one strike will use the 70 strike. Obviously, what works for the 70 strike also works for the 75, 80, 85, and 90 strikes.

Examples involving two strikes will use the 70 / 75 strikes. What works for the 70 / 75 strikes also works for the 75 / 80, 80 / 85, 85 / 90, as well as the skip "one" strike relationships, namely the 70 / 80, 75 / 85, 80 / 90. It is perhaps necessary to mention that it also works for skip "two" and "three" strike relationships, etc. Examples involving three strikes will use the 70 / 75 / 80 strikes. Examples involving four strikes will use the 70 / 75 / 80 / 85 strikes. Examples involving five *strikes* will use the 70 / 75 / 80 / 85 / 90 strikes.

Long Call

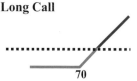

70

Long 70 Call (+70*c*)

Long 70 Put / Long Underlying (+70*p* / +*u*)

"Married Put"

Short Call

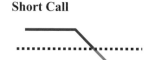

70

Short 70 Call (−70*c*)

Short 70 Put / Short Underlying (−70*p* / −*u*)

Long Put

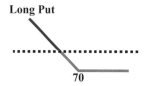

70

Long 70 Put (+70*p*)

Long 70 Call / Short Underlying (+70*c* / −*u*)

Short Put

70

Short 70 Put (−70*p*)

Short 70 Call / Long Underlying (−70*c* / +*u*)

"Covered Write" or "Buy-Write"

Long Straddle

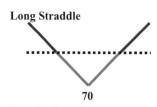

70

Long 70 Straddle

Long 70 Call / Long 70 Put (+70*c* / +70*p*)

Long 2*70 Calls / Short Underlying
  (+2*70*c* / −*u*)

Long 2*70 Puts / Long Underlying
  (+2*70*p* / + *u*)

Short Straddle

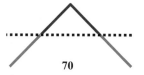

70

Short 70 Straddle

Short 70 Call / Short 70 Put (−70*c* / −70*p*)

Short 2*70 Calls / Long Underlying
  (−2*70*c* / +*u*)

Short 2*70 Puts / Short Underlying
  (−2*70*p* / −*u*)

Long Strangle

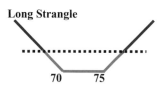

70   75

Long 70/75 Strangle

Long 70s and Long 75s

Long 70 Put / Long 75 Call (+70*p* / +75*c*)

Long "Guts" Strangle

Long 70 Call / Long 75 Put (+70*c* / +75*p*)

Short Strangle

70   75

Short 70/75 Strangle

Short 70s and Short 75s

Short 70 Put / Short 75 Call (−70*p* / −75*c*)

Short "Guts" Strangle

Short 70 Call / Short 75 Put (−70*c* / −75*p*)

Bull Spread

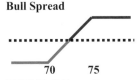

70/75 'Bull Spread'
Each has Long 70s and Short 75s
Long "Call Spread" or Long Call "Vertical"
Long 70 Call / Short 75 Call (+70*c* / −75*c*)
Short "Put Spread" or Short Put "Vertical"
Long 70 Put / Short 75 Put (+70*p* / −75*p*)
"Bull Collar"
Long Underlying / Long 70*p* / Short 75*c*
   (+*u* / +70*p* / -75*c*)
Short Underlying / Long 70*c* / Short 75*p*
   (-*u* / +70*c* / -75*p*)

Bear Spread

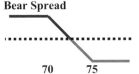

70/75 'Bear Spread'
Each has Short 70s and Long 75s
Short "Call Spread" or Short Call "Vertical'
Short 70 Call / Long 75 Call (−70*c* / +75*c*)
Long "Put Spread" or Long Put "Vertical"
Short 70 Put / Long 75 Put (−70*p* / +75*p*)
"Bear Collar"
Long Underlying / Short 70*c* / Long 75*p*
   (+*u* / −70*c* / +75*p*)
Short Underlying / Short 70*p* / Long 75*c*
   (-*u* / -70*p* / +75*c*)

Long "the Wings" Butterfly

Long 75 Butterfly
Long 70s, Short 75s, Long 80s
Long "Call" Butterfly
Long 70 Call / Short 2*75 Calls /
   Long 80 Call
(+70*c* / −2*75*c* / +80*c*)
Long "Put" Butterfly
Long 70 Put / Short 2*75 Puts /
   Long 80 Put
(+70*p* / −2*75*p* / +80*p*)
Short** "Iron" Butterfly
Long 70 Put / Short 75 Put /
   Short 75 Call / Long 80 Call
(+70*p* / −75*p* / −75*c* / +80*c*)
Long "Gut Iron" Butterfly
Long 70 Call / Short 75 Put /
   Short 75 Call / Long 80 Put
(+70*c* / −75*c* / −75*p* / +80*p*)

Short "the Wings" Butterfly

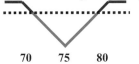

Short 75 Butterfly
Short 70s, Long 75s, Short 80s
Short "Call" Butterfly
Short 70 Call / Long 2*75 Calls /
   Short 80 Call
(−70*c* / +2*75*c* / −80*c*)
Short "Put" Butterfly
Short 70 Put / Long 2*75 Puts /
   Short 80 / Put
(−70*p* / +2*75*p* / −80*p*)
Long** "Iron" Butterfly
Short 70 Put / Long 75 Put /
   Long 75 Call / Short 80 Call
(−70*p* / +75*p* / +75*c* / −80*c*)
Short "Gut Iron" Butterfly
Short 70 Call / Long 75 Put /
   Long 75 Call / Short 80 Put
(−70*c* / +75*c* / +75*p* / −80*p*)

** Short Iron vs. Long Iron

Most traders refer to Irons as "short" when short the body and long the wings because the spread generates a credit but the risk profile is that of a long "the wings" butterfly.   The opposite is true for long irons.

Long "the Wings" Condor

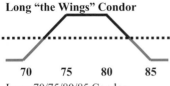

| 70 | 75 | 80 | 85 |

Long 70/75/80/85 Condor
Long 70s, Short 75s, Short 80s, Long 85s
Long "Call" Condor
Long 70 Call / Short 75 Call /
    Short 80 Call / Long 85 Call
(+70c / −75c / −80c / +85c)
Long "Put" Condor
Long 70 Put / Short 75 Puts /
    Short 80 Put / Long 85 Put
(+70p / −75p / −80p / +85p)
Short** "Iron" Condor
Long 70 Put / Short 75 Put /
    Short 80 Call / Long 85 Call
(+70p / −75p / −80c / +85c)

Short "the Wings" Condor

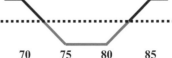

| 70 | 75 | 80 | 85 |

Short 70/75/80/85 Condor
Short 70s, Long 75s, Long 80s, Short 85s
Short "Call" Condor
Short 70 Call / Long 75 Call /
    Long 80 Call / Short 85 Call
(−70c / +75c / +80c / −85c)
Short "Put" Condor
Short 70 Put / Long 75 Puts /
    Long 80 Put / Short 85 Put
(−70p / +75p / +80p / −85p)
Long** "Iron" Condor
Short 70 Put / Long 75 Put /
    Long 80 Call / Short 85 Call
(−70p / +75p / +80c / −85c)

Long "Stretched-Out"[23] Condor

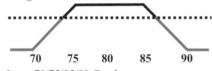

| 70 | 75 | 80 | 85 | 90 |

Long 70/75/85/90 Condor
Long 70s, Short 75s, Short 85s, Long 90s
Long "Call" Condor
Long 70 Call / Short 75 Call /
    Short 85 Call / Long 90 Call
(+70c / −75c / −85c / +90c)
Long "Put" Condor
Long 70 Put / Short 75 Put /
    Short 85 Put / Long 90 Put
(+70p /−75p / −85p / +90p)
Short** "Iron" Condor
Long 70 Put / Short 75 Put /
    Short 85 Call / Long 90 Call
Call (+70p / −75p / −85c / +90c)

Short "Stretched-Out" Condor

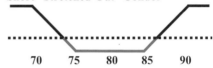

| 70 | 75 | 80 | 85 | 90 |

Short 70/75/85/90 Condor
Short 70s, Long 75s, Long 85s, Short 90s
Short "Call" Condor
Short 70 Call / Long 75 Call /
    Long 85 Call / Short 90 Call
(−70c / +75c / +85c / −90c)
Short "Put" Condor
Short 70 Put / Long 75 Put /
    Long 85 Put / Short 90 Put
(−70p / +75p / +85p / −90p)
Long** "Iron" Condor
Short 70 Put / Long 75 Put /
    Long 85 Call / Short 90
(−70p / +75p / +85c / −90c)

** **Short Iron vs. Long Iron**
See Explanation for Irons on the bottom of the previous page.

---

[23] **"Stretched Out" Condor**
The most common Condors cover a range of 4 strikes but a Stretched Out covers a range of 5 strikes or more. A condor is a bull spread against a bear spread so stretching the distance between the verticals stretches the condor to cover a wider range of strikes.

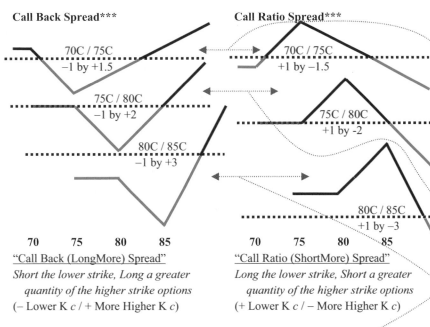

Call Back Spread***

70C / 75C
−1 by +1.5

75C / 80C
−1 by +2

80C / 85C
−1 by +3

70   75   80   85

"Call Back (LongMore) Spread"
Short the lower strike, Long a greater
quantity of the higher strike options
(− Lower K *c* / + More Higher K *c*)

Call Ratio Spread***

70C / 75C
+1 by −1.5

75C / 80C
+1 by -2

80C / 85C
+1 by −3

70   75   80   85

"Call Ratio (ShortMore) Spread"
Long the lower strike, Short a greater
quantity of the higher strike options
(+ Lower K *c* / − More Higher K *c*)

***The top ratio spread profile (opposite for the back spread) represents the **70C/75C** (**80P/85P**) spread with a ratio of 1:1.5 (1/ 1.5) and selling less than 2 for each 1 bought (in this scenario) generates a debit but has less risky unlimited exposure.

The middle ratio spread profile (opposite for the back spread) represents the **75C/80C** (**75P/80P**) spread with a ratio of 1:2 (1/2) and assumes the spread was executed at an even money (no debit or credit) cost represented by the left part of the spread profile being equal to and overlapping the dashed zero profit and loss line.

The bottom ratio spread profile (opposite for the back spread) represents the **80C/85C** (**70P/75P**) spread with a ratio of 1:3 (1/ 3) generates a credit but has more risky unlimited exposure.

Put Back Spread**

"Put Back (LongMore) Spread"
Short the higher strike, Long a greater
quantity of the lower strike options
(−Higher K *p* / + More Lower K *p*)

80P / 85P
+1.5 by −1

75P / 80P
+2 by −1

70P / 75P
+3 by −1

70   75   80   85

Put Ratio Spread**

'Put Ratio (ShortMore) Spread'
Long the higher strike, Short a greater
quantity of the lower strike options
(+Higher K *p* / − More Lower K *p*)

80P / 85P
−1.5 by +1

75P / 80P
−2 by +1

70P / 75P
−3 by +1

70   75   80   85

Call Christmas Tree

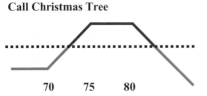

Put Christmas Tree

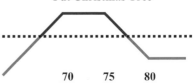

70 75 80	70 75 80

<u>Long Call Christmas Tree</u>
Long 70s, Short 75s, Short 80s
<u>Long 70 Call / Short 75 Call / Short 80 Call</u>
$(+70c\ /\ -75c\ /\ -80c)$

<u>Long Put Christmas Tree</u>
Short 70s, Short 75s, Long 80s
<u>Short 70 Put / Short 75 Put / Long 80 Put</u>
$(-70p\ /\ -75p\ /\ +80p)$

Long Semi Future or Semi Stock

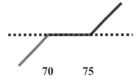

Short Semi Future or Semi Stock

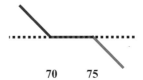

70 75	70 75

<u>Long "SemiStock" or "SemiFuture"</u>
Short 70s and Long 75s
<u>Short 70 Put / Long 75 Call</u> $(-70p\ /\ +75c)$
<u>Long Underlying / −70 / +75 Bear Spread</u>
(both *c* or both *p*)

<u>Short "SemiStock" or "SemiFuture"</u>
Long 70s and Short 75s
<u>Long 70 Put / Short 75 Call</u> $(+70p\ /\ -75c)$
<u>Short Underlying / +70 / −75 Bull Spread</u>
(both *c* or both *p*)

Risk Conversion

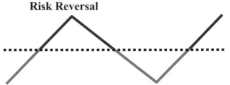

Risk Reversal

70 75 80	70 75 80

<u>"Risk" Conversion</u>
Long 70s and Short 80s
<u>Long some 70 Puts / Short equal amount</u>
<u>of 75 Calls / Long an appropriate amount</u>
<u>of Underlying in order to be Delta Neutral</u>
$(+X*70p\ /\ -X*75c\ /+u)$ [Delta Neutral])
<u>Bull Spread / Short Underlying</u>
(Delta Neutral)
$(+70s\ /\ -80s\ /\ +u)$ both *c* or both *p*
(Delta Neutral)

<u>"Risk" Reversal</u>
Short 70s and Long 80s
<u>Short some 70 Puts / Long equal amount</u>
<u>of 75 Calls / Short an appropriate amount</u>
<u>of Underlying in order to be Delta Neutral</u>
$(-X*70p\ /\ +X*75c\ /\ -u)$ [Delta Neutral])
<u>Bear Spread / Long Underlying</u>
(Delta Neutral)
$(-70s\ /\ +80s\ /-u)$ both *c* or both *p*
(Delta Neutral)

OTHER RISK PROFILES

Long Calendar Spread	Short Calendar Spread
Long Time (Serial)∞ Spread	Short Time (Serial)∞ Spread

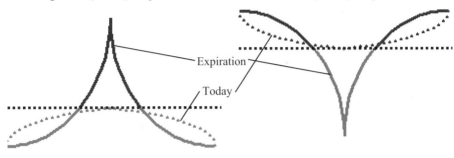

	70	**70**

Long "Time Spread" (Delivery for same underlying)	Short "Time Spread" (Delivery for same underlying)
Long "Calendar∞ Spread" (Delivery for different month futures contract)	Short "Calendar∞ Spread" (Delivery for different month futures contract)
Long Far Month 70s, Short Near Month 70s (Both Calls or Both Puts)	*Short Far Month 70s, Long Near Month 70s (Both Calls or Both Puts)*
Long Far 70 Call / Short Near 70 Call	Short Far 70 Call / Long Near 70 Call
(+Far Month 70*c* / −Near Month 70*c*)	(−Far Month 70*c* / +Near Month 70*c*)
Long Far Month 70 Put / Short Near Month 70 Put	Short Far Month 70 Put / Long Near Month 70 Put
(+Far Month 70*p* / −Near Month 70*p*)	(−Far 70*p* / +Near 70*p*)

There are a variety of inter-month spreads that combine the attributes of calendars and the common spread strategies already mentioned;

A "Diagonal Spread," which can be extremely versatile as far as profiles go, acts like a vertical and a calendar spread that have been merged.

A "Double Diagonal" also known as a Straddle Strangle Swap or a Calendarized Iron Butterfly or Calendarized Iron Condor usually involves a straddle or strangle short in the nearer term options and long further dated, further away strikes as outside (less time decay) strangles.

There are also ratioed butterflies and condors as well as Slingshot variations that behave like butterflies and condors with extra wings. The

∞ Calendar Spreads Synonymous with Time Spreads

These days, the terms calendar spread and time spreads are often used interchangeably or synonymously and describe the same strategy but in the past there was a difference. Be careful that an options on futures calendar spread has intermonth spread risk (could represent different crop years in grains, for example, that can move in opposites directions because when the options are exercised, each delivers a different futures contract. Serial refers to options deliverable to the same futures contract.

most exciting thing about options is that any Options Only Strategy (OOs) can be emulated by an Advanced Hybrid Hedge Strategy (AHHs). The strategy profiles pictured below, in Exhibit 1-12, are just a few of the over 1000 patent pending DARTs™ (Dynamic Adjustable Risk Transactions) that offer a vast array of underlying hedge opportunities that, at present have to be legged into, but someday can be filled in a single click (electronic transaction) of the mouse.

E X H I B I T   1 – 1 2

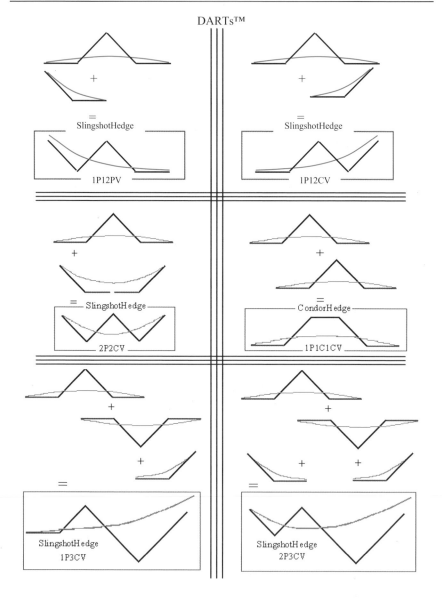

CHAPTER

2

A JUST CAUSE FOR ADJUSTMENTS

This chapter starts with a realistic series of trades from the perspective of an advanced retail customer. We witness how he speculates and manages a position in a particular stock. His position drastically changes as his market opinion changes. Readers should not be overly concerned about not being able to follow these trades the first time through, because the lessons that follow will help to develop the necessary thought processes to grasp it the second time around. Instead, it might be interesting to note what the reader's self-assessment might be. Is he or she able to follow the scenario and is it generating new ideas? Moving on, we will get a healthy dose of the thought processes involved in position adjustment in general, and we will see how positions evolve in Options Metamorphosis.

The reader will then be prepared to delve into Chapter 3 for the "Nuts and Bolts of Options", a more in-depth look into the usefulness of the Greeks.

TRADING BARRAGE

Gil Bates thought XYZ was a good value. It was down by over 50% from its 52 week high in July and Gil, fully clothed, began writing (selling short) 10 August 50 puts naked. When they expired worthless he did the same trade with the September options. In October he did it with the 45 puts and was almost assigned but the stock popped back up above the strike. He went back to the 50 strike again with the November options. Gil's trades, starting with the Nov 50 puts (Trade A), are denoted on the candlestick chart in Exhibit 2-1. Up until then, all the puts had expired worthless allowing Gil to keep the premium that he had collected. However, in November, on the last day of expiration, the stock was trading at around 48. Gil was assigned, put the stock, and therefore became long 10oo shares at 50 (Trade X). The stock dropped a few points over the next week but Gil wasn't too worried because he liked the stock long-term and his cost was a lot lower owing to all of the premiums that he had collected over the past few months.

The stock worked its way back to 51 by the next week, so Gil wrote (sold short) 10 January 55 calls (Trade B) giving him a covered write, in anticipation of the market running out of steam. He considered his position, at that point, to be synthetically short 10 Jan 55 puts. That was good because the market rallied further and the real 55 puts traded down to 4.00. He considered covering them (buying them back) at 4.00 because he thought that the market would have trouble getting through a resistance level. He did, however, first look at the price of the Feb 55 puts, Jan and Feb 50 and 60 puts, in case there was a better do (trade). After a little homework, Gil decided that he liked the value of buying the Jan 50/55 put bear spread for 2.00, twice as many times (20) (Trade C) for the same money, rather than buying back the 10 lot of Jan 55 puts for 4.00. This put him into the Jan 50/55 (+1 by −2) put ratio spread, synthetically, 10 times for a total of +10 by −20 (he also carried the Jan 55 conversion 10 times).

E X H I B I T   2 − 1

Trades by Gil Bates

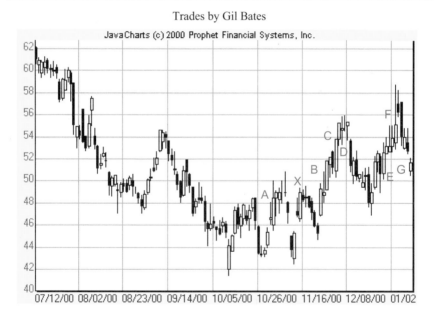

About a week later, after a breakout fake-out it looked ugly to Gil. He bought another 20 of the Jan 55 puts (Trade D) outright. The market moved lower and then began to bottom out over the next two weeks. Gil decided to buy the Jan 50 calls 20 times (Trade E). After a week of up-ticks he bailed out his 10oo stock (Trade F). It went a little bit higher but failed again, and so when it dropped a few bucks over the next few days he shorted another 30 lot of 50 puts that were almost at-the-money (Trade G).

Gil started to get confused about his position, which is what sometimes happens, and decided to dissect the position that he had. In Exhibit 2-2 we can see a list of the trades and the overall position after each trade.

In Exhibit 2-3 we can see the reasoning behind each trade and the position's basic risk exposure following each trade, by looking at the synthetic relationships.

Further analysis of this position continues on the next page in 'An Argument For Box Dissection'.

E X H I B I T   2 – 2

Trades and Overall Position After each Trade

Buy (+) Sell (−)	Trade	Position After the Trade
−10 Nov 50p	A	−10 Nov 50p
+10oo u via eXercise	X	+10oo u
−10 Jan 55c	B	+10oo u / −10 Jan 55c
+20 Jan 55p / −20 Jan 50p	C	+10oo u / −10 Jan 55c / −20 Jan 50p / +20 Jan 55p
+20 Jan 55p	D	+10oo u / −10 Jan 55c / −20 Jan 50p / +40 Jan 55p
+20 Jan 50c	E	+10oo u / +20 Jan 50c / −10 Jan 55c −20 Jan 50p / +40 Jan 55p
−10oo u	F	+20 Jan 50c / −10 Jan 55c −20 Jan 50p / +40 Jan 55p
−30 Jan 50p	G	+20 Jan 50c / −10 Jan 55c −50 Jan 50p / +40 Jan 55p

E X H I B I T   2 – 3

Reasoning Behind each Trade and the Basic Risk Exposure for Gil Bates

Reasoning	Trade	Basic Risk Exposure
Cheap way to buy stock if assigned	A	Short 10 Nov 50 puts
After several expiration Gil was assigned	X	Long 10oo u
Resistance and to enhance his return	B	Short 10 Jan 55p
Wanted an orderly down move over time	C	(+10 Jan 55p / −20 Jan 50p)
Turned really bearish when rally fizzled out	D	+10 Jan 55p / 20 Jan 50/55 Bear Spreads
Higher low after a bounce	E	Long ratioed 55 straddle (+20c by +10p)
Getting short at double top area	F	Long ratioed 55 straddle (+10c by +20p)
Taking profit but still in a strategy	G	See Exhibit 2 - 4

AN ARGUMENT FOR BOX DISSECTION

We can see why some market makers want to understand the intricacies of position dissection and go through the process, but what does a retail investor/trader do with this knowledge? Good question! The answer is that one does not necessarily have to get out of the trades that one gets into. By trading different options rather than liquidating the ones one has, the position changes to suit one's new opinion of market conditions. Some adjustments can create a minor change while others can reverse the position completely. The best way to explain this point is continue with the realistic trading scenario, earlier in the chapter, where Gil Bates has had a barrage of trades.

Gil has now got to sort it all out. After a number of trades, the practice of position dissection can help him to determine some possible next moves. It is good to be prepared before the fact. The market takes no prisoners. One has to be decisive and be ready to act fast when a market created opportunity arises. The total premium on the table is $15,000, but that number is totally misleading. Most of that money is tied up in boxes and is not going anywhere. We shall soon see what remains on the table, but keep in mind that these figures do not include a contingent liability (put side of this position) that could develop as a result of a market drop far below 45. Although it is common for traders to refer to naked puts as having unlimited risk we really cannot say that it is unlimited because the underlying can only go to zero. The raw position in Exhibit 2-4 shows what trader Gil Bates has on after about two months of trading.

E X H I B I T   2 – 4

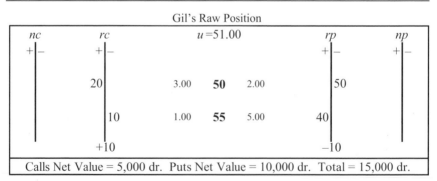

Gil's Raw Position					

Calls Net Value = 5,000 dr. Puts Net Value = 10,000 dr. Total = 15,000 dr.

Simply, this position is the result of Gil's accumulation of inventory (longs and shorts) that resulted from the market's behavior (in Gil's mind anyway). The market's behavior presented opportunities that advertised, to Gil, values that were, from a risk / reward standpoint, attractive enough to entice him into each trade. There were seven actual trades and one obligatory transaction where an option was assigned (shown as 'Trade X').

There are an infinite number of ways to dissect this position. I will start by introducing four specific ways. These use the BoxTool to remove each of the four corners of the box, one at a time. This means that Gil will imaginarily liquidate the +20*50 calls with an imaginary box trade and see what remains. Gil then will do the same, in a completely new set of dissections, with the –10*55 calls. He will do the same with the –50*50 puts and the +40*55 puts.

Let us review, compare and judge the net positions in Exhibit 2–5. Which of the five looks like the most desirable position to have from a risk management standpoint? Or does the Raw Position, the way it is, seem more manageable?

Although each position has been derived from the Raw Position, the way that each is viewed can undoubtedly lead to different decisions on what the next trades might be.

Examine the dissections 1 through 5, which follow in Exhibits 2–6 to 2–10. They each display the BoxTool as a template overlaying the original position to create five new and different perceptions. The current market prices are listed to help Gil consider his options (alternatives).

E X H I B I T   2 – 5

Review and Compare the Net Positions

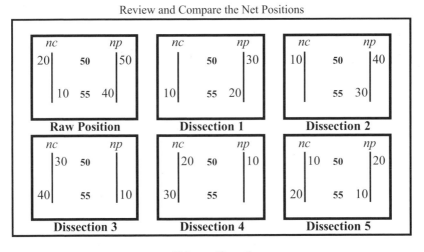

| Raw Position | Dissection 1 | Dissection 2 |
| Dissection 3 | Dissection 4 | Dissection 5 |

Dissection 1

This creates long 10 OTM calls at 1.00 and 10 put ratio spreads, each (+2 by –3) for a 4.00 debit. I prefer to think of the ratios in terms of a common denominator of one and consider that there are 20 spreads (instead of 10), each (+1 by –1.5) instead of (+2 by –3), for a 2.00 debit, (i.e. paying 5.00 once and collecting 2.00 one and a half times [which is 3.00] netting out to a 2.00 debit). This method is discussed further in Chapter 5.

E X H I B I T   2 – 6

1.) Long 10 OTM Calls at 1.00 Debit and
a Put Ratio Spread 20*(+1 by –1.5) at a 2.00 Debit

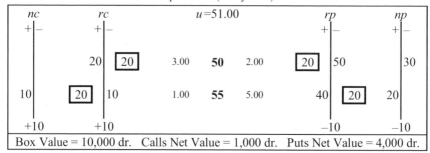

Box Value = 10,000 dr.   Calls Net Value = 1,000 dr.   Puts Net Value = 4,000 dr.

If Gil chooses to view his position as in dissection 1 (Exhibit 2–6), he can easily see that there is some potential liability from the open ended puts, exposure to the downside, and the value of the calls could be lost.

Dissection 2

This creates long 10 ITM calls at 3.00 and a put ratio spread (+1 by – 1.33) 30 times for a 2.33 debit (i.e. paying 5.00 once and collecting 2.00 one and a third times [which is 2.67] netting a 2.33 debit).

E X H I B I T   2 – 7

2.) Long 10 ITM Calls at 3.00 and a Put Ratio Spread 30*(+1 by –1.33) at a 2.33 Debit

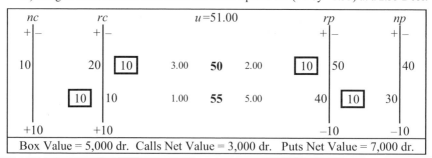

Box Value = 5,000 dr. Calls Net Value = 3,000 dr.   Puts Net Value = 7,000 dr.

If Gil chooses to view his position as in *dissection* 2 (Exhibit 2–7), and feels like taking a bit of money off the table, he may want to sell 10 of the 50 straddle to be left with a steeper 50/55 put ratio spread (+30 by –50) each (+1 by –1.6) for a 1.80 debit (5.00 minus [1.6*2.00]).

This position could profit in four possible scenarios: a decline in implied volatility, and / or a potential slow move downward to 50, sitting still for a while, or a small rally in the underlying but not above 53.20 because the break-even price is where the 55 puts will still be worth 1.80 at expiration. A move higher would cause some or all the 1.80 per spread to be lost. The worst scenario would be a large gap downward far below the short strike.

Dissection 3

This creates 30*(−1 by +1.33) call back spreads, each at a 1.67 credit and short 10 ITM puts at 5.00 (the back spread is derived by multiplying 1.33 x 1.00 for a debit, versus a credit of 3.00 for the sale of each 50 call).

E X H I B I T   2 – 8

3.) 30*(−1 by +1.33) Call Back Spread at 1.67 Credit and Short 10 ITM Puts at 5.00

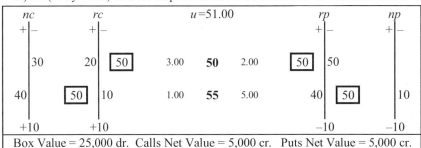

Box Value = 25,000 dr. Calls Net Value = 5,000 cr. Puts Net Value = 5,000 cr.

If Gil chooses to view his position as in dissection 3 (Exhibit 2–8), he may want to buy 10*55p leaving the 30*(−1 by +1.33) call back spread. This would only be prudent if the trader thought it likely that the underlying would spike up with an extended move, without, or in spite of, a collapse in implied volatility. Breaking down hard would also allow the 1.67 credit to be kept, if both calls go out worthless. A slow move upward to 55 would be the worst case for this position.

Dissection 4

This creates 20*(−1 by +1.5) call back spread at 1.50 credit and short 10 OTM puts at 1.00 (the back spread is derived by multiplying 1.50 x 1.00 for a debit, versus a credit of 3.00 for the sale of each 50 call).

E X H I B I T   2 – 9

4.) 20*(−1 by +1.5) Call Back Spread at 1.50 Credit and Short 10 OTM Puts at 1.00

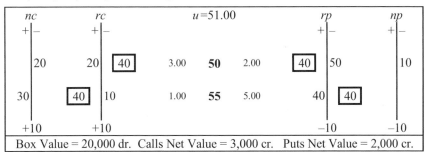

Box Value = 20,000 dr. Calls Net Value = 3,000 cr. Puts Net Value = 2,000 cr.

If Gil chooses to view his position as in dissection 4 (Exhibit 2–9), he may want to buy 10*50*p* leaving the 20*(–1 by +1.5) call back spread. Again, this would only be prudent if he thought it likely that the underlying would spike up. Since the ratio is not very steep, the rally must be huge, and happen very quickly. A slow move up to 55 would be the worst scenario for this position.

Dissection 5

The fifth dissection also uses the BoxTool with a quantity other than one of the position quantities (i.e. 20 from the 50 calls, 10 from the 55 calls, 50 from the 50 puts, or 40 from the 55 puts) in each of the box's corners. One might use, for example, the average position quantity of the four corners for the dissection or a number that seems to make sense from a position size and ratio aspect. The idea is that the imaginary trade of the box offsets the largest possible quantities of position inventory. In this case, three corners of the box get reduced while both puts maintain their long/short status, and the position of the 50 calls shifts from long to short but reduces in size. The position of the 55 calls shift from short to long, but the quantity increases a bit.

E X H I B I T   2 – 1 0

5.) 10*(–1 by +2) Call Back Spread at 1.00 Credit and
10*(+1 by –2) Put Ratio Spread for a 1.00 Debit

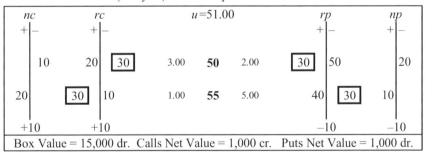

Box Value = 15,000 dr. Calls Net Value = 1,000 cr. Puts Net Value = 1,000 dr.

This creates 10*(–1 by +2) call back spread at 1.00 credit (2 x 1.00 debit versus a 3.00 credit) and 10* (+1 by –2) put ratios spread for a 1.00 debit (2 x 2.00 credit, versus a 5.00 debit).

By viewing the position that results from dissection 5 (Exhibit 2-10), it is evident that buying 10*45*p* would turn the put side into a long butterfly, which would limit the exposure to an amount equaling the cost of the 45 put. This purchase could easily be financed by capturing excess premium from the sale of up to 10*55 calls. If the trader likes the value of the butterfly and/or it meets with his or her market opinion, the above dissection leads to a rather simple adjustment.

Following dissection, the trader's choice of position depends on what the he or she feels comfortable with and what meets his or her market objectives. By dissecting the position, the trader is searching for inappropriate aspects of it. This activity serves to optimize the potential of that position.

Dissection can be a valuable tool even for the simplest hedging strategies. When dissecting a position, do not forget about the locks that are removed. To have a complete understanding of synthetic positioning it is necessary to be aware of the nuances involving arbitrage "locks". A locked position is theoretically fully hedged. It is usually not necessary for anyone except market makers and risk managers to know about locks in great detail. The reason that it is mentioned here is that the concept must be accepted as valid before embracing the methods of position dissection. The fact that these positions are not as secure as many believe is of consequence to those only with very sizable positions where a minor loss multiplied by a huge quantity of contracts can really add up.

Next Move? Gil needs to be prepared for his next move. What should he do if: the market rallies, the market breaks, if it sits still for a while or he becomes edgy due to uncertainty before an important company information announcement? The thing is to be ready for when a market created opportunity arises.

ADJUSTMENT ALTERNATIVES

There are various ways to adjust an options position and we now see why many traders seldom get out of their position the way they got into it. How to adjust has traditionally depended on one's commission structure because those paying high commissions (e.g., retail customers) did not adjust so readily. Now that stock and options markets have moved closer toward commission-less trading, retail investors can utilize the power of adjusting. There comes a point when it is time to take a profit, take a loss, or exit the trade because the reason for holding the position is no longer valid, and high commissions should no longer keep the retail trader from making the trades.

Whenever traders wish to try something new with options, they should proceed with caution. If they trade too big too soon, they can be ruined. Trading small is best for testing new ideas. When traders start to profit consistently and are able to manage positions with very little anxiety, it may be time to increase the size of the trades.

Do What You Know and Know What You Do.
Do It Right and Be Comfortable With It.

Imagine going into a dark cave for the very first time; you would go slowly and feel your way around. If you go too fast, you might trip and either fall into a hole or bang your head on a stalactite. Small steps are best to test the path. Once you have traveled the path enough times and started seeing a new light, you can follow it and can walk a little faster. With more light, you can even run.

MANAGING THE BEAST

With so many alternatives *(options)* available, it may be prudent to change the "nature of the beast" (i.e., adjust the position) instead of exiting the initial trade due to a new market opinion or pricing considerations. We saw how Gil Bates made his trades but let's examine closer just what we can do with a simple 10 lot of calls. The following example illustrates when it makes sense to adjust the initial position.

Suppose that a trader has a bullish call position, for example, long the 10 Oct 50 calls at $2.00, that was initiated when the underlying market was at $49.00. The market then rallies to $54.00. The call value has now appreciated by 3.00 to 5.00. Looking at the grid of prices on the next page, the trader can choose from an infinite number of alternative strategies in an attempt to take profits while remaining in the market with a new strategy. Scenarios A to I, which follow, demonstrate some possible strategies. Note: the actual cost[1] and the "fair cost[2]" (prices presently available in the market) will be discussed in the next section. Stock and Options Prices with the Underlying at $54.00

Stock $54.00

Call $	Strike	Put $
9.25	**45**	.25
5.00	**50**	1.00
2.00	**55**	3.00

Long 10 Oct 50 calls @ $2.00

50

---

[1] **Actual Cost**

Actual or synthetic cost based upon the put call parity equation, assuming cost of carry until expiration equals the dividend: $k + c = s + p + i - d$, or stri**K**e + **C**all price = **S**tock price + **P**ut price + **I**nterest − **D**ividend.

[2] **Fair Cost**

This is what it would cost to put the position on at present market prices. This term is only used when the trader decides to make an options trade as an adjustment to an existing position. Since the position being adjusted has been executed in the past, one would make a biased evaluation (in the present) if they used prices particular to those transactions made in the past.

A.   Sell 10 Oct 55 calls at 2.00. The result is **10*50/55 bull call verticals,** each for even money (fair cost = 3.00 debit). The trader is still long, but not as aggressively so, and has limited the possible gain.

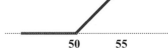

50   55

B.   Sell 10 Oct 50 calls and buy 10 Oct 55 calls for a 3.00 credit (sell 50/55 call vertical i.e., bear spread). The result is **long 10 Oct 55 calls,** each for a 1.00 credit (fair cost = 2.00 debit). The trader is still long, but for a price that is cheaper than free, and has limited risk.

50   55

C.   Sell 10 Oct 45 calls at 9.25. The result is **10*45/50 bear spreads,** each for a 7.25 credit (fair cost = 4.25 credit). The trader anticipates a downward move.

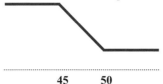

45   50

D.   Sell 20 Oct 55 calls at 2.00. The result is a **50/55 call ratio spread** (+10 by – 20), each (+1 by –2) for a 2.00 credit (fair cost = 1.00 debit). The trader would now like the market to stay around 55.

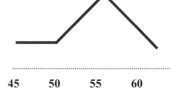

45   50   55   60

E.   Sell 5 Oct 45 calls at 9.25. The result is a **45/50 call back spread** (+10 by – 5), each (–1 by +2) for a 5.25 credit (fair cost = .75 debit). The trader now hopes for a large move in either direction, preferably upward.

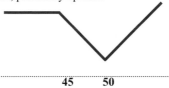

45   50

F.   Buy 10 Oct 55 puts at 3.00. The result is **long 10 Oct 50c / 55p "guts" strangle,** each for a 5.00 debit (the minimum possible value for this gut strangle is 5.00) (fair cost = 2.00 debit). This will win if there is a large move in either direction.

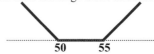

50   55

G.   Buy 10^3 Oct 50 puts at 1.00. The result is **long 10 Oct 50 straddle**, each for a 3.00 debit (fair cost = 6.00 debit). This will win if there is a big move in either direction. Since the underlying is already at 54.00, a continued move upward will generate a profit. A break from here would most likely be a loss until the underlying goes below 47.

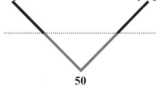

50

H.   Sell 10oo shares at 54.00 (10 calls x 1oo shares each). The result is synthetically **long 10 Oct 50 puts** for a 2.00 credit[4] (fair cost = 1.00 debit). The trader anticipates a downward move.

50

I.   Selling only 8oo shares at 54.00, assuming a hedge ratio of .80 for the Oct 50 calls, results in **long a synthetic** ratioed straddle [5] **at the 50 strike** $(+2*50c/+8*50p)$. Each of the $2*(+1c$ by $+4p)$ spreads, for a 6.00 credit [6] (fair cost = 9.00 debit[7]). The trader would profit from a large move in either direction, but eventually more so from a downward move.

50

---

[3] **10**

At this point, it might warrant purchasing more than 10 to achieve market neutrality. This would be called a ratioed strangle.

[4] **2.00 Credit**

Selling the 1oo stock at 54.00 is the same as selling 1 combo, which is selling the call and buying a put for a 4.00 credit. Since the original call cost 2.00 debit and we now receive 4.00 credit, the puts are synthetically owned for a net 2.00 credit. (For a cost of 2.00 better than free.)

[5] **Ratioed Straddle**

A ratioed straddle is not 1 : 1, meaning one call for every one put.

[6] **6.00 Credit**

Selling the 8oo stock (.80*1oo) at 54.00 is the same as selling 8 combos for 4.00 credit (5.00 credit for the calls and a 1.00 debit for the put). That's a total credit of 32.00 versus the original purchase of 10 calls for a 2.00 debit (20.00) leaves a running credit of 12.00. Since the result is $2*(+1c$ by $+4p)$ spreads, each is for a net credit of 6.00.

[7] **9.00 Debit**

Selling the 8oo stock (.80*1oo) at 54.00 is the same as selling 8 combos for 4.00 credit (5.00 credit for the calls and a 1.00 debit for the put). That's a total credit of 32.00 versus the present purchase price of 10 calls for a 5.00 debit (50.00) leaves a running debit of 18.00. Since the result is $2*(+1c$ by $+4p)$ spreads, each is for a net debit of 9.00.

This could go on and on, but by now one should have the idea. Once the trader has any of these aggregate spreads on, the strategy could evolve into many alternative configurations or risk profiles. Unlike a stock trader, who generally uses stop orders or mental stops to limit his or her risk, an options trader often adjusts rather than exits a position, providing that the position does already contain built in stops, as it were, by virtue of its design. This way he or she may be able to recoup some or all of the loss (where applicable) and even go on to profit. The adjustment turns the original strategy into a more appropriate one given current price levels, even though the trader's position is (perhaps temporarily) running at a loss.

When the nature of the beast is changed, it is essential that traders realize that any adjustment is identical to the liquidation of their old strategy and the initiation of a new strategy without all of the trades. One new trade changes the nature of the strategy and a new position exists at that point.

To decide whether an adjustment is really something that traders want to do, it is important to realize that they must like the current price (alternative cost) of the adjusted spread. In other words, they should look at the spread that they will end up with synthetically, and then assess its value and their reason for putting it on. This is the point where understanding the concept of synthetics separates the women from the girls. It is better to think about the most basic risk profile in the most simple[8] terms (i.e., synthetic terms) as opposed to the actual price terms.

At every stage in the analysis of the alternatives and adjustments to a position, traders should ask whether they would put this spread on having had no position whatsoever. They must make the decision based upon the "fair cost" disregarding all the previous prices paid or received (actual cost) on the aggregate spread. If the answer is that they "would not put on the trade", then this particular adjustment is not right for them. Their thinking should be consistent whether the position has just been initiated or has already been on for some time. The trader should get out of the position if the risk / reward profile is not attractive from this point forward. Some of the most important revelations for traders occur when they understand at what point they are contradicting themselves. This is when the "lights go on" and they really learn from their misperceptions.

---

[8] **Simple Terms**

Example: A "fenced" position (+u / + lower strike put and short higher strike call) is best viewed in its simplest terms, namely, a bull spread. Manage the bull spread by watching either the long call spread or the short put spread, whichever is more liquid.

ADJUSTMENT COSTING

The following tables examine trades A to I from the perspective of actual and fair cost.

Actual Costs

First Trade and Second Trade = Total for each spread
A. 10 @ 2.00 debit and 10 @ 2.00 credit = 10 @ 0 or even
B. 10 @ 2.00 debit and 10 @ 3.00 credit = 10 @ 1.00 credit
C. 10 @ 2.00 debit and 10 @ 9.25 credit = 10 @ 7.25 credit
D. 10 @ 2.00 debit and 20 @ 2.00 credit = 10 @ 2.00 credit
E. 10 @ 2.00 debit and 5 @ 9.25 credit = 5 @ 5.25 credit
F. 10 @ 2.00 debit and 10 @ 3.00 debit = 10 @ 5.00 debit
G. 10 @ 2.00 debit and 10 @ 1.00 debit = 10 @ 3.00 debit
H. 10 @ 2.00 debit and 10oo @ 54.00 credit = 10 @ 2.00 credit
I. 10 @ 2.00 debit and 8oo @ 54.00 credit = 2 @ 6.00 credit

Fair Cost (3.00 more times 10) [9]

Present Value of First Trade and Second Trade = Total
A. 10 @ 5.00 debit and 10 @ 2.00 credit = 10 @ 3.00 debit
B. 10 @ 5.00 debit and 10 @ 3.00 credit = 10 @ 2.00 debit
C. 10 @ 5.00 debit and 5 @ 9.25 credit = 5 @ 4.25 credit
D. 10 @ 5.00 debit and 20 @ 2.00 credit = 10 @ 1.00 debit
E. 10 @ 5.00 debit and 5 @ 9.25 credit = 5 @ .75 debit
F. 10 @ 5.00 debit and 10 @ 3.00 debit = 10 @ 8.00 debit
G. 10 @ 5.00 debit and 10 @ 1.00 debit = 10 @ 6.00 debit
H. 10 @ 5.00 debit and 10oo @ 54.00 credit = 10 @ 1.00 debit
I. 10 @ 5.00 debit and 8oo @ 54.00 credit = 2 @ 9.00 debit

Obviously all the current costs look less attractive than the actual costs because it costs 30.00 (10 contracts times 3.00) more. The important point here is that it may not make sense for some players to make any adjustment. Take scenario A for example. If there was a poll taken from the viewers of CNBC which asked whether or not they would ever buy a 5 point vertical for $3.00 (current cost) the results would probably be a resounding 100% saying "*NO WAY!*" Even if a professional group were polled, probably 70% would concur. Therefore, scenario A is rolling into a situation where one would have 3.00 on the table and it can go up to 5.00 or down to zero. That is risking 3.00 to

---

[9] **3.00 more times 10**

Had there been no prior position, the calls would have otherwise cost 5.00 instead of 2.00 meaning 3.00 more for 10 calls each turning into 10 spreads, 6.00 more for 10 calls turning into 5 spreads, and 15.00 more for 10 calls turning into 2 spreads.

make 2.00. A discussion in Chapter 6 discusses what on earth the other 30% might be thinking when compelled to risk 3.00 to make 2.00. Scenario B, on the other hand involves a strategy with unlimited upside potential. It is therefore difficult to say definitively how much the premium is worth. Its value would be calculated using the usual variables such as time to go, proximity to the money and volatility.

RULE THE BEAST

1. Predetermine strategy based on market opinion.
2. Predetermine point of entry based on an attractive price level.
3. Predetermine profit-and-loss objective based on pain threshold.
4. Enter the market.
5. Ongoing "live" reassessment of the position at current price levels.

Would the trader execute the same trade now if he or she were not already in the market? If the answer is yes, then the traders should do nothing and stay in the position. If the trader would never execute the trade at this point, this is where he or she should either exit the trade or change the nature of the beast. When looking to adjust the prevailing prices must represent a good value as if it were a fresh new initiation price. If not, one should exit. Failure to do so is a contradiction of desires. In example A, again, the trader would have to like the idea of having a long call vertical at the current price of $3.00 which can only go to $5.00. If he or she had no position and prefers not to buy that spread for $3.00, then it is pointless to stay in the trade. It would be inappropriate to stay in the trade just because it was legged[10] into for free. Long-term consistent winnings in the market have much to do with taking profits. If that spread goes from $3.00 to worthless, the trader will wish that he or she had taken the profits. There is no justification for adjusting into positions that the trader normally would not put on at current prices. If there is an adjustment to the position it should be managed like it is new without past consideration to accumulated profits or loss on the prior setup.

Rule the Beast (continued)

6. Redetermine strategy based on new market opinion.
7. Predetermine point of entry for adjustment (changing the beast).
8. Predetermine a profit-and-loss objective.
9. Exit or adjust the position.
10. Ongoing "live" reassessment of the basic position profile in simplest terms at current price levels.

---

[10] **Leg, Legging, Legged**

Legging is trading into a spread on separate orders. When the quoted spread price is too wide or not a desirable price, traders will do what is referred to as legging into the position by executing one side first and then at a later time entering an order to transact the second leg (the other side). There is transaction risk in getting 'caught between legs'. As an example, the market moves a large amount adverse to the first leg of the position resulting in the price of the overall spread to be executed being at undesirable levels. It can be dangerous to leg spreads but sometimes that is the only way in or out of a spread position.

When thinking about speculating with any options strategy (e.g. purchasing calls, puts, straddles or verticals) remember that the trader should not only think in terms of the maximum cost of that strategy. For example, the trader decides to buy a straddle (put and a call at the same strike price) because he or she believes that the market will make a large move in one direction or the other (but does not know which). The trader is willing to risk $10,000. The straddle is going for $1,000, which means that the trader can afford ten spreads and ride them through to expiration. An alternative would be to buy the straddle 6 or 7 times, leaving $3,000 or $4,000 to have in reserves for adjustment purposes.

OPTION METAMORPHOSIS

As time goes by and the market unfolds, positions evolve. The most common position held worldwide is long underlying. There are many hedging strategies available to the holder of the underlying. The most popular, which is not a true hedge, is to sell calls against the underlying to enhance the investor's rate of return on the investment. As many readers may well know, this is a "covered write." The risk profile is that of a short put. If the real put is eventually purchased to lock in a profit, the position evolves into a conversion. Instead of the same strike put being bought, the higher or lower strike may be bought, and the position evolves into a bear or bull spread.   These are examples of options metamorphosis.

Exhibit 2–11 shows in great detail how positions can evolve into new spreads with a minor adjustment.   Exhibit 2–11 (the dissection proofs are in the appendix).   Strategies are presented in the form of a flowchart that starts in the center of the diagram with a risk profile of a long underlying position (like a forward slash at a 45 degree angle) in the red stylized square. The 4–sided shape in the center indicates that there is a choice of four directions in which to go. Small investors, brokers, and institutional hedgers will find this exercise particularly useful. An initial hedge of selling calls or buying puts can take on one of four alternative forms:

1. In quadrant I, the investor turns the long underlying into a long straddle by purchasing two puts against the position. He will profit if the market becomes volatile and moves significantly in one direction or the other.

2. In quadrant II, the investor turns the long underlying into a short put by selling a call against the position to enhance the rate of return on the underlying investment. Profit will result from a stable to higher market.

3. In quadrant III, the investor turns the long underlying into a short straddle by selling two calls against the position. He will profit if the market does not move or if implied volatility declines.

4. In quadrant IV, the investor buys a put. The investor turns the long underlying into a long call by purchasing a put for downside protection while maintaining the upside profitability potential.

E X H I B I T   2 – 1 1

Options Metamorphosis
Transforming a Long Stock Position

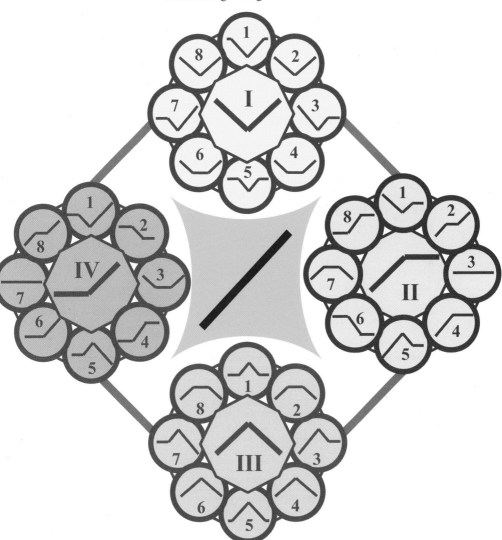

E X H I B I T   2 – 1 2

Explanation of Options Metamorphosis

Transforming a Long Stock Position

See Appendix for all Dissections for Proof

I LONG STRADDLE by BUYING twice the number of PUTS

1 SHORT BUTTERFLY with a 4 strike value range: by SELLING a STRANGLE two strikes out.
2 LONG STRADDLE rolled to a higher strike: by TRADING twice the amount of BEAR SPREADS with the sale strike = to the original hedge strike.
3 PUT (LongMore) BACK SPREAD: by SELLING a higher strike CALL
4 LONG STRANGLE : by TRADING a BEAR SPREAD with the sale strike = to the original hedge strike.
5 SHORT BUTTERFLY with a 2 strike value range: by SELLING a surrounding STRANGLE.
6 LONG STRANGLE : by TRADING a BULL SPREAD with the sale strike = to the original hedge strike.
7 CALL (LongMore) BACK SPREAD: by SELLING a lower strike PUT.
8 LONG STRADDLE rolled to a lower strike: by TRADING twice the amount of BULL SPREADS with the sale strike = to the original hedge strike.

II SHORT PUT (Covered Write) by SELLING a CALL

1 PUT (LongMore) BACK SPREAD: by BUYING twice the number of lower strike PUTS.
2 LONG SEMI-STOCK: by BUYING a higher strike CALL.
3 CONVERSION (Flat): by BUYING a same strike PUT.
4 SHORT PUT rolled to a different strike: by TRADING a VERTICAL SPREAD with the sale strike = to the original hedge strike.
5 PUT (ShortMore) RATIO SPREAD: by BUYING half the amount of higher strike PUTS.
6 BEAR SPREAD: by BUYING a higher strike PUT.
7 SHORT STRANGLE: by SELLING a different strike CALL.
8 BULL SPREAD: by BUYING a lower strike PUT.

III SHORT STRADDLE by SELLING twice the number of CALLS

1 LONG BUTTERFLY with a 2 strike value range: by BUYING a surrounding STRANGLE.0
2 SHORT STRANGLE : by TRADING a BULL SPREAD with the purchase strike = to the original hedge strike.
3 PUT (ShortMore) RATIO SPREAD: by BUYING a higher strike CALL.
4 SHORT STRADDLE rolled to a higher strike: by TRADING twice the amount of BULL SPREADS with the purchase strike = to the original hedge strike.
5 LONG BUTTERFLY with a 4 strike value range: by BUYING a STRANGLE two strikes out.
6 SHORT STRADDLE rolled to a lower strike: by TRADING twice the amount of BEAR SPREADS with the purchase strike = to the original hedge strike.
7 CALL (ShortMore) RATIO SPREAD: by BUYING a lower strike PUT.
8 SHORT STRANGLE : by TRADING a BEAR SPREAD with the purchase strike = to the original hedge strike.

IV LONG CALL by BUYING a PUT

1 CALL (LongMore) BACK SPREAD: by SELLING HALF the number of lower strike CALLS.
2 BEAR SPREAD: by SELLING a lower strike CALL.
3 LONG STRANGLE: by BUYING a different strike PUT.
4 BULL SPREAD: by SELLING a higher strike CALL.
5 CALL (ShortMore) RATIO SPREAD: by SELLING twice the amount of higher strike CALLS.
6 LONG CALL rolled to a different strike: by TRADING a VERTICAL SPREAD with the sale strike = to the original hedge strike.
7 CONVERSION (Flat): by SELLING a same strike CALL.
8 LONG SEMI-STOCK: by SELLING a lower strike PUT.

CHAPTER

3

NUTS AND BOLTS OF OPTIONS

This chapter explores the variables that are the life-blood of option pricing. After a brief encounter with profit and loss scenario interpretation, we will cover the variables that measure options risk called the "Greeks". The Greeks help sort out almost all of the confusion about how profits and losses occur. We will examine the effects that dividends and interest rates have on options pricing, and then look at how 'early exercise' works and can be played.

PROFIT AND LOSS (P&L) SCENARIOS

If the reader has not previously seen the theoretical P&L graphs for all of the option strategies, he or she should become familiar with them. Every exchange and most brokerage firms have produced pamphlets on them.

The first two Exhibits show profit-and-loss graphs, one of long 1 at-the-money put (Exhibit 3–1) and the other of long 1 at-the-money call (Exhibit 3–2). There is a 2-dimensional graph (above) and a 3 dimensional graph (below) showing what happens over time on the z-axis. The profits or losses for this particular day would be for a constant implied volatility (no skew) if the underlying were to trade at each point between and including 93.00 and 107.00.

The put (Exhibit 3–1) and call (Exhibit 3–2) graphs are basically mirror images of each other. Simply remember that long calls are exactly the opposite of short calls and that they are basically the opposite of long puts (i.e. as far as directional aim and deltas go).

The put and call would be perfectly opposite were it not for the probability assumption, which implies that calls can theoretically go further in-the-money than puts and therefore have bigger deltas than puts when they are both at-the-money or equidistant from the money.

Some readers will cite minuscule differences between the Greeks of puts and the Greeks of calls at the same strike prices using various software platforms. For all intents and purposes, gamma, theta, and vega are the same for long calls and long puts. A fair wager would be that there is no way to make or save money by playing for any differences.

E X H I B I T   3 – 1

1*100 Put Theoretical P&L--91 Days, 10% Volatility, (.01% Interest) IV = 10%
Using Black-Scholes Futures Style Margin

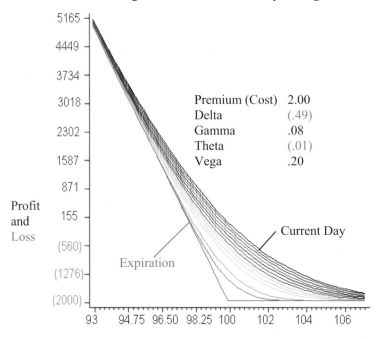

Premium (Cost)	2.00
Delta	(.49)
Gamma	.08
Theta	(.01)
Vega	.20

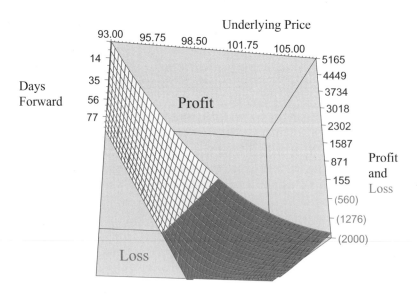

E X H I B I T   3 – 2

1*100 Call Theoretical P&L--91 Days, 10% Volatility, (.01% Interest) IV = 10%
Using Black-Scholes Futures Style Margin

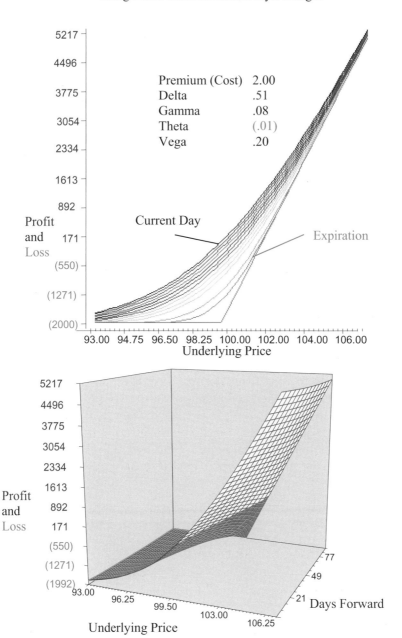

Premium (Cost)	2.00
Delta	.51
Gamma	.08
Theta	(.01)
Vega	.20

The Greeks for the current day are displayed (i.e. the theoretical delta, gamma, theta, and vega[1]), but are theoretical assumptions, only as good as the data input. Stress testing[2] with changes in overall implied volatility and at each individual strike should be carried out. The best data input can come only as a result of trading experience in the market in question. However, to rely totally on that experience would be foolish because new experiences are made every day, and sometimes the market has a way of treating traders as though it were their first day of trading.

GLANCING GREEK TO GREEK

The Greek letters derived from statistical models, such as the Black-Scholes, represent the various sensitivities of options behavior. These are delta (Δ), gamma (Γ), theta (Θ), omega (Ω, better known as vega) and rho (P). Successful traders from all over the world have varying degrees of understanding about 'Greeks,' how they can be used, and when they should be disregarded. It is common to find traders with sound mathematical backgrounds becoming so immersed in the formulas that they do not actually use the derivatives objectively. Some traders avoid using them because they do not fully understand their implications. Without a doubt, it is important to be fully versed in all of the types of risk to which one is exposed.

The purpose of this chapter is to explain how the Greeks change when the *underlying* moves, what happens to them over time, and why they are an indispensable tool for an investor. It is most important that traders understand the difference between how these tools are expected to and actually do affect their profit-and-loss profile (P&L). They should also be very aware of where there is Greek exposure in their position, so that any elements of the position that work against the trader's intended strategy can be eliminated. In addition, the traders' position could be neutral with regard to all of the Greeks, but have extreme multi-expiration exposure.

---

[1] Vega

Vega is not a Greek letter but it is widely accepted as 'a Greek' in the derivatives business. It is also known as omega (Ω).

[2] Stress Testing

Performing tests on a position to see how much the profit or loss would be with certain market scenarios. What-if assumptions examine many possibilities for implied volatility levels as well as underlying price changes. The risk analyser, testing these same generic contract examples, would use the Black-Scholes model for calls, and the Binomial model for puts with the interest rate set to 0%. The contract value is $100 for each point (1.00). Each tick (.01) is equal to $1.00 as in most U.S. equities.

Throughout this book, there will be discussions about various types of positions, commentaries on how the Greeks affect those positions, and exhibits of graphs depicting them. The variables that affect the Greeks are time, implied volatility, and the position of the underlying in relation to the strike prices. Most example position will use at least 100 contracts in order to prevent rounding errors from distorting the analyses.

Memorizing each Greek's definition, exhibit, and property will help but it is also important to understand their interrelationships. Some general rules follow:

1. All of the Greeks except delta (Δ) are at their greatest value when they are at the money. (Scientifically speaking, this may not be the case, but for all practical intents and purposes it is true).

2. Gamma (Γ) has an inverse relationship with theta (Θ). The more positive gamma there is, the more negative theta (time decay) there will be.

3. The effect of decreasing volatility is vega or omega (Ω) and is similar to the effect of time moving forward. Increasing volatility has the effect of time moving backward (if that were possible), i.e. increasing time until expiration is increasing volatility and vice versa.

IMPLIED VOLATILITY

Implied volatility is a market driven factor and an extremely ambiguous component of the pricing model. It is very often talked about when options are discussed. Real rocket scientist, well capitalized, professionals try to predict the stability of the market from a statistical standpoint and play the odds. It is a dangerous game. Retail investors can use it to help them to line up all the options values in their analysis software in order to determine opportunities based upon a historic reference and make a play from there. The factors that go into calculating option theoretical values are the underlying price, time until expiration, the risk-free rate of return (interest), dividends (where applicable), the strike price, and a chosen volatility level. Assume that an actual option's price and all of the factors used to determine its price are known except for the volatility level. Using algebra, the missing volatility level can be determined. This factor is known as implied volatility because the option's price implies something about the anticipated volatility of the underlying over a certain period of time in the future. Implied volatility is often interpreted as though it is actual money, because premium levels vary directly with implied volatility levels (i.e. the higher the implied volatility, the higher the option price). An option price can be analyzed to learn what is expected about the future volatility of the underlying instrument. If the option's premium is running at high-implied volatilities, then supply and demand is suggesting that the underlying will fluctuate in a volatile manner. Alternatively, if implied volatility is low, then traders believe that the market will not be so volatile in the near future. Although this prediction could be totally inaccurate, it is the buying and selling pressure of the options themselves that are reflecting market sentiment on the price volatility of the underlying in the future.

Implied volatility is only similar to money for a brief moment in time and with all other variables frozen. For example, if a trader buys options with an implied volatility of 20% and sells them in the next moment, with all other variables remaining equal, at 21%, the trader should profit by 1%. However, since implied volatility changes differ according to the level of the underlying and the amount of time remaining, one's point of reference disappears and it is difficult to gauge values. For example, IBM is priced at $75.00 with 31 days to go and a 20% implied volatility. The 75 call is valued at $1.75. At $74.00 with 22% volatility, the call is worth only $1.45. If IBM is at $76.00 with 30% volatility and 11 days to go, the call is worth only $1.57. We can see from the above that volatility figures are best used for relative pricing purposes (relative to the other options as alternatives).

RISK

Many aspects of risk must be considered when trading an options position. The following acronym may be useful to ensure that you are not overlooking anything:

GLAD SNIP (be happy to cut down your risk).

Greek risk— i.e. the derivatives' sensitivities, delta, gamma, theta, omega or vega and rho, as covered in this chapter.

Liquidity risk—When traders have too many contracts to get out of or into, or trade larger than the market will allow them to trade out of at fair value, they face liquidity risk. It can also happen that market makers accumulate positions that are heavily weighted predominantly at one strike, and are not able to get out of them. If traders believe that an option is undervalued or overvalued, they often hoard it. This makes it difficult for a retail investor to get out of that same position.

Assignment risk—Options are exercised because there is an economic benefit in doing so. If traders are assigned, they may lose out on collecting interest income or save on interest expense. They may receive or pay dividends and as in the case of cash settlement index options, lose positive or negative deltas.

Dividend risk—Although it is better to collect a dividend than to have to pay one, many profit opportunities justify the short selling of stock. Entities that are short stock on the date of record have to pay the dividend to the shareholder. There is a risk of a change in the ex-dividend date[3], which has an effect on the cost of carry. Additionally, there is a risk of being subject to a greater or lesser dividend payment if the amount of the dividend changes while one is holding the stock position.

Skew risk—Skew, or the smile, refers to the possibility that implied volatilities can vary at different strikes. The risk is that the implied volatility for the strikes of long options can decrease while those for the strikes of short options can increase. It is therefore necessary to monitor the option's sensitivity to the P&L and the Greeks as implied volatility changes at the various strikes.

Net contracts exposure—Number of net calls and *puts* including the underlying, as calculated in Chapter 1 (long underlying counts as long calls and short puts and short underlying counts as short calls and long puts for this purpose).

Indigenous risk—Nuances that are specific to a given market. For example, OEX exercise of deep in-the-money options is based on what happens to the S&P 500 futures and the OEX (S&P 100) combos (synthetic futures) in the last few minutes of the day.

Pin risk—The dilemma of not knowing whether the short options will be assigned or whether one should exercise the long options of an at-the-money combo at expiration.

---

[3] **Change in the Ex-Dividend Date**

Cost of carry is the finance charge for carrying a position. Certain positions generate negative carry when there is a credit balance, resulting in an interest rebate because the proceeds from short sales earns interest.

NEUTRALITY DEPENDS ON ONE'S PERCEPTION

Being neutral is usually associated with being a market maker, because they generally trade flat (with little market exposure in their position). Investors flatten up to reduce their exposure when they need time to figure out their next move.   No one is really happy about taking everything off. If there were one or two trades that one could make to get reasonably flat, traders could neutralize their position in order to get through an economic announcement or an earnings report without too much damage being done to the position. A major distinction to be made is that there is a big difference between current and eventual neutrality. Positions change over time, even when no trades have been made, because the underlying moves farther from some strikes and closer to others, and *implied volatility* changes. It is an art for traders to adjust their position to where they want it while all the variables are changing.

It can be helpful to understand what a market maker has to go through because sometimes it seems as though they will not provide a quote. Sometimes, they just need a little time to sort things out when the market gets busy. In many respects, because of all of the variables that have to be managed, market makers are much like performers in the circus who try to get eight plates spinning all at once on top of eight poles. They get a few started, but before they get to the fourth or fifth one, they have to go back, give numbers one and two another spin, and then proceed to the next. They must continually monitor the activity of all of them as they go along, because plates start to wobble, fall, and crash to the floor. The circus performers have to ensure that each one stays balanced. Option traders make a trade and find that all of a sudden one aspect of their position is no longer neutral, which necessitates another trade that could throw their position off with respect to some other sensitivity. This may explain why they seem unwilling, sometimes, to honor markets. Trades have to be made to neutralize and diversify the risks. At the same time, traders have to keep abreast of each level in GLAD SNIP, any speculative bias, and technical factors in the market.

Some other risks to be aware of in trading are: basis risk, collateral risk, credit risk, cross-market risk, currency risk, hedging risk, modeling risk, negotiating risk, position limits risk, regulatory risk, reinvestment risk, systems risk, tax risk, technology risk, transaction risk and yield-curve risk.

When teaching the Greeks, certain points can be made without the clutter of dividends and interest getting in the way. The following examples will therefore use a generic contract without dividends and with the interest rate set to 0% (making calls equal to puts at the strike). These examples can then be further stress-tested by performing 'What-if' scenarios using a risk analyzer.

DELTA (Δ)

Delta is the rate of change of an option's *theoretical value* as the underlying changes in value. A common definition for delta is the rate of change of an option's theoretical value in relation to a one-point move in the underlying. An option's theoretical value actually changes with the most infinitesimal move in the underlying. Another problem with the one-point definitions is that one point means different amounts in different markets, (e.g., strikes are five points apart in the OEX, S&Ps, and many U.S. equities, but there are ten strikes in one point of CBOT corn, four strikes in one point of Eurodollars, and one strike per point in T-notes).

Many veteran traders believe that delta represents the probability that the underlying will move sufficiently to bring the option in-the-money at expiration and that a .50 delta means that there is a 50% chance that the option will be in-the-money even if it is by only one tick. However, I am told that that is incorrect, mathematically speaking. The delta is used as the hedge ratio to determine what could be traded against the underlying. It is often considered to be equivalent to an amount of underlying at a specific price and at a specific point in time. Calls have a positive delta and puts have a negative delta. The sum of the absolute values of deltas add up to 1.00 (in this case, .51 for the call and –.49 for the put). Some option pricing models calculate the sum of the deltas to be slightly above or below 1.00, but this is not significant to the discussion of delta at this point.

Look at the two sets of delta graphs for puts in Exhibit 3-3 and calls in Exhibit 3-4. The call delta and the put delta at the same strike change at the same rate but inversely. This is the first indication that calls can be puts and puts can be calls. They become synthetically each other when either is offset by an equal amount of the underlying.

Suppose that the expiration is tomorrow and that a call is just out of the money. It looks as though it is going to expire worthless and the delta will be close to zero. If, in the last few moments of the trading day, the market were to rally, bringing the call in-the-money, then the delta would change immediately to 1.00.

When there is a longer period of time to expiration, deltas change more gradually. Their properties are similar to what happens to deltas when implied volatility increases.

Just knowing that if volatility goes down it is like time going by faster makes it easy to guess what would happen to in-the-money and out-of-the-money deltas as volatility changes.

E X H I B I T   3 – 3

100*100 Puts Delta--91 Days, 10% Volatility, .01% Interest and Using Black-Scholes Futures Style Margin

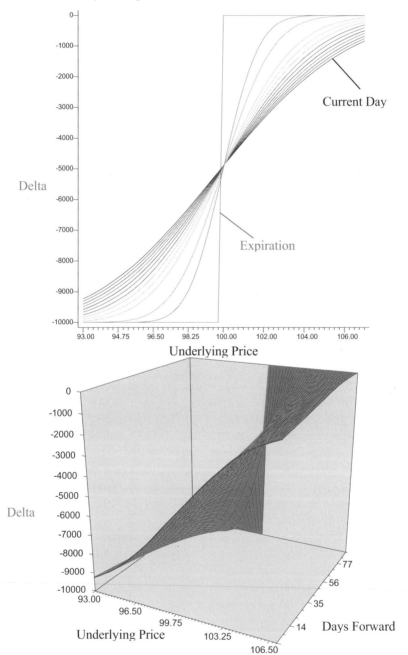

E X H I B I T   3 – 4

100*100 Calls Delta--91 Days, 10% Volatility, .01% Interest and Using Black-Scholes Futures Style Margin

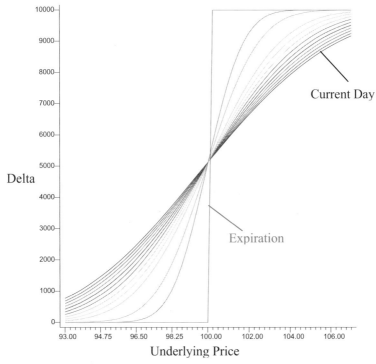

Current Day

Delta

Expiration

Underlying Price

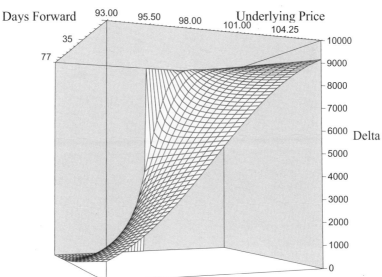

Days Forward

Underlying Price

Delta

E X H I B I T   3 – 5

100*100 Strike Delta with changes in Implied Volatilities --91 Days, 10% Volatility, .01% Interest and Using Black-Scholes Futures Style Margin

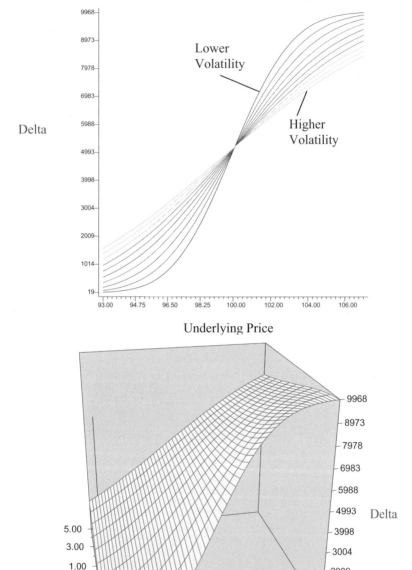

Without looking it up, most readers would guess that out-of-the-money deltas go down as time goes by because there is less and less chance that they will go in-the-money. When volatility goes down (See Exhibit 3-5), the implication is that there is little chance for those out-of-the-money options to also go in-the-money. If in-the-money options stay in-the-money over time, their delta will move toward 1.00 (–1.00 for in-the-money puts) at expiration.

If volatility decreases, it makes sense that in-the-money calls will have more of a chance of staying in-the-money, and so their deltas will also move toward 1.00. The effect of changes in implied volatility is often considered to be the most difficult sensitivity to comprehend. However, it is not complicated if one remembers that a decrease in implied volatility has the same effect on the option value as time going by, and that an increase in implied volatility has the opposite effect.

GAMMA (Γ)

Gamma is the rate of change of the delta in a one-point move. Professional traders interpret gamma values as the number of underlying deltas or contracts that will be generated from a 1-percent move[4] in the underlying price. The deltas change as a result of a move in the underlying (up or down). Positive gamma in a delta neutral position generates deltas that are favorable to the direction of the market. As the market moves lower, the position produces short deltas, while long deltas are produced as the market moves higher. For example, a trader owns 50 straddles, each call (+.50Δ) and put (-.50Δ) has a gamma of positive .08 for a total gamma of 8 (.08 x 100 options). Positive 8 means that if the underlying moves 1 point from 100 up to 101, the trader's net delta position will move from delta neutral to a new delta of +8F or +8ooS at 101. If the market declines to 99, the net delta of the position will be -8F or -8ooS. The trader gets longer when the underlying moves up, and shorter when it drops. Long gamma provides an opportunity to scalp gammas. A scalp trade is one where a trader gets in and out of the market very quickly. In this context, the trader takes advantage of selling out the long deltas manufactured on the way up and buying in the shorts manufactured on the way down for a small profit on each trade.

Exhibit 3–6, shows the theoretical values (premium) and the Greeks for a 100 call at the underlying stock price of 100 with various volatility assumptions. Gamma would be the same for a 100 put.

---

[4] 1-Percent Move

Some software allows the user to define the range that the gamma covers, for example, one percent, one-point or a one-stike. Most software available to retail customers calculates based upon a one-point move in the underlying.

E X H I B I T   3 – 6

100 Call Information at Many Implied Volatilities with 91 Days to go, Underlying at 100

Volatility	5%	6%	7%	8%	9%	10%	11%	12%	13%	14%	15%
Premium	0.9960	1.1951	1.3943	1.5935	1.7926	1.9918	2.1909	2.3900	2.5891	2.7882	2.9873
Delta	0.5050	0.5060	0.5070	0.5080	0.5090	0.5100	0.5110	0.5120	0.5129	0.5139	0.5149
Gamma	0.1598	0.1331	0.1141	0.0999	0.0888	0.0799	0.0726	0.0666	0.0614	0.0570	0.0532
Theta	(0.0055)	(0.0066)	(0.0077)	(0.0088)	(0.0098)	(0.0109)	(0.0120)	(0.0131)	(0.0142)	(0.0153)	(0.0164)
Vega	0.1992	0.1992	0.1992	0.1992	0.1991	0.1991	0.1991	0.1991	0.1991	0.1991	0.1991

Gamma as the Underlying Changes and Over Time: The graph in Exhibit 3-7 illustrates that as the underlying moves away from the strike, gamma gets smaller and smaller. With a lot of time to go or with high implied volatility the gammas of the in-the-money, out-of-the-money and at-the-money options are relatively similar as can be seen in Exhibit 3-8.   Toward expiration the away-from-the-money gammas dwindle, while the at-the-money gammas explode.   In fact an in-the-money option with a delta of .99 requires a larger move in the underlying to change to 1.00 than does an at-the-money option with a .50 delta to change to .55.

At-the-money gamma goes up and away-from-the-money options' gamma goes down. At expiration the at-the-money option's gamma is at it highest while the rest are virtually zero.

E X H I B I T   3 – 7

100*100 Strike Gamma over Time -- 91 Days, 10% Volatility, .01% Interest and Using Black-Scholes Futures Style Margin

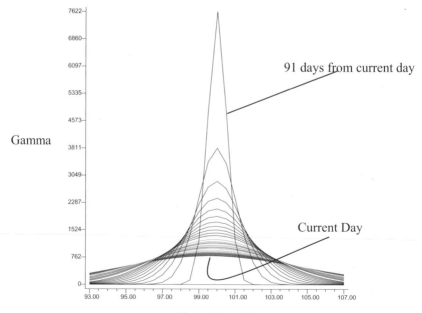

Underlying Price

E X H I B I T   3 – 8

100*100 Strike Gamma over Time – Side View -- 91 Days, 10% Volatility,
.01% Interest and Using Black-Scholes Futures Style Margin

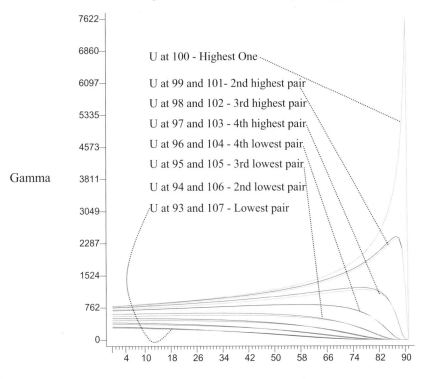

Days Forward

Keep in mind that on the day of expiration the king, the at-the-money
strike, can fall and one of the dirty old rascals, the away-from-the-money strikes
(Exhibit 3-8), could become king for a day.

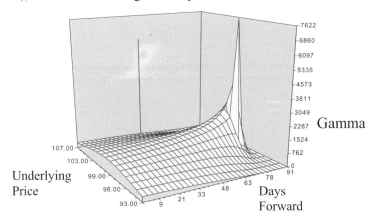

E X H I B I T   3 – 9

100*100 Strike Gamma with Implied Volatility – 91 Days, 10% Volatility, .01% Interest and Using Black-Scholes Futures Style Margin

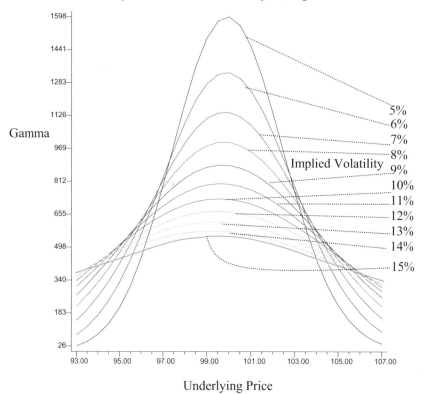

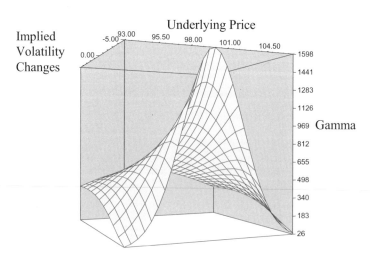

Gamma as Implied Volatility Changes: Gamma over time (from 91days to 1 day) is similar to the graph (Exhibit 3-9) depicting the effect of an implied volatility change from 5% to 15% (by increments of 1%) as the underlying changes in price.

Volatility going down has the same effect as the passage of time does. The farther the drop, the faster time goes by, so the at-the-money gamma goes up and the others dwindle a bit. Implied volatility increasing is like putting more time back on the clock; the at-the-money gamma falls and the other gammas are given a boost.

Remember: With a lot of time to go or with high implied-volatility the gamma of the in-the-money, out-of-the-money, and at-the-money options are relatively similar. Toward expiration, the away-from-the-money gamma dwindles, while the at-the-money gamma explodes.

Relativity of Gamma

When comparing the gamma of 100 straddles for three different strikes, 100, 105 and 200 as in Exhibit 3-10, one can see that the higher the strike price, the lower the gamma. The values have an inverse relationship. As the underlying doubles in price, the gamma halves in value.

Consider the graphs of gamma values at three different at-the-money strikes. Compare the three positions in Exhibit 3-11, i.e. the 100*100 calls when the underlying is at 100, 105*105 calls when the underlying is at 105, and 200*200 calls when the underlying is at 200. All three positions generate exactly the same graph. A higher priced underlying (e.g. $200) is expected to fluctuate (two times) more than lower priced ones (e.g. $100 and $105). The percentage move is the same, however. Price and gamma are therefore relative. The only difference between all three of theses graphs is the absolute price range that the underlying covers. However, the price range is the same in relative terms (7% up or 7% down). The price range for the 100*200s is 28 points from 186 to 214, the price range for 100*100s is 14 points from 93.00 to 107.00, and the price range for the 100*105s is 14.70 points (7% x 105 in each direction) from 97.65 to 112.35.

In the case of a 2 for 1 stock split, when the strikes become half their previous value, gamma doubles at each strike. That is simply because a 1 point change in a stock that trades for $50 amounts to the same percentage change as a 2 point change in a stock that trades for $100.

An important thing to remember is that a position can consist of unlimited risk gammas and limited risk gammas. It is possible to have a neutral position with respect to gamma and suffer devastating losses due to the fact that the position was short unlimited risk gammas and long limited gain gammas against them.

E X H I B I T   3 – 1 0

Comparison of Absolute Gamma Values of 100 At-the-Money Options

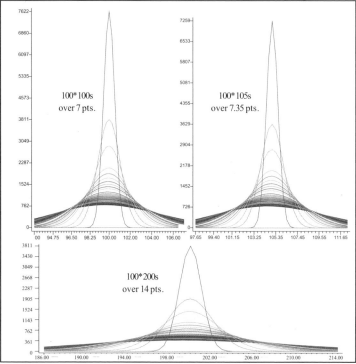

E X H I B I T   3 – 1 1

Comparison of Relative Gamma Values of Equivalent Quantities At-the-Money Options

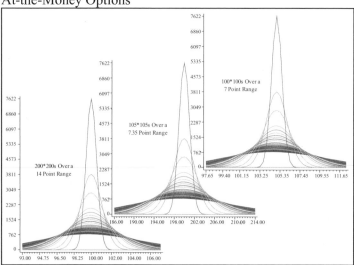

THETA (Θ)

Theta measures the amount of premium that will theoretically decay each day. It can be said that positive theta has the risk of negative gamma, and that the price of positive gamma is negative theta. The inverse of these is also true. There is a trade-off that has to be handled based on experience, comfort and discipline. No two people will handle any position the same. It boils down to how much heat you can take, and how you handle the valleys and peaks in your trading. Some traders will hold positions of positive gamma that generate losses daily, until the loss can be made up by either a large move and/or gamma scalping opportunities.

When theta is positive and the market is volatile, traders either cross their fingers and hope that the underlying eventually returns to close to unchanged, or they play defense by selling into dips and by buying on rallies in order to maintain delta neutrality. The idea is to lose a lesser amount on these hedges than that which is being received in the way of time decay. Some traders day-trade from the short gamma side and either cover on a break-out or get flat before the close. The graphs in Exhibit 3-12 from right to left show theta as the underlying moves while Exhibit 3-13 shows theta as time passes, and Exhibit 3-14 shows how theta is affected by changes in implied volatility.

Most software programs factor interest income and expense into the theta value. This can be misleading to a novice because the interest amount may be offset by either a charge to the account or a payment to the account at the end of the month. It is therefore important to differentiate between each item, otherwise the hedge may be inaccurate.

Many traders who use the old school approach to risk management, and want to be long premium to take advantage of a big price move in the underlying in either direction, look at their time decay and calculate a maximum level of negative theta that they will tolerate (this is usually 1% of their capital). This is not to say that they will leave the position on for 100 days (1% is one 100th) and that at the end of the 100 days they will have exhausted all of their trading capital. Theoretically one could never lose all of the money. Realistically one would still have almost 37% of the initial capital, even after the 100 days has passed. See Exhibit 3-15. This method is preferred as a guideline and a trading parameter in order to prevent traders from becoming overzealous when waiting for a move in the underlying.

E X H I B I T   3 – 1 2

100*100 Strike Theta as the Underlying Changes– 91 Days, 10% Volatility,
.01% Interest and Using Black-Scholes Futures Style Margin

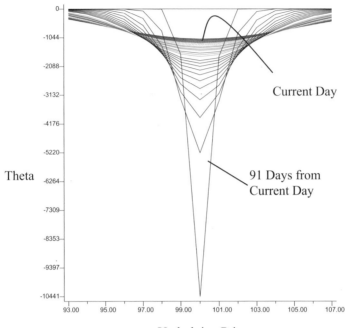

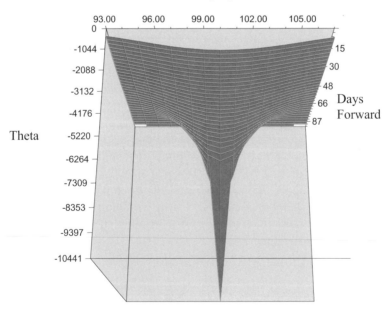

E X H I B I T   3 – 1 3

100*100 Strike Theta as Time Passes – 91 Days, 10% Volatility, .01% Interest and Using Black-Scholes Futures Style Margin

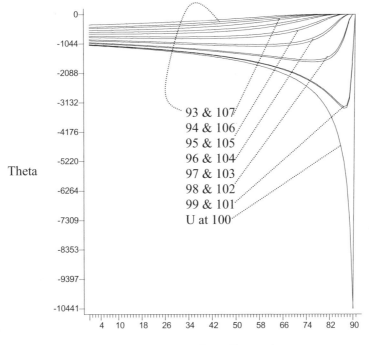

93 & 107
94 & 106
95 & 105
96 & 104
97 & 103
98 & 102
99 & 101
U at 100

Days Forward

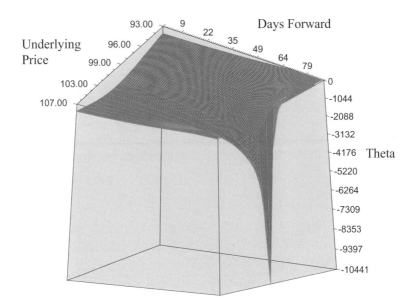

E X H I B I T   3 – 1 4

100*100 Strike Theta with Volatility Changes – 91 Days, 10% Volatility, .01%
Interest and Using Black-Scholes Futures Style Margin

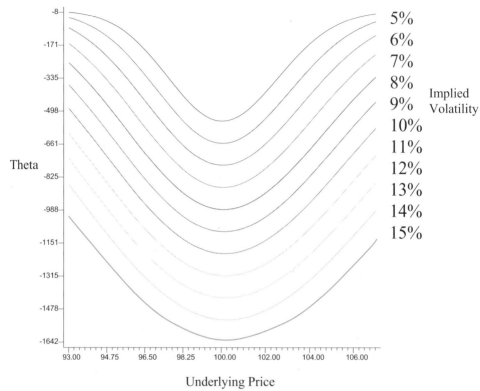

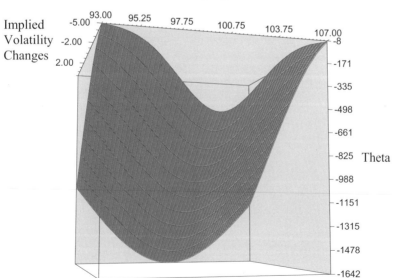

EXHIBIT 3 – 15

Equity Balance with Theta Equal to 1% of Capital for 100 Days

Day	Equity	1%	Day	Equity	1%	Day	Equity	1%	Day	Equity	1%	Day	Equity	1%
1	100000.00	1000.00	21	81790.69	817.91	41	66897.18	668.97	61	54715.66	547.16	81	44752.32	447.52
2	99000.00	990.00	22	80972.79	809.73	42	66228.20	662.28	62	54168.51	541.69	82	44304.80	443.05
3	98010.00	980.10	23	80163.06	801.63	43	65565.92	655.66	63	53626.82	536.27	83	43861.75	438.62
4	97029.90	970.30	24	79361.43	793.61	44	64910.26	649.10	64	53090.55	530.91	84	43423.13	434.23
5	96059.60	960.60	25	78567.81	785.68	45	64261.16	642.61	65	52559.65	525.60	85	42988.90	429.89
6	95099.00	950.99	26	77782.14	777.82	46	63618.55	636.19	66	52034.05	520.34	86	42559.01	425.59
7	94148.01	941.48	27	77004.31	770.04	47	62982.36	629.82	67	51513.71	515.14	87	42133.42	421.33
8	93206.53	932.07	28	76234.27	762.34	48	62352.54	623.53	68	50998.57	509.99	88	41712.09	417.12
9	92274.47	922.74	29	75471.93	754.72	49	61729.01	617.29	69	50488.59	504.89	89	41294.97	412.95
10	91351.72	913.52	30	74717.21	747.17	50	61111.72	611.12	70	49983.70	499.84	90	40882.02	408.82
11	90438.21	904.38	31	73970.04	739.70	51	60500.61	605.01	71	49483.87	494.84	91	40473.20	404.73
12	89533.83	895.34	32	73230.34	732.30	52	59895.60	598.96	72	48989.03	489.89	92	40068.47	400.68
13	88638.49	886.38	33	72498.03	724.98	53	59296.64	592.97	73	48499.14	484.99	93	39667.78	396.68
14	87752.10	877.52	34	71773.05	717.73	54	58703.68	587.04	74	48014.15	480.14	94	39271.10	392.71
15	86874.58	868.75	35	71055.32	710.55	55	58116.64	581.17	75	47534.00	475.34	95	38878.39	388.78
16	86005.84	860.06	36	70344.77	703.45	56	57535.47	575.35	76	47058.66	470.59	96	38489.61	384.90
17	85145.78	851.46	37	69641.32	696.41	57	56960.12	569.60	77	46588.08	465.88	97	38104.71	381.05
18	84294.32	842.94	38	68944.91	689.45	58	56390.52	563.91	78	46122.20	461.22	98	37723.66	377.24
19	83451.38	834.51	39	68255.46	682.55	59	55826.61	558.27	79	45660.97	456.61	99	37346.43	373.46
20	82616.86	826.17	40	67572.90	675.73	60	55268.35	552.68	80	45204.37	452.04	100	36972.96	369.73

VEGA OR OMEGA (Ω)

Vega or Omega is a measure of the amount that theoretical values will change in relation to a one percentage point change in implied volatility. Note that we are concerned with a 1% move, and not 1% of the implied volatility amount, that is where implied volatility is 10%, the move is to either 9% or 11% (not 9.99% or 10.01%).

It is difficult to maintain perfect vega neutrality with a position in several strikes due to the following factors:

1. Vega levels are different at each strike and change at different rates (see the graphs in Exhibits 3-16 to 3-19).

2. Supply and demand nuances (influenced in many cases by open interest) cause some strikes to trade at higher implied volatilities, while others may trade lower or remain unchanged.

3. The implied volatility levels between months do not always correlate with each other because the further months are part of a vega play and the closer expirations are more of a theta vs. gamma play.

Exhibits 3-16 to 3-19 show some interesting characteristics of vega. At-the-money options have the greatest price sensitivity to the changes in implied volatility (Exhibit 3-16). Far-term options are more sensitive than near-term ones (Exhibit 3-17).

E X H I B I T   3 – 1 6

100*100 Strike Vega Over Time – From 91 Days to Expiration, 10% Volatility, .01% Interest and Using Black-Scholes Futures Style Margin

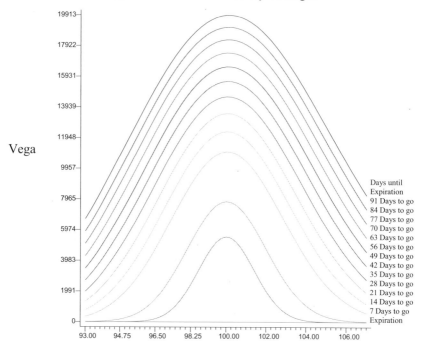

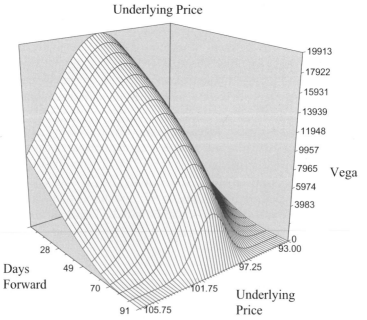

E X H I B I T   3 – 1 7

100*100 Strike Vega as Time Passes – 91 Days, 10% Volatility, .01% Interest and Using Black-Scholes Futures Style Margin

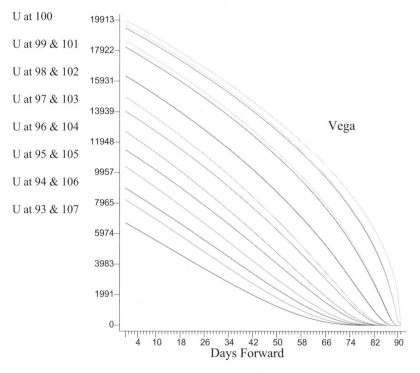

U at 100

U at 99 & 101

U at 98 & 102

U at 97 & 103

U at 96 & 104

U at 95 & 105

U at 94 & 106

U at 93 & 107

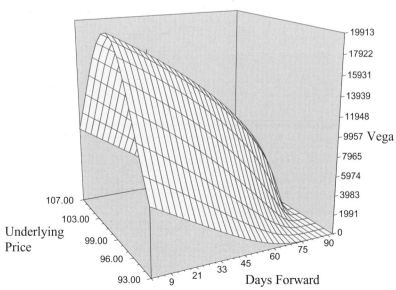

E X H I B I T   3 – 1 8

100*100 Strike Vega as Implied Volatility Changes – 91 Days, Starting at
10% Volatility, .01% Interest and Using Black-Scholes Futures Style Margin

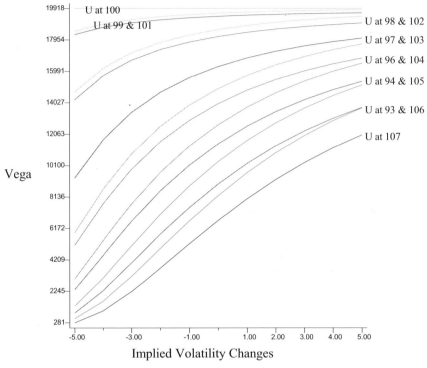

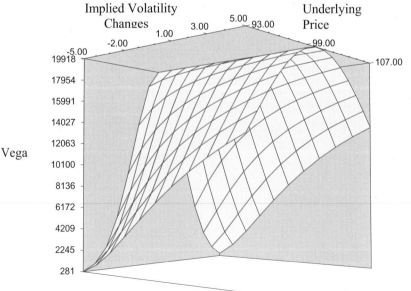

E X H I B I T   3 – 1 9

100*100 Strike Vega as Implied Volatility Changes – 91 Days, Starting at
10% Volatility, .01% Interest and Using Black-Scholes Futures Style Margin

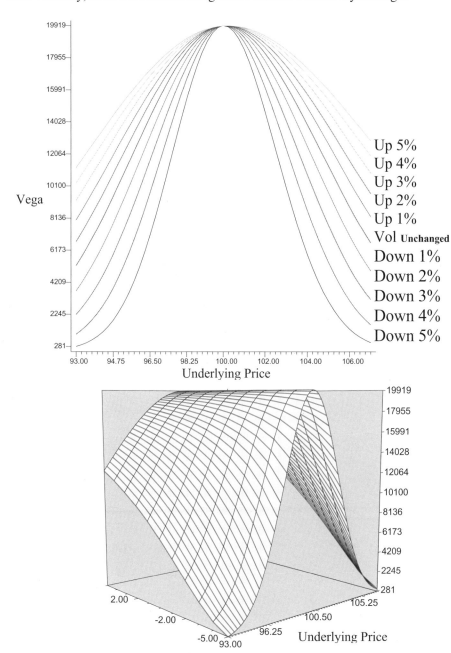

Exhibits 3-18 and 3-19 display what happens to vega as implied volatility changes. The most important lesson here is that at-the-money (ATM) vegas are not affected (that is, vega remains constant) in the way that in-the-money (ITM) and out of-the-money (OTM) vegas are. Go back and see the vega values in Exhibit 3-6 that show that it does not matter what the implied volatility is for that ATM 100 strike option. It means that each option should change by .199 (on that point in time) for every 1 percentage point change in implied volatility, i.e. from 5% to 6% represents the same .199 vega as from 14% to 15%. This is graphically indicated by the straight line for the ATM options at the top of Exhibit 3-18. This is also shown in the top center of Exhibit 3-19 where all the lines converge. Furthermore, the fact that this relationship does not hold for away-from-the-money options is of profound significance. When the option, in this example, is either 7 points ITM or OTM, as seen in the extremes (93.00 and 107.00) of all the graphs, the vega amount varies by about .00281 for every 1% change. This may not seem like a lot, but think again because it grows exponentially with each 1 percentage point increase. Consider the effect that it would have on a ratio spread where the OTMs, in greater quantity, increase exponentially while the ATMs increase linearly. Implied volatility, in the bond options, screamed to 36% in seconds during the Rocket to Quality coinciding with the Stock Market Crash of '87 and stayed there long enough to drag the victims out of the pits forever.

RHO (P)

Rho is to interest rates what vega is to implied volatility. Most of the time it is of little concern, and is usually a trader's lowest priority. However, in periods when interest rates are volatile, rho can affect the market maker's profit and loss considerably. This is especially true in places like Brazil, where greater attention was placed on rho risk than delta risk because of the huge swings in interest rates that occurred in the mid 90's. The sensitivity is greater for the instruments with more time until expiration, as it is in the case of vega. The more time there is, the more borrowing or lending is impacted by a change in interest rates.

DIVIDENDS

When a stock has a dividend, there are a myriad of considerations for traders who have, or anticipate having, a position in that particular stock. Dividends have an unusual impact on the valuations of not only the everyday strategies but also on the locks. A change in the amount of the proposed dividend, the sudden declaration of a dividend, or a change in the ex-dividend date can create either unanticipated profit or loss for anyone having an existing position. An important lesson to be learned for anyone considering initiating a trade based on a deviation from a fair valuation is to check first to see whether something is wrong, whether a variable has not been considered, or whether any of the variables have changed. On the other hand, hesitating could result in a missed opportunity if nothing was wrong in the first place. This is a luxury that no trader can afford. Because of these unknown factors, there is a huge gap between the practical and theoretical approach to using options. Besides the list of variables that affect the valuations of every options strategy, the biggest and the most obvious unknown is: Where will the stock be when it is time to exercise? This unknown means that there is an opportunity for a rent-a-put early exercise play.

Dividend-paying corporations make an announcement of the dividend's particulars on a quarterly basis in the United States. In many countries, however, dividends are paid only once or twice a year. The announcement states the amount declared and the pertinent dates, important for both shareholders and market players, to consider. Along with the variables of time until expiration and the interest rate, these dates are required for valuation purposes. They are record date, payable date, ex-date or ex-dividend date, and the settlement dates for both the stock and the options. The latter two subject the trader not only to the dividend but also to the cost of carry.

Record Date

The record date is the date set by the corporation paying the dividend and the stockholder must own "settled[5]" stock in order to be considered the "owner of record" so that he or she can receive the payment.

Payable Date

The payable date, also set by the paying corporation, is the day when the cash payment will be paid to the owners of record. It is announced when the dividend amount and record date are declared.

Ex-Date or Ex-Dividend Date

On or before the ex-dividend date or ex-date (this date is set by the paying corporation) the stock has to have been bought, sold, or shorted for it to be subject to the dividend. Keep in mind that dividends must be paid if the trader is short stock because the transaction needs time to settle, and that happens on the settlement date.

---

[5] **Settlement**

Settlement refers to the actual payment and transfer of ownership for the shares.

Settlement Date for Stock

This is the date that the buyer becomes the owner of record. Stock settles in three business days in the United States[6] (e.g. a stock traded on Tuesday settles on Friday). Settlement is postponed a day for each holiday in between. For stock to be subject to the dividend it must be settled by the record date. On Friday, in this example, the buyer becomes the owner of record for dividend purposes.

Agreements at the time of transaction can be negotiated between the buyer and seller to alter the date. Stock traded for cash "same day settlement"[7] causes the buyer to become the owner of record by the same day's close.[8] Similarly "next day settlement" causes the buyer to become the owner of record by the next day's close.

The settlement of stock as a result of an option exercise also settles in three business days.

Settlement Date for Options

Options settlement is the next day after the transaction. If an option is exercised on the same day that it is transacted, it follows that the option settlement will take place the next day and the stock settlement will take place in three days.

Keep in mind that if a stock is purchased, or an option is exercised, prior to the weekend, two extra (sometimes more if there is a holiday) days without carry should be factored into, or rather out of, the valuation.

Countries other than the United States have other variables to consider. First, in many countries[9] there is a different tax rate for

---

[6] **Settlement Procedures**

Settlement procedures vary from country to country.

[7] **Cash Settlement**

Based upon an agreement between buyer and seller at the point of sale, the stock will be settled by the end of the business day that it was transacted.

[8] **Settlement by Agreement**

Based upon an agreement between buyer and seller at the point of sale, the stock will be settled by the end of the business day that it was transacted.

[9] **International Dividends**

Germany, for example, factors other variables into the valuation. These include the following:

Doppelbesteuerungsabkommen, an agreement between countries to avoid double taxation on dividends for foreign shareholders.
Kapitalertragssteuer, a tax reduction for foreign investors.
Bruttodividende, the gross dividend received by a German resident.
Bardividende, the net dividend paid by the company to the shareholder.
Courtage, a transaction fee paid to a broker (Amtliche Makler or Freimakler).
Körperschaftssteuer, or *Steuerguthaben*, the amount of tax credit for shareholders who are German residents.

dividend income (or expense) than there is for interest income (or expense). There may also be different tax rates for foreign and domestic investors. Long-term and short-term capital gains may be treated differently. There may also be different levels of taxation for corporations relative to individuals.

EXERCISE NUANCES INVOLVING EQUITIES WITH DIVIDENDS

Puts are usually exercised after an ex-dividend date so that the person exercising them does not have to pay out the dividend. They are also exercised for the same reasons that normal puts are exercised, namely when the corresponding call becomes cheaper than the carry amount (do not forget about the rent-a-call option). No trader would be motivated to exercise puts before that date unless the carry on the stock, up to the ex-dividend date, is greater than the short call to be covered plus the dividend to be paid or lost. (Dividends are paid if the exercise results in a short sale, and lost if the exercise results in a long sale.) Keep in mind that the carry rate depends on whether the exercise resulted in borrowing (at say 7.5%) or lending (at say 5%) more or less capital.

Fair Value Equation: $k + c$ vs. $s + p + b$

k = strike price, c = call price, s = stock price, p = put price, b = banking
Banking is the interest payments or receipts minus the dividend payment.

Calls are usually exercised when the corresponding put dips below the dividend less the carry amount. This can be an opportunity for a rent-a-put situation unless, for the same reasons mentioned earlier, there is a very remote chance that the cheap options will go higher than (in this case) dividends less interest. Therefore, calls should only be exercised before the ex-dividend date so as to receive the most (when already short) or pay the least (when becoming long the stock upon exercise) amount of interest.

NUANCES OF DIFFERENT STYLES OF CONTRACTS

Every options contract, apart from futures-style options, has nuances that affect the value of the conversions/reversals and boxes. The variables that allow the prices of locks to fluctuate, causing risks and opportunities, are interest (cost of carry) as it relates to Rho risk (price sensitivity to fluctuations in interest rates), dividends, takeovers and tender offers, supply and demand nuances, and exercise nuances as they relate to interest expense reduction or interest income enhancement. Some stocks are hard to borrow for shorting purposes, which puts price pressures on options (upward pressure on puts and downward pressure on calls) that differ from those in normal situations. American-style, deep in-the-money options, especially those with cash settlement, can be exercised before their expiration date because of an economic benefit to the holder.

EXERCISE NUANCES AS THEY RELATE TO INTEREST INCOME OR EXPENSE

The economic benefit to someone who exercises deep in-the-money options can be a reduction in interest expense or an enhancement to interest income, depending on their position. This can be accomplished by exercising puts or calls in futures, but only puts in equities. The point of exercise is not arbitrary, but the decision concerning whose contracts get assigned is random. If the out-of-the-money option becomes valued at less than the cost of carry on the deep in-the-money option plus the underlying, then the options may be worth exercising. It is for this reason that locks also change in value. Only American-style exercise allows options to be exercised before expiration, causing deep in-the-money options to always be worth at least parity (the in-the-money amount). Otherwise the "deeps" could trade below parity as they do in European-style options.

Story: Mishandled Reversal: In the summer of 1992 a group of traders, who had dissected their reversals out to the side and treated them as if there was no exposure, assumed that they were Greek and contract-neutral on the reversals. Although it was a limited risk problem, a large sum of money was involved because they had a huge size on. The reversal emulated a miniature bull spread and when the market collapsed, so did this bull spread. When the calls were trading significantly lower than the synthetic calls (cost of carry on the puts and stock), their puts were assigned. This left the traders with a loss of the difference between the calls and the carry costs. Since they had so many on, it cost them more than $2 million. This nuance is discussed in detail in the section on equity reversals. **End**

The Black-Scholes model will value locks at significantly different values than the models that start to account for the early exercise possibility long before the threat of exercise. The Modified Black-Scholes model for American-style options has the deep in-the-money options adjusted back up to parity, while the Black-Scholes model for European-style options will discount them (pricing the deep options below parity) in order to keep the price of the conversion/reversal equal to the cost of carry.

TO EXERCISE OR NOT TO EXERCISE?

It should become clear after reading about early exercise nuances why it is beneficial to be in control of the exercise by being long the deep in-the-money options. There is a good reason to be willing to pay a little extra when buying them and charging a little more when selling / shorting.

Calls are almost never exercised early unless there is a dividend (payable to holders of long stock) with a greater amount than the interest to carry that stock plus the cost of the corresponding (same strike) OTM put. This OTM put needs to be purchased in order to keep the trader's market exposure the same as it was before the exercise.

Puts are commonly exercised so that traders can save on the carrying costs of their long stock, or so that they can earn interest on being short stock (called short stock rebate). Exercise happens when the corresponding OTM call can be purchased for an amount less than or equal to the carry costs involved with the deep ITM put. The OTM call needs to be purchased in order to keep the trader's market exposure the same as it was before the exercise.

Exhibit 3-20 displays positions in the first column. Each position's exposure before an exercise is detailed. The next column shows the position and exposure after exercise of the option. The last column, 'Lost Attribute', identifies the missing element, which is needed in order to maintain the position exposure that one had prior to exercise. One therefore needs to purchase the corresponding out-of-the-money option in the same quantity.

E X H I B I T   3 – 2 0

Consequence of Exercise

Position Before Exercise : Exposure	Position After Exercise : Exposure	Lost Attribute
Long Call : Limited Risk Long	Naked: Long Stock : Unlimited Risk Long	OTM Put
Long Call / Short Stock : Limited Risk Short	Flat : None	OTM Put
Long Call / Short Stock / Short Put : Flat	Short Put : Unlimited Risk Long	OTM Put
Naked Long Put : Limited Risk Short	Naked: Short Stock : Unlimited Risk Short	OTM Call
Long Put / Long Stock : Limited Risk Long	Flat : None	OTM Call
Long Put /Long Stock / Short Call : Flat	Short Call : Unlimited Risk Short	OTM Call

Obviously, it would be wise to buy options closer to the money, but prices available at the time of exercise may not be agreeable. In spite of this, the purchase should be made before one exercises, otherwise one will have the exposure of the lost attribute.

Understanding how the exercise can be used as a very high-reward for a low-risk strategy can be useful when an opportunity arises. Professional traders exercise in order to save on carrying costs that are greater than the amount that can be synthetically achieved with a different position configuration, or to collect a dividend when it is greater than the corresponding put plus the carry costs of the stock. This is because carrying costs and dividends can be translated into synthetic premium as a component of an option's value.

A lot of traders exercise deep in-the-money puts (in order to receive interest on short stock) when the corresponding out-of-the-money calls of the same strike become cheap enough to buy. However, it is often beneficial to cover those cheap out-of the-money calls but hold off exercising. It may be advantageous to wait a while before exercising because the remaining position generates a relatively low-risk / high-reward speculative position to the upside. The following story is about a favorite trade of my career. It was in the CBOT US Treasury Bond options and works a little different than a similar trade in a stock options contract. In the case of stocks, interest is calculated on the stock and the options. In the case of futures contracts, interest is only calculated on the options. Having said that, interest income and expense are also based upon movement in the futures, as I explained in the discussion of futures margin variation.

RENTING OPTIONS

Story: Better to be Late for Early Exercise: This story from 1985 relates the first time that I capitalized on the early exercise nuance. It will help you to understand how the exercise can be used as a very high reward, low risk strategy. The trade started on March 1st and the saga lasted until May 20th.

It all began when a trader standing next to me in the bond options pit mentioned that he was going to exercise his 74 puts that night (76 days before expiration). He said this because he had just covered (meaning bought back the shorts) his 74 calls at 6 ticks (.06 = 6/64) = ($93.75 where each tick is worth $15.625). Since the bonds were at 67.00, his 74 puts were at parity or 7.00 ($7,000) each. The carry cost of each put, with the interest rate at 9.7%, was about 9 ticks ($141). The calculation is $7000 x 76 days /365 @ 9.7% which equals $141 (call it 9 ticks). He was going to profit (or save) an extra $47 ($141–$94) for each conversion on the put exercise.

Sometimes this concept is difficult to fully understand. Think of it this way: he bought back calls at 6 ticks that he was synthetically short at 9 ticks. Long futures at 67.00 and long the 74 puts at 7.00 means that $7000 will either have to be borrowed, or will deplete capital that could be sitting in the bank earning interest of 9 ticks until expiration $(f + p - k + \text{carry in ticks}) = (67.00 + 7.00 - 74.00 + .09)$. About a day earlier when those calls were trading for 9 ticks each, the conversion was valued at a 9-tick credit $(f = 67.00, p = 7.00, c = .09)$. Plug these amounts into the conversion equation:

k = strike c = call price f = futures price p = put price

Day 1   *(k + c)*   –   *(f + p)*
                   Short   **Long**
                   (74 + .09) – (67 + 7.00) = .09 (9 ticks) debit

The trader bought the calls back at 6 ticks (.06).[10] To profit through exercise, the trader has to exercise the puts, which sells the futures at the strike, and in so doing he forfeits the put premium. This transaction unwinds the conversion by doing the reversal for a 6-tick (.06) debit. The profit is therefore 3 ticks (.03).

Day 2   *(k + c)*   –   *(f + p)*
                   Buys   **Sells**
                   (74 + .06) – (74 + zero) = .06 (6 ticks) debit

When the trader said that he was going to exercise the puts, I asked him to not exercise them, but to offer them out at parity with the futures (i.e. sell both at a total price of 74.00) because I wanted to buy them. He looked at me, a little bit confused, and yelled out "74 puts and futures at parity!" I said, "done". He asked how many. I told him that I would take all that he had (700 spreads). No one else in the pit wanted any. I then yelled out to the crowd, "74 puts and bonds 74.00 bid at

---

[10] **European-Style versus American-Style**

In European-style options the puts would be worth 6.61 (6 61/64, that is 3 ticks under parity) if the calls were worth .06. The C/R value would remain at .09, as opposed to the American-style C/R, the value of which changes as the underlying moves.

74.00" to see if anyone else wanted to participate one way or the other. No takers. We carded up the trade and I thanked him (the transaction costs to him were equal to the cost of exercising). He wondered why I wanted to do this, thinking probably that I had made a mistake because if I sold the real calls at .06 (the current price), I would have locked in a loss. This would be a loss because even though this would be the conversion for a 6-tick credit, it would cost me 9 ticks in interest to carry it until expiration.

Why did I do it? Hint: these were synthetic calls because I was long puts and futures 1:1. I was bullish because 67.00 was a former resistance point, which I believed would serve as a support level.

I could have bought 700 real calls for 6 ticks each, totaling 4,200 ticks equal to $65,625. Instead I bought the puts and futures for 74.00. The total cash outlay for the puts was $4.9 million (700 x $7000). The carry cost for 76 days was $98,967 (700 puts x $7000 x 76/365 x 9.7 percent financing cost).

Any answer yet as to why I did it this way? Was it a mistake?

Before I tell you why, let me first tell you what happened next and draw a comparison with a trader named Austin, who will have hypothetically bought 700 real calls for 6 ticks at the same time that I bought the synthetic calls.

The original trade was initiated at about 67.00 on the bonds (+700*74p / +700f at parity + carry).

The bonds rallied to 68 and change, and I sold 700 real 74 calls at 12 ticks. Assume that Austin sold out at 12 ticks as well.

Examine the reward to risk ratios for Austin and myself:

700 calls	Austin's Trade	My Trade
Risk	6 ticks ($65,625)	9 ticks ($98,439)
Reward	6 ticks ($65,625)	3 ticks ($32,813)
R/R Ratio	1 to 1	3 to 1

Austin bought at 6 ticks and sold for 12 ticks, making a profit of 6 ticks. 6 ticks risk divided by 6 ticks reward, yields a 1 to 1 risk/reward ratio. I bought the futures and the puts for the synthetic price of 9 ticks (f+p–k+carry). It seems as though I only profited 3 ticks when I sold the real calls at 12 ticks, that is 9 ticks risk divided by 3 ticks reward, which yields a 3 to 1 risk/reward ratio.

Based upon this information, it would seem better to have taken Austin's trade, the real calls, as opposed to my trade, the synthetic calls. Most of you are probably wondering why I am still talking about this, but I will ask one more time: which is the better trade?

If it still seems as if Austin's trade was the better of the two, one might want to reconsider after having understood the non-transparent aspect of the trade. Non-transparency is a major cause of deception in options trading. The carry is the deceptive aspect in this case. It is assumed that I would have had to carry the position until expiration to have a synthetic cost of about 9 ticks. The advantage that I had over Austin was that if the market had dropped that day and he had sold each option at a price of 3 ticks, his total loss would have been $32,813. If the market had dropped the day that I bought my synthetic calls I would have lost nothing because I could have exercised my puts. Exercising (selling futures at 74.00) would have gotten me out at my spread cost of 74.00 (67.00f + 7.00p). My loss would have been the carry charge. There would have been no carry charge and therefore no loss if I had not carried it overnight.

The next day I sold the real calls at 12 ticks. The futures were up at 68.00, and so the conversion was worth about 7.65 ticks ($120) ($6000 x 75/365 x 9.7%). The carry charge on $4.9 million at 9.7% for one night was $1302. That is $1.86 per contract or .119 of a tick. Now recalculate the transparent risk of 0.119 tick to the transparent reward of 4.35 ticks (12–7.65):

700 calls	Austin's Trade	My Trade
Risk	6 ticks ($65,625)	0.119 ticks ($1,302)
Reward	6 ticks ($65,625)	4.35 ticks ($47,578)
R/R Ratio	1 to 1	1 to 36.54

If it had been 2 days until I locked in the value, the carry charge would have been twice as much, and the risk/reward ratio would have been half as great, that is, 1 to 18.27. That is still a lot better than 1 to 1. In fact 50 days of carry would have still beaten the real call purchase. In my mind, I had decided to risk about $4000 on the whole play (three days of carry). In the interim, if the futures had dropped a good amount, I would have exercised my puts to avoid the carry charges.

I call this strategy 'renting a call'. It also works for renting puts. Renting calls works in a very similar way in stock options, when the out-of-the-money call trades lower than the carry cost of the stock versus the put. Renting puts in equities works when the out-of-the-money put trades less than the dividends minus the carry. These early exercise plays are the very reason that the Black-Scholes model is inappropriate to use for American-style options pricing and analysis. The market activity that followed this trade was quite interesting. Although I cannot really say what Austin would have done with his trades, my position was on automatic pilot. The bonds broke for the next two days and the calls traded back down to 6 ticks. I bought them back at 6.

The profits at this point were roughly $60,416, which was $65,625 (6 ticks x 700 calls in and out) minus $5,209 (carry for 4 days). Who knows whether Austin would have gotten long again there after he had sold out. The calls were lower than carry for me, and so I scooped them up, as the trader who had sold the puts and futures to me had done. I did not exercise as he did because there was a chance that the market would rally and that the calls would then trade above the cost of carry again. If the market continued to break, I could exercise my puts and be done with it. It bounced again three days later, and I sold the calls out at 12 ticks a second time. "KA-CHINGGGG!" Ring that cash register! This trade locked in another 6 ticks profit 700 times, less 3 more days of carry for roughly, $60,000. I bought those calls back at 6 ticks again six days later. I was back to square one with about $117,000 profit after carry costs and 65 days to go.

Sometimes you get to a point in a trade where your profits will still exceed your losses even if everything goes wrong from that point forward. In this case there were 65 days to go and I was borrowing about $4,9 million (with the futures at 67.00). This type of loan decreases as the futures move toward profitability. A decrease in the loan amount decreases the interest expense and therefore increases the profit. If the futures had moved the other way, the loan could have gotten larger unless I had exercised the options to liquidate the loan. Assuming that I just let this ride and paid the carry charge for 65 days on the $4,900,000, my profit of $117,000 would have been reduced by $84,643. I still would have had about $32,357 in profits.

Some traders would say that I am "playing with their money" (they mean the market's money), and that if I made $117,000 then lost $15,000, that I made only $102,000. I look at it another way. If I make $117,000 from a trade, it is a profit from that trade. If subsequently I lose $15,000 while maintaining my position, I would say that I lost $15,000 on that new trade.

A friend of mine was on a diet. He proudly told me that he had lost 25 pounds from his all time high weight. One week later when I asked him how his diet was going he said with a smile that he was 20 pounds lighter than the highs. I asked him how low off the highs he had gotten. When he answered 27 pounds, I said that meant that he had gained 7 pounds. He stopped smiling, realized that he was now managing a loser and not a winner, and went back to the discipline that had lost him the weight in the first place. The same attitude has to apply to the preservation of capital.

Back to the position of (+700*74p/+700f): There were 65 days to go. The last on the futures was about 67 and a half (67.16). The carry was $1247 per day, which equals about 7.4 ticks per spread ($6500 x 65/365 /15.625) until expiration. The futures rallied again, as did the calls that I sold in a scaling-up fashion. At a price of 12, I sold only half of my calls this time (350). It seemed to me that the bonds had built a base, and so I decided to be a scale-up seller. Further up at 15 ticks, I sold half of what was left (175 contracts), at 19 ticks I sold 75. Up at 21, I let 50 more go, and at 24 ticks I sold 25 more. This brought my profits to well over $170,000. Exhibit 3–21 shows a chart of the bonds and all the points where I made the trades.

E X H I B I T   3 – 2 1

Chart of the Bonds and the points of the trades.

In trades A, B, C, D and E it looks as though I was playing the market perfectly, but in reality it just happened that at points A, C and E the calls were trading at less than carry. Points B, D and F were just where the calls doubled in price, tempting me to take profits.

PIN RISK

As you can see from Exhibit 3–22, I was left with 25 long synthetic calls. In addition, the futures were at 73 and a half (73.16 or 73 16/32), just 16 ticks out of the money. My concern now was pin risk. If the bonds were at 74 the next day, I would have a dilemma. Should I exercise my puts to liquidate my futures (leaving the calls to die worthless) or wait to be assigned on my calls to liquidate my futures (let the puts die worthless)?

The dilemma is that if I do not exercise my puts and my short calls are not assigned, I will come in on the following Monday with a position of long 700 futures. I hate it when that happens. If on the other hand I exercise the puts and then I am assigned on the calls as well, I will have a position of short 700 futures. I hate that too. What did I do? I found someone to trade the C/R at even money with me. I did the Reversal (*R*) with a guy named Frank, who did the conversion. This left me with long 25*74 real calls that were a half a point out of the money.

EXHIBIT 3 – 2 2

The Day Before Expiration, My Position Was: +700*74*p* / +700*f* / –675*74*c*.

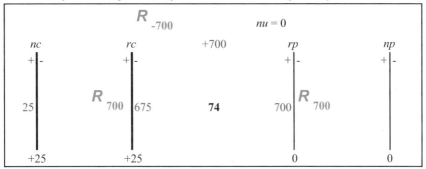

AFTER EXPIRATION NEWS EVENTS

The expiring bond options stopped trading at noon on Friday, May 17, but we had until 8:00 A.M. the following Saturday to exercise. Bond futures continue to trade until the 2:00 P.M. close on Friday. If one exercises, one takes delivery of the futures, which still trade for a few more weeks. At 11:58 A.M. on Friday, the bonds were at 73.28 (73 28/32), making the 74 calls just 4 ticks (4/32) out-of-the-money. The calls which I was long were also trading at 4 ticks (4/64), $62.50. I could have sold them and salvaged the remaining value of $1,562.50, but I wanted to play for a cheap scalp. I had been waiting to play it ever since I had come down to the CBOT from the CBOE.

Below the strike my calls were just out-of-the-money. I wanted to play the market in a way similar to the way I did one month earlier, when I scalped the calls over and under the carry value of 6 ticks. I was hoping that the market would rally up so that I could sell up to 25 futures and turn my calls into puts. Once filled, I would then hope that the market would break, so that I could buy the futures back under the strike, taking a profit on the futures and turning the position back into plain naked long calls. This game differs from the usual scenario of buying and hoping for a rally or selling and hoping for a break. For example, if I had the chance to sell the 25 futures up at 74.05 (74 5/32), that would be synthetically selling my calls at 10 ticks (10/64) and buying puts for zero. If the market continued to move higher after the sale, I would just exercise my calls and the futures would disappear, leaving me totally flat.

It was a nice dream to buy at below the strike, sell above it, buy again at below it, sell again above, and then buy again below. However, the market just fizzled out and slowly drifted to 73.22 by 2:00 P.M. There was still life though. The cash market was open until 4:00 P.M. Brainstorm! I could play the free scalp with the cash equivalent. I called a broker in New York to find out the basis and the conversion factor for cash bonds versus futures. It turned out that a $1 million cash bond was equal at that time to 14 CBOT futures. The first price that I would have liked to sell at in the futures was 74.05, and, I was told by a basis trader, what the equivalent cash bond price would be. Although it was a beautiful warm spring Friday and there was a band playing at the Limit-Up bar near the CME, I decided to stay on the floor and watch the cash screens, hoping to see my price on the bond. I did my homework for Monday and printed out my theoretical value sheets as the custodial squad cleaned up all the papers from the day's trades. By 3:45 the floor was spotless and I was the only one in the room. All you could hear was the click tick clicks from the time stamp clocks. The cash market had thinned out as the dealers were shutting down their operations for the weekend. I was sorry that I missed the band, the beer, and the banter over at the Limit-Up as I walked toward the door. Passing the T-note pit, I looked up as the cash screens went blank. I took a last look at the news screen and all of a sudden the words came across the tape: FED CUTS THE DISCOUNT RATE.

The cash screens suddenly lit up and the bonds were trading almost 2 points higher than I wished to sell at. I have always been pretty conservative so I thought, do not look a gift horse in the mouth, take the money and run. This represented more than $40,000 in additional profits. I was afraid that there might have been an overreaction and that there could be a sell-off. I called New York and sold $1 million in bonds and $1 million in 10-year Treasury notes. The T-note conversion factor was 12 futures for $1 million of cash notes. The market stayed at that level until the extended trading session ended at 4:30. I exercised my calls to have a basis trade (futures vs. cash) in the bonds and a basis trade in the notes.

On Sunday night (Monday morning over the phone to London), I sold the one bond future left at 75.24. On Monday, it was a simple task to allocate the positions to four separate arb[11] brokers for liquidation on a not held[12] basis. By the way, bonds opened up limit, but I was already out. No guts no glory.

DO NOT FORGET TO EXERCISE

The story does not end there. On Monday morning, a trader came into the pit and walked up to Frank with whom I had traded the C/R. The trader said, "I forgot to exercise my 1000*74 calls on Friday and I heard that your calls were not assigned. So can you have someone in your office please write a check payable to us in the amount of $2 million?" Frank said, "Sorry, that trade is history." He turned around, made a trade, and never said another thing about it. There was nothing the other guy could do about it except go and close up his operation. He was obviously unaware of the discount rate cut and the cash market rally, so he just assumed that he would be assigned on his puts. Don't be a pinhead. Wait a minute, that $2M could have been mine if I had not done the reversal with Frank. Easy come, easy go. The last time that I talked to Frank, he was building a 12,000 sq. ft. house. **End**

RENTING STOCK OPTIONS

The rent-a-call strategy becomes available in stock options when an out-of-the-money call trades lower than the carry cost of the stock versus the same strike put. It is for this very reason that the Black-

---

[11] Arb

Arbitrage

[12] Not Held

'Not held' means that the filling broker is not held responsible if he or she does not get the best price available. This kind of an order is placed when the customer knows and trusts the ability of the broker. Many times the broker can get a much better price than was available at the time of the order, because he or she has a good feel for the market. 'Best can' means best effort.

Scholes model is inappropriate for use in American-style options pricing and analysis.

After real options are sold against rented options, the result is a conversion in the case of rented calls (long stock and long puts) or a reversal in the case of rented puts (long calls and short stock). Subsequently, an opportunity may arise where the real option that has been sold declines in value lower again than the banking amount (carry for rented calls or dividend minus carry for rented puts). In that case there is a chance to cover that option for a scalped profit, and to hope to play the rented option again.

The length of time that one finances the position is the risk in rented options. The beautiful thing about the strategy is that if the market is volatile many scalps can be performed. If the market moves against one, one needs only to exercise the deep in-the-money option, thereby liquidating the stock, in order to stop the finance charges from accruing.

One other concern is, of course, pin risk if the position is a conversion, reversal, box or jelly roll. If the stock were at the money on Friday expiration, besides a possible automatic exercise[13], one would have the pin-risk dilemma (explained earlier) if one's position were a reversal, for example. What can be done to avoid this dilemma? One can place an order to do the conversion, in order to completely liquidate one's position. This can be done for even money if you have a position that is opposite to that of the crowd. However, most often members of the crowd are carrying reversals, and you will have to pay a few cents or so to entice them into adding to their dilemma.

COST OF DOING BUSINESS

As with any strategy, traders should factor the costs of doing business into their equations. Margin costs and commissions change all the time and are different for each trader based upon his or her brokerage relationship. The math is getting easier now that prices trade in decimals. For example, if the commission for 10 contracts is $30 that works out to be about $3.00 per contract for 100 shares. As a result of this calculation, the trader recognizes that an option purchased at $3.20, effectively costs $3.23 [($3.20 x 100 shares + 30 commission)/10 contracts]. The net proceeds of a sale at 7.40 will be 7.37 [($7.40 x 100 shares – $30 commission)/10 contracts].

---

[13] **Automatic Exercise**

At-the-money stock options at expiration are automatically exercised for retail customers when $US0.25 in-the-money. It was changed in 2004 from .75 but, for decades, market makers have enjoyed the automatic exercise at $0.25 in-the-money.

A FINAL WORD

The Greeks of a position will help one to be prepared for situations before the fact, if one does just a little bit of analysis. A good time to do this is at or near the end of the trading day. If one is in a hurry, one can try to complete this work prior to the close. Sometimes the market can keep a trader busy up until the close though. In this case, the preparation for the next day could be done after the close, or before the opening on the following day. If one takes the time to prepare after the close, there will be more time to think about it and sleep on it. Adjustments to the position could then still be made before the market opens on the following day.

When dissecting a position, make the distinction between the gammas that have naked risk attributes and those that are part of limited risk spreads. To distinguish between the two, refer to the limited risk gammas as "*grammas*." The positions that they are part of do not have as strong an impact on P&L as the positions with unlimited risk.

CHAPTER

4

STRANGLES AND STRADDLES

When discussing strangles, straddles, and ratioed straddle strategies, it is necessary to understand the buying and selling of 'premium' (not the cost of an option). Sellers of premium want the market to sit still and buyers of premium want the market to move. It is important to understand the role that gamma and the other derivatives play in managing premium. Hence, there will be a presentation on gamma scalping, spread scalping and setting up break-even grids.

REASONS FOR BUYING PREMIUM

Why does someone buy strangles or straddles (i.e., premium)? The following are some responses I've had:

1. In anticipation of an implied volatility increase.
2. To have long gamma.
3. In the hope that either the put or the call, or both[1], goes far enough in the money to make it intrinsically worth more than the call and the put originally cost.
4. To scalp gamma[2] (basically fading the market as the position manufactures deltas).
5. Traders buy at-the-money straddles because they usually have the lowest implied volatilities compared with the other strikes.

   The simplest reason is that long strangles and straddles become long deltas if the underlying rallies, and short deltas if the underlying breaks. A trader loves to be long on the way up and short on the way down. This happens automatically with long premium spreads. The opposite occurs with a short premium.

---

[1] **Both call and put go in-the-money**

In equities, this could happen in a partial cash tender.

[2] **Scalping Gamma**

Many newcomers to options think Gamma Scalping is the Bees Knees but it is not very practical in a retail sense in most markets. It is more of a defensive strategy for market makers to protect themselves against time decay when caught long premium.

E X H I B I T   4 – 1

Profit and Loss Profile of 100*101 Straddles with 11% Implied Volatility and 47 Days to go and .01% Interest

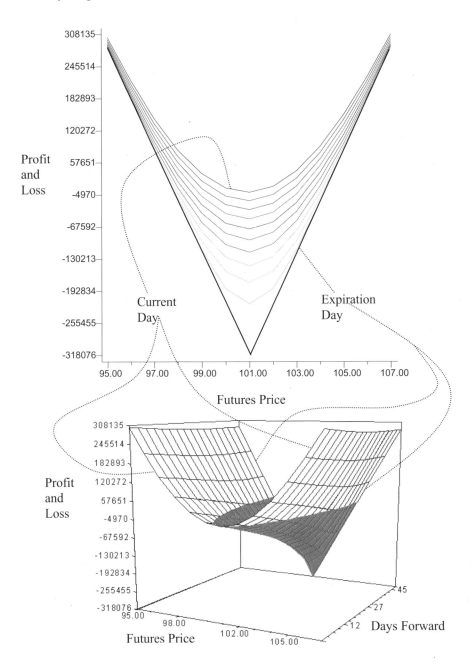

E X H I B I T   4 – 2

Profit and Loss Profile of 100*99/103 Strangles with 11% Implied Volatility and 47 Days to go and .01% Interest

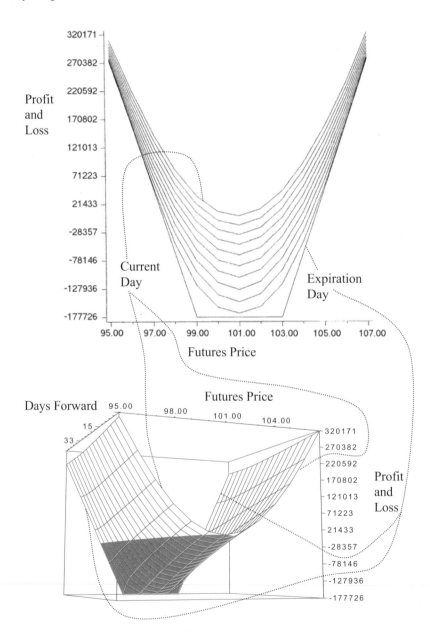

REASONS FOR SHORTING PREMIUM

Why does someone sell premium?

1. In anticipation of an implied volatility decrease.
2. In anticipation of a tight trading range for the underlying.
3. To have positive theta. (Time decay makes money in stable markets).
4. In the hope that both the put and the call, both go out worthless.
5. There is the impression that the Implied volatility level shorted will be greater than the actual volatility in the market allowing for a profitable 'negative gamma scalping' scenario.

There are, of course, safe ways and dangerous ways to be short premium and still manage it successfully. **Bottom Line: Limited-Risk-Short-Premium is the only way to go.** Shorting premium is a way that many derivatives traders consistently make money. On average they win more often than they lose. However, when they lose, it is usually by a much greater amount than their average gain, owing to the high-risk nature of selling naked premium. Selling naked premium should only be for the too wealthy or the too crazy. Too wealthy could be defined by taking a severe beating in the market and it still makes no material difference to the wealth of the individual. The only other reason to sell naked premium is if the person is too crazy. There will be times when there is no chance to manage it, for example the huge gapping market situations. The ideal situation for a premium seller is to go to sleep after initiating the trade and to wake up at expiration with the price of the underlying at the short strike price. It is of course not that easy because the market stretches out the trader's wallet from time to time, causing him to react for protection. Be careful when selling premium. If at the end of a trading day, the trader has a naked short premium, he or she is in the hands of fate. It is often too late to turn back especially when earnings warnings are announced, unusual surprise events or other great or horrible news.

In some cases, after options prices have become inflated, traders who were not accustomed to selling premium have come in and sold, and made huge profits once price levels have returned to normal. Another example of such a situation turning out well for some is that those insolvent traders who were not forced to liquidate during the 1987 crash did get their money back when the market recovered. However, many who tried to top pick[3] the high in premium levels were unsuccessful. It is not easy to sell naked premium and then wait and see where the strike ends up at expiration, although many traders wish that they could. One just has to get lucky, and have a large amount of trading capital, or both, in order to be able to carry this type of risk.

PONTIFICATION: SHORTING NAKED PREMIUM

In attempt to make a point about shorting naked premium during a recent response to a strategy question in one of the weekly Ri$k Doctor webinars (web based seminars), an individual suggested to:

"Short a December Strangle (120 calls and 100 puts) with the stock trading 110 for a 2.80 credit, a delta of (.01), a gamma of (.04) and adjust as necessary and hope the CEO doesn't die."[4]

Ri$k Doctor Response:

That would do well if the market stabilized but how would you be doing if it did not? While playing with options, don't forget that your mind gets played with while in the positions. Your proposed position has naked exposure and it's not like playing futures with a stop. Most less capitalized traders end up panicking and puking because the leverage of OTM options expands on them. Options positions should not be used with a day trader mentality. Options are better suited for a 'week' trader or a 'month' trader approach. Therefore (and please develop the good habit of limiting risk exposure, if not for you, for your family and dependants), for .10 or .15 less of a credit you can have the outside protection in the way of the November 95P/125C strangle (for 7 days anyway just until expiration) instead of taking on the short DEC strangle naked. By then, perhaps you will have made a bit of money or you can roll into a long OTM DEC strangles for a reasonable price. I don't think that I would buy the NOV but I would definitely buy some wings (either 1 for 1 or ratio them long) somewhere (learn to force yourself). I don't see any need to have net short options (I have taken one too many beatings for doing otherwise). Better to receive a lesser credit and have long wing insurance. Because of this, it means you have to trade a little bigger but you have less exposure.

---

3 **Top picking**

Top picking means to guess the top of a market while bottom pickers try to pick the bottom. Top and bottom pickers become cotton pickers!

4 **CEO Dying**

I think this individual was inferring that that would be bad for the stock.

Here is a little insight from the other side of the options business -- the market maker / proprietary market taker side: How do you think professional market makers/takers, who are well capitalized consistently make money? Why are they well capitalized? In other words, why do banks back these guys? Remember, bank directors have a fiduciary responsibility, mandates and have to answer to management, shareholders, the SEC the NASD, yada, yada, yada. One hint is they don't make money the new fashioned way – not the pie in the sky way – not the way that your 10 emails a day - peddling the $3000 options seminars - way. You may already know that the answer is that Pros are, by and large, premium sellers. They can be, because they are well diversified through the products allowing for the occasional bloody beating when a stock does a tap dance on their wind pipe. But what happens when the whole market goes…you know…goes really big, in one direction, fast and far, across the board, in all the products? Meaning: you can throw the idea of diversification out the window.

Insight: Wings. By owning, that is being long cheap wing premium (either 1 for 1 or ratioed long), one is given permission to short closer to the money, beefier premium. The proof is in the implied volatility (IV) skew…you know…the smile. To John Q. Public and speculators high implied volatility represents an over-priced opportunity motivating them to sell OTM options. The smile is caused by options inventory guys, that is, market makers, hoarding the wings. Did you ever notice the price, in terms of dollars and cents, of those high implied volatility options? They are the cheapest options available in those underlying instruments and this is the reason that market makers can sell premium across all sectors, and the reason that the banks can back them and remain comfortable with the firm's exposure. They may lose money here and there, but when the nightmare hits, these institutions with extra long wings score big. They avoid getting destroyed like victims of derivatives debacles. Why? Their wings kick in and it rains money.

PROPERTIES OF STRANGLES AND STRADDLES

From a theoretical standpoint strangles and straddles have very similar properties with regard to gamma, vega, and theta.

Any disparity between the Greeks deviates further as time passes or the market moves away from the strikes involved. They will, however, come close together again as the underlying moves to a point where both spreads are deep in-the-money.

Curvature refers to gamma. A position is said to have positive curvature when it is long gamma. It is quite common to have analyzer software that shows the curvature over time in one graph. This means that you will often see a curve for the current day, a week from today, two weeks from today, and so forth, and none for the day of expiration where the lines are quite angular (creating a 'hockey stick' graph -- see Exhibit 4-1). The settings are usually flexible so that you can choose the time increments.

Sometimes I ask my participants in class, "What is the difference between a long straddle and a long strangle; for example, long the 101 straddle and the +99*p* / +103*c* strangle with the underlying (this could be bonds or the DJX or the Diamonds (DIA)) at 101?" Some of the responses are:

1. The straddle is at the money while the strangle is out of the money.

2. Gamma, vega, and theta are all larger for the straddle.

3. The implied volatility of the straddle options is usually lower because of the skew.

4. The straddle costs more.

5. The straddle will have some exercise value at expiration while the strangle will be worthless if the underlying is at, 103, for example.

6. The straddle is more readily quoted and therefore is more liquid for trading.

All of these are correct, but the answer that I am always looking for is simply "a butterfly." The difference between these two spreads is the 99/**101**/103 butterfly (equivalent to a call butterfly, put butterfly, iron butterfly, a "gut" iron butterfly or any other butterfly configuration as long as it is buying the outside wing options and selling the inside body options). Simply though, if one is long a straddle and trades an iron butterfly (selling the 'straddle' body and buying the 'strangle' wings) they end up with a long strangle (the 'difference' – something minus something).

Since the price sensitivity[5] of a butterfly with more than a month to go is rather stable, the price of a strangle changes at virtually the same rate as that of a straddle (on a ratioed basis). Differences between the Greeks and price sensitivities of the straddles and strangles start to become very apparent during the last few weeks before expiration. Exhibit 4-3 shows the differences with eight days to go. In this example, there are 100 straddles versus 100 strangles for comparative purposes.

---

5 Sensitivity

If implied volatility is extremely low, the price sensitivity becomes higher.

For a one-percent move in either direction from 100, the 100 straddles outperform the 100 strangles by roughly $12,000. For a six-point percentage move in either direction, the 100 straddles outperform the 100 strangles by over $86,000. This is kind of obvious and about what you would expect.

E X H I B I T   4 – 3

Comparison of 100*101 straddles to 100*99/103 strangles with 8 days to go

	100*101 Straddles												
Price:	95.00	96.00	97.00	98.00	99.00	100.00	101.00	102.00	103.00	104.00	105.00	106.00	107.00
P&L	468771	368845	269449	172823	86006	22994	0	24074	87246	173562	269719	368909	468781
Delta	-9998	-9981	-9866	-9347	-7775	-4533	66	4603	7746	9290	9833	9971	9996
Gamma	5	41	237	914	2352	4086	4851	3980	2281	923	266	55	8
Theta	-7	-62	-370	-1456	-3820	-6772	-8202	-6864	-4011	-1655	-486	-103	-16
Vega	10	90	538	2117	5557	9850	11930	9983	5835	2407	708	150	23
	Differences Between 100 Straddles and 100 Strangles with 8 Days to go.												
Price:	95.00	96.00	97.00	98.00	99.00	100.00	101.00	102.00	103.00	104.00	105.00	106.00	107.00
P&L	86347	84903	79287	64593	39143	12007	0	11590	37785	62625	77695	84105	86086
Delta	-56	-281	-933	-2051	-2885	-223	-11	2157	2787	2040	1006	353	31
Gamma	-102	-394	-929	-1179	-254	1592	2535	1522	-218	-1066	-888	-427	-137
Theta	153	603	1449	1876	412	-2639	-4286	-2625	384	1912	1622	794	260
Vega	-222	-876	-2108	-2729	-600	3839	6234	3818	-558	-2781	-2359	-1155	-379
	100*99/103 Strangles												
Price:	95.00	96.00	97.00	98.00	99.00	100.00	101.00	102.00	103.00	104.00	105.00	106.00	107.00
P&L	382425	283942	190162	108230	46863	10986	0	12483	49461	110937	192024	284804	382696
Delta	-9942	-9700	-8933	-7296	-4890	-2305	77	2445	4960	7251	8827	9617	9906
Gamma	107	435	1166	2093	2605	2493	2316	2458	2499	1989	1154	482	145
Theta	-159	-665	-1819	-3332	-4233	-4133	-3916	-4239	-4395	-3566	-2108	-897	-276
Vega	232	967	2646	4846	6157	6012	5696	6165	6393	5187	3067	1305	402

From a theoretical standpoint strangles and straddles have very similar properties. Let us now consider how many 99p/103c strangles it takes to have the equivalent gamma, vega and theta levels (the life force that flows through all the options in the matrix) of 100*101 straddles. To start off with a similar gamma, theta and vega equivalent, it requires 113*99/103 strangles to have the same fire power of the straddles. The difference in premium erosion (negative theta) is $12 ($3383 versus $3371) for the whole position and a 1% move in either direction is only 1%, to 100.00 or 102.00 for example. The profit and loss differences are about $400 (not much on 100 plus spreads).

Many people are mainly concerned with the quantity of contracts that might eventually go into the money but when dealing with premium, the decision to go with straddles versus strangles will vary depending on time to go and volatility levels. With a very large 6% move in the underlying, the 113 strangles will outperform 100 straddles by $12,036 on the upside and $8,572 on the downside, as can be seen from the extreme values, in Exhibit 4–4. If the move is smaller, after some time passes, the 100 straddles will outperform the 113 strangles. The natural question then arises: How about a certain number of straddles long or short versus short or long strangles? Straddle Strangle Swaps will be discussed in Chapter 6 and inter-month ones in Chapter 7.

E X H I B I T   4 – 4

Comparison of 100*101 Straddles to 113*99/103 Strangles with 47 Days to Go

	100*101 Straddles												
Price	95.00	96.00	97.00	98.00	99.00	100.00	101.00	102.00	103.00	104.00	105.00	106.00	107.00
P&L	302051	218357	144129	82482	36427	8425	0	11477	41981	89600	151742	225525	308135
Delta	-8744	-7946	-6845	-5431	-3735	-1833	160	2123	3947	5537	6846	7865	8617
Gamma	659	944	1259	1564	1814	1968	2001	1911	1717	1454	1163	879	630
Theta	-985	-1443	-1964	-2490	-2947	-3261	-3383	-3296	-3020	-2607	-2125	-1638	-1196
Vega	8418	12329	16782	21277	25179	27871	28912	28162	25804	22281	18162	13997	10217

	Differences Between 100 Straddles and 113 Strangles with 47 Days to go.												
P&L	-8572	-3696	-783	514	724	412	0	-368	-839	-1800	-3729	-7051	-12036
Delta	590	385	202	65	-14	-41	-39	-37	-64	-136	-257	-413	-585
Gamma	-206	-199	-164	-109	-51	-7	7	-9	-48	-98	-141	-169	-175
Theta	309	303	255	173	82	13	-12	14	84	175	258	313	331
Vega	-2636	-2592	-2177	-1480	-707	-111	106	-126	-724	-1491	-2200	-2675	-2832

	113*99/103 Strangles												
Price	95.00	96.00	97.00	98.00	99.00	100.00	101.00	102.00	103.00	104.00	105.00	106.00	107.00
P&L	310623	222053	144912	81968	35703	8013	0	11845	42820	91400	155471	232576	320171
Delta	-9334	-8331	-7047	-5496	-3721	-1794	199	2162	4011	5673	7103	8278	9202
Gamma	865	1143	1423	1673	1865	1975	1994	1920	1765	1552	1304	1048	805
Theta	-1294	-1746	-2219	-2663	-3029	-3274	-3371	-3310	-3104	-2782	-2383	-1951	-1527
Vega	11054	14921	18959	22757	25886	27982	28806	28288	26528	23772	20362	16672	13049

GAMMA SCALPING

Often, when I ask; "What is the best position for a market maker to have?" (I am looking for the answer; "a flat position") students say, "Long gamma." It is true that a long gamma position creates deltas favorable to the market direction. That is a wonderful thing to have happen, but remember that there is a luxury tax attached to this position and can be very costly. The exposure is negative theta, which means that your asset is wasting away and is also subject to potentially devastating decreases in implied volatility. Gamma scalping methods can be used to recapture some or all of the lost premium, but it is more of a defensive play (money saver) than a money maker.

Gamma scalping is basically fading the market as the position manufactures deltas. Gamma scalping is not for everyone, but the following discussion will surely tie up a lot of loose ends regarding options behavior. The gamma scalping type of neutralization, also referred to as "delta hedging", is performed on an as needed basis by market makers whether it be from the long side or short side. The following experience will illustrate the strategy.

Story: Scalping Gammas in My Sleep: One afternoon I left the exchange with a net exposure equivalent to 110 at-the-money (3800) straddles in the CME Swiss Francs. Although I had a position consisting of thousands of contracts, after dissecting the position, I was net long the same number of gamma as 110*3800 straddles would have been. I simply took the net gamma of my total position and divided into that figure the gamma for one 3800 straddle. The product was my net at-the-money straddle equivalent. The net at-the-money straddle equivalent is the amount to liquidate when you want to take a break from trading or want to flatten out your exposure. Since the at-the-money straddle options are usually the most liquid, it is generally easy to get a fair price. In my case I would have had to sell 220 of the 3800 options against futures to neutralize the position. That night there was a Group of Five Nations meeting, and some news that could move the market was expected, so I decided to speculate for a big move and an increase in implied volatility.

Each at-the-money straddle settled at 222 ticks ($2,775.00) at the close for a total cost of $305,250.00. I had no intention of risking even 5% of that figure. My maximum risk as far as I was concerned was going to be $10,000.00 (about 7 ticks per straddle). My only concern was my cost, 222 ticks. I hoped to reduce that cost by making a small profit through gamma scalping opportunities.

Positive gamma scalping can take place when a position is long premium and negative gamma scalping can be carried out when a position is short premium. My total gamma was 3054 @ SF3790 for a one point move. Notice that if the market had rallied about a point to 3890, the delta would become long 2978 deltas (or 30 futures worth). About a point lower down at 3690 we would have been short 3019 (or 30 futures worth). See Exhibit 4–5.

E X H I B I T 4 – 5

Profit and Loss for 110 Straddles in the Swiss Franc with 104 Days to Go

Price:	36.90	37.10	37.30	37.50	37.70	37.90	38.10	38.30	38.50	38.70	38.90
P&L	18899	12086	6775	2985	725	0	801	3118	6932	12219	18946
Delta	-3019	-2422	-1817	-1206	-593	20	629	1232	1826	2409	2978
Gamma	2961	3009	3043	3063	3067	3057	3032	2994	2943	2879	2805
Theta	-1279	-1318	-1351	-1377	-1396	-1407	-1411	-1407	-1396	-1378	-1353
Vega	19911	20468	20931	21297	21562	21723	21781	21735	21588	21344	21007

The market had previously developed into a symmetrical triangle formation as in Exhibit 4–6. I thought that the Swiss Franc would open either with a gap up or a gap down causing implied volatility to explode, a continuation of its current rising trend. The longer dated (104 days until expiration) straddle seemed to be a good strategy for gamma scalping.

E X H I B I T 4 – 6

Symmetrical Triangle formation in CME Swiss Francs

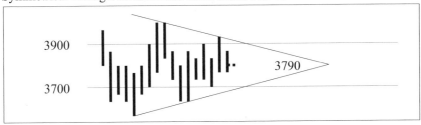

If I had been looking for a gamma play alone, a shorter dated straddle with 13 days to go would have been more appropriate because it had a higher gamma (8712 vs. 3057) and was therefore capable of manufacturing more deltas in the same move in the Franc (Exhibit 4–7).

E X H I B I T   4 – 7

Profit and Loss Grid for 110 Straddles in the Swiss Franc with 13 Days to go.

Price:	36.90	37.10	37.30	37.50	37.70	37.90	38.10	38.30	38.50	38.70	38.90
P&L	58813	40148	24482	12311	4053	0	288	4882	13588	26068	41888
Delta	-7994	-6900	-5597	-4108	-2475	-755	986	2680	4265	5693	6932
Gamma	4958	6028	7030	7866	8447	8712	8635	8230	7547	6664	5670
Theta	-2206	-2733	-3238	-3675	-3999	-4175	-4186	-4033	-3736	-3328	-2853
Vega	4285	5234	6137	6912	7484	7796	7816	7548	7025	6304	5458

There are several trade-offs to consider when buying a straddle. As it was, I had approximately one-third of the theta to worry about (-1,407 per day vs. -$4,175) and almost three times the vega (a double-edged sword), which was what I was playing for with the far month straddle versus the near month straddle ($21,723 per 1% change vs. $7,796).

Because the Swiss Franc futures also trade in Singapore, I decided to put overnight orders in to scalp some futures if the market gyrated between 3700 and 3900. The reason that I had picked 3700 and 3900 was that these points represented breakout levels. Outside of this range I no longer had any desire to "fade"[6] the market. At 3900 I would be fairly neutral, primed to take advantage of a move in either direction, because from my analysis that point either continued to be resistance or changed to become a new support level. At 3700 I would be fairly neutral and ready for a bounce off from the support or a break through it. Until the Swiss Franc did break out though, I intended to scalp gammas.

Remember that my gamma was 3054 for a one-point move. The most difficult aspect of gamma scalping is deciding how and at which point you are going to do your scalps. The 'how' in this case was easy because I was doing it in Singapore and they only had futures contracts at the time. It was tougher to decide at which point to scalp because this is an individual matter. What is too small and/or too early for one trader might be too big and/or too late for another. The answer varies according to comfort level, experience and risk tolerance. Gamma scalping is basically fading the market as the position manufactures deltas.

At the time that the market was opening in Singapore I was dining out and called my broker. I had calculated that if the market went up to

---

[6] **Fade the Market**

Fading means challenging the market while hoping for a rebound. If the market is falling, fading means buying on the dips. If the market is rallying it means selling on the way up.

3900, I would be long over 30 futures, while down at 3700, I would become short about 30 futures. My trading size was 6 at the time so I decided to fade with 6 futures at 20 tick intervals (30oo deltas in 100 ticks is about 6oo deltas every 20 ticks). Incidentally, trading 6 every 20 assumes that gamma is linear, which it is not. It appears to be linear because these are longer dated gammas.

The gamma graph (See Exhibit 4–8) looks like a hump with the peak just before the strike price. As we move further from the strike the gamma gets smaller. Therefore, to maintain the size 6 (lots to scalp) when gamma is say, down to 2400, that will stretch the increment to 25 ticks (24oo deltas in 100 ticks is about 6oo deltas every 25 ticks), The hump gets taller and narrower as time goes by. Notice that with 13 days to go the gamma is 8712. At this point I would have had to trade 6 futures at 7-tick intervals (87oo deltas in 100 ticks is about 6oo deltas every 7 ticks). Notice the delta changes if my position had a shorter term to expiration, I would have had to trade at either smaller tick intervals or increase my size to wait for bigger intervals.

E X H I B I T   4 – 8

Gamma Graph for 110 Straddles: Swiss Franc Between 13 and Zero Days to go.

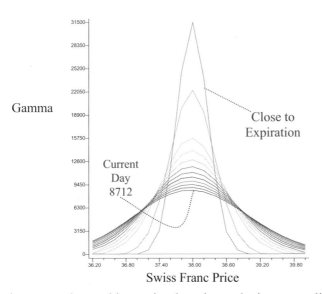

It is better to keep things simple when placing complicated orders (especially if you might upset your dinner date by spending the whole night trading).

The order that I placed was:

"Buy 6 SEP (September Futures) every 20 ticks and/or sell 6
SEP every 20 ticks starting at 3790" (the closing futures
price in Chicago).

"If you sell 6 and it drops 20 buy them back".

"If you buy 6 and it rallies 20 sell them out".

"If they get past 3900 on the upside, stop selling and pray for me
that the Swiss Franc goes to the moon".

"If they get past 3600 on the downside, stop buying and pray for
me that the Swiss Franc plunges into the toilet".

The broker could not understand how I could possibly wish for the
market to continue in the same direction subsequent to either selling all
the way up or buying all the way down. I asked him to leave that to me
and to please give me a 5:00 A.M. wake up call with any fills.
When the phone rang at 05:00, I hoped that the broker would tell
me that the results of the G5 meeting sent the Swiss Franc over 4000. He
told me that the futures were at 3790, exactly where they had closed the
day before. I was immediately getting geared up to sell out all of my
premium and get short some on the opening bell at 07:20 because
implied volatility would undoubtedly be annihilated. The broker then
proceeded to tell me that I had had a nice night and that I was a genius
because I had sold 18 futures on the way up to the high of 3855, and
bought each 6 lot back for a 20-tick profit, then bought another 18 on the
way down to the low of 3725, and sold each 6 lot for a 20-tick profit,
totaling a 720 tick profit. Exhibit 4–9 shows the transactions.

E X H I B I T   4 – 9

Market Action and Transactions Overnight

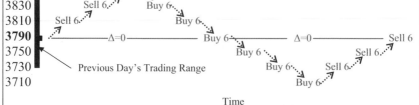

What seemed ingenious to the broker was simply going to cover the loss that I was about to take on the underlying opening unchanged.

On the opening bell I was able to sell 110 straddles at 216 (a good sale because it closed that afternoon at 205), 6 ticks lower than where they settled the day before, for a 660 tick loss, almost all of the profit from the gamma scalping. This was the luxury tax that I mentioned earlier. **End**

Implied volatility is a prediction of actual volatility in the future. When the future becomes the present, the actual movement of the underlying has an uncanny way of erasing option premium equivalent to the extent of the movement. It is frustrating to see gamma scalps earn only what was lost when the premium gets crushed, but it is a necessary defense.

Often when long premium, the erosion of value is far greater than the profits from gamma scalping. This suggests that having positions of short premium profit more often than long premium positions. It is true that one wins more often when short premium, but losses can be severe if safe strategies are not employed. Outright naked short premium is not for everyone. One must be prepared for extreme market conditions as well as disciplined and quick to adjust the position when necessary. Examine Exhibit 4-10.

E X H I B I T   4 – 1 0

The Effect of the Gamma Scalp Trades

Futures Price	cΔ	pΔ	Delta Per Straddle	Delta of 110 Straddles	Flat Δ After Trades:		Trades if Traded 18 Every 60 Ticks:	
3890	+.625	-.355	+.270	+2972				
3870	+.599	-.381	+.218	+2403				
3850	+.573	-.407	+.166	+1821	C		A -18	
3830	+.546	-.434	+.112	+1227	B D			
3810	+.519	-.462	+.057	+625	A E			
3790	+.491	-.489	+.002	+16	F	L	B +18	D -18
3770	+.463	-.517	-.054	-596	G	K		
3750	+.435	-.545	-.110	-1208	H	J		
3730	+.407	-.572	-.165	-1818	I		C +18	
3710	+.380	-.600	-.220	-2423				
3690	+.353	-.626	-.273	-3006				

In retrospect, it would have been better to have ridden my deltas further, and to have traded 18 futures at 60 tick intervals. This would have yielded a profit of 2160 ticks during the night minus 660 ticks the following morning for a net profit on the trade of 1500 ticks instead of 60 ticks. However a problem occurs when the size and increment are too wide for any subsequent move. If my size were 30 every 100, then I would have missed out on any gamma scalping opportunities that night because the high was only 3855 and the low was only 3725. If it is carried out with a smaller size and narrower increments the losses from the premium can exceed the gamma scalping profits.

For each futures price observe the implied call and put deltas. The next two columns show the net delta of each straddle and the total delta of 110 straddles. The fifth column shows where the scalps were traded to flatten out the delta. The last column depicts where the scalps could have been traded if I wanted to take more risk.

A trader can never know in advance the size and increment of his 'pure' gamma scalps. "Pure" because there is nothing from stopping anyone from overbuying or overselling the amount of deltas produced. Sometimes I will sell into a rally more deltas than are generated simply because if I am right, I will make more money and if I am wrong, or too early, any continued move will generate the contracts that I need to absorb the over-trades. For example, I may decide to trade 7 futures instead of 6 at each point. In this case I would also have ended up with a greater profit than we have in the example discussed. However, consider what would have happened if the futures had rallied to 38.90. At 3890 (see Exhibit 4-5) I would have had a straddle delta of +2419 against -35oo deltas (5 trades x 7oo contracts each) from my futures trades up to and including sales at 3870 and 3890, for a total net delta of -1081. (At about 3900 I would have stopped selling because of the breakout through technical resistance.) To calculate where the futures would have to be in order to generate enough deltas to absorb the excess short detlas due to this aggressive over-gamma scalping start at 3890, the last scalp point. Being short 1081 deltas and having positive gamma of 2805 at that point, divide 1081 by 2805 and get .39 ticks higher or at almost 3930 and the position would begin to get long again from that point forward.

Exhibit 4-11 shows another perspective where each sale of the 6 futures is synthetically selling 6 calls and buying 6 puts.

E X H I B I T   4 – 1 1

Dissections of the Gamma Scalps

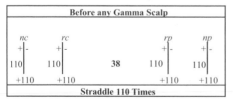

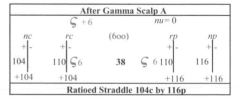

As you can see in the net call and net put columns, the ratio of the straddle changes with each of the gamma scalps, A, B, & C from 110x110 to 104x116, 98x122, and 92x128 respectively. Exhibit 4-12 shows the P&L graphs before the first scalp with of 110 straddles that were neutral at 3790 and another graph depicting the P&L profiles after Gamma Scalp A, B and C.

E X H I B I T   4 – 1 2

Straddles and Ratioed Straddles after Gamma Scalps A, B and C

Before any Gamma Scalps

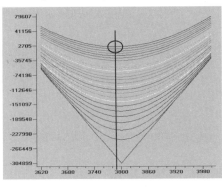

After Gamma Scalp A

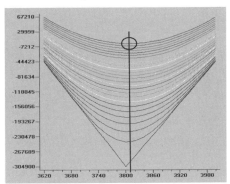

After Gamma Scalp B

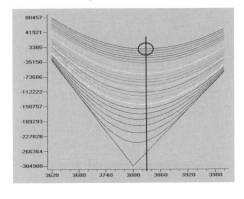

After Gamma Scalp C

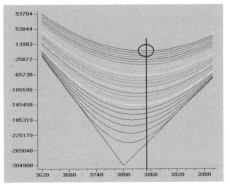

The straight lines in Exhibit 4-12 represent the expiry profile, while each curve represents the current P&L profile. Notice what happens to the curve as each gamma scalp trade is made (the shifts are to the right in these illustrations). The lowest point of the curve shifts to the point where neutrality is achieved (depicted by the black circle 'O'). After trade A at 3810, it looks as if the position is long a straddle with a new strike, the 3810 even though there is no 3810 strike. At 3830 when we neutralize again it looks as though the straddle's new strike is 3830.

If time goes by and the underlying does not move, the thick red circles 'O' and the curves will move toward the strike vortex, over time, as depicted in Exhibit 4-13.

E X H I B I T   4 – 1 3

As Time Passes, Premium Erodes

The Circles Representing Delta Neutrality Moves Toward the Vortex

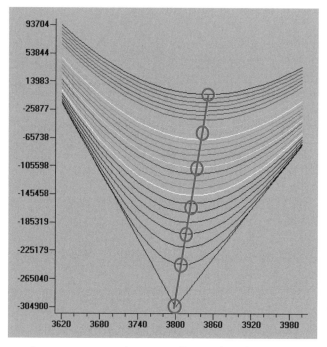

If the market were to continue to rally so that short deltas were not being generated and you continued to sell, it would not be possible to cover gamma scalping sales. Eventually, with the sale of 110 futures, the position would turn into long 220 puts which would be significantly out-of-the-money, perhaps even worthless. This would most certainly be a losing trade because the average sale of all of those futures would have had to be greater than 4022 (3800 +222), i.e. the strike plus the original straddle cost, in order to make a profit. Conversely, if the market moved in a slow grind downwards, the average purchase price of the futures would have to be 3578 (3800 - 222, the strike minus the original straddle cost) in order to break-even. The position would eventually be net long 220 calls which would most likely be worthless.

The straddle originally cost 222 ticks each. To calculate the net premium, multiply 222 by the quantity of 110 for a result of 24,440 ticks. Each trade on the gamma scalp serves to reduce that net outlay. The future, a synthetic combo, is synthetically generating a credit with each sale above 3800 and each purchase below 3800. Selling 6 futures at 3810 is like selling 6 calls and buying 6 puts for a total credit of 10 ticks,[7] six times. At 3830 there is a credit of 30, six times. At 3850 there is a credit of 50 six times, etc. By the time we have rallied to 3850, we have reduced our original cost of 24,440 by 6x10 + 6x30 + 6x50 to 23,900. If the futures are bought above the strike, the cost is obviously being added back and is increasing even though there is a profit on the isolated scalp. Buying the futures back below the strike reduces the cost because a synthetic combo (buying calls and selling puts for a greater amount) is being bought for a credit.

Suppose I had been constantly hedging deltas trading 1 future every 3 ticks instead of 6 futures every 20 ticks. The profit during the night would in this case have been 126 ticks from 42 scalps each with a 3 tick profit (21 sales on the first leg up to 3855, 42 buys on the way down to 3725 and 21 more sales back up to 3790). I do not have a chart of exactly what happened that night, but I am sure there were opportunities to scalp many one lots as the Swiss Franc bounced around. It would however have taken a lot of bouncing for that profit to exceed the 720 ticks produced with the 6 futures every 20 ticks, let alone the 2160 ticks produced with 18 every 60. As I stated earlier, when long premium, trades are most profitable if you can wait for the widest possible increment on a large size without missing the opportunity to scalp. This is the most profitable strategy in each direction.

Now consider what strategies a trader could employ if he is short premium and his position is manufacturing deltas against the market direction. His position manufactures long deltas with each down-tick or becomes short deltas with each up-tick. Suppose that a trader, Shorty, was short 110 straddles the night of my Swiss Franc trade. He may have handled the position in a number of ways:

1. He may have done nothing and reaped the reward of an unchanged market followed by a decline in implied volatility.

2. If he had been overly cautious he would have placed an order to buy 1 every 3 ticks on the upside and sell 1 every 3 ticks on the downside. The result would have been a loss of 126 ticks overnight, followed by the larger profit in the morning.

3. Or he may have placed orders every 50 ticks to cover the deltas manufactured (15 the first 50 ticks and 13 the next 50 ticks, etc.). In this case he would have lost 1500 ticks overnight.

---

7 **Selling Futures has a Call/Put Combo Equivalent**

Actually it is equivalent to the present value of the in-the-money amount of 10.

4. He could have placed a stop 100 ticks away to trade twice as many contracts (60), thereby reversing the position. This would have enabled him to absorb the futures manufactured against his position. His stop order would not have been filled, and he would have profited as a result of the unchanged opening price.

There are as many different techniques for scalping gammas as there are traders. Each method is based upon the individual trader's experience or lack thereof, and the amount of risk that he is willing to take.

DYNAMIC GAMMA SCALPING

As we saw earlier in my gamma scalping example, trading futures against long straddles can be very limiting. If on that overnight trade I had had more alternatives, I could have altered my premium profile or avoided the dampening effect on my net contracts.

If the move from 3790 up to 3850, then down to 3730 and back to 3790, had happened during the day, I could have sold calls when the market was moving up and puts on the way down. In this way much of the premium erosion that I suffered would have been avoided.

An alternative can be to buy premium with each adjustment. This strategy can work well if the futures move in one direction. One buys the delta equivalent amount of puts on the way up and the delta equivalent amount of calls on the way down. However, if this strategy had been used in my example, a large loss would have been incurred because of the premium decline on the opening. On days when implied volatility increases, traders profit very well from buying options to scalp their gamma because their hedges either do not lose as much as the futures would have lost, or they do not lose anything at all. On days when volatility is very high and the market goes up, the puts can increase in value as well, and the strategy will be extremely profitable.

A dampening effect occurs if only futures are being scalped, and they move predominantly in one direction causing a loss of net contracts in that direction. For example, if the market is in a bull trend, futures are sold into that rally in anticipation of buying them back lower. If they are not bought back because the rally continues, but more and more are sold, all net long call contracts (which you wish you would have had on an extended move up) will have been depleted.

Suppose that you choose to neutralize your deltas in a different way. You can achieve this without changing your premium or losing any net contracts. You have the option of adding or removing premium at different strikes and/or for different months. You can shift your premium elsewhere and even add to the net contracts while removing premium using calendar spreads, diagonals, back spreads and ratio spreads ("Let your dreams run wild...").

SPREAD SCALPING

Most traders would rather go home with a flat position. Day traders, scalpers, position traders, options speculators, and market makers would all be delighted if the market were to do what they expected before the closing bell, so that they could get flat. They would rather not have to worry about it overnight and enjoy the fact that they had had a good day. The next section is devoted to the concept of getting "in" and "out" of spreads which do not have a transparent price level.

A transparent price is one that is displayed on the boards of the exchanges or on computer screens via price feeds. When something is nontransparent, an additional amount has to be factored in to derive its true value. The biggest non-transparencies in the markets today have to do with embedded qualities, such as dividends, cost of carry, and features of delivery. Those who can calculate non-transparent spread values faster than the competition make profits.

Prices are certainly not displayed if the spread is some sort of ratio of different contracts. Any relationship can be made transparent today with the sophisticated software or market-linked spreadsheets that are available. The user can define relationships that update dynamically as individual contract prices change.

To be able to maintain a reference to cost levels while trading spreads, with or without these tools, one must have a system to monitor and evaluate price relationships between the instruments that are being traded.

The next few examples have little to do with options. They are provided to help promote certain conceptual ideas for spread tracking. It is useful to comprehend this because similar techniques can be used to scalp in and out of relatively liquid options that are traded against the underlying on a delta-neutral basis.

BREAK-EVEN ANALYSIS

Break-even analysis is used to create and monitor break-even points. It is very similar to scalping a futures spread. For example, assume that a spread in the S&P 500 futures has a fair value[8] between the March and

---

[8] **Fair value**

Fair value is the cost of carry between the two time periods minus the present value of the dividend cash flow.

June contracts of $2.00. The spreader tries to buy below $2.00 or sell above it. Suppose, for example, that he or she legged it and paid $1.85 [bought SPM (June) for 1358.85 and sold SPH (March) for 1357.00]. He or she may have a calculator or a little spreadsheet in a handheld computer or may write some prices down on a card. The grid of numbers in Exhibit 4–14 is set up for a spread price of $1.85.

E X H I B I T   4 – 1 4

Intermonth Spread Scalp: 1

SPH	SPM	
-1	+1	The trader has established at what points he or she will
1355.30	1357.15	break even on the SPH (March contract) vs. SPM (June
1355.25	1357.10	contract). All prices in column 1 are 1.85 lower than the
1355.20	1357.05	prices in column 2. This grid of numbers represents some
1355.15	1357.00	break-even prices. If the trader sells SPM for a value in the
1355.10	1356.95	right-hand column vertically higher than what he or she
1355.05	1356.90	pays for the SPH in the left-hand column, the trader will
1355.00	1356.85	profit. If the two prices are at the adjacent level, the trader
1354.95	1356.80	will scratch the trade, that is, break even.
1354.90	1356.75	
1354.85	1356.70	
1354.80	1356.65	

This is merely a way to pre-calculate the break-even levels so that while trading, the trader can concentrate on other important matters, such as seeing what else is happening in the market while waiting for a potential trade at a critical moment. Exhibit 4–15 shows how the trader might exit the trade.

E X H I B I T   4 – 1 5

Intermonth Spread Scalp: 2

SPH	SPM	
-1	+1	The original price is 1.85 but a 2.00 could be easily
1355.30	1357.15	calculated in your head (1356.95 minus 1354.95 = 2.00).
1355.25	1357.10	If the trader gets out of the trade with the relationship
1355.20	1357.05	shown, three prices higher, the trade will profitable. The
1355.15	1357.00	profit will be .15 or 3 ticks for each spread that he or she
1355.10	1356.95	bought.
1355.05	1356.90	
1355.00	1356.85	
1354.95	1356.80	
1354.90	1356.75	
1354.85	1356.70	
1354.80	1356.65	

This is an easy example, but even this gets tough for many when the pressure is on. It gets even tougher when you are trading products in fractions like 32nds and 64ths, even when they are displayed in decimal form (e.g., OTCBB[9] stocks, U.S. Treasury bonds and notes). For example, where traders do a spread with a tail or on a ratio, it becomes almost impossible to calculate break-even points in their heads. A tool or a program is needed that tells the break-even price of one contract at each tick price of the other contract. Exhibit 4–16 shows a spread with a simple ratio of 2 to 1.

E X H I B I T   4 – 1 6

InterStock Spread Scalp

ORCL	MSFT
2	1
24 1/4	53 1/2
24	53
23 3/4	52 1/2
23 1/2	52
23 1/4	51 1/2
23	51
22 3/4	50 1/2
22 1/2	50
22 1/4	49 1/2
22	49
21 3/4	48 1/2
21 1/2	48
21 1/4	47 1/2
21	47
20 3/4	46 1/2

A stock spread trader might trade 2oo shares of ORCL for every 1ooshares of MSFT. For example, a trader buys MSFT 50 and sells twice as many ORCL at 22 1/2. Each 2x1 spread was bought for 5.00 (50 minus (2*22 1/2)). A \$5.00 grid is then set up. To do this, make a list of consecutive prices, such as every 1/4 in the first column. If ORCL is 22 1/2 put that price in the middle, add 1/4s going up and subtract 1/4s going down. To determine the relationship between ORCL and MSFT prices, multiply 22 1/2 times 2 and add 5.00 (the spread cost) to arrive at 50.00 (the break-even price with ORCL at 22 1/2). Now realize that if 2oo ORCL each change by 1/4, 1oo MSFT must change by 1/2 to keep up. So add 1/2s to 50 to the upside and subtract 1/2s to the downside. Once you complete this process, check for errors by seeing that the differences are 5.00 at the two extremes (53 1/2 minus (2*24 1/4)) and (46 1/2 minus (2*20 3/4)).

MISSING THE HEDGE

Often traders get into the habit of squeezing their orders, especially when they miss their hedge or get caught between legs. Squeezing means that they avoid going to the market (paying up) on the underlying when hedging and sometimes let the stock or futures go far against them. Some traders get so addicted to this that they do it on every order. In a tight options market they may squeeze the futures for 2 and 3 ticks in order to make a half tick in the options.

Story: **Missing The Hedge:** On my birthday in 1986, an S&P option broker legged a combo spread to unwind an error which cost him $450,000 because the futures were down 5%. To liquidate, he bought overpriced calls and sold the puts dirt cheap to a few of us. This trade (selling 100 combos) required that I buy 100 futures to lock in a profit. When I turned to my broker, I noticed that he had

---

9 OTCBB

Over the Counter Bulletin Board Stocks are shares in small companies that are not listed on the big board..

left for the day because he was fed up. To compound the problem, trading in the SEP futures (SPUs) had switched over to the back month area as DEC futures (SPZs) had become the front month. It seemed that I was not really prepared to handle 100 S&Ps at that moment. It was the first futures trade of the day for me. Up until that point, every trade that I had made was on an options-to-options basis. I could not get anyone's attention, so I had to physically run around the S&P futures pit to the place where you can enter it. It seemed that the futures were faster than I. As I ran, I watched the SPUs rallying by whole points (1.00) as opposed to the usual .05 increment (which was about the first time that this had ever happened—today it seems to happen almost every day). Each point on 100 lots equals $50,000—327, 328, 329, 330. Finally, I made it to the point where I was supposed to be (20 seconds and $200,000.00 later) and asked Jimmy, a spread trader, for a market. He could see the anguish in my face, smiled and casually said, "331–332" (another $100,000). TIME OUT!

What would you do in this situation? In a split second, I was reminded of the time when I went into the back months of the bonds to buy 100 contracts (also for a hedge). The market was "10–12" so I tried to 'middle' it with an 11 bid but the spreaders stood their ground "at 12" and smiled that same smile. I made an obscene gesture and left the pit without buying any, only to find myself two seconds later running back in to pay 17 (that disgruntled moment of hesitation cost me over $15,000)

TIME IN! "Buy 100 at 332" I said. He said, "Done," and turned to buy DEC against it and watched as the SPZs rallied another six points (6.00) against him. I guess he thought that I knew something (yes, I knew that I hated myself when it cost me 15 grand in the bonds that other time). That was a trade from hell. When the smoke cleared I was lucky to be ahead $70,000 from the great edge on the combo. **End**

The lessons from the above example are:

If you ever catch yourself smiling after a trade,
it might be already too late to get out.

Indecision and hesitation are luxuries that traders can ill-afford.
Timing is everything.

CHAPTER

5

VERTICALS (BULL AND BEAR SPREADS) & COLLARS

Verticals (Bull Spreads and Bear Spreads) are the option trader's most versatile directional speculative tool. They are also instrumental in volatility trading. Retail investors can now expect to enjoy this versatility as well, since commissions have come down to level the playing field between retail customers and professional traders. Verticals are very popular for playing for time decay owing to their limited risk nature and although they have limited profit potential they can, in certain configurations, still reward a trader many times the risk taken. Since the crash of 1987 it has been too costly, from a margin standpoint, to sell naked options. In addition, during periods of high implied volatility, options premium becomes too expensive to buy. So where does that leave traders? Verticals are the bread and butter of the industry and are narrowly quoted, tighter than what is implied by the natural quotes displayed in options chains. Market makers get motivated to tighten the market quotes in order to invite two way order flow and enjoy a greater edge per delta than on wider quoted naked options. Verticals offer investors a more economical way to enter and exit the market and market makers are attracted to the type of inventory that is easier to manage as far as his or her whole position is concerned. It is certain that the competition by the six exchanges for this type of inventory has caused the bid/ask spreads to become as narrow as can be such as in the Quad-Qs (QQQQs - The Nasdaq-100 Tracking Stock) and in other issues, as well, bringing about better execution prices, further leveling the playing field between retail traders and professionals. Therefore, find the mid-value (averages between bids and offers) of the spread and from there, motivate the market maker by bidding a little more (.05, .10, .15. or a tick or two depending on liquidity) when attempting to buy and offering a little less when wanting to sell.

A vertical may be used for rolling risk and can be a useful weapon in avoiding an early assignment. Risk-averse investors and fund managers who want to participate in the upside (and even downside) of the market can put on a particular hedge, called a collar, that turns their stock investment into a synthetic vertical (collar) during periods of uncertainty. Although verticals can also be useful for complex trades such as gamma scalping, the most obvious use for verticals is that of speculating on direction. It can also be helpful to become familiar with how premium (time decay) is affected as the underlying travels between and beyond the strikes of a vertical.

The following P&L profiles in Exhibit 5–1 demonstrate how verticals behave over time and underlying fluctuations. The 95/100 bull spread is a mirror image of the 95/100 bear spread. Remember from Chapter 1 that a vertical can be comprised of a call spread, a put spread or a synthetic vertical, known as a collar (bear collar). A collar spread consists of calls, puts and the underlying stock. The differences between the three types of verticals are minor because, as mentioned earlier, one spread is only a box or a conversion/reversal away from one of the others.

E X H I B I T   5 – 1

P&L Graphs of Vertical Spreads

Bull Spread   **Bear Spread**

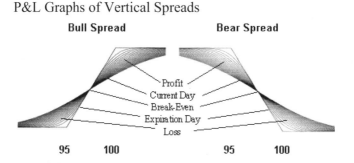

SPECULATIVE CONSIDERATIONS FOR VERTICALS

It is not enough to know that a bull spread is used when one is bullish, and that a bear spread is used when one is bearish. Additional considerations are warranted before applying a strategy to a market prognosis, such as:

1. Should one be considering an in-the-money (ITM), at-the-money (ATM) or out-of-the-money (OTM) vertical?[1]

2. Does the trader have an opinion on direction, or does he or she want to exploit changes in implied volatility?

3. How soon does the trader expect the market to move?

Direction, time and volatility levels must all be considered.

---

[1] **ITM, ATM or OTM Vertical**

With respect to the stock's current level, a vertical might have one option ITM and one OTM, making it what this book will refer to as an ATM vertical. In addition, in this book an ITM vertical refers to one where both options are currently ITM, and an OTM vertical refers to one where both options are currently OTM.

Exercise: Position: DJX (CBOE's Dow Jones Contract) is at 105 and the 90c/100c in-the-money (ITM) Bear Call Credit Vertical Spread is shorted for $6.70 ($670) credit. How much will the credit spread's profit or loss be if the Dow stays at 105 by expiration? _____ [*]

PREMIUM: TIME AND IMPLIED VOLATILITY EFFECTS

It is helpful to understand how the call vertical spread and the put vertical spread relate to each other and the best way to understand is to learn how the box spread works. Although retail customers do not consider trading into boxes for any particular purpose, revisiting the BoxTool will enhance one's risk management capabilities and help to prevent misperceptions. In addition, if the investor knows a little about butterfly prices, he or she can also compare vertical prices to the next adjacent vertical up or down, in order to create a greater sense of where the prices belong and are worth considering for a trade. Compare the in-the-money (ITM), at-the-money (ATM) and out-of-the-money (OTM) 10–point verticals in Exhibit 5–2 showing two sets of valuations for each vertical with the stock at a price of 105.00 (middle column). Let us first become familiar with the structure of the exhibit. The call spread values are shaded with blue forward slashes /////// representing their portion of each 10 point box. Red back slashes \\\\\\\ are used to represent the put spread portion of each box. Call spreads have an inverse correlation to put spread values due to relationships they both have to each individual box spread valuation. If you were to add together the shaded areas, for example, between the 100 and the 110 strikes, you would see that they make up almost the complete distance (*basic value*) between the strikes, i.e. 10 points. The remaining value, a thin (lavender colored) "▩" line, is based on the cost of carrying[2] the box and takes up more space on the left with more time than on the right side with less time (there are exceptions[3] to this). The 'Current Day' spread values (left column) can then be compared with spread values at a 'Later Date' (right column).

---

[*] **Answer**

Most people think it is $670 Profit but the answer is a $330 Loss.

[2] **Cost of Carry**

Cost of carry is of huge importance to market makers because of their pricing practices. Every penny counts. For a retail investor, it usually does not matter so much if a $10 box is valued at the present value of its basic value of $9.88 or $9.94.

[3] **Exceptions**

Early exercise opportunity (related to dividends and interest) premium cause boxes to trade above the basic value.

E X H I B I T   5 – 2

Vertical Bamboo

Current Day   Later Date

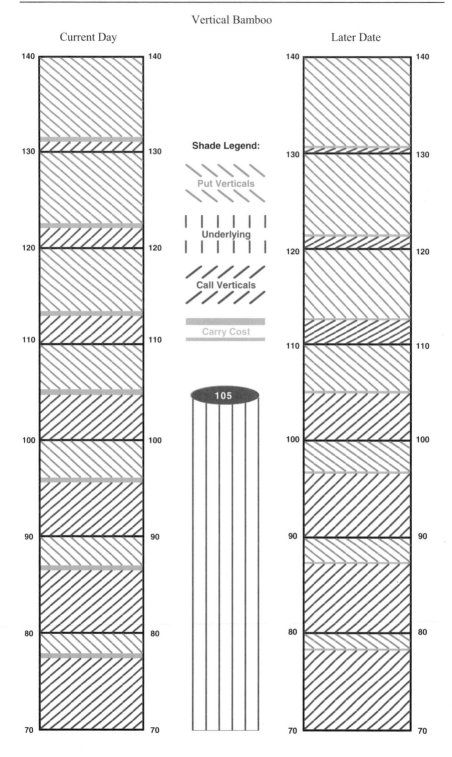

Shade Legend:

Put Verticals

Underlying

Call Verticals

Carry Cost

105

Notice that, in both groups, the ATM verticals have equal values, at about half of their potential basic value of 10.00. About 5 points of the value is, again, shaded /////// for the call spreads and the remaining 5 points of the value is shaded \\\\\\ for the put spreads. This mid-point of a box has a special property in that the verticals have almost no exposure to premium changing owing to unilateral shifts in implied volatility because the options involved in the spreads are equidistant from the stock price. The market nuance called 'skew'[4] will however cause values to deviate to some degree from straight options theory.

The values on the right represent values when either time passes (a 'Later Date') or if there was lower implied volatility prevailing in the market. As one can see, the amount of time left and the overall implied volatility[5] do influence vertical values differently according to whether the spread is ITM, ATM or OTM. Cost of carry is not affected by changes in implied volatility.

OTM vertical spreads (call verticals with strikes above the stock price and put verticals with strikes below the stock price) have more value 'Current Day' (left column) than with a 'Later Date' or lower implied volatility (right column), as you would expect. **However,** ITM verticals (call verticals with strikes below the stock price and put verticals with strikes above the stock price), on the other hand, go against normal logic and instead have greater values at the 'Later Date' or lower implied volatility (right column) than the 'Current Day' with more time to go (left column).

As a consequence, the lower strike box values are dominated by the call spreads, taking up more value the further they are ITM. The opposite holds true for the spreads in the upper half where the OTM call spread values are reflected with a lesser amount of area as they become further OTM.

The lost values in the call spreads migrate to the put verticals, which are increasingly ITM, the higher their strike prices. This is simply

---

[4] **Skew**

Skew or smile, refers to the fact that implied volatilities can vary at different strikes. The risk is that the implied volatility for the strikes of long options can decrease while those for strikes of short options can increase. It is therefore necessary to monitor the option's sensitivity to the P&L and the Greeks as implied volatility changes at each strike.

[5] **Overall Implied Volatility Level**

Since not all series of options trade at the same implied volatility, it is hard to say that one implied volatility represents a single month, but people do, and they usually refer to the at-the-money series or the average of the closest three series. Skewing of the volatilities plays a role in vertical valuations. When the underlying is exactly between the strikes, using the same implied volatilities for all strikes produces a call spread that is cheaper than the put spread, owing to the fact that OTM calls have greater value than OTM puts with equal proximity to the money. Volatilities are sskewed lower for the higher strike in this example, causing the two spreads to be of virtually equal value.

a result of the box valuations, and it is also evidence that a long call vertical's P&L performs identically to a short put vertical's P&L and vice versa.

The Thing to Remember: Without regard for skew which affects all verticals, time and unilateral shifts in implied volatility affect the ITM and OTM verticals, not ATM spreads. Time passing has a similar effect as a decline in implied volatility; the OTM spreads lose value while the ITM spreads increase in value. Remain cognizant that an ITM call vertical's price will change an equal amount to the corresponding OTM put spread (one up and the other down), owing to their relationship to the box spread. This is due to the fact that buying both the call spread (bull spread) and the put spread (bear spread) leaves the trader with a long box, while selling both results in a short box.

One obvious way to capitalize on this knowledge is when an investor is holding a spread that is deeply ITM. Since both options are trading with a high delta it follows that their bid/ask spreads are quoted wider than OTM options. Rather than liquidate a deep ITM spread, traders traditionally have transacted the low priced OTM corresponding spread that should ordinarily have a tighter (bid/ask spread is narrower) market. The result of this 'locking in' effect is, of course, a box that may require later transactions such as exercises/assignments or to avoid pin-risk. Even thought at least one of the options will expire worthless the commissions will be the same as simply liquidating the original position. Perhaps a consideration for exercise/assignment (E/A) fees[6] can deter a smaller trade but for larger positions it is a no-brainer because of the huge savings in market prices.

It is useful to think in terms of "extrinsic" premium because there is a natural tendency to judge intrinsic value spreads incorrectly. It may be more intuitive to think about an ITM call spread in terms of, or in relation to, an OTM put spread. When a put spread is out-of-the-money, it is natural to think, any increase in implied volatility should give that out-of-the-money spread more of a chance to go into the money. If a vertical has more of a chance of going in the money, it will be worth more.

PREMIUM PERSPECTIVE

Suppose that someone is bullish, the stock is trading at 105, and he or she decides to buy a 10-point vertical call spread. The pricing in the market across all the strikes allows for a choice of buying any ATM, in any

---

[6] **Exercise/Assignment (E/A) Fees**
Say the E/A fee is $15 per strike. It is cheaper, then, to go through the E/A process than to liquidate a large position. E.g., The E/A fee ($30) equates to a .30 trade price for one vertical spread but only a .03 trade price for 10 verticals and only a .003 trade price for 100 verticals.

month for about 5.00 or one of several OTM options that are priced at a lesser value, or one of the ITM options that is valued higher. Which bull spread should it be?

The investor also has to consider whether the option should be Long Premium (OTM), Short Premium (ITM) or Neutral Premium (ATM). As the underlying market moves, not only will the price of the vertical fluctuate, but so too will the premium stance change.

Limited Gain - Long Premium (OTM)
(Time working against the spread)

It is natural to consider the simple risk reward tendencies of vertical spreads. For example, if the investor pays 1.00 for an OTM vertical that can eventually go to 10.00, he or she can earn a lot more than he or she can lose. Looking at the right column in Exhibit 5–2, this may be represented by the 120c/130c spread. Paying 1.00 for something that can go to 10 is a 'risk 1.00 to make 9.00' scenario. It seems as though there is not much time left for that to happen, but it is possible. In a memorable expiration, with a week to go in the YHOO (Yahoo) July 2000 expiration there were options that were priced similarly. Within 3 days YHOO went from under 100 to over 135. That may be too much of a long shot for someone expecting a smaller advance. A 10-point spread a bit closer to the money (right column's 110c/120c) that is going for about 2.00 which would be a 'risk 2 to make 8' scenario may be more realistic. Judging from Exhibit 5–2 again, a 'risk 2 to make 8' scenario may also be represented by the left column's 120c/130c spread. In each of these speculations, the spreader would have to be aware of the fact that, until the bounce happens, time is working against the spread's valuation. Also a decline of implied volatility would decrease all of the OTM spread values. That particular week Yahoo's earnings were to be announced, and so anything could happen.

Limited Risk - Short Premium (ITM)
(Time working for the spread)

Not many option neophytes would often consider paying 7.00 for a call vertical spread that could only go to 10.00. That would 'risk 7 to make 3'. It would have similar pricing to the left column's 70c/80c spread or the right column's 90c/100c spread. If the stock rallies, it would profit. If it sits still, it would also win. If the stock declines but stays above the higher of the two strikes, it still wins. Obviously, it loses if the stock drops like a stone, but who is to say that it would not be liquidated on the way down to salvage a good portion of the cost? Suppose that it is sold at 5.00, when the underlying was trading half way between the two strikes. The '7 to make 3' scenario just changed into a 'risk 2 to make 2' scenario. Perhaps the key to all of this is to bear one's thinking and regard the long call spread for 7.00 debit as a short put spread at 3.00 credit. Of course this is risking 7 to make 3 here also, but somehow the credit of 3.00 seems more appealing. Now, it is more intuitive to hope that the put spread goes worthless (the call spread maximizes), staying above the higher of the two strikes at expiration. Again, a rally, sitting still, or not dropping too much would all help in this scenario.

For stocks that seem to have a world of support at certain levels the long ITM debit spread or short OTM credit spread may make a lot of sense. In this case, one should avoid getting wrapped up in the idea that risk reward ratios need to be favorable. Having said that, in the last quarter of 2000 and early 2001, there did not seem to be much support even for stocks that appeared to have a world of support. Like everything else, timing is everything.

Temporarily Purely Directional - Neutral Premium (ATM)
(Time has not much effect at current stock price)

Suppose, for example, an opinion is bullish with no expectations of volatility one way or another. To buy any month's ATM 10-pointer for about 5.00 would be a 'risk 5 to make 5' scenario. Logically, one might think at first that it may be better to buy the further dated spread because of more time. Throw out the logic because more time left means that the bull spread will not maximize (also won't minimize) in price as fast as a nearer term spread will. While the front month spread goes from 5.00 to 10.00 on the upside or to 0.00 on the downside the deferred month may have traveled only to 7.00 on the upside and 3.00 on the downside. The all important question is "what is the appropriate time frame?"

PRICING AND THE GREEKS

It is useful to remember the graphs of the Greeks from Chapter 3. Gamma, Vega, and Theta are greatest at the strikes that are the closest to-the-money, and get increasingly smaller the further the strike is from-the-money.

Exhibit 5-3 shows the P&L profiles for a bull spread along with graphs for each of the Greeks (delta, vega, gamma and theta) and the Greeks in tabular format.

E X H I B I T   5 – 3

P&L Profile and Greeks for 100*70/75 Bull Spreads over 44 Days, Futures-Style Margin
Black-Scholes, 10% Implied Volatility and .01% Interest

Price:	65.00	66.25	67.50	68.75	70.00	71.25	72.50	73.75	75.00	76.25	77.50	78.75	80.00
P&L	-21310	-19357	-16685	-13286	-9242	-4732	0	4687	9081	12991	16302	18975	21038
Delta	1295	1843	2433	2995	3450	3732	3803	3663	3342	2898	2394	1887	1424
Gamma	405	464	472	417	302	144	-30	-191	-314	-388	-411	-393	-346
Theta	-94	-111	-118	-108	-81	-40	9	57	97	124	135	133	121
Vega	413	491	518	475	357	176	-38	-250	-426	-544	-596	-587	-533

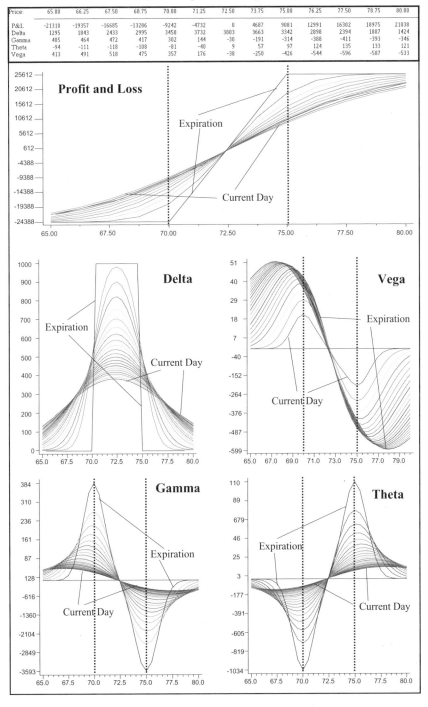

The straight lines in the graphs depict the expiration day calculations. The furthest line in each graph that has a slight curve to it is the calculation for the current day. The vertical dashed lines represent where the strikes are. You can see that a vertical has properties that are very different from those of individual options. For example, you can see in the gamma graph that the spread goes from long premium (at $70.00) to neutral premium (at $72.50), to short premium (at $75.00), as the underlying passes through the range of the two strikes from $70.00 to $75.00. Gamma and theta look as though they are mirror images of each other.

Notice that the peaks and troughs of each graph occur at either of the strike prices in all cases except for when there is a lot of time to go. Although vega is also greatest at the strike price (see Exhibit 5-4) for the individual options, the vega of a spread is not necessarily highest at the strikes. In a spread the extreme maximum and minimum values are distant from the strike but move closer over time. The values between the strikes are more similar for vega than they are for gamma and theta.

E X H I B I T   5 – 4

Vega for the 70s, 75s and the 70/75 Bull Spreads Over Changes in the Underlying Price

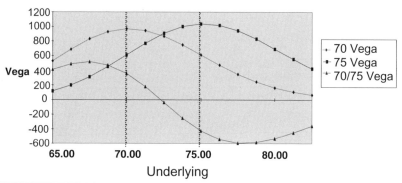

Underlying	65.00	66.25	67.50	68.75	70.00	71.25	72.50	73.75	75.00	76.25	77.50	78.75	80.00	81.25	82.50
70 Vega	529	689	830	929	969	946	868	750	612	474	348	244	163	104	64
75 Vega	116	198	312	454	612	770	906	1000	1038	1018	944	831	696	556	425
70/75 Vega	413	491	518	475	357	176	-38	-250	-426	-544	-596	-587	-533	-452	-361

When deciding on a vertical strategy, most people think about the risk / reward ratios, potential cost or proceeds. Do not forget to anticipate your time-frame and / or an implied volatility scenario.

HEDGING BY COLLARING UNDERLYING INTO A VERTICAL

The most common strategy used by retail investors is the 'Zero-Cost Collar', which is a synthetic bull spread. A collar[7] is a combination of long underlying against an off-strike combo[8] (Short a call for each 1oo underlying and long a lower strike put in the same quantity). Customers will apply the call and put trade against their long underlying if they believe it is necessary to have limited downside risk but do not want to pay the expensive premium for a protective put.

The most common collar order is to sell an OTM call and buy an OTM put, for even money, against an existing stock position, but many individuals, who learned this from a seminar or read an article on zero-cost collars, are always bullish when placing these orders and, in fact, feel quite bearish. Many do not know that there intended trade would convert their stock investment into a synthetic bull spread when their opinion could be manifested in converting their stock investment into behaving like a bear spread (a bear collar) instead. That is easily achieved by switching the two strikes involved as shown in Exhibit 5-5.

A hedger using a collar or bear collar intends to purchase puts and finance them with the sale of calls and should be willing to give up some of the upside potential. It may be easier to understand this conceptually by first grouping the underlying with either a short call (covered write) or with a long put (married put). The short call and the long underlying create a synthetic short put. When this synthetic short put is coupled with a long put at a lower strike, the result is a bull put vertical profile. A bull call vertical, on the other hand, results from the synthetic long call (long put plus long underlying) coupled with the actual short call at a higher strike.

If the call strike is higher than the put strike, the resulting position is a bull spread. A bear collar, on the other hand, is where the call strike is lower than the put strike, resulting in a synthetic bear spread. Remember that in both strategies the calls are sold and the puts are bought. Besides choosing the direction that one wants to be aiming, one should pay some attention to whether to be long premium (risking less to make more), neutral premium (ATM spread that has no imminent time decay), or short premium (favorable time decay but risking more to make less) as an additional consideration for the intended hedge.

---

[7] **Collar**

Collar is synonymous with 'caps and floors', tunnel, barrier, fence or squash, depending on what market it is traded..

[8] **Off-Strike Combo**

An off-strike combo is simply a combo using the call and put at different strike prices. Short a call for each 1oo underlying and long a lower strike put in the same quantity.

E X H I B I T 5 – 5

Bull Collars and Bear Collars

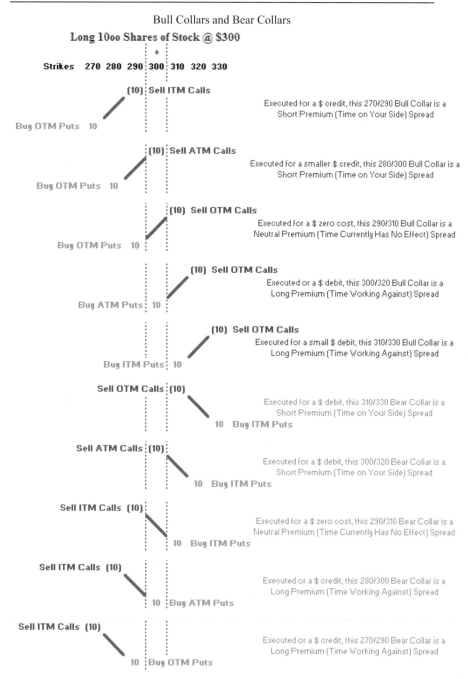

Long 10oo Shares of Stock @ $300

Strikes   270 280 290 300 310 320 330

(10) Sell ITM Calls

Executed for a $ credit, this 270/290 Bull Collar is a
Short Premium (Time on Your Side) Spread

Buy OTM Puts   10

(10) Sell ATM Calls

Executed for a smaller $ credit, this 280/300 Bull Collar is a
Short Premium (Time on Your Side) Spread

Buy OTM Puts   10

(10) Sell OTM Calls

Executed for a $ zero cost, this 290/310 Bull Collar is a
Neutral Premium (Time Currently Has No Effect) Spread

Buy OTM Puts   10

(10) Sell OTM Calls

Executed or a $ debit, this 300/320 Bull Collar is a
Long Premium (Time Working Against) Spread

Buy ATM Puts   10

(10) Sell OTM Calls

Executed for a small $ debit, this 310/330 Bull Collar is a
Long Premium (Time Working Against) Spread

Buy ITM Puts   10

Sell OTM Calls (10)

Executed for a $ debit, this 310/330 Bear Collar is a
Short Premium (Time on Your Side) Spread

10   Buy ITM Puts

Sell ATM Calls (10)

Executed for a $ debit, this 300/320 Bear Collar is a
Short Premium (Time on Your Side) Spread

10   Buy ITM Puts

Sell ITM Calls (10)

Executed for a $ zero cost, this 290/310 Bear Collar is a
Neutral Premium (Time Currently Has No Effect) Spread

10   Buy ITM Puts

Sell ITM Calls (10)

Executed or a $ credit, this 280/300 Bear Collar is a
Long Premium (Time Working Against) Spread

10 Buy ATM Puts

Sell ITM Calls (10)

Executed or a $ credit, this 270/290 Bear Collar is a
Long Premium (Time Working Against) Spread

10   Buy OTM Puts

An ITM can lose more than it can make but profits over time if the underlying sits still.

An ATM can profit and lose equal amounts and remains unchanged over time if the underlying sits still.

An OTM can profit more than it can lose but loses over time if the underlying sits still.

Many customers have convinced themselves that it is better to do the hedges valued at a credit[9] (selling a higher valued call than the value of the put being bought), however they may be synthetically taking on more risk than desired. It is a situation of give and take. If the investor wants more protection and more upside, it will cost more and can be achieved by trading an off-strike combo.

Although the more protective combo produces a debit, it synthetically leaves the investor with a cheap out-of-the-money (OTM) spread that may go on to profit at a higher reward but with low probability. If one is set on the idea of a credit, that is fine, but they should realize they have changed their play into a long in-the-money (ITM) vertical which, from that point on, could lose more than it can make but with favorable probability. We have seen this in the earlier example where 7 was the risk to make 3. Some investors are not aware of this, and others may not want to take the risk. The probability is that in the 'risk more to make less' scenario, investors will win in spite of themselves because time is working for them in this case.

It is worth mentioning here that unlike a collar, a SlingshotHedge (Chapter 10) accomplishes the downside protection with unlimited gain potential.

ROLLING / ADJUSTING SPECULATIVE TRADES USING VERTICALS

Rolling means that a strategy is shifted into a different month or to a different set of strikes. Verticals also provide traders with many rolling strategies. Take for example (from Chapter 2), a trader who had a position of long 10 Jan 50 calls at $2.00. The stock went up far enough for the call to be trading at 5.00. Exhibit 5–6 uses this example to demonstrate three rolling strategies. In **A**, the trader adjusts the long calls into a 50/55 Bull Spread. In the middle example, **B**, a Bear Spread is used to roll out of the 50 calls and into the 55 calls. In **C**, the trader adjusts the calls into a 45/50 Bear Spread.

A. Sell 10 Oct 55 calls at 2.00. The result is **10*50/55 bull call verticals,** each for even money (fair cost = 3.00 debit). The trader is still long, but not as aggressively so, and has limited the possible gain.

B. Sell 10 Oct 50 calls and buy 10 Oct 55 calls for a 3.00 credit (i.e. sell 50/55 call vertical or bear spread). The result is **long 10 Oct 55**

---

[9] **Credit**

Credit refers to the net amount received for the spread.

calls, each for a 1.00 credit (fair cost = 2.00 debit). The trader is still long, but for a price that is cheaper than free, and has limited risk.

C. Sell 10 Oct 45 calls at 9.25. The result is **10*45/50 bear spreads,** each for a 7.25 credit (fair cost = 4.25 credit). The trader anticipates a downward move.

Continuing with the same position of long 10 Jan 50 calls at $2.00, another strategy that I have not yet mentioned, is to trade 10*45/50 bull spreads (i.e., buy 10*45 calls and sell the 10*50 calls). This trade rolls the long 10*50 calls down to long 10*45 calls when the 50 calls may have become considerably out-of-the-money. The strategy can be used to achieve two different purposes. The first motivation to do this is when anticipating higher prices, but after either the market has dropped or time has nearly run out, leaving the 50 calls with a remote chance of seeing daylight. Although this trade adds to the overall cost of the original trade, it discounts the purchase price of the 45 calls by capturing the salvage value on the dying 50 calls. An investor will often have the opportunity to roll closer for even money but into half of the amount of closer contracts. For example, buy one-half as many of the 45 strike while selling the 50s (ratio spread +1 by –2 for even money or a credit) in order to conserve capital.

E X H I B I T   5 – 6

Rolling Into or Adjusting Using Verticals

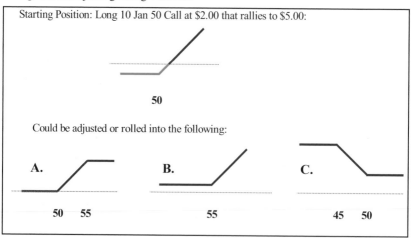

The second purpose of this trade is to bring the 50 calls closer to the underlying. Suppose that an investor is long 50 calls as part of any spread. He or she may find that the 50 calls become inadequate in the event of an upward move. In other words, certain elements (e.g. contracts in the spread) may require enhanced protection. For example, if the stock is 43.00, the trader could roll the 50 calls down to the 45 strike (closer-to-the-money) in order to bring potential fire power nearer to the underlying price.

At some point in the life of any position, it becomes prudent to roll some options closer in. On the other hand investors can decrease the cost of their position by rolling their protection a little farther away and collecting some premium to boot. Investors can use verticals to roll away options that have a higher chance of being assigned and roll closer options that they hope to exercise shortly.

The vertical is also an excellent vehicle to use for scalping positive gammas, much more dynamic than the examples outlined in Chapter 4, chiefly because you will not deplete the net contracts that you need for any extended moves in the underlying. For example, consider long 10 of the 50 straddle at the price of 50.00. The stock rallies to 52.50, and one wants to adjust. An investor may roll the calls to the next strike by selling 10*50/55 call spreads (see Exhibit 5–7) or buying 10*50/55 put spreads and winding up with 10*50p/55c strangles or 10*50c/55p gut-strangles. This is ignoring deltas, but it is pretty intuitive that with the underlying at 52.50, the 50 calls have quite a bit more value and firepower than the 50 puts. To even things out, in order to take advantage of a move from the new price of 52.50, a more balanced approach would be to have the strangle on where both options are equidistant from the underlying. This is achieved synthetically with the bear spread adjustment, 10 times.

E X H I B I T   5 – 7

Original Trade: 10*50 Straddles (in bold)—No Synthesis
Adjustment: Sell 10*50/55 Call Vertical Spreads (in italics)
Result: 10*50/55 Strangles (in net columns)

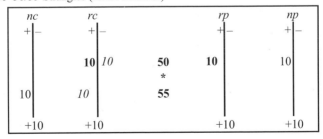

Suppose that the rally continued to 55 and the trader sold another 10 call spreads for a total of 20 bear spreads as an adjustment. The result of this dissection is in Exhibit 5–8.

E X H I B I T   5 – 8

Original Trade: 10*50 Straddles (in bold)—Synthesis: Buy 10*50/55 Boxes
Adjustment: Sell another 10*50/55 Call Vertical Spreads for a total of 20
Result: 10*55 Straddles (in net columns)

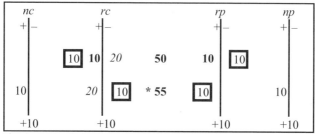

Verticals, calendar spreads (time spreads), certain back spreads and diagonals are dynamic ways to adjust gammas because they do not hinder the performance of the original strategy on extended moves as happens when gamma scalping is done with pure stock.

. The strangle will be fairly neutral with the stock at 52.50 as will the new straddle at 55.00. The advantage of gamma scalping with verticals is that the long 10 net call contracts and the long 10 net put contracts are maintained after each trade. Exhibit 5–9 illustrates the results of the adjustment.

E X H I B I T   5 – 9

Using Verticals: Shift the Initial 50 Straddle to the 50/55 Strangle then to the 55 Straddle.

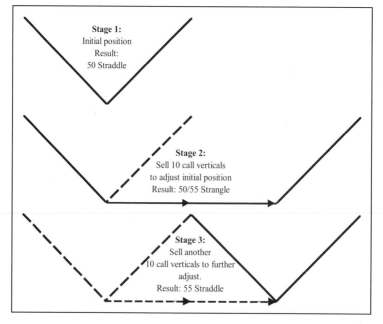

Note: At the crucial time of making adjustments, there might not be an opportunity to trade a vertical, so trading a stock equivalent first and replacing it later with a vertical based on a delta-neutral trade might be prudent. Do not miss the chance to make an adjustment because the stock price spikes up and then falls back before you get a chance to trade anything. This often happens in opening rotation[10] or when a number comes out that shocks the market.

LEGGING OPTIONS IN A CLICK

It was once considered sound advice not to leg into and/or out of options spreads. Most investors still shy away from doing this. It was good advice when orders were physically handled in the pits on the options floors around the country and one had very little control over the transactions. Levels of frustration ran high when people are waiting for floor procedures to be carried out (clerks trying to get information from busy brokers, about impending fills, canceled orders or even a simple quote). Now the world has changed, and immediate gratification has become more attainable. Options can be clicked into and out of in a matter of seconds and therefore the transaction risk has been greatly diminished. It is important to keep the following nuances in mind when legging:

1. The electronic realm, allows you to gain control by legging spreads, because you avoid the archaic floor procedures.
2. With an understanding of the synthetic relationships you have other ways in or out of a position.
3. You can save money while still motivating market makers to take the other side of your orders.
4. You should not be afraid to use stock to 'stop the bleeding' (or at least change the nature of it).

Which Side First?

Normally, the hard side should be done first. One leg of the spread can be considered harder than the other side when there is lower liquidity in one of the components. To help determine the level of liquidity, check the volume and open interest, and make sure that there is some trading

---

[10] **Opening Rotation**

On some exchanges, there is a procedure called *opening rotation* where one option is opened at a time instead of all of them at the same time. An option that has not officially been opened cannot be traded until after the opening. In the meantime, the underlying market is moving and could rebound, which may mean that the trader cannot trade out of the unopened options at favorable prices.

going on in those options. Note the widths of the individual market quotes in order to indicate what you might be faced with when trying to make subsequent adjustments or liquidating the trade.

For calendar spreads (also known as time spreads) the hard side would almost certainly mean trading the deferred month first and then the closer dated month. The front month moves faster (higher gamma) but the options are usually more liquid. There are those, more experienced 'leggers', who prefer to enter their buys and sells to work at the same time, but that is not recommended for everyone. Either way, many traders can prepare orders and store them in an order queue ready for sending.

For a Ratio/Back (ShortMore/LongMore) spread, I like to grab the greater quantity side first. It is easier to pull the trigger on the smaller quantity especially if it starts to get away. However, from a margin and risk standpoint, you may have no choice but to execute the buy side first (funds may be insufficient or you may want to avoid naked exposure). If you have the experience, capital and discipline, by all means, go ahead and leg from the sell side. Don't forget that you need to remain consistent with your market opinion. You might want to consider executing the synthetically equivalent position as an alternative to achieve your objective. If you are bearish, then buy a put vertical (bear spread) instead of selling a call vertical (also bear spread). When at the same strikes, the synthetic equivalents move at about the same rate and maintain a fairly constant relationship via the box. It is also wise to consider that the out-of-the money synthetic equivalent options' bid/ask spreads could be considerably narrower, and would therefore reduce the cost of doing business.

Risk and Money Management

Suppose that you have Long 10 March 90/95 call spreads (bull spreads), that is long 10 MAR 90C and short 10 MAR 95C and want to liquidate it (with a bear spread). Exhibit 5–10 shows that on the natural[11] markets, the spread but you can easily motivate the market makers for a better price. The components involved in the BID price of each vertical are in (Blue Ovals) and the components involved in the ASK price of each vertical are in [Red Rectangles]. The natural implied BID of the verticals are in ((Double Blue Ovals)) and the natural implied ASK of the verticals are in [[Double Red Rectangles]]. Thus the implied market

---

[11] **Natural Bid and Ask Prices**
The actual worst case prices to trade on. The 'Naturals' surround fair value. Spreads involving two or more different legs have unreasonably wide 'Natural' bid / ask spreads because they are the some of all the individual bid / ask spreads involved.

quote is (bid) 3.60 − 4.00 [ask] and is 40 cents wide. It is a pretty good bet that the spread is worth about 3.80 when 3.80 is the current average between bid and ask prices. The inside or actual market would be something like 3.70 − 3.90, or possibly even 3.75 − 3.85 if the crowd felt that they had to be a bit more competitive with one another or the other exchanges. By the way, the 3.60 bid is derived from 8.60, the bid price of the 90 calls, minus 5.00, the ask price of the 95 calls.

The call vertical's 4.00 ask price is derived from 8.80, the call vertical's ask price of the 90 calls, minus 4.80, the bid price of the 95 calls. Incidentally, you should always consider the corresponding put spread and in this case the MAR 90/95 put spread is 1.10 − 1.30, only 20 cents wide (half as wide as the call spread) on the naturals and most likely something like 1.15 − 1.25 when the fair value is 1.20. The put vertical's 1.10 bid is derived from 2.25, the bid price of the 95 puts, minus 1.15, the ask price of the 90 puts. The put vertical's 1.30 ask is derived from 2.35, the ask price of the 95 puts, minus 1.05, the bid price of the 90 puts.

E X H I B I T   5 − 1 0

The Natural Implied BID of the Verticals are shown in the ((Double Blue Ovals)) and the Natural Implied ASK of the Verticals are shown in the [[Double Red Recatangles]].

Very seldom does one have to "pay up" to "take" the natural ask price or "sell down" to "hit" the natural bid price. Often traders like to middle the market in hopes that the market will move to their price. The market would almost certainly have to move because there is little incentive for market makers to meet in the middle unless the trade happens to fit their position. For example, a market maker may need to get rid of premium (vega and gamma) and meet in the middle to sell an OTM credit spread.

Remember that the reason market makers come to work, in the first place, is to buy under-value and sell over-value. Customers with the exactly opposite opinion are usually not counter parties to each other on a trade, but it happens.

A current ask price at the middle, i.e., 3.80 would prove fruitless temporarily but could get bought in the event of a market rally high enough to motivate a market maker to buy it. This spread happens to have a delta of about .20 so a 50-cent rally in the stock may increase the spread's value by about 10 cents meaning that it would then be worth 3.90 making the 3.80 a better buy and accordingly 'scooped up'.

Back to the trade...remember that you are no longer bullish, or you are now bearish, or you have enough profit, and you now want out. From a market opinion standpoint it doesn't make sense to leg by buying your short 95 calls back first. It may also be prohibitive, from a risk and margin standpoint, to sell out your long 90 calls because this will leave you naked short the 95 calls. What oh what is a legger to do? Buy the 90/95 put vertical spread instead and if you are filled, you will be long the 90/95 box. It may become necessary to sell the box later due to the potential pin risk. Don't worry, because the box can usually be sold just prior to expiration for a nickel (.05) or two (.10) less than the 5.00 value. It is reasonable to first try to bid 2.25 for the 95 puts (middling), and if filled, to offer the 90 puts at 1.10 (again middling). Even if you have paid the ask price and sold at the bid price, the net price of 1.20 for the spread is synthetically equivalent to selling the call spread for 3.80 when the box is worth around 5.00[12]. Not bad. The crucial trade is to get the 95 puts, and then you can relax and offer the 90 puts at the ask price or even higher, or just sit on them for a few days, because only 1.10ish is at risk from that point forward. You would then have the 3-legged box waiting for the sale of the last corner (Exhibit 5–11), and this is consistent with your market opinion.

E X H I B I T   5 – 1 1

BoxTool Applied to Three-Legged Box Reveals Synthetic Missing Corner

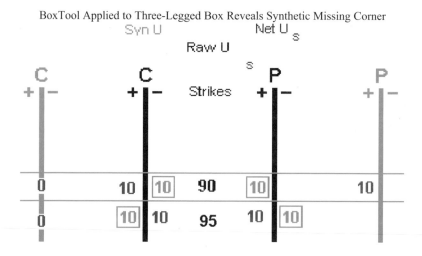

---

[12] **5.00 Box**

Actually a box is worth the present value between the strikes with some exceptions. See more about boxes in Chapter 8.

Adjusting the Leg Size

What if you had no position and wanted to just get long 10 put spreads for about 1.25? That would be $1250 of risk. Therefore, when legging, you do not want to risk more than that amount (assume the worst). This means that you can only leg about 5 contracts at a price of 2.30 on the first leg, get filled and wait for the fill on the other side's sale before going for the next set of five lot legs. Legging 5 at a time instead of legging all 10 at once ($2300) will end up costing a bit more in commissions (depending on ticket charges), but it is a safer money management approach in the long run.

The immediate accomplishment, along with the fact that you are more assured of getting in or out of the market, will make legging well worthwhile if you have a disciplined approach. Remember also that the reason for legging in the first place is to get a fill at possibly better price or manifesting a short-term opinion. Better prices for spreads will save more than the extra commissions spent.

Remember: The biggest problem with legging is the stubbornness of the trader. Be disciplined and pull the trigger. Don't be greedy. When you mess up, spread it off, and move on.

VOLATILITY TRADING

Ratio (front) spreading / back spreading in the traditional sense involves a vertical with extra contracts at the more distant strike. If the spread has more long contracts than short contracts, it is a back spread (LongMore). If there are more short contracts than long contracts, it is a ratio (front) spread (ShortMore). Any ratio is possible, but to keep it simple most people start at first with 1 by 2 spreads. When naming either type of spread, the smaller quantity is usually mentioned first and the bigger quantity second, so +1 by –2 for ratio spreads and –1 by +2 for back spreads. In addition, the lower strike is generally stated first, whether it is long or short. For example:

Ratio (Front) Spreads	Back Spreads
Calls: 100/102: +1*100C/-2*102C	Calls: 100/102: -1*100C/+2*102C
Puts: 100/102: +1*102P/-2*100P	Puts: 100/102: -1*102P/+2*100P

Keep in mind that there are a lot of traders who refer to back spreads as '2 by 1s' and '3 by 2s' (the larger quantity first) and ratio spreads as '1 by 2s' and '2 by 3s' (the smaller quantity first).

Most market makers these days do not quote or trade these spreads in the traditional manner. If they do make a market on the spreads and get the trade, they will hedge the excess deltas with underlying and merge the whole spread into the rest of their position. To most market makers, any spread that is long gamma is considered to be a back spread, and any spread that is short gamma is considered to be a ratio (front) spread.

An older style of trader, who specializes in either ratio (front) spreads or back spreads, is known as a ratio (front) spreader or a back spreader. Other traders will make markets on these spreads and will attempt to trade each neighboring strike cheaper, thereby molding the whole package into a butterfly of sorts. This adjustment is important because it may be the best and quickest trade that one can make when the market starts to heat up.

The object of the ratio (front) spread game is to buy some options and finance their purchase with the sale of options that are out of the money. Many traders will only do a ratio spread if it is for a credit, but to do that it would mean in some instances that the ratio has to be quite steep (i.e., many more short options than long, which is not a safe position). Since the out-of-the-money options are cheaper (but not necessarily in terms of implied volatility), traders have to sell more to recoup most of, all of, or even a greater amount than the purchase cost of the long option. This strategy is almost like a butterfly except that it does not include the long options at the next strike out. The missing element - the long options at the next strike out - serves as an insurance policy by turning the package into a limited risk spread. Again, note that that little insurance policy is good to monitor as a potential failsafe measure.

The ratio (front) spread strategy can treat a trader well if he or she gets the opportunity to neutralize and plays by very strict rules. **Be warned!** - Never get comfortable or complacent when naked short premium. Monitor ratio (front) spreads daily and have a failsafe plan that can be enacted at a moment's notice. It should be like having a fire extinguisher nearby in case of a fire. Be prepared for the worst. The steeper the ratio, the more the risk grows exponentially.

In Exhibit 5-12 are graphs for call spreads on the right and put spreads on the left. The back spreads are on the top half and the ratio (front) spreads are below. The underlying price is at 100.00 for each position with 44 days to go, at a flat volatility of 10%. Each contains 100 options which are 2% out-of-the-money versus 200 options 4% out-of-the-money (102c/104c and 96p/98p).

The center point of the four graphs acts almost like a mirror. The ratio spread prices are the inverse (i.e. debit versus credit) of the back spread prices. However, you may have noticed from the graphs that the starting price of the call spread is not the same as that of the put spread. Even though this contract is of the generic futures-style margin type, there is still the statistical attribute that the underlying has unlimited upside potential while the downside of the underlying is limited to zero.

As you can see in Exhibit 5-13, the call spread is 16.2 ticks and the put spread is 19.6 ticks. They are both debits (meaning a cash outlay) if we refer to them as ratio spreads. Conversely they would each be priced at a credit if they were backspreads. Time, implied volatility, the volatility skew, and the proximity of the spread to the underlying price will determine what the amount of the debit or credit will be.

E X H I B I T   5 – 1 2

Mirror Images of Ratio (Front) and Back Spreads

-100 x +200*+96/-98 Put Backspread   **-100 x +200*-102/+104 Call Back Spread**

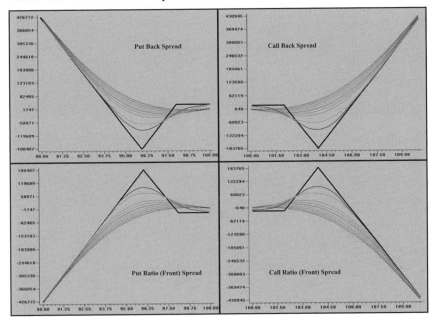

+100 x -200*-96/+98 Put Front Spread   **+100 x -200*+102/-104 Call Front Spread**

You should also notice that the spreads are not Greek neutral at the moment. As the underlying moves positive Greeks can become negative and vice versa. Butterfly spreads also behave this way, however, ratio spreads and back spreads are unlike the butterfly because a butterfly has a limited gain and a limited loss potential.

Various strategies are more consistent with regard to the Greeks. For example, a call is long delta and always remains long delta. A long call's gamma and vega are also always long and theta is always negative. We saw how a bull spread always stays long delta but the premium and Greeks can flip from positive to negative. It is different for ratio spreads and back spreads.

E X H I B I T   5 – 1 3

Greeks and Prices for Individual Contracts and +1 by -2 Ratio (Front) Spreads, Futures-Style Options with Futures = 99, 44 Days to go, Flat Volatility of 10% and .01% Interest

Puts			F=99.00	Calls		
96	98	-96/+98	Strikes	100	102	+100/-102
0.201	0.597	+1 x -2	Premium	0.6204	0.229	+1 x -2
20.1	59.7	19.6	In Ticks	62.0	22.9	16.2
(0.116)	(0.275)	(0.042)	Delta	0.2901	0.133	0.024
0.0564	0.0960	(0.017)	Gamma	0.0986	0.0619	(0.025)
(0.008)	(0.013)	0.002	Theta	-0.0135	-0.0085	0.004
0.068	0.116	(0.020)	Vega	0.1189	0.0746	(0.030)

As the underlying moves, positive Greeks can become negative and vice versa, including the delta. Butterfly spreads and time spreads also behave in this way, however, they have a limited gain and a limited loss potential, unlike the unlimited nature of spreads that are not one-to-one.

Let us examine the properties of the other Greeks by illustrating each using the call back spread as an example. Exhibit 5-14 displays the delta, gamma, theta and vega of the call back spread.

It may be helpful to place a mirror at the bottom of each graph so that the reflection of each graph is just below it, and then to the right of each graph. This way, the basic properties of the other spreads become apparent. When the mirror is below the graph it is as if looking at the same analysis as for the call ratio spread. If what is going on is understood, it will be easy to discern what the measurements for the other three spreads would look like using the same method. When the mirror is on either side of the graph, the analysis of the call spread will depict the properties of the put back spread. Two mirrors are required to see the put ratio spread.

The purpose of positioning with a back spread is to profit on a quick extended move toward, through, and beyond the long strike. The expiration P&L graph depicts a valley where losses will occur. The current day has no valley when neutral or long in the case of a call back spread, but over time a valley forms and gets deeper and deeper. The odds are against the back spreader, but when he or she finally wins, a huge profit can be taken. The graph's ends are pointing to the sky because the sky is the limit with a back spread. The purchase of a quantity of long options is financed by the sale of a lesser quantity of short options. The danger is that since the short options are closer to or in-the-money, they might grow faster than the long out-of-the-money options. The out-of-the-money options may dwindle and die worthless.

E X H I B I T   5 – 1 4

Greeks and Prices for individual Contracts and -100 by +200 Back Spread, Futures-Style Options with Futures = 100, 44 Days, Flat Volatility of 10% and .01% Interest

The Greeks of the -100 x +200 * -102/+104 Call Backspread

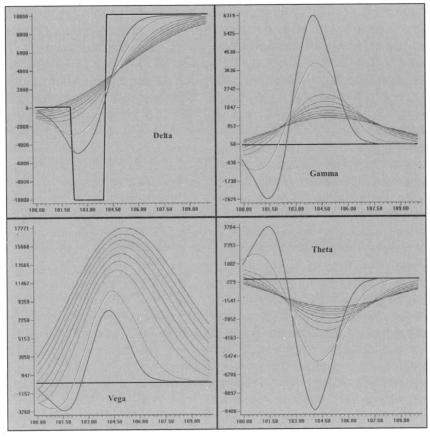

If the market moves in the other direction, the back spreader will make a small profit if the spread was executed for a credit, which is what a back spreader generally tries to do. The back spreader suffers most days from time decay while waiting for a large, profitable move.

Ratio (front) spreads are the most infamous of all spreads because they are strategies that often ruin traders. Trading them is like playing hot potato with a time bomb. The object is to not be holding it when it explodes. Huge wealth has been created with these plays over the years, sometimes only to be donated back to the market all in one day, with bankruptcy proceedings to recoup any amount that exceeds the trader's capital, his or her family's capital, the investors' capital, and the trader's houses, computers, cars, yachts, airplanes, RV, motorcycle, and children. Most traders like to trade them for a credit, so that if both options go worthless they can keep the credit. That modus operandi is penny-wise and pound-foolish. An ever growing popular spread methodology is that of ratioing vertical spreads against one another which is an unbalanced or a ratioed butterfly of sorts and will be covered in Chapter 6.

PRICING OF RATIOS

Unfortunately, as of writing this book, the options world does not have any standards with regard to the quoting and pricing of ratios. It is getting closer but entering orders can still be confusing for customers. It is necessary for the customer to hammer out a method for their order takers to get their orders filled. With the advent of online trading, we have seen some change in this regard consistent with what is presented here. Suppose that a trader has a put ratio spread on and wants to get a quote on it, or to determine where it is trading. Keep in mind that this person may wish to unwind it or add more to it. He or she will undoubtedly want to monitor it as well, by checking its price as often as necessary using quotes posted either online or in the newspaper.

The strikes in this example will be the 95 puts worth about 2.20 and the 100 puts worth about 3.00. **Question:** What is the going price of the spread based on a position size of 10 by 15? Some beginners stumble here because they think that they need to know which option will be bought and which will be sold. However, it is better to get into the practice of calculating without knowing. One really does not want to let the market makers know which way the order is going to come in because they will price it accordingly. If, on the other hand, they are asked purely for a two-sided market they have little choice but to be fair. To emphasize this point without getting hung up on the concept of two-sided markets, suppose that something is worth 5.00. If a market maker does not know which way an order will come in, he or she may provide a .20 wide market, for example, of 4.90–5.10. If the market maker knows that order is be a buy order, he may quote 5.00–5.20. If the order is sell order, he may quote 4.80–5.00. (He can always use the extra cash.) It is always best to ask for a two-sided market, the size that that price is good for and be sure to call it a "ratio/back" spread so as not to show your hand on which way you are going.

If asked to quote 10 by 15 on a 95/100 put ratio/back spread, most market makers will look at their values and perhaps quote 2.10–2.30 on the 95s and 2.85–3.15 on the 100s. The broker may ask, "But what is the spread?" They usually do not respond with a spread price, but only repeat their individual market quotes hoping that they get the *edge* on both sides (bid price on buy side and ask price on sell side). At best, they may say, ".70–.90 on the 10 put vertical spreads embedded in the ratio/back spread and provide a separate quote for the extra 5 of the 95s, 2.10–2.30." This is done to save time thinking and avoid missing other market opportunities. Even most professional ratio spreaders keep their ratios to 1 by 2s and 2 by 3s because of the simplicity and ease of execution.

The basis of one method is a pricing method that has a chance of becoming more universal, and is preferred by many practitioners. This method allows any ratio to be priced quickly and easily. A novice investor may derive the going price using a calculation of the aggregate amount of the package: (10 x 3.00) versus (15 x 2.20) is a difference of 3.00 (30.00 versus 33.00). The calculation on a per spread basis, uses one as the least common denominator, i.e. for every one contract traded, 1.5 of the other contract will be traded against it. 30 divided by 20 equals 1.5, and 1.5 multiplied by 2.20 (the price of the option with the lower value) is 3.30. Compare 3.30 to the price of the option with the higher value, 3.00 to get .30 1 by 1.5 spread. A reasonably tight spread market quote would be something like .20–.40. The market maker is saying that he will do the back spread and pay .20 but wants to receive .40 to do the ratio spread.

There are at least three ways to price the spread using 2.20 and 3.00:
>   10 by 15—1 spread = $3.00 (10 x 3.00 versus 15 x 2.20)
>   2 by 3—5 spreads = .60 (2 x 3.00 versus 3 x 2.20)
>   1 by 1.5—10 spreads = .30 (3.00 versus 1.5 x 2.20)

Which way to price the spread is best? Well, if a broker is splitting the order up between several traders, the first way is no good because it is based upon the aggregate amount. 2 by 3 in this instance might be considered the best way since a broker cannot split the order amongst 10 traders (a trade cannot consist of 1.5 contracts).

This method becomes more obvious when a ratio is bizarre, something like 20 by 34. The spread can be quickly calculated on a 1 by 1.7 basis for 20 spreads. That's 1 by 1.7—20 spreads = .74 (3.00 versus 1.7 x 2.20). The trader can quickly compare many of the other put spreads with the same ratio to see what the price that his or her spread might go to in order to help assess risk. For example, he or she might look at a couple of the spreads a little bit closer (the 100/105, 105/110 or 110/115) to hint at what his or her spread might be priced at in the event of a big move down. He or she could check the values of the spreads further out-of-the-money (the 90/95, 85/90 or 80/85) as an indication of how his or her spread might be priced on a huge rally.

The other advantage to this method is that traders can quickly determine profitable levels of the individual legs. If, for example, someone else offers to sell some 95s at 2.50, and the trader wants to leg out of the spread, he or she can see whether 2.50 is a good price by multiplying it by 1.7 (= 4.25). The trader would then subtract the .74, the credit that he or she would have received (if initiated using 2.20 and 3.00 on the spread), and can then offer the 100s at 3.52 or better to get out for a profit (4.25–.74 = 3.51 the equivalent cost based on the current 2.50 offer on the 95s).

DEFENSIVE FLATTENING OF RATIO SPREADS

The beginning position in Exhibit 5–15 is long 10*85 puts and short 30*80 puts for a ratio of +1 by −3. There are 2 adjustments that the trader makes, in this example, as the market grinds its way lower. The first time a bear spread is traded on a +1 to −1 basis for 10 contracts. After the 'first adjustment' the ratio is flattened to +1 by −2. The second adjustment is for 20 bear spreads flattening it down to +1 by −1.5. This sort of management assumes that the market is orderly as opposed to a crash or stock take over. In the event that one is able to get a trade off in a wild market, it may be wise to stop the bleeding on the excess shorts by covering them or purchasing an equal quantity at a different strike.

A ratio (ShortMore) spread is one of the most dangerous options plays on the street. This type of approach for defense may not be good enough to ward off severe damage to one's trading capital. It may be wise never to employ such a strategy in the first place. Some longer term investors can afford to and are comfortable taking such risks with put ratio spreads.

E X H I B I T   5 – 1 5

Flattening a Ratio Spread with a Vertical

Option	Beginning	First	After 1st	Second	After 2nd
Strikes	Position	Adjustment	Adjustment	Adjustment	Adjustment
80p	**(30)**	**(10)**	**(40)**	**(20)**	**(60)**
85p	10	10	20	20	40
Ratios	**+1 by -3**	**+1 by -1**	**+1 by -2**	**+1 by -1**	**+1 by - 1.5**

Put Ratio Spreads

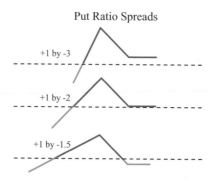

ASSESSING RISK IN RATIO SPREADS AND BACKSPREADS THROUGH RATIO ANALYSIS

Here are a few guidelines for assessing risk that traders may want to use to enhance their creative approach:

1. Use as shallow a ratio as possible. Consistently successful ratio spreaders, when initiating or adjusting, try to keep the steepness of the spread to a ratio less than 1 by 2, and often use a ratio of less than 1 to 1.4. It also depends on how far apart the strikes are from one another.

2. Be sure that a 20% move in the underlying can be withstood without losing very much money. This should be of greater concern than doing the spread for a credit. (A good tolerance level is 20% for most stocks where the strikes are relatively farther apart, and 6% for an index or futures contract. This is based on his trading style and experience, but levels vary from 10% to 50% for stocks, and 1% to 10% for an index or futures contract, depending on the trader.)

3. Stress test[13] the spread, assuming that a move will occur immediately.

4. When trying to assess how a spread may perform, look at the spreads of deeper in-the-money options for an indication of relative prices. Should a what-if analysis reveal that traders could lose an uncomfortable amount of money, they should either flatten out their ratio, wait for another opportunity in the cycle, or look for a spread in another stock. This must be monitored daily, always checking the prices of the relationships a few strikes deeper. The ratio should be adjusted as necessary, always testing for the chosen tolerance level.

5. If the spread has earned a significant profit and is currently valued at an expensive debit (a large credit if liquidated), one should consider taking profits. Look at the cheaper options of the strikes further away from the money for an indication of the value of the spread in case the market turns around. At such a point, it may be tempting to steepen the ratio of the spread to improve proceeds (either by increasing the initial credit or reducing the initial debit), but sometimes it is better to take the profits and to trade another day instead of adding more exposure to the position.

When steepening the ratio, consider doing it with a vertical instead of with naked options, so that in case of a devastating move, you will not be faced with exponentially increased exposure.

Anyone trading during the last year has seen tremendous moves in stocks. Often the pricing in the options reflects an even bigger move

---

[13] **Stress Test**

To stress test is to run an options analysis, including what-if scenarios.

than was experienced, because volatility exploded. The options can easily act as though the stock has moved 30% when in fact the stock has only moved 20%. It is necessary to adjust to the market concerned, but the short options (aggregated) that are farther away from the money are more sensitive to implied volatility changes than options that are almost at-the-money (aggregated).

Taking a closer look at several spreads gives the trader a sense of where the market believes that these ratios belong over time and with a movement in the underlying. The same exercise can be performed with butterflies to start building a mental database of price relationships.

Using historical implied volatility levels and skew shapes for pricing can be inaccurate because it is nearly impossible to maintain a frame of reference. Suppose that with two weeks to go on the XYZ options, the implied volatility is 60% for out-of-the-money puts. It is important to consider how far out of the money they are, what the volatilities of the other strikes are, and what the market is doing at that particular time (rallying, breaking, or choppy?). Do not forget that implied volatility levels are not absolute values. They represent different absolute values over each time period. The use of implied volatility serves as a relative pricing mechanism.

Volatility is not money. There is a different frame of reference for it every day, and strikes have different proximities to the underlying stock price. Spreads, on the other hand, are easier to keep track of. The frame of reference is all of the other spreads. This kind of analysis gives us a different perspective on price relationships and an insight into what back spreaders and ratio spreaders can do.

One more reminder about the steepness of the ratio: many out-of-the-money put ratio spreads perform in a similar fashion when the market takes a nosedive, making it seem as though no adjustments should be made to the ratio. It won't take long before the options start to emulate those with higher strike prices, so don't just sit around waiting. One can easily stress test that a ratio of 1 by 1.333 (quite shallow) profits more on a decline and loses a lot less than a 1 by 2 in a nosedive. Is it not better to pay a little extra to have the bigger cushion of protection?

In an emergency, the safest thing to do is to buy an amount equal to the quantity of net short options at a far out strike (but close enough to be of any help) to control the open-ended risk. Often traders dislike this idea because those options trade at higher and higher implied volatilities. Realize that this is the most inexpensive insurance that can be bought, although it could be a waste of money.

The best-case scenario would be to have very deep pockets, so that one can ride out the storms and not have to pay crazy prices for protection or liquidation. Most people do not have large amounts of cash available, so they need a plan if the market turns against them. Keep in mind that having excess capital can give some an artificial sense of security. Even large institutions go under with derivatives debacles.

UNBELIEVABLE MOVES

Story: Crashes, Takeovers, Shortages, and Flight to Quality: A ratio (front) spreader's worst fear is a crash, takeover, shortage, and flight to quality. What can one do if one has a call ratio spread in a stock that is suddenly the candidate for a company takeover? Unfortunately, there is no answer to this. It would have been better not to have had net short call contracts in the first place. Some of the scariest horror stories to come out of the industry have come from the pits where stock options are traded.

One of the first most famous stories comes from the late 1970s where out-of-the-money Kennecott Copper options were expected to go out worthless on the day before expiration. Instead, they went from a "teeny" 1/16 or $.0625 ($6.25) to over $30 ($3,000). Being net short only 100 extra contracts meant a loss of $300,000. If the Kennecott options had gone out worthless, the gain would have been $625. This is obviously not a good risk-reward ratio.

There was a huge flight to quality on the Tuesday following the stock market crash of 1987. The Eurodollars, for example, blew through 12 strikes in a single print, because investors were willing to take 3% less on their 90-day money than they could lock in the day before. When the bonds were rallying out of control, I was lucky to get a 500 lot of 90 calls at 15 ticks (.15 or 15/64), when one second later someone paid me the same price for a 500 lot of the 92 calls. I bought the call spread for free at a time when it was going for about 10 ticks ($156.25 each). That was a 5,000-tick ($78,125) savings, because I was in the middle of flattening a huge ratio spread that I had inherited from a former partner. The ratio warranted going from 1 by 1.8 down to 1 by 1.65, based on the spreads that were 6 percent deeper.

Before the trade, my position was +2200 by –3960. After I had bought the vertical 500 times, the ratio was 1 by 1.652 (+2700 by –4460), right where I wanted it to be because the price of the last trades of the 84 calls divided by the last price in the 86 calls was 1.65, which meant that 1.65 times the price of the 86 calls equaled the price of the 84 calls. This also meant that that spread was trading at even money on a ratio of 1 to 1.65.

I like to buy verticals to flatten a ratio because it is the cheapest way to do this, and therefore is the easiest way for me to justify paying for the cost of protection. Out-of-the-money options tend to be astronomically priced during a panic. When I buy verticals cheap, I consider it to be adding to a winner. If the market moves higher, the original trade will win and so will this extra bull spread. If it starts to fall, I simply sell the extra calls out to reduce the cost of the adjustment, which means that the spread regains the necessary steepness of the ratio. Verticals are great vehicles for compromise. You can reach into your tool chest at any time to see which vertical application can provide you with what you need at that particular moment.

The above method would have not worked on the put side during the stock market crash of 1987. There was plenty of time on the Friday to liquidate when the Dow was down 100 points. You just have to decide beforehand that if you are in a dangerous spread and the market begins to do something extraordinary, you are not going to be cute and outthink the market, but bite the bullet and get flat before you get flattened. It is a terrible and unnecessary shame when disasters occur such as those that buried Barings Bank and once bankrupted Orange County.

In the S&P 500 Index, I liquidate when there is a 3 percent move irrespective of a win/loss or break-even situation. If there is not much liquidity, I will not hesitate to take the chance to liquidate. I immediately buy enough naked options to cover all net short contracts. You can do this without undoing all of your deltas if the puts are far enough out of the money. In that case, should the market rebound, you will not miss out on recuperating some of the losses. It is important to free yourself from anxiety, so that you can take advantage of the free money when the market is acting crazily.

There were such pickings on my birthday, September 12, one year. I slept in, but called into the market and found that the S&Ps were down 2%. My position was a put ratio spread +1 by -1.7 * 300 times (+300 by -510). I had Jimmy, my broker, buy 50 put spreads to flatten the ratio down to +1 by -1.6 (+350 by -560). I had to get to work fast. I called from the car and the S&Ps were down over 3%. I had Jimmy buy another 50 put spreads so that my ratio would be +1 by -1.525 (400 by 610). By the time I got into the pit, we were down over 4%. I calculated that at this point I was breaking even from the previous close. I had Jimmy buy 210 strangles to make me fairly neutral before I physically stepped into the pit. As far as I was concerned, I was flat enough to make markets without a nagging agenda. It is like picking *money* off trees when everyone else is panicking and there is nothing that you *need* to do. By the time the market was down almost 6%, I was one of three people making two-sided markets (i.e., providing a bid and an ask).

When brokers' eyes are bulging out of their heads, you can tell that they have to fill an order to save their lives. On the day when investors took flight to quality in the bond market, a broker named Bill had to sell a lot of 78 puts at 11 ticks (.11 or about $172). At the same moment, another broker, Pat, was bidding 9 ticks (.09 or about $141) for the 76 puts. That meant that I could do the ratio spread 1 by 2 for a huge 7-tick credit (buy 1*78*p* at 11 / sell 2*76*p* at 9). I said "done" to Bill and he dumped 1100*78 puts on me. I could not say "no" because I had made the mistake of not putting a size on it. I turned to hit Pat on the .09 bid for 2200 but he only had 100 to buy. I looked over to the bond futures pit and, during the next 10 seconds, watched the bonds rally a whole point. By the way, that is bad when you are long an extra 1,050 puts (50 went against the 100*76 puts). Before I could decide what to do, another broker, John, was grabbing me by both lapels (his eyes were bulging out of his head slightly) shouting, *"78 puts - .17 bid for a thousand!"* Talk about being saved. "SOLD!" KA-CHINGGGG! 6,000-tick ($93,750) profit in 30 seconds. You read correctly that the bonds went up, but that did not diminish the demand for those puts, fortunately for me.

Brokers needed to fill customer orders and most traders were, at that moment, looking at their sheet values (the numbers on the page just looked like dots), which told them nothing. When the markets are moving so fast, locals often cannot establish where the underlying is to lock in a value. The option markets are nonexistent at such times because nobody likes to stick his or her neck out while swords are slashing. When trades are made and hedged in the market, prices often come back that are surprisingly worse than the traders anticipated—that is, if they can even get a report from the filling broker. Half of the crowd is paralyzed because they do not know where they stand. Most of us are clueless concerning whether we are long or short, what strikes we need to buy and sell, whether we are up or down, and whether we are coming or going. The only way to operate in a sea of panic like that is to trade option to option, to think ratio spreads and back spreads, and trade accordingly. **End**

CONCLUSION

I Love Verticals.

6

WINGSPREADS

This chapter covers butterfly spreads and other wingspreads such as irons, condors, stretched out condor skip-strike butterflies and unbalanced butterflies. They all have similar risk/reward characteristics and sensitivities. In addition, there are pregnant (multi-strike) butterflies that have many single-strike butterflies inside them.

Wingspreads are strategies that traders employ when they believe that the market will land within a specified range and within a specified time frame. In addition to examining the Greeks and the P&L profiles of butterflies, we will see how they can overlap and create what looks like hills or mountains for long configurations which would be ravines or valleys for short configurations. I will then examine how to adjust and dissect various wingspread configurations by relating a story about how greed let a butterfly fly off with $300,000, and another more recent scenario from the live RD3 Webinar series where Diamonetrics was used to forecast a likely butterfly expiration range.

BUTTERFLY STRUCTURE

Butterflies, condors and wingspreads are so-called because their expiration date risk profiles look like something that could fly. When talking about butterflies, et al., you will hear about options as the "body" and the "wings". The body refers to options with strikes in between the two outermost strikes (they are most often sold short). The wings refer to options at the outermost strikes (they are most often purchased long). I would like to make the point right now that very few speculators sell a butterfly. (I am not talking about selling an iron butterfly yet.) **Very Important: Speculators always buy the wings.** The only people who sell the wings on a wingspread are market makers when providing liquidity. The remainder of the chapter refers only to *Long the Wings* wingspreads, which includes short irons.

A butterfly is a wingspread that has options at three equidistant strikes. A long butterfly is long 1 low strike option, short 2 middle strike options and long 1 high strike option, and a short butterfly is short 1 low strike option, long 2 middle strike options and short 1 high strike option.

A condor or other wingspread has options at four strikes, with the same distance between the options at each end. Condors look like butterflies whose bodies have been stretched wider apart.

The P&L profile for a long 99/**100**/101 butterfly in Exhibit 6–1 depicts the most common illustration of a butterfly. The top of Exhibit 6–2 shows the same butterfly over time but from the side (a great amount of time on the left and expiration on the right). Notice that the price can become very sensitive to changes in the underlying with less than two weeks to go. Obviously, a short butterfly graph will be the mirror image of the hill or mountain depicted in the graph shown. The numbers on the x-axis at the bottom of the graph are underlying prices. As can be seen, the butterfly has its highest value when the futures price is at the middle strike of $100. The butterfly has its minimum value at expiration day, when the underlying is either below the low strike of the butterfly ($99) or above the high strike ($101).

E X H I B I T   6 – 1

Theoretical Risk P&L Profile of a **(Long the Wings)** 99/**100**/101 Butterfly—View over Underlying Price Movement. Futures-Style Margining, 57 Days, 10% Flat Volatility and .01% Interest

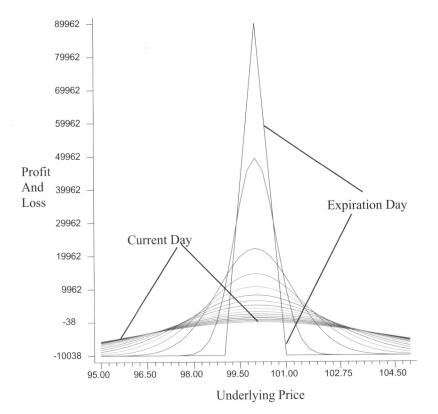

Underlying Price

E X H I B I T   6 – 2

Theoretical Risk P&L Profile of a **(Long the Wings)** 99/**100**/101 Butterfly—View over Time.
Underlying at 100, Futures-Style Margining, 57 Days, 10% Flat Volatility and .01% Interest

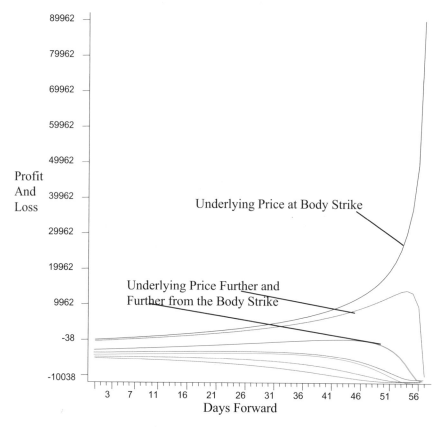

The risk and potential reward of a wingspread is limited. If one buys a butterfly, the most he or she can lose is the amount paid for it. The most value the spread can achieve is the difference between the body strike and a wing strike. Therefore, the greatest value is at the middle strike, 100, in this example. Incidentally, to reinforce the point made in Chapter 5, a +1 by –2 call ratio spread shares the point of greatest value at the short strike. Again, the addition of the cheap call 'wing' (the newly added third strike) serves as an insurance policy, creating the butterfly.

Wingspreads' sensitivity to movement in the underlying price is related to the time to expiration. For example, the closer a butterfly is to expiration, the more sensitive its price is to a change in the price of the underlying. What this means is that butterflies and wingspreads that are far from expiration don't change in value that much when the underlying fluctuates a relatively small amount.

This means that wingspreads are not the best tool for exploiting changes in the underlying price. The spreads can be bullish and turn bearish or bearish and turn bullish, or they can benefit from an unchanged market.

Wingspreads reach their maximum value when the underlying price is at (in the case of butterflies) or between (for other wingspreads) the middle or body strike(s) at expiration. They are at their minimum value when the underlying price is either above the higher wing strike or below the lower wing strike at expiration. Therefore, wingspreads can be effective when you believe that an underlying's price will land within a specified range and within a specified time frame. When you believe that an underlying will stay at a single price, long butterflies might be a good choice. When you think an underlying will stay in between two prices, a long condor with body strikes at the low and high prices of the underlying's range might work best. In this sense, long butterflies and wingspreads are like short straddles and strangles, but without the unlimited risk. Look at the graph of the value of a long butterfly at expiration in Exhibit 6–1 again. The middle of the butterfly looks like a short straddle. This will be discussed more in the "Structure" section.

Conversely, if you think the price of an underlying is going to move away from a specific point or outside a specific range of prices, short butterflies and wingspreads might be a choice, but, unlike long straddles or strangles, they have a limited profit potential.

It is sometimes useful to think of a butterfly (or any wingspread) in terms of two vertical spreads: one bullish and the other bearish (see Exhibits 6–3 and 6–4). This will enable you to calculate wingspread prices faster. It will also help you to understand how to make adjustments to positions like ratio or back spreads and, where necessary, turn them into butterflies.

E X H I B I T   6 – 3

A Combination of Call or Put Bull Spreads and Bear Spreads Creates Butterflies

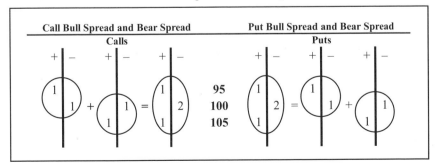

It makes sense that a combination of the two P&L graphs of a bull spread at one strike and a bear spread at the next higher strike will form a butterfly spread.

Remember that a bull spread can be either long a call vertical or short a put vertical (see "Verticals"). A bear spread can be either short a call vertical or long a put vertical. Therefore, any combination of bull spread at the lower strikes and bear spread at the higher strikes results in a long butterfly. A bear spread at the lower strikes and a bull spread at the higher strikes results in a short butterfly.

E X H I B I T   6 – 4

Formation of a Butterfly Spread

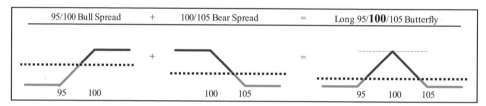

| 95/100 Bull Spread | + | 100/105 Bear Spread | = | Long 95/**100**/105 Butterfly |

Given three equidistant strikes, a long butterfly can be a call butterfly, a put butterfly, an iron butterfly (the credit version), or a "gut" iron butterfly, and they all have expiration P&L graphs that look the same. No matter what kind of butterfly it is, its maximum profit will be reached if the underlying price lands at the middle strike price at expiration. At that point, the lower strike bull spread will maximize in price (the difference between the strikes), and the higher strike bear spread will be theoretically worthless.

To prove the basic equivalency of call and put butterflies, let's look at the resulting position if you buy a call butterfly and sell a put butterfly at the same three strikes. The position will be more or less neutral (see Exhibit 6–5) because the result is a long box and a short box. With American-style options, boxes often have slightly different values. It follows that if the two boxes have different values so will the two butterflies. If the 100/105 box is worth .05 more than the 95/100 box because of an exercise aspect[1], then the put butterfly will be worth .05 more than the call butterfly. This may be of concern to a market maker with thousands of contracts on, but immaterial to a retail customer.

---

[1] **Exercise Aspects**

Boxes can expand beyond the difference between the strikes. (See Chapter 8)

E X H I B I T   6 – 5

100 Call Butterfly Versus 100 Put Butterfly is the 95/100 Box Versus the 100/105 Box

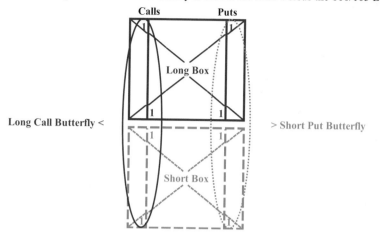

IRON WINGSPREADS

A note about short "iron butterflies" and "iron condors": despite the fact that they are *short,* they act the same as long call or put wingspreads in that they are a play for the same trading range that the strikes cover. Iron butterflies and iron condors are a seeming contradiction: you receive a credit to be long the range that you want the underlying to reside in.

Is the credit for the short iron butterfly better than a debit for a regular long butterfly? A short iron butterfly has the same risk/reward profile as a long call or long put butterfly, both of which cost money to be long. As can be seen in Exhibit 6–6, an iron butterfly is simply a long butterfly and a short box and for that reason a good reminder is to refer to it as a "long the wings butterfly". The credit comes from the short box embedded into the package. A short iron butterfly can be seen as either a long call butterfly plus a short box, whose strikes are at the lowest and middle strikes of the butterfly, or a long put butterfly plus a short box, whose strikes are at the middle and highest strikes of the butterfly.

E X H I B I T   6 – 6

An Iron is: a Call Butterfly and a Lower Strikes Box **OR** a Put Butterfly and a Higher Strikes Box

Iron = Call Bfly - Lower Strikes Box					Iron = Put Bfly - Higher Strikes Box				
C +/−	C +/−	Strikes	P +/−	P +/−	C +/−	C +/−	Strikes	P +/−	P +/−
	10	32.5	10				32.5	10	
	10	35	10			10	35	10	
10	10	37.5		10	10	10	37.5	10	10

The bull spread consists of a put vertical (at a credit) and the bear spread consists of a call vertical (also at a credit). Whichever way one looks at it, the two spreads make up an iron butterfly.

An iron butterfly is therefore a regular butterfly plus a short market-neutral box spread. Adding a short box to a butterfly does not necessarily change its risk/reward profile. It simply adds a cash loan from the market (which is what a short box is).

A 'long the wings' iron butterfly can also be identified as a short straddle at the middle or body strike and a long strangle at the wing strikes. This corresponds exactly with the middle part of a price graph of a long butterfly at expiration, which looks like a short straddle. The straddle strike (100) is located right between the strangle strikes (99 and 101). Looking back at Exhibit 6–1, the short straddle can be discerned in the area of the graph just above and below the middle strike price (100). The credit of the iron butterfly or iron condor is not significant and provides no real advantage. Iron condors work in the same way. A long iron condor would be a long condor plus a short box, or a short strangle surrounded (protected) by a long strangle at the outer wing strikes.

Note: For the rest of the chapter, butterflies, condors and other variations of wingspreads may not identify whether it is a call configuration, a put configuration or an iron configuration. From now on, we should think about them as verticals vs. verticals, i.e. bull spreads versus bear spreads, because the important aspect of the wingspread is the range that it covers. Where is (are) the short strike(s)? That is where the win zone is located.

THE GREEKS OF A BUTTERFLY

Note that the price of the butterfly can become very sensitive to changes in the underlying price with less than two weeks to go. The Greeks of the butterfly can also change very dramatically as the underlying price moves up and down. **This discussion will concentrate on butterflies, but the same principles can be applied to all wingspreads.**

Explore the Greeks in the following exhibits; delta in Exhibit 6–7, gamma in Exhibit 6–8, vega in Exhibit 6–9 and theta in Exhibit 6–10, over time (57 Days) as the underlying moves with implied volatility at a flat 10%. Obviously, if a trader has a short butterfly, he wants the market to be far away from the middle strike. Short butterfly Greeks' graphs will be the mirror images of Exhibits 6–7 to 6–10.

DELTA Δ

The delta of a butterfly (Exhibit 6–7) is quite interesting in that when the underlying price is below the middle strike of the butterfly the delta is long. When the underlying is at the strike the delta is flat, and when it is above the strike the delta is short.

E X H I B I T   6 – 7

Delta of 100*99/**100**/101 Butterfly - View - Over Price Movement
Futures Style Margining with a Flat Volatility of 10% for 57 Days

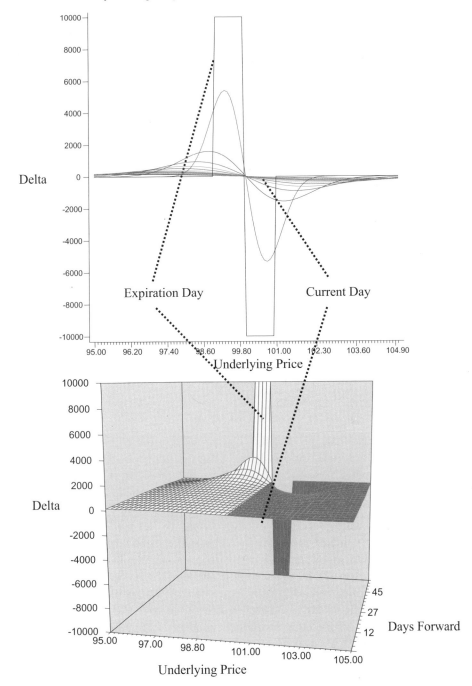

It is helpful to personify any spread that a trader has on to help understand what it wants and needs to make money. For example, an at-the-money butterfly wants the market to sit still and an away-from-the-money butterfly wants the market to go toward the strike price. The Greek profiles in the remaining three graphs, in Exhibits 6–8 to 6–10, also confirm these attributes. What causes the delta to flip from positive to neutral to negative? Gamma.

GAMMA Γ

The gamma of a long butterfly can flip from positive to negative or vice versa. At the outer strikes of the butterfly, gamma is positive, indicating that the butterfly wants the underlying price to move back to the strike price, because further away from the strike price it becomes worthless. This corresponds exactly to the way that the delta of the long butterfly works as described above. The gamma (Exhibit 6–8) and vega (Exhibit 6–9) are both negative when at-the-money while the theta (Exhibit 6–10) is positive, which confirms the butterfly's desire for the market to sit still. This indicates that the butterfly will manufacture negative deltas if the underlying price rises, and positive deltas if the underlying price falls. The butterfly will still have a chance to blossom because time and implied volatility can continue to add value within the long butterfly price range.

When the underlying moves away-from-the-money the gamma and vega turn positive, while the theta turns negative, suggesting a desire for a move back to the level of the middle strike.

VEGA ν

A wingspread can be a good choice to exploit changes in implied volatility in a limited risk fashion. Like the other Greeks, the vega of a butterfly changes depending on where the price of the underlying is relative to the strike prices of the butterfly. When the underlying price is at the middle strike, the vega of the long butterfly is negative. That means that any increased implied volatility in the underlying will decrease the value of the butterfly. This makes sense, because as will be discussed later, a butterfly's value depends on the likelihood that the underlying price will be at the middle strike of the butterfly at expiration. A higher implied volatility implies a decrease in the likelihood that the underlying will sit still. Therefore the value of ATM butterfly would decrease with an increase in implied volatility. Higher volatility means OTM butterflies have more of a chance of becoming ATM, while ATM butterflies have less of a chance of remaining ATM.

E X H I B I T   6 – 8

Gamma of 100*99/**100**/101 Butterfly - View - Over Price Movement
Futures Style Margining with a Flat Volatility of 10% for 57 Days

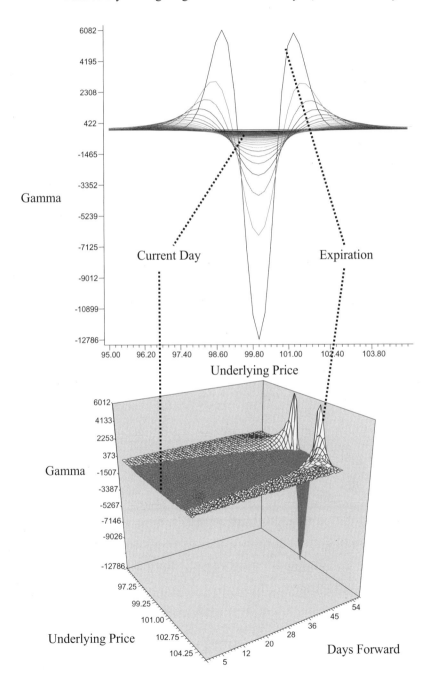

E X H I B I T   6 – 9

Vega of 100*99/**100**/101 Butterfly - View - Over Price Movement
Futures Style Margining with a Flat Volatility of 10% for 57 Days

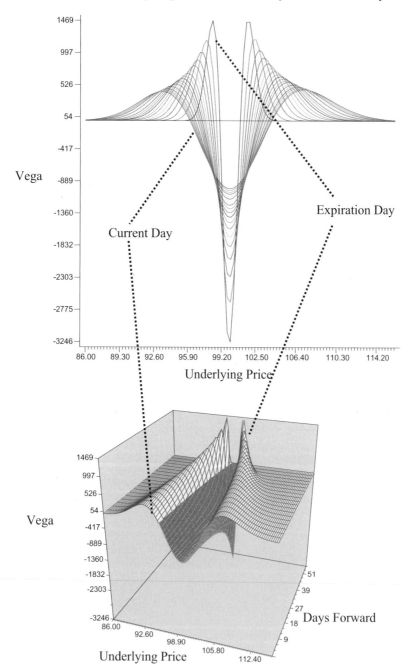

E X H I B I T   6 – 1 0

Theta of 100*99/**100**/101 Butterfly - View - Over Price Movement
Futures Style Margining with a Flat Volatility of 10% for 57 Days

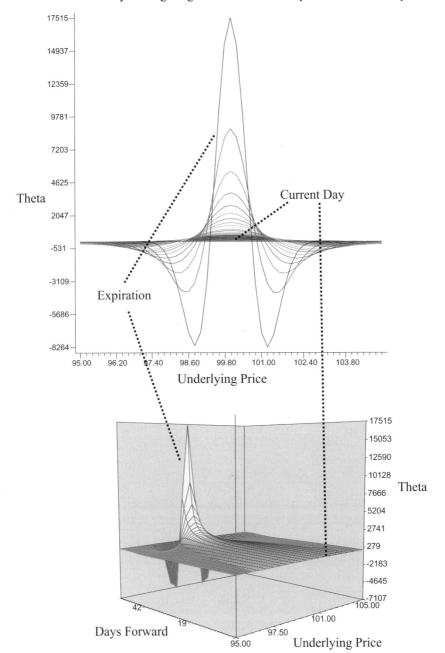

Therefore, an increase in implied volatility of the underlying increases the value of the butterfly because of the greater likelihood that the underlying will move toward the middle strike by expiration.

Butterflies and other wingspreads are interesting positions to test in the analyzer because their Greeks, although somewhat complex, make intuitive sense if you know how and when a butterfly increases and decreases in value. The Greeks can then confirm analytically what you know about butterflies intuitively.

THETA Θ

The theta of the long butterfly (Exhibit 6–10) is the mirror image of the gamma. Along with the negative gamma comes positive theta, and vice versa. Theta is positive when the price of the underlying is at the middle strike, indicating that time passing helps the long butterfly reach toward its maximum value. At the outer strikes theta is negative, indicating that the butterfly is losing value as time passes.

COMPARING THE PRICING OF BUTTERFLIES

Prior to expiration, wingspread values depend largely on the likelihood of the underlying being at a certain strike price (in the case of butterflies) or between two strike prices (in the case of other wingspreads) at expiration. The more time there is until expiration, the less certain you can be of where the underlying price will be at expiration. The less time there is to expiration, the more certain you can be of where the underlying price will be at expiration (Exhibit 6–1 and 6–2). Examine the prices in Exhibit 6–11. The individual call prices and deltas are displayed along with the prices of one strike butterflies (i.e. the difference between the wings and the body) and two strike butterflies.

E X H I B I T   6 – 1 1

One-Strike and Two-Strike Butterfly Prices Futures-Style Margining
56 Days Remaining at 10% Implied Volatility – No Skew

Strike	94	95	96	97	98	99	100	101	102	103	104	105	106
Call Premium	609	517	429	348	275	211	156	112	78	52	33	20	13
Delta	0.9451	0.9081	0.8558	0.7873	0.7038	0.6088	0.5078	0.4073	0.3135	0.2312	0.1631	0.1101	0.0710
1 pt. Butterfly		94/95/96	95/96/97	96/97/98	97/98/99	98/99/100	99/100/101	100/101/102	101/102/103	102/103/104	103/104/105	104/105/106	
1 pt. Butterflies $		4.68	6.29	7.86	9.14	9.95	10.13	9.67	8.67	7.31	5.83	4.72	
1 pt. Butterfly Delta		-0.0153	-0.0162	-0.0150	-0.0115	-0.0060	0.0005	0.0067	0.0115	0.0142	0.0151	0.0139	
2 pt. Butterfly		93/95/97	94/96/98	95/97/99	96/98/100	97/99/101	98/100/102	99/101/103	100/102/104	101/103/105	102/104/106	103/105/107	
2 pt. Butterflies $			25.12	31.15	36.09	39.17	39.88	38.14	34.32	29.12	23.69		
2 pt. Butterfly Delta			-0.0627	-0.0577	-0.0440	-0.0230	0.0017	0.0254	0.0439	0.0550	0.0583		

Interestingly, the graphs (Exhibit 6–12) of the prices of consecutive butterfly prices in a single expiration month form an arc which looks very much like a single butterfly P&L graph. The peak at the center represents the at-the-money butterfly, and as you go further from the center the butterflies become successively cheaper.

The graph would look flatter the more time there is until expiration. The reason for this is that when there is more time to expiration, there is more uncertainty about what the price of the underlying will be at expiration. This results in uncertainty over which butterfly will have the maximum value at expiration.

E X H I B I T   6 – 1 2

Plot of One-Strike and Two-Strike Butterfly Prices Futures-Style Margining
56 Days Remaining at 10% Implied Volatility – No Skew

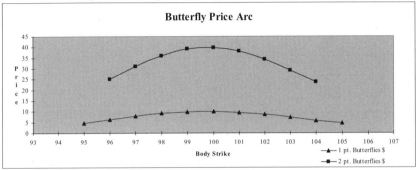

Remember that a butterfly reaches its maximum value when the underlying price is at the middle or body strike of the butterfly at expiration. This means that butterflies far from expiration have roughly the same value as each other because any one of them could be the big "winner" or "loser" at expiration.

When there is less time to expiration, there is somewhat more certainty where the price of the underlying is going to be at expiration. For those options months that are near expiration, the graph would begin to develop a "hump" at or near the current underlying price. In fact, the closer you get to expiration, the more the graph of all the consecutive butterfly prices begins to look like the P&L graph of a butterfly itself. The "hump" on the graph is the price of the most expensive butterfly. The at-the-money butterfly is the most expensive because it is the one most likely to be closest to the underlying price at expiration.

Condors are more expensive than butterflies, but they have a much larger profit range. Whereas a butterfly maximizes its value if the underlying price is exactly at the middle strike price of the butterfly, a condor maximizes its value over a range of underlying prices.

USING BUTTERFLIES TO SPECULATE DIRECTIONALLY CAN BE A CHALLENGE

The reason that one may want to speculate with a butterfly is that it is usually very cheap. It can be for example, a long call vertical (bull spread) partly funded with the sale of a short call vertical (bear spread) further out. If a trader insists on going this route he or she should learn from the blunder in the following paragraph. First of all, anticipate the need to adjust using additional capital, and secondly, realize that as expiration approaches it may be difficult to find an appropriate hedge. Here is an ugly tale.

Story: The Ugly Butterfly: By mid 1985 the T-Bonds had completed the right shoulder of a reverse head and shoulders pattern in the monthly bar chart (Exhibit 6–13). In a classic reverse head and shoulders pattern after breaking through the neckline, the market will retrace to the neckline and then bounce upwards. By November the market broke out of its continuation pattern.

E X H I B I T 6 – 1 3

U.S. T-Bonds Monthly Chart: Reverse Head and Shoulders Pattern with Price Projection to 88

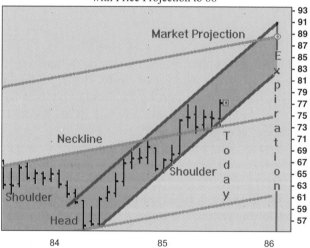

Buying premium outright seemed to be out of the question because my projections, based on the distance from the head to the neckline, were that by the time the June contract expired the bonds would be at 88.00. An 86/88 ratio spread would be too dangerous with so many days to go, but the June 86/88/90 butterfly was fairly cheap (5 ticks or .05 or $78.125), so I bought that instead. 5 ticks x 15.625 per tick seemed reasonable to me because if bonds reached 88 at expiration, each spread could be worth $2,000.00 and my total profit would be over $3,000,000.00 for the quantity I planned to buy. I reached into my right pocket and pulled out a crisp

$125,000.00 bill (a real collectors item), slapped it on the table and said "1600 please" (I was a cocky kid).

Within four and one-half weeks the bonds had rallied five points to 83. I went back to the pit and bought another 800 spreads at 10 ticks, pyramiding my investment while increasing my size by 50%.

One month later, bonds had rallied another five points and were trading at 88. This was too soon for the butterfly to maximize in value because the options still had almost four months to go (see Exhibit 6–14).

I thought that I may as well take my profits because a lot can happen in four months, and so I went to the bond options pit where the deferred months trade, and asked for a market on the "6,8,0 butterfly". I was waiting to hear something like 16 bid – at 20. The traders seemed to be waiting for me and responded with a smile, "10–12" (10 ticks bid, at 12 ticks) all that you want at 12". I thought they were joking because they knew my position, so I said "12 for 400".

E X H I B I T   6 – 1 4

Bonds Met the Projection a Few Months too Soon.

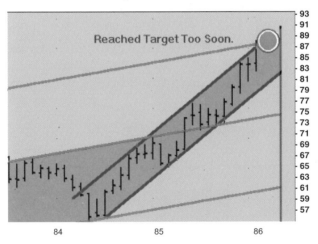

When they climbed all over themselves to sell them to me, my first thought was to buy even more, but it dawned on me that I already had 2800 at-the-money butterflies.

Time Out for a Quick Lesson:
Why were these guys selling the butterfly so cheap? They were quoting their bids and offers surrounding fair value. Volatility had exploded from about 9% to over 13%[2] during the last eight weeks.

---

[2] **Bond Volatility shift from 9% to 13%**

E X H I B I T   6 – 1 5

Theoretical Profit and Loss Risk Profile of 100*99/**100**/101 Butterfly – Underlying and
Implied Volatility Changes--Futures Style Margining, 57 Days to Go and .01% Interest

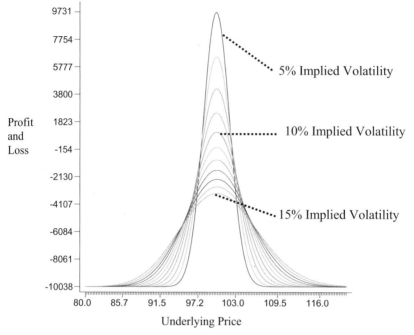

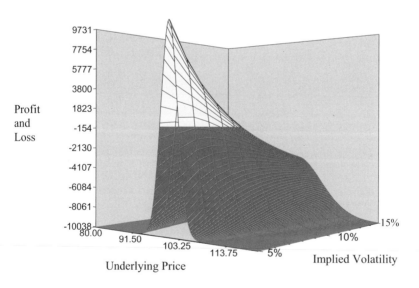

When volatility increases it is like adding time to the clock, which
theoretically implies that the market level could visit many strikes. If the
market perceives a wide price distribution, it makes sense that an at-the-

money butterfly will be of less value, because who will want to buy it if the market is not going to stay there? Exhibit 6–15 demonstrates how implied volatility affects 100*99/**100**/101 butterfly spreads.

Time In:

Quickly I determined that the 2800 butterflies' gamma was equivalent[3] to being short about 466 at-the-money straddles, and that I should buy at least 200 straddles in order to protect my butterfly. This would create a position with net long contracts but maintain a positive theta. I talked to my partner Joe, who said that the straddle which had been trading at 5.00 this morning was now (at noon) trading at 5.06. He thought that I should wait until the afternoon to buy straddles because implied volatility would probably bring the price down to 5.00 again. I agreed that volatility was a little too high and decided to wait a little while, since it was a Friday and traders usually take out the premium before the weekend. Wrong! OOPS! Not only was I stubborn about not buying the 200 straddles, but I also failed to look at the big picture over a longer period of time. There happened to be an even larger head and shoulders pattern (Exhibit 6–16) that I had not noticed until it was too late.

E X H I B I T   6 – 1 6

The Bonds Never Looked Back.
The arrow points to where the 200 Straddles should have been bought.

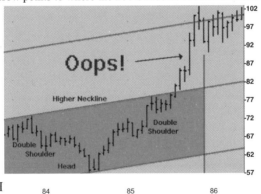

T   84   85   86   the 200
straddles.

Over the next two months the 88 straddle went from 5.00 to 16.00 and the bonds sailed over 104. $2.2 million (11 point profit

---

[3] **Straddle Equivalent**

The outside strikes had gammas of about .05 while the body strike was about .06 so each butterfly had a negative gamma of .02 (.05–(2x.06)+.05) totaling –56.00 "gramma" (limited risk gamma). Divide the straddle gamma of .12 (2 of the 88s) and you arrive at the equivalent of 466 straddles

on 200 straddles) down the toilet, not to mention the $325,000.00 of worthless butterflies that I had. I hate it when that happens.
End

OPTIONS MATRIX

Let us take a look at how the 'Options Matrix' (Exhibit 6–17) helps to place all these related spreads in perspective. Many of the following exhibits use these prices in the matrix. You can see the relationships between the individual call and put prices and the impact they have on verticals, butterflies, condors and so on. The strikes are labeled in the center horizontal line. Call and call spread prices are in the upper half of the exhibit.

E X H I B I T   6 – 1 7

Options Matrix

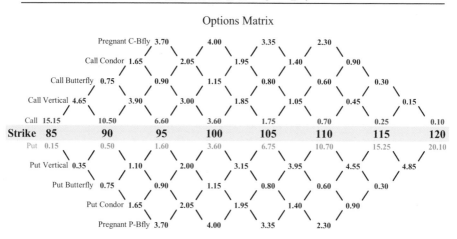

Put and put spread prices are displayed in the lower half of the exhibit while call and call spread prices are in the upper half. The butterfly prices are in the third set of rows further out from the center. The fourth rows out have the condor prices, which are simply the sums of the two adjacent butterfly prices from one row closer to the center. The top and bottom rows show values of the pregnant or two-strike butterflies. In this example, there are 4 baby butterflies in each two-strike butterfly.

Note that when you add the call verticals to the put verticals they all add up to 5.00, the box value (zero interest rate for simplicity). Also note that the call wingspreads equal the value of the put wingspreads.

The first rows away from the center row show each of the individual call prices (above) and put prices (below). The next rows out have the vertical values, i.e. the difference between the two adjacent strikes.

CONDORS AND STRETCHED – OUT CONDORS

Condors and other wingspreads can be understood as combinations of bull spreads and bear spreads. But condors can also be seen as being made up of a row of butterflies. The more butterflies that one has in a row, the wider the wingspread is, and the more the profit zone is stretched-out. See Exhibit 6–18 to see how 2 butterflies create a condor involving 4 strikes, and 6–18 to see how 3 consecutive butterflies create a condor involving 5 strikes. Every time a butterfly is added the vertical is pushed farther away and the profit range is stretched out further. The really stretched-out condor manifests in the common form of a trader wanting to short a strangle, but so as not to have naked exposure purchases a further out strangle (wings).

E X H I B I T   6 – 1 8

2 Butterfly Spreads in a Row Stretches Out the Profit Range, Risking 1.65 to Profit 3.35
Condor Involving 4-Strikes from Wing to Wing

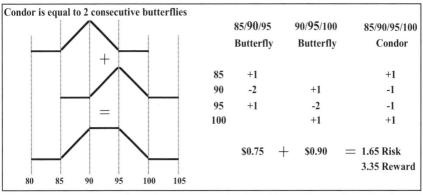

Condor is equal to 2 consecutive butterflies		85/90/95 Butterfly	90/95/100 Butterfly	85/90/95/100 Condor
	85	+1		+1
	90	-2	+1	-1
	95	+1	-2	-1
	100		+1	+1
		$0.75 +	$0.90 =	1.65 Risk 3.35 Reward

Exhibit 6–20 takes the concept further illustrating when Soybeans were trading at very high implied volatilities and a student wanted to sell short the 720p/880c strangle (displayed in the purple box (cell C12 for the put and K10 for the call) and purchase the 700p/900c strangle (B12 for the put and L10 for the call) for outside protection. Say for example, this double credit spread is going for a 4 cent credit (.04 x $50 = $200.00). Remember that it is equivalent to the all call (row 1) or all put (row 21) condor debit trade of about 16 cents ($800.00), which is calculated by taking the 20 cents[4] (900-880 or 720-700) minus the credit generated by the two OTM credit spreads (4 cents). Any way it is done, it all amounts to buying all the butterflies in between. Call butterflies

---

[4] **About 20 Cents**

The difference between each strike in Soybeans is 20 cents and, because there are 5000 bushels in the contract, 20 cents equals $1000. This example ignores carry cost.

illustrated in rows 4, 5, 6 and 7 along with put butterflies illustrated in rows 15, 16, 17, 18 along with the Iron butterfly with the call side in row 8 and the put side in row 14.

E X H I B I T   6 – 1 9

3 Butterfly Spreads in a Row Stretches the Profit Range, Risking 2.80 to Profit 2.20

Condor Involving 5-Strikes from Wing to Wing

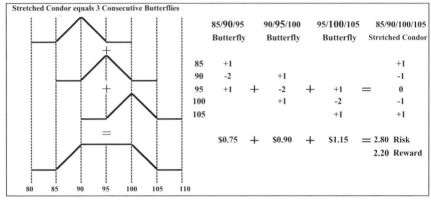

Stretched Condor equals 3 Consecutive Butterflies

	85/90/95 Butterfly		90/95/100 Butterfly		95/100/105 Butterfly		85/90/100/105 Stretched Condor
85	+1						+1
90	-2		+1				-1
95	+1	+	-2	+	+1	=	0
100			+1		-2		-1
105					+1		+1
	$0.75	+	$0.90	+	$1.15		= 2.80 Risk
							2.20 Reward

E X H I B I T   6 – 2 0

9 Butterfly Spreads in a Row Stretches the Profit Range

Condor Involving 11-Strikes from Wing to Wing

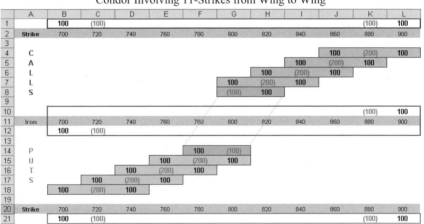

#	A	B	C	D	E	F	G	H	I	J	K	L
1		100	(100)								(100)	100
2	Strike	700	720	740	760	780	800	820	840	860	880	900
3												
4	C								100	(200)	100	
5	A							100	(200)	100		
6	L						100	(200)	100			
7	L					100	(200)	100				
8	S					(100)	100					
9												
10											(100)	100
11	Iron	700	720	740	760	780	800	820	840	860	880	900
12		100	(100)									
13												
14	P				100	(100)						
15	U			100	(200)	100						
16	T		100	(200)	100							
17	S		100	(200)	100							
18		100	(200)	100								
19												
20	Strike	700	720	740	760	780	800	820	840	860	880	900
21		100	(100)								(100)	100

EMBEDDED BUTTERFLIES IN WIDE BUTTERFLIES

Exhibit 6–21 shows a 2-strike butterfly with a cumulative risk of 3.70 for a possible reward of 6.30. One can use this knowledge to help decide whether to unload one or more of the embedded butterflies whenever the price is attractive or the adjustment is warranted because of market conditions.

Butterflies with strikes with greater distances between the wings and the body are used to cover a bigger range of prices. An interesting aspect of this type of butterfly is that it has smaller (1-strike) butterflies embedded into it, and therefore it has the nickname, 'pregnant butterfly'. If one takes the distance between the wing and the body and squares that number of strikes, one will identify the quantity of smaller butterflies embedded in the larger one. In other words, a two-strike butterfly will have 4 'baby' butterflies (two at the center strikes, and two more, one at each end). A 3-strike butterfly will have 9 babies (three in the center, two adjacent ones in each direction away from the body and one more set in each direction) further toward each wing. A 4-strike butterfly will have 16 babies, and so on. They stack up on top of each other, forming a mountain, with most of them being at the body and the least amount being near the wings.

E X H I B I T   6 – 2 1

Pregnant Butterfly (Two-Strike Butterfly) Contains 4 Baby Butterflies
with 3.70 Risk and 6.30 Reward.

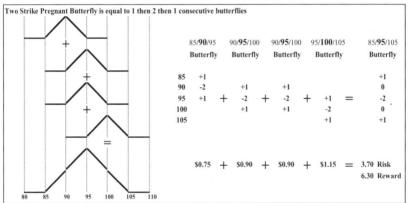

Exhibit 6–22 shows the configuration of 100 five-strike butterflies and by squaring the amount of strikes (5) from wing to body creates 25 embedded butterflies for a grand total of 2500.

How does an understanding of these concepts help one to trade? By seeing where the inventory of butterflies exists the trader can then scrutinize the values embedded and perhaps sell off blossoming butterflies as the underlying visits different bodies, or cover (buy back) cheap synthetic verticals, as components of butterflies, when they are too cheap to remain short. We know that butterflies have their greatest value when they are ATM. They may reach an attractive enough level motivating one to sell, harvest profits and reduce costs.

Certainly, with 30 days or more left in the expiration cycle or in scenarios of high implied volatility, it may not be opportune to unload even an ATM butterfly, simply because it is the most valuable butterfly in the inventory at the current time. Individual market sentiment would have to play a roll in the decision making process.

E X H I B I T   6 – 2 2

Pregnant Butterfly (Five-Strike Butterfly) Contains 25 Baby Butterflies
100 Pregnant Butterflies has 2500 Baby Butterflies.

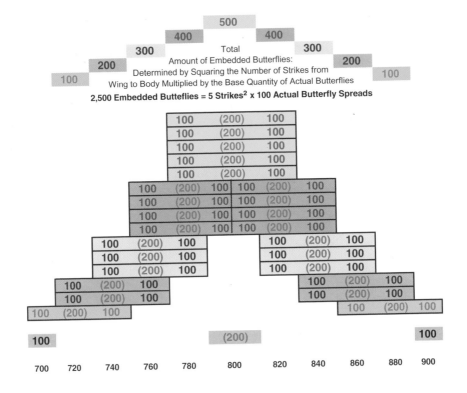

WINGSPREAD DISSECTION IN PRACTICE

We are going to follow an initial trade and the subsequent adjustments made in the RD3 Webinar Series, where we forecasted a likely expiration range with the Diamonetric™ Grid[5] (Exhibit 6–23).

GOOG (Google) was trading at $296 with 23 days to go and a target price of 280, while staying within the range of 260 to 300. The initial trade warranted either a 280 calendar spread, or a Butterfly with a

---

[5] **Diamonetrics™**

Technical analysis tool used to determine profit opportunities based on forecasting probable trading ranges, at particular options expiration dates.

280 body strike. We chose the AUG 260/**280**/300 Put Butterfly for 6.50 debit (10 spreads cost $6,500) because the class wanted to see how to adjust butterflies over time.

Wingspread dissection involves imaginarily selling or buying butterflies and condors against the position and placing the opposite trade in another area called the 'Butterfly Basket'. The reason that the dissector buys one and sells one is because he or she is not really making a trade, and therefore the net effect is zero. It is like debiting a trade in one account and crediting it to another.

E X H I B I T   6 – 2 3

Diamonetric Grid Identifies AUG Expiration Range of 260 to 300 with 280, Target Price.

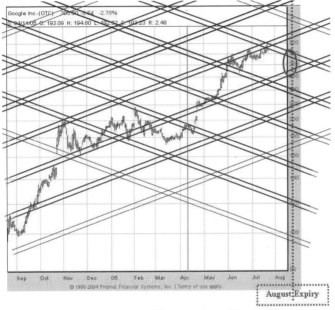

Chart courtesy of **ProphetFinance.com**

Dissecting out wingspreads by hand can be very messy, so it is important to be methodical. This trade was a 2-strike butterfly but was managed as 4 embedded baby butterflies (see Exhibit 6–18).

The WingTool 'ω' is used to denote the extraction of a butterfly from the position, just as the SynTool and BoxTool extract conversions/reversals and boxes. Exhibit 6–24 demonstrates a method that can be performed by hand. Simultaneously, the extracted butterfly is offset by the opposite transaction in the basket (left side of the hand dissection). The butterfly basket is where the opposite transaction shows up so that we can monitor our inventory of butterflies.

Trying to understand this concept can be difficult at first, but once it has been grasped it can become second nature. The initial trade is in the black font, immediately to the right of the strikes. The Stage 1 dissection, in the red font, is applied to the initial position (black font) and the results (displayed in red) and moved to the right. The Stage 2 dissection, in the blue font, is applied to the red results and moved further to the right (new results displayed in blue). The Stage 3 dissection, in the green font, is applied to the blue results and in this case nothing remains as can be seen in the far right net columns (green results).

E X H I B I T   6 – 2 4

Butterfly Hand-Dissection of Initial Trade – GOOG AUG 260/280/300 Put Butterfly

BSB +|-	C +|-	Strikes	Stage 1 P +|-	Stage 2 P +|-	Stage 3 P +|-	Net P +|-
		260	10	10|10ω		
10		270		20ω	20|20ω	
20		280	20|10ω	30|10ω	40ω|40	
10		290	20ω	20	20|20ω	
		300	10|10ω			
		310				

What follows is a spreadsheet method (Exhibit 6–25) which is much faster and can avoid errors. There are three separate stages, in Red, Blue and Green, in order emulate and match up with the hand-dissection performed above. The butterfly dissections occur in the three of the middle columns (J, K & L) and the sum is displayed in column I. Realistically, one would go through all the stages during the process, but only have the last stage showing in the end. The two methods or formats differ but yield exactly the same results.

Thirteen days passed and GOOG traded down to 290 causing the 280/**290**/300 baby butterfly to blossom to a reasonably attractive liquidation level (3.50). Many often ask, "What is an attractive level?" and my answer is pretty consistent, "Would I initiate, whatever it is, at the current price?" If the answer is "No", then the position warrants being adjusted. If the answer is "Yes", that I would initiate the trade at the current price, then it is attractive. If I am undecided because it is not obvious one way or another, then I will watch it until I get a better conviction.

Having sold the 280/**290**/300 baby butterfly, Exhibit 6-26 shows the hand dissection displaying a Skip-Strike-Butterfly which is the topic of the next section. Stage 1 dissection, in the red font, is applied to the evolved position (black font) and the results (displayed in red) are again moved to the right. The Stage 2 dissection, in the blue font, is applied to the red results and also moved further to the right (net results displayed in blue) where, in this case, nothing remains.

E X H I B I T 6 – 2 5

Butterfly Spreadsheet-Dissection of Initial Trade – GOOG AUG 260/280/300 Put Butterfly

Stage 1

	C	D	E	F	G	H	I	J	K	L	M	P	R	T
11								Net Contracts						
12		PivotK	300								PivotK	300		
13	Month							Butterfly						
14	Raw Position							Dissector				WorkSheet		
15	nC	rC	K	rP	nP	K	Bfly1	Bfly2	Bfly3	K	C		K	P
32			260	10	10	260				260			260	10
33			270			270				270			270	
34			280	(20)	(20)	280				280			280	(30)
35			290			290	10	10		290			290	20
36			300	10	10	300				300			300	
37			310			310				310			310	
58			Net			Net	10	10		Net			Net	

Stage 2

	C	D	E	F	G	H	I	J	K	L	M	P	R	T
11								Net Contracts						
12		PivotK	300								PivotK	300		
13	Month							Butterfly						
14	Raw Position							Dissector				WorkSheet		
15	nC	rC	K	rP	nP	K	Bfly1	Bfly2	Bfly3	K	C		K	P
32			260	10	10	260				260			260	
33			270			270	10	10		270			270	20
34			280	(20)	(20)	280				280			280	(40)
35			290			290	10	10		290			290	20
36			300	10	10	300				300			300	
37			310			310				310			310	
58			Net			Net	20	20		Net			Net	

Stage 3

	C	D	E	F	G	H	I	J	K	L	M	P	R	T
11								Net Contracts						
12		PivotK	300								PivotK	300		
13	Month							Butterfly						
14	Raw Position							Dissector				WorkSheet		
15	nC	rC	K	rP	nP	K	Bfly1	Bfly2	Bfly3	K	C		K	P
32			260	10	10	260				260			260	
33			270			270	10	10		270			270	
34			280	(20)	(20)	280	20	20		280			280	
35			290			290	10	10		290			290	
36			300	10	10	300				300			300	
37			310			310				310			310	
58			Net			Net	40	40		Net			Net	

Exhibit 6–27, the spreadsheet method, shows both stages combined. This will reconcile with the hand-dissection performed above. Again, the butterfly dissections occur in the three of the middle columns (J, K & L) and the sum is displayed in column I.

This evolving trade went on to more than double the original investment and the all the trades and dissections are discussed in "Miracle in August GOOG" at the Diamonetrics Forum at www.riskdillustrated.com. We Coulda Woulda Shoulda left this one alone because GOOG expired at exactly 280.00. However, during my 25 years at options, I have never ridden a butterfly right to the strike at expiration, and I cannot recommend that, because the risk of losing the accumulated profits is too great.

E X H I B I T 6 – 2 6

Butterfly Hand-Dissection of Adjusted Trade – GOOG AUG Skip-Strike-Butterfly

BSB		C			Stage 1		Stage 2		Net	
					P		P		P	
+	–	+	–	Strikes	+	–	+	–	+	–
				260	10		10	10ω		
10				270		20ω	20ω	20		
20				280	40ω	30	10	10ω		
				290	20	20ω				
				300						

E X H I B I T 6 – 2 7

Butterfly Spreadsheet-Dissection of Adjusted Trade GOOG AUG Skip-Strike-Butterfly
Stages 1 and 2 Combined

	C	D	E	F	G	H	I	J	K	L	M	P	R	T
11							Net Contracts							
12		PivotK	300									PivotK	300	
13	Month							Butterfly						
14	Raw Position							Dissector				WorkSheet		
15	nC	rC	K	rP	nP	K		Bfly1	Bfly2	Bfly3	K	C	K	P
32			260	10	10	260					260		260	
33			270			270		10	10		270		270	
34			280	(30)	(30)	280		20	20		280		280	
35			290	20	20	290					290		290	
36			300			300					300		300	
37			310			310					310		310	
58			Net			Net		30	30		Net		Net	

By the way, as the underlying drops, conversions / reversals and boxes are removed and synthesized to the at-the-money Pivot Strike[6].

---

[6] **Pivot Strike**

Destination strike, to where ITM options are 'boxed'. ITM Calls (Puts) are dissected to OTM Puts (Calls) via boxes that involve a user defined pivot (usually the ATM) strike.

SKIP – STRIKE – FLIES

Quite a popular spread in the OEX is the Skip-Strike-Fly or 1 by (skip–strike) 3 by 2 (see Exhibit 6–28). It is merely a way to extend the profit range from 5 to 10 points and save a little bit of money by, in effect, leaving out the last baby butterfly of a 2-strike butterfly. The difference between Exhibits 6–21 and 6–28 is the missing 95/**100**/105 butterfly priced at 1.15.

E X H I B I T   6 – 2 8

Adding 3 Butterfly Spreads, 1 at a First Set of Strikes and Two at an Adjacent Set of Strikes to Form a Skip-Strike Butterfly with 2.55 Risk and 7.45 Reward

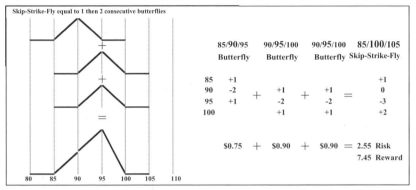

There are some really cool variations of Skip–Strike–Flies where more strikes are skipped and for each, an additional short vertical is required. To help to understand how it works, Exhibit 6–29 shows a series of dissections beginning with a normal butterfly followed by the first skip-strike-fly shown a little differently than the previous exhibit.

These different configurations are overlaid and compared in the (color coded) Hockey Stick Graphs at the bottom of Exhibit 6–30.

The +1 by 0 (skip–strike) by –3 by +2 has a distance of 2 strikes between the wings where the short strike is the peak of the value zone. That is a 2-strike bull spread against 2 (1-strike) bear spreads where all the short options share the same strike. Stretching further, it will be a 3-striker versus 3 single-strike verticals, then a 4 versus 4 singles and so on.

The nice feature of these configurations is that the positions are not only limited risk but the larger long vertical is financed to a degree by the sale of a number of smaller verticals without creating a liability like there would be in unbalanced butterflies.

E X H I B I T   6 – 2 9

Skip–Strike Butterfly Configurations – Dissected

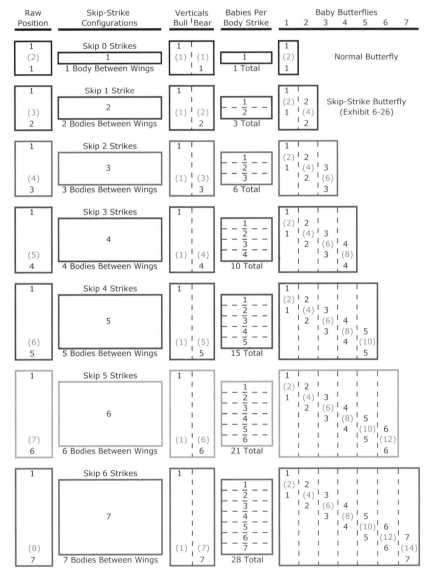

An unbalanced butterfly, for example, would be a call vertical debit spread financed by the sale of a greater number of call vertical credit spreads, and all the verticals involved have equal strike widths. This creates a potential liability when the underlying moves higher, above the butterfly aspect of the trade (the debit spread against only one of the credit spreads) increasing the liability of the extra credit spreads shorted.

E X H I B I T   6 – 3 0

Skip–Strike Butterfly Configurations – Hockey-Stick Graphs

RATIOED VERTICALS / UNBALANCED BUTTERFLIES

Sometimes called Broken Wing Butterflies (BWB), the next group of wing spreads (Exhibit 6–31) show properties similar to skip-strike-flies but differ in one respect. They can lose more than the cost. Let's be perfectly clear here and understand that cost includes the synthetic equivalent cost.

Remembering that a butterfly is a vertical against a vertical and a skip-strike-fly is a wide vertical against more smaller verticals whose sum equals a wider vertical, both of which have only the amount paid (synthetically paid) at risk. When you have a vertical versus more verticals of the same size you create a liability equal to the distance of each extra short vertical. Through wing spread dissection we can identify the locations of the long and now short butterflies embedded in the position.

This approach to ratio spreading is much safer than the open-ended risk of a ShortMore ratio spread discussed in Chapter 5, because the net units are zero.

E X H I B I T   6 – 3 1

Various Ratioed Verticals or Unbalanced Butterfly Configurations – Hockey-Stick Graphs

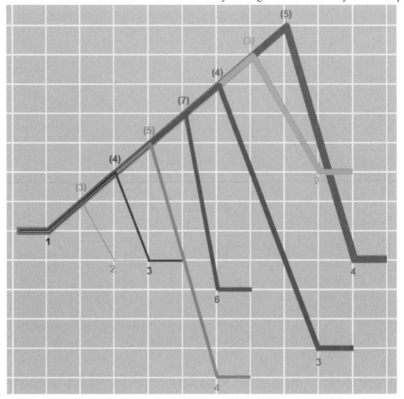

WHY MARKET MAKERS USE DISSECTION

Dissecting out wingspreads can play an important role in the Market Maker's decision making process because when insensitive, limited risk components are removed, it is easier to see what is leftover. The first questions that should be addressed in dissection are whether it is necessary to neutralize the current risk, and if so, what quantity of options should be bought or sold in order to neutralize about 95% of it (where possible). If a market maker can neutralize with one trade (always be one trade away from comfort) it is a good situation to be in. He or she will have the flexibility to turn his position around in an instant if necessary. One can solve a number of confounding questions that have plagued many successful traders by simply dissecting one's positions.

Wingspread dissection helps achieve two vital objectives: to establish priorities for trading and risk management, and to give the market maker ideas about ways that he can better proceed in the market. It makes sense to get to the heart of the position by removing it's less sensitive attributes. Once the limited gain/risk spreads have been removed, the more aggressive part of the position becomes easier to identify. If butterflies have been dissected out of the position, they should be merged back into it with less than two weeks to go or in periods of low implied volatility. During such times butterfly prices can fluctuate considerably, as demonstrated in the Greeks and profit & loss profiles of prior exhibits.

Keep in mind that when wingspreads are removed from a raw position and placed into either a general spread, butterfly basket or speculation basket, whatever has been removed must be regarded as still being alive. They still have risk, perhaps significant risk. The butterflies are removed because those spreads have the least worrisome attributes at that particular moment, based upon the Greeks, the trader's market opinion and his or her sense of how the spreads will behave in conjunction with the remnant position. The trader should prioritize by category: primary risk (consisting of the imminent risk involving naked or unfavorable risk/reward aspects and any other unwanted bias); secondary risk (consisting of definable or limited risk/reward spreads); and cheap (almost worthless) long options and cheap spreads that can profit more than they can lose. The amount of risk that is removed should be monitored relative to the risk remaining.

Analyzing multi-leg option positions is a bit like playing chess. It's a good idea to think a few moves a head, but more importantly you need to see the whole board. Dissection helps you to do just that.

CONCLUSION

Dissection is used to help generate decisions that can be acted upon. In order for a trader to make informed decisions he needs to learn as much as possible about his position. He can do this by dissecting it. He can isolate the subsets of his raw position and differentiate between them. Sometimes a trader does not gain any useful ideas from dissection. There are three possible reasons for this. The first is that the dissection has confirmed what he already knows. The second reason is that he may not have tried enough possibilities and there may be another way to dissect the position that will generate ideas. The third reason is that for that particular position it may be a waste of time and not worth the trouble.

Traders should continually 'rotate the chess board', or turn their positions around so that new perspectives are gained. Dissection is clearly invaluable to traders who need ideas on how to better proceed in the market. Many would feel helpless without it.

CHAPTER

7

MULTI-EXPIRATION SPREADS

Spreads involving two or more expirations come under the category of multiple expiration spreads. They include jelly rolls, time spreads, calendar spreads, diagonals, double diagonals (also known as straddle-strangle-swaps or calendarized iron wing spreads) and spreads involving one or more OTC[1] (over-the-counter) or flex[2] options. Originally, a calendar spread was, and often still is, called a 'time spread', consisting of two calls or two puts of the same strike but with different expirations where one is long and the other is short. They must be assignable to the same underlying instrument (i.e., equity options or the serial[3] month futures contracts). Traditionally, calendar spreads had options representing two different index months[4], futures or forward contracts and when exercised/assigned delivered different underlying month contracts. Please note that throughout this chapter, the term 'time spread' will be used to represent what most people in the industry call a calendar spread. Make no mistake about it, in this discussion time

---

[1] OTC

Over the counter options refer to privately guaranteed deals made by and between financial institutions and those customers who apparently have sufficient credit. Counter-party risk is the major consideration, especially for the holder of the option, because he or she must rely on the financial strength of the writer to pay for the in-the-money amount should the option be exercised.

[2] Flex

Flex options are exchange-regulated options contracts with flexible expirations. They are similar to OTC options in nature, but different in that they are guaranteed by the exchange and are backed by the financial integrity of the exchange's membership.

[3] Serial

A *serial month option* delivers into a quarterly futures contact, that is, the January, February, and March options receive a March futures contract when exercised, while the April, May, and June options deliver into the June futures contract.

[4] Index Months

Although it appears that options on an index are for the same underlying, they are actually not. The options in a given month are priced off a non-transparent synthetic futures contract via each combo (strike plus call minus put). Combos are synthetic futures and are theoretically valued based upon the interest to carry the basket of stocks minus the dividend stream for the cycle, which is different for each expiration month.

spreads involve contracts with delivery for the same underlying stock or futures contract month upon exercise or assignment.

Margin requirements are quite small for long time spreads compared to most other options strategies, because they are limited to what you pay. Short time spreads, on the other hand, can be quite prohibitive for retail customers because regulators treat them as naked shorts. It seems a little ridiculous, but they are concerned that after the closer term option expires worthless the remaining short will be naked. This is also a concern if the front month option is exercised and the new underlying position, combined with the remaining short option creates a synthetic that has naked exposure.

The basic long time spread strategy is to play for market stability or to target a trading range. It is even better if implied volatility is low for the longer dated option being bought. For some reason, novices think that it is better to buy LEAPs against the expiring month because they have more time. It does give them more time, but often it is more time to lose money. Their intent is to roll the nearly worthless short option (buy it back…) to the next month (shorting the next month), in order to take more advantage of time decay (positive theta). What the novice may not realize is that, first of all, they have to be right about the target, which is an art in itself, and then secondly, they have to be right again and again and again for as many expirations as there are in between the long month and the short month. In effect, the trader is buying all those time spreads in between with the object of being right every single expiration. The more time spreads bought, the more the trader is at risk. Exhibit 7–1 displays the actual long 10 one-year, JAN06 / JAN07 time spread position in the large bold font at either end (columns A and M). Here there are twelve embedded time spreads (each in a colored pair) within the two JANs. The long 10 and short (10) in each column, B to L, indicates that each is not a real trade, but is only used as place holders for dissection purposes.

E X H I B I T   7 – 1

A One Year Time Spread Equals 12 Consecutive One Month Time Spreads

A	B	C	D	E	F	G	H	I	J	K	L	M
JAN07	DEC	NOV	OCT	SEP	AUG	JUL	JUN	MAY	APR	MAR	FEB	JAN06
10	(10)	10	(10)	10	(10)	10	(10)	10	(10)	10	(10)	
	10	(10)	10	(10)	10	(10)	10	(10)	10	(10)	10	(10)

JELLY ROLLS

The concepts relating to jelly rolls and jelly-roll structures are presented here because they are directly involved in the structure of time spreads and reveal synthetic relationships useful in risk management and the decision making process. The interrelationships of the structures of jelly rolls and time spreads are shown in Exhibit 7–2. The structure of this short jelly roll consists of a long 100 strike call time spread against a short 100 strike put time spread, which is also equivalent to a far month long combo (synthetic underlying) versus the near month short combo. A call time spread is synthetically a put time spread when a jelly roll is dissected out.

E X H I B I T   7 – 2

Structure of Long Jelly Roll as it Relates to the Structure of Call and Put Time Spread

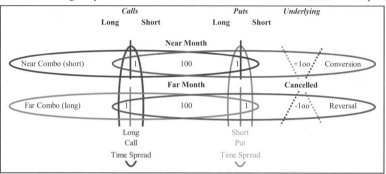

The key to understanding whether a time spread or jelly roll is long or short lies in whether the long option (for time spreads) or combo (for jelly roll) is in the near month or the far month. For one of the spreads to be short, the further term option or spread (in the case of a combo as part of a jelly roll) has to be short. Remember that when we refer to time spreads, *short* denotes that the further month is the short month, and the near-term month is the long month, because when the further month is short and the closer term is long, the position is known to be short time.

Jelly rolls in equities are interesting because the early exercise feature causes put spreads to collapse when cheap calls approach a value that is less than the cost of carry. The prices in Exhibit 7–3 and the graph in Exhibit 7–4, use the binomial model with 60 and 151 days to go and a flat implied volatility of 20%.

E X H I B I T   7 – 3

Values Using a Binomial Model with a Flat Implied Volatility of 20 Percent

Strike	55	60	65	70	75	80	85	90
60 Day Calls	15.59	10.68	6.11	2.64	0.81	0.17	0.03	0.00
151 Day Calls	16.51	11.89	7.78	4.55	2.36	1.08	0.44	0.16
Call Timespread	**0.93**	**1.21**	**1.67**	**1.90**	**1.55**	**0.91**	**0.42**	**0.16**
Jelly Roll	0.87	0.93	0.98	0.99	0.98	0.90	0.42	0.16
Put Timespread	**0.06**	**0.28**	**0.69**	**0.91**	**0.57**	**0.01**	**0.00**	**0**
60 Day Puts	0.00	0.04	0.43	1.96	5.24	10.00	15.00	20.00
151 Day Puts	0.06	0.32	1.12	2.87	5.81	10.01	15.00	20.00
60 Day Combo	15.58	10.63	5.68	0.68	-4.43	-9.83	-14.97	-20.00
151 Day Combo	16.45	11.57	6.66	1.68	-3.46	-8.93	-14.56	-19.84

The differences between the call and put time spread prices become larger as the strikes increase, and then they start to collapse.

E X H I B I T   7 – 4

Plot of Values from Exhibit 7–3

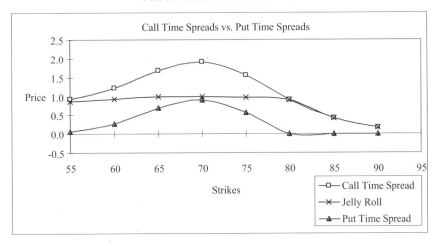

JELLY ROLLER

The jelly roller "⌡" is a dissection tool for rolling combos from one month to another (synthesizing out a jelly roll). Starting with the original position on the left side in Exhibit 7–5, a jelly roller is used to demonstrate how to synthesize a short December 70 combo into a short September combo. Of course, one would have to account for a short jelly roll in the position after synthetically purchasing it in the dissection on the right, because afterwards the net position is the September combo.

E X H I B I T   7 – 5

Dissection Using Jelly Roller to Roll Combos Between Months

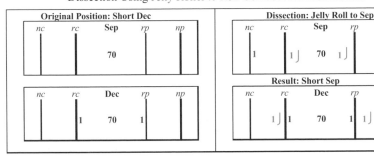

Another obvious purpose for a jelly rolling synthesis is to turn a call time spread into a put time spread, or vice versa, when moving inventory around to accommodate liquidity in the market (Exhibit 7–6).

E X H I B I T   7 – 6

Dissecting a Long Call Time Spread into a Long Put Time Spread Using the Jelly Roller

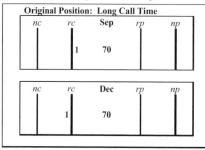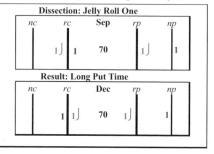

There are other practical uses and some fascinating discoveries that this tool could help to uncover. For example, a jelly roller proves that two long call time spreads are synthetically the same as a straddle long in December against a short straddle in September, as shown in Exhibit 7–7.

E X H I B I T   7 – 7

Dissecting 2 Long Call Time Spreads into a Long DEC Straddle vs. Short SEP Straddle

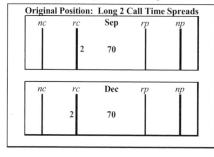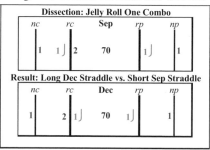

CALENDAR SPREADS : BRIEFLY

The kind of calendar spread that involves options representing different futures contracts contain what we originally called 'calendar risk', which is otherwise known as inter-month spread risk. This type of risk can be huge. A group of neutral spreaders in Eurodollar options in 1989 suffered a $12 million loss when their short premium month's futures were moving more than their long premium month's futures. Although they knew what they were doing, and had made money for years doing just this, the group had to be bailed out by another firm.

I do not have much to say about calendar spreads, except that they are a considerable gamble because their price fluctuations are heavily influenced by large players in the market. That is not to say, don't use them but K.I.S.S. Keep it simple sweetheart. Trade apples to apples and oranges to oranges. Calendar spreads are mostly an implied volatility play, and they require a lot of delta adjustments to keep it that way. One more thing, although OEX and other index options are quoted as time spreads, they are priced off synthetic futures and have calendar risk.

TIME SPREAD VALUE

Time spreads are very much like butterflies in many respects, and this is why, when considering either one as a strategy, it is also appropriate to consider the other.

Once again, "long" a time spread refers to time spreads where the deferred month is long while the closer month is short, so that the trader is long more time. The P&L graph, displayed in Exhibit 7–8 (using a 0% interest rate for illustrative purposes) looks similar to the butterfly spread. A major difference, however, is the aspect of premium.

E X H I B I T   7 – 8

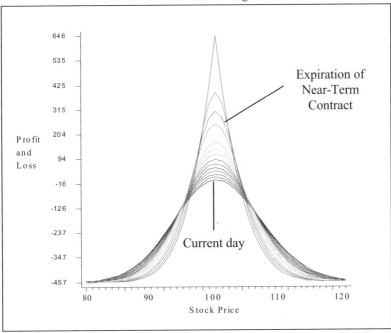

Theoretical Risk Profile of a Long 100 Strike Time Spread
View over Price Movement Using 0% Interest

Note that long any time spread will always have a positive vega, but depending on whether it is in-the-money, at-the-money, or out-of-the money, the gamma can be positive or negative. Recall that a butterfly's gamma and vega are both short for a long ATM butterfly, but may become long when the butterfly has gone ITM or OTM. The opportunities, as seen by time spreaders, are threefold. They can either play directionally (delta), for implied volatility changes (vega), or for time decay (theta). Gamma comes along for the ride in most cases, except for in diagonal and diagonal back spread plays (inter-month back spreads).

Don't forget that equity options include interest (see Exhibit 7–4). Unlike a worthless OTM put time spread, a deep ITM call time spread (same strike) will still have a value equal to the difference between the costs of carry between the two months involved. Also, ITM put time spreads will go to zero faster the higher the interest rate is, because both puts will go to parity sooner owing to the early exercise nuance discussed in Chapter 3.

TIME SPREAD PRICE ARC AS A PRICING TOOL

Time spread prices (Exhibit 7–9) are useful in determining value and risk. Prices for 'time butterflies' are also provided to give you an idea of how they may behave as the underlying moves. A time butterfly is a spread consisting of three expirations. The first and third month expirations are either both long or both short, while twice as many of the second month expirations are the inverse (e.g., +1 JAN (14 days left) 95c / –2 APR (105 days left) 95c / +1 JUL (196 days left) 95c). One could say that this is a near term time spread (+1 JAN 95c / –1 APR 95c) spread against a far term time spread (–1 APR 95c / + 1 JUL 95c). Each spread shares a common expiration (APR) and the "wing" (outside) expiration options are either both long or (as in this case) both short.

E X H I B I T   7 – 9

Call Prices and Deltas, Call Time Spread Prices and Time Butterfly Prices

Implied Volatility: 60% Interest Rate: 7%.

Strike	70	75	80	85	90	95	100	105	110	115	120	125	130
Call Premium 14 Days	30.20	25.23	20.32	15.63	11.33	7.68	4.82	2.80	1.50	0.75	0.34	0.14	0.06
Timespread 14/105	2.69	3.68	4.87	6.19	7.45	8.37	8.82	8.74	8.23	7.41	6.48	5.50	4.63
Call Premium 105 Days	32.89	28.91	25.19	21.82	18.78	16.05	13.64	11.54	9.73	8.16	6.82	5.64	4.69
Timespread 105/196	3.14	3.65	4.12	4.54	4.89	5.14	5.25	5.36	5.33	5.22	5.11	4.92	4.74
Call Premium 196 Days	36.03	32.56	29.31	26.36	23.67	21.19	18.89	16.90	15.06	13.38	11.93	10.56	9.43
Time-Butterfly	0.45	(0.03)	(0.75)	(1.65)	(2.56)	(3.23)	(3.57)	(3.38)	(2.90)	(2.19)	(1.37)	(0.58)	0.11

The prices plotted in Exhibit 7–10 form an arc just as butterflies do, with the most expensive spreads at-the-money (if there is no implied volatility skew). The time butterfly is simply the sum of differences between each respective time spread.

E X H I B I T   7 – 1 0

Plot of Time Spread and Time Butterflies

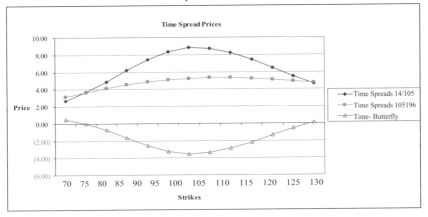

Time Spread Prices

WARNING: DON'T BE A SUCKER!

Now and then, in certain situations, (for example when a bio-tech company is expecting a decision from the FDA[5]) a stock may experience a large move, and implied volatility explodes. This creates what looks like an opportunity, but one can lose a lot of money in these sucker plays. Here is a common scenario; a stock that normally has an implied volatility of, for example 30, explodes in anticipation of FDA approval. The front month implied volatility increases to 100% and deferred months only go up to 60%. The sucker, using a limited risk, long time spread, buys the 60% volatility in the back-month and shorts the 100% volatility in the front-month hoping to clean up on the correction. The correction comes and both months come back down to say 40%. The sucker thinks that because his shorts came down 60% and his longs only came down 20% that he or she is a huge winner. WRONG! The vega of the deferred longs are so much greater that they represent more money per percentage point of implied volatility than the front month options vega does. For example, front month vega is .05 per one percentage point in implied volatility change while the deferred month's vega is .30. When the front month corrects by 40% it means that the option drops $2.00 (40 x .05). The back month however, although correcting the lesser amount of 20% volatility, represents $6.00 (20 x .30), losing $4.00 per spread. The poor sucker is bewildered and rarely understands where the damage came from. It works like long-term interest rates versus short-term rates changing. A 1% fluctuation in 30-year bonds is huge

---

[5] **FDA**
Food and Drug Administration

while a 1% fluctuation in 30-day T-Bills is almost like nothing. Bottom Line:

Volatility is not Money!

DIAGONALS

A diagonal is a long call (put) in one month and a short call (put) in another month with different strikes. It is usually preferable to sell the near month options and buy further dated ones in order to have favorable time erosion (time on our side). Usually investors would prefer to own a far dated ITM Call (unlimited risk) rather than the stock that has a lot more down side risk. Then they sell a closer dated OTM Call to enhance their return. Exhibit 7–11 shows the Diagonal's theoretical risk profile.

E X H I B I T   7 – 1 1

Long a Call Diagonal Spreads—Long 10*65 Call (173 Days)/Short 10*75 Call (82 Days)

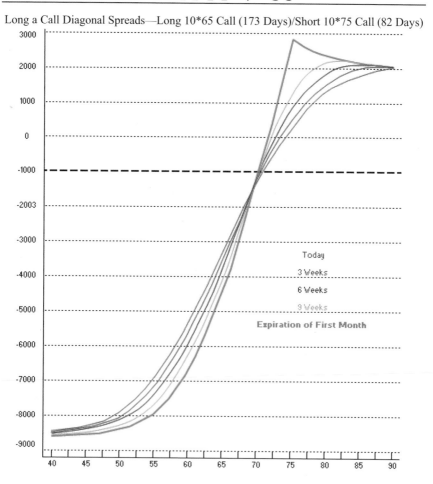

The following dissection in Exhibit 7–12 demonstrates the 65/75 call diagonal is synthetically a 65/75 put diagonal.

E X H I B I T   7 – 1 2

10 Call Diagonals Dissected to a Put Diagonals via a Jelly Roll and a Box

JAN (82)

Net Calls	Raw Calls	Strikes	Raw Puts	Net Puts
		65		
		70		
	10J 10	75	10J	10

APR (173)

Net Calls	Raw Calls	Strikes	Raw Puts	Net Puts
	10 10	65	10	10
		70		
	10 10J	75	10J 10	

Since diagonals can be confusing, to make it more intuitive, it can be useful to realize that a diagonal is simply a vertical spread that intersects with a time spread. Exhibit 7–13 shows a crossed out imaginary trade in a light blue box (long and short the same thing). This reveals an embedded vertical and an embedded time spread.

E X H I B I T   7 – 1 3

Call Diagonal Spreads Dissected into Verticals and Time Spreads (Two of the 16 Ways)

10 APR 65 / -10 JAN 75 Call Diagonal With Imaginary Trade Applied		Equals	10 APR / JAN 75 Call Time Spread Plus APR 65 / 75 Call Bull Vertical		OR	10 APR / JAN 65 Call Time Spread Plus JAN 65 / 75 Call Bull Vertical	
Calls	JAN		Calls	JAN		Calls	JAN
	65			65		10 10	65
	70			70			70
10	75		10	75		10	75
	APR			APR			APR
10	65		10	65		10	65
	70			70			70
	75		10 10	75			75

This APR/JAN 65/75 call diagonal can be the vertical in either month accompanied by a time spread at one or the other strikes. Either you have the April vertical with the 75 time spread or you have the January vertical with the 65 time spread. Perceiving diagonals in this way will help you to understand how to tweak gamma, theta, and vega more to your favor. There are 16 ways to construct the same diagonal because there are 4 different verticals times 4 different time spreads.

It will be best understood if you already have entry criteria for individual vertical and calendar spreads. Obviously, if the criteria are met for both or are rather close, there is a strong case for entering the diagonal. The price will simply be the debit price for the time spread minus the credit for the vertical. Prices will vary depending on the underlying price, the strikes involved, time until expiration and implied volatility levels.

Using a diagonal spread is a way to control how time will affect a vertical spread. To put it more simply, it is another way for a trader to optimize his or her market objectives based on an analysis of implied volatility levels and may provide the trader with alternative, less costly, and even creative ways to lock in value or eliminate risk.

EXERCISE / ASSIGNMENT

At expiration, if the front month option expires worthless, one will be left with only the deferred month's position. Exhibit 7–14 shows the results from the front month's Exercise / Assignment.

E X H I B I T   7 – 1 4

Result from Exercise / Assignment of Front Month Option

Original Position	Option Exercised
Long Call Time Spread	Long Synthetic Put
Short Call Time Spread	Short Synthetic Put
Long Put Time Spread	Long Synthetic Call
Short Put Time Spread	Short Synthetic Call

When the underlying is delivered the resulting position is the opposite type of option, as shown above. *This may be counter-intuitive to some people.*

DOUBLE DIAGONALS
STRADDLE - STRANGLE - SWAPS
CALENDARIZED WING SPREADS

A double diagonal is two diagonal spreads, one in the calls and the other in the puts. This strategy wins in a stable market. It consists of short a straddle or a strangle in the current month and long a further dated strangle at strikes further away. It is a trading vehicle that combines the best characteristics of time/calendar spreads and short iron (long the wings) spreads (butterfly for 3 strikes and condor for 4 or more) and is betting for the underlying to stay within a certain range. The object is to keep rolling the shorts to the next month as the front months become nearly worthless. The iron reduces the cost of the time spread but don't forget that there is a liability (which is the distance between the short and the long strike).

The advantage of using time spreads in conjunction with butterflies or condors is that time spreads create additional positive theta creating cash flow (time decay in your favor) every day. Butterflies will only have a significant positive theta when the underlying trades within the strikes during the last couple of weeks, or if the wings are far enough from the body in the case of a large butterfly.

The original position is created on a fairly delta neutral basis and adjusted periodically by using vertical spreads or calendar spreads depending upon market conditions. Prior to entering positions a range of acceptable deltas should be established. This range is the basis for making position adjustments. So you may ratio more on one side than the other for balancing and adjusting. In order to remain reasonably market neutral, a professional trader will always try to keep positions within this delta range. The bigger the position size the more important this becomes. In addition, keeping gamma within a range is just as important as keeping the deltas within the specified range, but the concepts and strategies needed to do so are more sophisticated. These gamma adjustments require the use of time spreads to achieve the desired gamma. The objective for a retail investor is different because he or she plays more for support and resistance levels and leans long or short accordingly.

The pricing of time spreads is mostly determined by monitoring the relationships between the volatilities that exist in all of the listed months. For our purposes, looking at the front month and the following three months is more than sufficient[6]. As a general rule, it is desirable to sell options in the front month at an implied volatility level that is higher than the back month options that you are buying. However, long time spreads often profit when the implied volatilities are not so favorable, simply because prices are built in to what may be obvious to the collective market participants. The basic volatility skew (an aberration between implied volatilities) that generally exists in most underlying equities and indices is less pronounced as you move out in time. The above guidelines will prevent traders from selling the front month options too cheap. Also basic probability assumptions can be used to determine the ideal strikes to employ when opening positions.

Exiting and rolling time calendar spreads involves several assessments. First of all, in a perfect scenario these positions would

---

[6] In my opinion, the majority of worthwhile technical analysis chart plays, conducive to options strategies do not extend beyond six months.

never have to be adjusted, so that when the front month options become cheap enough, it is advisable to either close or roll the shorts to the next month where premiums are meatier and therefore a better short candidate. Secondly, what is a good price? And finally, what should we look for when exiting and rolling time calendar spreads?

How do we determine an attractive opportunity to enter a short (long the wings) iron condor and buy a cheap calendar spread? If you know your entry criteria for a long butterfly or condor and your risk threshold for a long calendar, merge the two concepts because the pricing criteria of both together will directly apply to the diagonal. Remember that a long condor for a debit acts the same as a short iron condor for a credit (provided that the credit is close to the short vertical's basic value minus the debit of the long condor). We also need to establish the entry criteria for entering an OTM time spread. Knowledge is power so all you have to do is combine the two separate understandings and this is best established over time by experience. Depending on implied volatilities and stock price, conservative traders look to get a credit (potential profit) roughly equal to the maximum loss. In other words, for a 4–strike, 5–point iron condor (example: 75/80/85/90) with $500 margin (liability), taking in (credit of) between 2.00 to 3.00 ($200 – $300 per spread) creates risk of 3.00 to 2.00, respectively (5.00 liability minus the credit). Although a 4–strike, 2.5–point iron condor (example: 37.5/40/42.5/45) has about half the credit and half the risk reward and half the liability, most people trade twice the size that they would trade a 5–pointer. This is why, when going through a 2 for 1 stock split with a 5–pointer, one ends up with twice as many 2.5–pointers. Considering that diagonals are somewhat ambiguous compared to simpler strategies, it will be no surprise to know that when we trade double diagonals we face the same issues. Exhibit 7–15 shows the profit and loss profile of a Double Diagonal (Iron Calendar).

With time to go the curved lines look like those of a condor or time spread. At expiration of the front month, the profile forms two peaks, one at each short strike. The day following expiration will result in a long strangle but most do not play for this because they get out.

Exhibit 7–16 shows the dissection of the position, showing what happens when 10 Short 101p/103p/105c/107c Iron Condors become combined with 10 Long 101p time spreads and 10 Long 107c time spreads. This configuration has basically the Iron condor's credit less the two long time spreads' debits. Therefore, if it is attractive to do a 2-point Iron for say a 1.00 credit and at the same time buy the two outer strike calendar spreads for .50 debit each, then the whole deal will be even money ($1.00 credit minus two $.50 debits).

E X H I B I T   7 – 1 5

Double Diagonal (Iron Calendar) for Even Money Flat Skew
Long 10 NOV 101p/107c Strangles /Short 10 OCT 103p/105c Strangles
NOV (56 Days) OCT (28 Days)

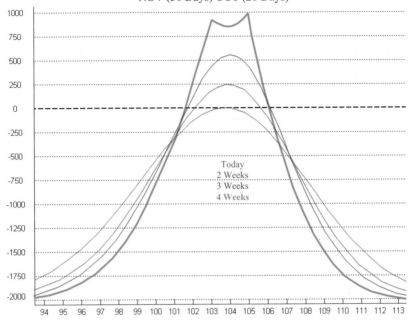

E X H I B I T   7 – 1 6

Dissection of Iron Calendar or Double Diagonal
Long 10 NOV 101p/107c Strangles /Short 10 OCT 103p/105c Strangles

	Calls				Strikes	Puts			
	NOV		OCT			OCT		NOV	
	+	-	+	-		+	-	+	-
101 Put Time Spread					**101**	10	10	10	
					102				
					103		10		
Short 10 Iron Condors					**104**				
				10	**105**				
					106				
107 Call Time Spread	10		10	10	**107**				

The Straddle Strangle Swap (depicted in Exhibit 7–17) is like a butterfly intersecting with the time spreads instead of a condor as described above. The profit and loss profile differs from the one above in that it is short the 104 straddle in OCT rather than the 103p/105c strangle. The extra profit potential is due to the greater credit the straddle affords even though the liability has a greater distance from body to wing. The trade-off is a narrower target for the maximum profit range.

EXHIBIT 7–17

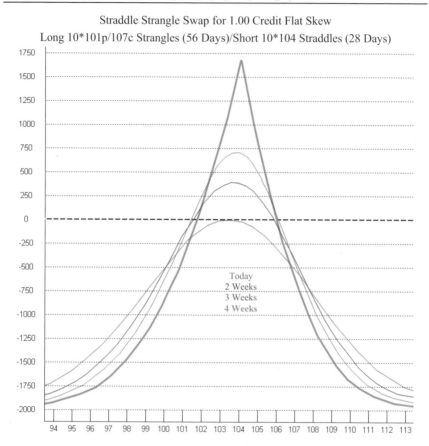

Straddle Strangle Swap for 1.00 Credit Flat Skew
Long 10*101p/107c Strangles (56 Days)/Short 10*104 Straddles (28 Days)

DOUBLE TIME SPREADS OR STRANGLE SWAPS

Another approach to play for a range or increased implied volatility in the deferred month is to buy a double time spread. However, in the name of diversification, you are giving up a lot by not picking either single time spread, because the potential profit amount of the winning time spread can be greatly decreased by the amount lost on the losing time spread. Unless the time spreads are far OTM and/or cheap, I prefer to pick one target or the other. I would use condors or double diagonals for range plays, instead.

Often advisory newsletters suggest to subsidize the cost of a strangle with the sale of a shorter dated strangle as a cheaper way to get into a long strangle. Frequently, I am asked whether I agree since it can be a large cost savings. The answer is no, because this strategy represents limited gain potential. These strategies, don't forget, play for a range. If there is a huge move in the underlying, the double time spread or strangle swap goes to nearly worthless (see Exhibit 7–18) because both the time spreads become far away from the money. A naked long strangle, on the other hand, would have made large profits.

I suppose that when there is a news event scheduled for after the expiration of the first month, an explosion could happen in the next, rewarding the then naked long strangle in the further month. Realistically though, how often does the market anticipate this sort of thing but begin to make its move earlier? That would surely spoil the outcome of the double strangle. If there is going to be a move then play for a move. If there isn't going to be a move then play for no move. Timing is hard enough without having to be right twice.

E X H I B I T   7 – 1 8

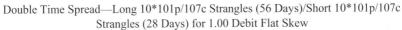

Double Time Spread—Long 10*101p/107c Strangles (56 Days)/Short 10*101p/107c Strangles (28 Days) for 1.00 Debit Flat Skew

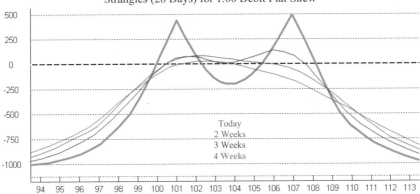

CONCLUSION

Time spread configurations, ratioed or otherwise, offer the trader a gamut of configurations from which to choose, and the margin requirements for them are quite small in comparison to other strategies. It is recommended to stress test ratioed time spreads and ratioed diagonal time spreads in an options analyzer in order to become familiar with their properties. Option volatility skews (Chapter 10) also play a big role but these options relationships are generally overlooked and have a tendency to become attractive for speculative strategies owing to the fact that inter-month volatilities can diverge quite a bit.

CHAPTER

8

MARKET MAKER INSIGHTS

This chapter will let the reader into the world of the market maker and how he or she sees and uses customer order flow. This should shed a great amount of light on certain trades or spreads that are easy or impossible to get filled. I remember thinking at the beginning of my career, in 1981, that there must be something magical about options, because profits could be squeezed out with little or no risk. I came to discover that by understanding relationships better than my market maker competitors, I could pick their pockets on sizable trades. Those opportunities are now few and far between but the concepts remain.

The reader should build a foundation of knowledge about locks. A lock, as mentioned earlier, describes a position that has a locked-in profit or loss and theoretically cannot lose any money from that point forward. Spreads that are commonly referred to as locks are conversions/reversals, jelly rolls, and boxes and can and do lose money although they seem to be neutral. In the grand scheme of things, a lock does not make or lose much money by itself but market makers tend to have them on in huge sizes, turning molehills into mountains or cracks into canyons. Understanding the similarities and differences between the European-style options, American-style options, and options with futures-style margining help traders to make trading decisions even though they may only be trading one product. There will be a discussion about exercise features of the OEX and nuances that are caused when a stock is in a partial tender offer. This chapter does not place much emphasis on models except to explain some of the differences between them and to suggest how to enhance their usefulness. Does that mean that the models are useless for retail customers? No. The models are great. The problem is not the models, though some are better than others. For certain applications, a model is not the Holy Grail, but merely a tool. One can use a shoe to pound a nail into the wall just like this book will try to pound important concepts into its readers' heads. One can also dig a hole with a hammer easier than a trader can dig his way out of the hole that he got himself into because he tried to pay for a Mercedes with the anticipated profits that his options model projected.

THE EDGE

The most profitable players in the options game over time are traders who turn themselves into machines and churn out the money day in and day out simply by getting the edge. Edge is the trader's markup or added premium when selling and markdown or discount when buying.

   With this understanding, it is easy to see why some stock trading brokerage houses have commission-free trading. They provide free trades to customers who are willing to use market orders (i.e., trading at the market, which is taking the ask price or hitting the bid price)[1]. There is no guarantee that the market maker will make a profit on the trade but he does have a head start in either spreading[2] it off, or scalping out of the trade. It is a lot easier for banks and other traders who do have a wide client base to take advantage of a wide bid-ask spread differential. Generally, it is made wide so that the trader can lay off the risk for an automatic profit. Normally the bid-ask spreads widen out when markets are illiquid and the trader has fewer routes to go in spreading it off. This also occurs when the market gets choppy:

Story: Liquidity and the Bid/Ask Spread: In 1985, I wandered over to the CME from the CBOT. In the Treasury bond futures market at the CBOT, if the market was 20 bid / asking 21 (verbally: 20–21, complete price: 104.20–104.21)) I would be satisfied to get filled at 20 if I put in a market order to sell. If DM futures were 20–21 (33.20–33.21 at the time), I had to learn to be satisfied with a fill at 17 (33.17) on a sell at the market order. This can happen in any market on any exchange when moments of illiquidity create a vacuum. Take Eurodollars, also at the CME, a very thick market where at almost every price there are thousands of contracts to buy and to sell. Many times, if you try to sell at the market while it is 20–21 (94.20–94.21), the broker can get the edge and give you the fill at 21 because the market hardly moves. Do not hang your hat on that last sentence because for about a week in April 1989, while trading in Euro options, there were serious vacuums when certain numbers were announced. Before 7:30 A.M., for example, the market would be something like 90.50–90.51, and then in an

---

[1] **Taking / Hitting**

Buying at the ask price is synonymous with "taking" and selling at the bid price is synonymous with "hitting."

[2] **Spreading / Scalping**

Spreading occurs when a trader makes some sort of an offsetting trade. Ostensibly, in the event that the market moves adversely to the original trade, there is a similar gain on the other side.

Scalping refers to the style of trade whereby the trader attempts to make a profit by getting in and out of the market very quickly; that is, either buying a contract low and selling it higher or short selling a contract high and buying it back lower.

instant, as the number was being announced, the market would widen to 90.40–90.60, then 90.80 bid. There were options traders in my pit waving orders to sell hundreds at the market when it was up there and getting filled at 90.20. Those who were trying to buy down there at the market hoping to get something close to 90.20, were getting filled at 91.00 (not 90.00). Eighty ticks ($25 per tick) on 100 Eurodollar futures is $200,000. Ouch! **End**

Fewer traders and customer orders create less liquidity, hence more risk. Market makers try to make wider markets but still close enough to compete with other exchanges and for customers to be attracted to the market. Customers hate the feeling of being ripped off. It is, however, unfair to state that customers think market makers are crooks just because they make wide markets. This is almost always a function of liquidity, often simply because it is lunchtime or a hot summer day when traders are not around to make markets. Fewer traders left to accommodate paper flow means added risk on the bigger orders when few are around to take down a sizable trade because they have fewer avenues on which to layoff the risk. The wide markets are a direct result of the fact that the trader expects a horrible fill price on his or her hedge. In effect, the trader is merely passing that hedge cost plus the negative-edge on to the customer.

It will soon become evident that options are a relationship game. If the relationships get stretched out far enough, they will eventually attract the attention of some great big force that will push them back into line. That force is the market as a whole, and it will do whatever it wants to do.

FAIR VALUE EQUATIONS INCLUDING BANKING[3]

As stated in Chapter 1, the conversion/reversal is a forward value because it represents interest or interest less dividend flows until expiration. Though there are different considerations for equities and futures and also between models, only equities (stocks or shares) have dividends, and indexes have stocks that are part of their valuation.

---

[3] **Banking**

Banking is a term that describes the flows of cash from interest and dividends.

The Black-Scholes fair value equations are as follows:

For equity options: $k + c = u + p + i - d$

where

k – the strike   p – the put
c – the call   u – the underlying
i – the interest amount   d – the dividend.

$$i = \text{cash flow} \times \frac{\text{days left}}{365^4} \times \text{interest rate}$$

Notice the difference of no d (dividends) in the futures options, and that the interest component is a positive or negative value on either side of the equal sign (=). The 'i' and the 'd' are nontransparent[5] variables that are accounted for differently depending on which model is used.

INTEREST RATE EXPOSURE

Interest rate exposure should not be ignored. Past increases in interest rates have significantly affected the profits and losses of equity option traders around the world, especially where they have held long-term options.

A group of my students in Scandinavia back during one of Sweden's first Euro votes made over $1 million of unanticipated profits when their short-term interest rates went from 15% to 75% overnight and then to 500% over the weekend (by collecting short stock rebate from a reversal). They were lucky because they could have had conversions on requiring them to borrow at 500% for the weekend. What about those on the other side who had conversions on? They had a bad weekend.

When working, be cognizant of both the interest rate aspects and the fact that each option trade either borrows money from or lends money to the marketplace. Each trader also has a relationship with a brokerage firm with which he or she does financing and investing. The properties that are inherent to all of these types of spreads will be presented before examining the particulars of each.

---

[4] **365 Days in a Year**

Some entities prefer to use 360 days in their calculations.

[5] **Non-Tranparency**

A nontransparent value is one that has other income or expenses associated with it and is not currently visible (e.g., if you buy stock today and hold it for one year the cost is greater than the purchase price today because you are either forgoing the interest—implicit interest—on the money you paid, or you have to borrow money to buy it with and pay interest on that. Of course, if you receive dividends, your cost is reduced to some extent).

BANKING:
THE CONCEPTS OF BORROWING AND LENDING

The concept of borrowing and lending should be of some interest to customers who may become quite large option traders. For example, traders who are carrying a lot of long stock, may have to borrow funds from their brokerage firm. When selling boxes, the sale raises cash thereby reducing the borrowing needs for the long stock or it creates the opportunity to invest the cash with the brokerage firm if not needed to reduce a debit balance. By selling boxes, traders are borrowing money from the marketplace. The actual transaction of buying boxes is actually lending money to the marketplace. In this respect, traders are much like banks that seek to borrow at low rates and lend at high rates. It is important to see that any cash debit or credit contains exposure to rho risk.

It is interesting to know the implied interest rate for each locked trade that one makes. We will see how the tick income or expense (trading gain or loss) is in effect interest income or expense (but not for tax purposes) when applied to the cash flow of the lock for the number of days left until expiration. For a box, the tick income or expense refers to the discount on the box from the box basic value (the difference between the two strikes). For a conversion/reversal, the tick income or expense refers to the conversion/reversal price. The cash flow is simply the . amount of cash credit or debit generated by the trade.

Generally, traders will regard a cash credit to have only positive implications, because they earn interest income on the cash credit balance. This is a false assumption. A cash credit can come from several different potential sources, some of which are straightforward and others that which are not. Some interest rate positions traders can hedge and others they cannot. If one intends to hedge, he or she first needs to be able to discern the source of the cash. Traders can still make huge profits by not paying attention to small details. However, small details sometimes have a way of destroying you with an innocent smile. A certain portion of a cash credit—for example, short deep in-the-money options, which should have already been assigned—is undeniably good. It is not, however, possible to hedge or lock this type of option in any way, because it may be assigned any day. In this case, one cannot assume a defensive posture.

Cash credits can be caused by short premium (vega and gamma). Because the big P&L fluctuations will be caused by that premium posture, interest rate sensitivity is not a material factor.

All the other cash credits produced by positions, such as short stock, conversions/reversals, jelly rolls, and boxes, are of no benefit unless the interest rate earned is greater than the interest expense implied by the trades. One is invisibly incurring the expense as the present value of the position grows to maturity. Although one receives an interest payment for that cash credit, it is being expensed in the way of "ticks" lost on the position.

Each option's intrinsic value and extrinsic value is sensitive to interest rates, but only the extrinsic value is subject to theta and the other Greeks, which cause it to erode in value. At the same time that the option value is eroding, there is an increase in value by a lesser amount due to the interest effect. If you put that option into a package that neutralizes the effects of the other Greeks, the interest aspects will remain. Therefore, for market makers who do not have an opinion on interest rates, it makes no sense to carry this additional exposure if they can neutralize it at fair value. They could spend the excess cash credit by purchasing the appropriate quantity of boxes or other Greek neutral packages at fair value instead of being subject to changes in overnight interest rates. It probably wouldn't pay for a retail customer to go to all the trouble but if the position size warrants it, it could be a definite consideration.

In the normal course of market making, it is of no material importance whether traders have a debit or a credit because if they have a debit it is likely that their subsequent trades will offset it. If by the nature of the trade or the effects of futures margin variation a sizable cash balance ensues, it becomes time to neutralize this element unless they intend to play the direction of interest rates. The longer the term of the contracts, the more the exposure, and if there are many expirations involved in one's position, there is yield curve risk.

SHORT STOCK INVENTORY PROBLEMS & SQUEEZES

When rumors circulate that a certain company is about to be taken over, it may become difficult to find anyone who is willing to loan stock for shorting. Those who do manage to find stock to borrow may take advantage of the attractive prices created by the market, such as once for a friend with March 1994 reversals, which could be transacted for large credits. Normally (based on fair value), it is worth paying (a debit) just a little less than what you would receive in interest payments. At this time, however, it was difficult to borrow any stock, and so stock was loaned only if the borrower agreed to forfeit his or her short stock rebate. Doing a reversal for .40 ($40) debit, would normally earn a half ($50) in interest as a short stock rebate, and yield a net profit of .10 ($10.00). When the rebate was removed, the .40 debit became a loss of $40 per spread. My friend just bailed out at even, but because of this strange occurrence fair value subsequently went the other way to .50 debit ($50) for the conversion, creating .50 credit for the reversal. That represented an amount of a $1.00 ($100.00) per conversion away from theoretical value. For traders with small capital, this can be a real problem in the interim because they may be forced out of their positions. Such a situation arises when the terms of the buyout have not yet been determined. The stock was finally taken over near the end of that year, nine months after the rumor started. Short squeezes happen a lot in highly speculative NASDAQ stocks that have a large short interest[6].

Lenders put a squeeze on the shorts by requesting their stock back.

EQUITY (STOCK) REVERSAL (WITHOUT DIVIDEND)

An equity reversal is valued by the difference between the strike and the present value of the strike. The present value of the dividend (if there is one) is added to the present value of the stock. An American-style reversal has P&L characteristics similar to those of a miniature bull vertical spread when there is no dividend. The following example will be for a 70 strike spread with 60 days to go at 6.5% interest. The short stock rebate[7] is $.75 ($.748 70 x 60/365 x 6.5%), which makes this a $.75 vertical. It can be materially inaccurate to use the strike price as the amount to finance because the real amount that the trader will have to finance[8] is the cash flow amount, which may be significantly different from the strike price (i.e., the stock price minus the combo price). In this case, it does not matter because the difference is insignificant. It would have been more accurate to use the cash flow, which is about $69.25, and get an interest rebate of $.74.

When looking at the Black-Scholes values for the 70 reversal in Exhibit 8–1, observe that the horizontal line starting at a stock price of $66 begins to level off at a $.75 debit, which is the short stock rebate for the reversal and also the difference between the strike and the present value of the strike. Assuming that there is no early exercise, the present value (using 6.5 percent) of the strike (70) is about $69.25 (at fair value).

---

[6] **Short Interest**

Amount of stock that is being held short.

[7] **Short Stock Rebate**

The interest received on credit balances generated by being short stock. It is usually an amount close to the T-Bill rate less an amount in the way of a fee to the stock lender. The fee is competitive and if stock to borrow is hard to find and in short supply (no punn intended), the fee goes up high enough sometimes to completely wipe out the rebate.

[8] **Options Finance**

The rate of interest for options financing is usually at a different rate than that of the rate for short stock rebate.

To trade the reversal, the real stock can be sold at $70 and the combo (synthetic stock) bought for .75. The equation works at other stock prices as well: at $71.00 the combo's fair value is $1.75. The fastest way to calculate where a combo should be is to take the differential between the stock and the strike and add it to the interest amount. The in-the-money amount is $1.00 (at $71) plus $.75 (the value of the reversal) gives a total of $1.75. This is how much the call should be greater than the put at fair value.

Exceptions to the above valuation will occur when the call price approaches a value less than the carry cost of the stock plus the put. In this case, the graph of an American-style reversal looks like it is falling off a cliff, losing money on the downside as the call gets further out of the money and becomes less than the rebate amount of $.75. At a stock price of $62, the calls decline to $.25 putting downward pressure on the price of the reversal. Having owned it at a value of $.75, it becomes theoretically worth a $.25 debit to the market place:

Buy Call and Strike vs. Sell Put and Stock
 + $.25 + $70   − $8.00 − $62.00 = $.25 debit

E X H I B I T   8 – 1

Reversal Using Modified Black-Scholes Model

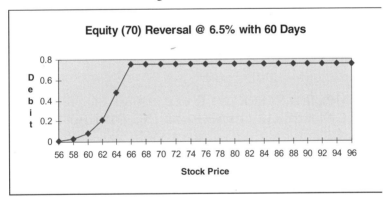

The trader carries a loss of $.50 per spread. This is not a lot for a small investor, but a huge amount for an arbitrageur who has 400,000 shares worth on (i.e., 4,000 reversals x .50 loss per reversal x 100 shares per option = $200,000). C/Rs are not dangerous because their prices change all at once or as drastically as in the last chart. The danger results from the fact that they are traded into and accumulated in a huge size, thereby making a small loss per spread really add up.

Story: Reversal's Revenge: Some traders in the German market had 4,000 reversals (200,000 shares worth) on in a 700 DM stock with carry costs of 20 DM per reversal. The market on the stock collapsed, as did the calls to 5 DM (15 DM below the carry), making it beneficial for the holders of the puts to exercise. When they were assigned, this group stopped receiving the interest that they paid to receive in the way of a 20 D-Mark debit on the reversals (i.e., 4,000 reversals x 15 DM loss per reversal x 50 shares per option[9] x $.67 per DM = about $2,000,000). Ouch! They thought they were flat. More like flattened, I would say. **End**

    Some models reflect "pumped up" theoretical values in pricing and position analysis. A more desirable model than the previous one is the binomial model. It is slower than other models because the number of iterations in the calculations. Some traders prefer to calculate their put values using the binomial model and use the modified Black-Scholes model for call values to cut down the calculation time, because the call values and deltas that these two models generate are very close. The binomial model attempts to smooth out the price fluctuations of conversions / reversals and alter the deltas so that one automatically trades more shares against each combo to hedge against an adverse move. Suppose that the delta of each combo is 1.02. A retail customer would not pay much attention to the extra .02 deltas per spread and would certainly not sell 2 extra shares per 1oo for protection, because of the size involved. The maximum possible valuation of the reversal will be the interest rebate at each given time interval and the least amount would be zero.

IMPLIED INTEREST RATE ON AN EQUITY CONVERSION / REVERSAL (NO DIVIDEND)

The implied interest rate of a trade is the value derived from the transacted price of the spread. To determine the implied rate, take the price of the conversion/reversal and divide it by the total cash flow, then multiply the result by 365 days per year divided by the amount of days left until expiration.

$$\frac{(C/R)}{\text{Cash flow}} \times \frac{365}{\text{Days left}} = \text{Implied interest rate}$$

---

[9] **Shares per Option**

Most DTB stock options each represent 50 shares.

Suppose that at an interest rate setting of 6 percent, the analyzer[10] has generated a value for the 100 conversion/reversal equal to $2.00 with 96 days to go. Prove this value using the above formula.

$$\frac{2.00 \text{ (C/R price)}}{98.00 \text{ (stock-combo)}} \times \frac{365}{96 \text{ (days left)}} = 7.75\% \text{ (implied interest rate)}$$

If the conversion/reversal is worth 2.00, a market maker's market might be $1.90 – $2.10. The implied interest rates of those potential prices are calculated below.

Bid:	Ask:
Reversal:	Conversion:
$\dfrac{1.90}{98.10} \times \dfrac{365}{96} =$	$\dfrac{2.10}{97.90} \times \dfrac{365}{96} =$
Borrowing from the market place:	Lending to the market place:
7.36%	8.16%

INTEREST RATE SETTING IN YOUR OPTIONS PRICING TOOL

Having a proper interest setting for generating theoretical values is essential for market makers, but again, purely because of the size involved, retail customers would be over doing it a bit if they were to worry about it. Many market makers use inappropriate rate settings. There are three, possibly four, different settings for the same underlying contract that traders could use; the borrowing rate, the lending rate, the average rate, or the short stock rebate rate.

How do traders know which rate to use? I have visited traders at some of the largest banks in the world and have seen that they do not understand this concept. Some were using two columns of values, one for conversion and one for reversals. At that time, the spread between their borrowing rate and short stock rebate rate was about 1.5 %.

Take a stock that is trading at $100 with 96 days to go (average rate = 7.75%, borrowing rate = 8.5% and lending rate = 7%). The bid and ask spread of the conversion/reversal with its rates 1.5% apart is equal to about $.40 ($100 x 1.5% x 96/365). The break-even market would be about $1.80–$2.20. That would mean that the spread width has to be $.60 wide ($1.70–$2.30) to lock in a profit of $.10 per trade. Anyone working with a market that wide is not working. All that they can do is stare at the screen because the live markets are too tight to

---

[10] **Analyzer**

Software designed to calculate options theoretical values and Greeks. Options analyzers can only estimate what would happen given the inputs. If the input assumptions are not good, neither will be the output.

compete for a conversion/reversal. Everyone else has a market that is no wider than $.25.

How can other traders be profitable if their markets are so tight that they cannot be profitable based upon their financing? One answer is that with a narrower market of $1.85–$2.10, if they could get out right after they have gotten in, they would have a $.25 profit. Another possibility is to get in for a $2.10 credit on Monday, hold it overnight, and then get out on Tuesday for a $1.85 debit with a profit of almost $.23 (the cost of financing is .$023 for one night i.e., 100 x 8.5% / 365). If they are unable to liquidate it within a day, even within a week, they could still scratch[11] after 11 days because the financing cost would be about $.25.

The most important point to be conveyed here is that traders should use the interest rate that is most appropriate to them at the time. They are either borrowing a lot, lending a lot, or have no significant cash balance one way or another until they have initiated a position.

Scenario 1. The Trader Is Already Borrowing Heavily at 8.5%

If she has a large number of conversions, has net long options value, or has a futures margin variation debit, then she has a huge total equity debit balance and needs to borrow money. She will probably borrow until the futures generate cash, until she sells some stock, or until her trades accumulate a total equity credit balance. In this scenario, she should set her interest rate to the borrowing rate (8.5%). When she collects cash by selling on subsequent trades at fair value, she will be reducing the balance of her 8.5% loan at the bank and will be borrowing in the marketplace at 8.5%. This reduction in the loan balance also reduces her exposure to interest rates. If those sales are made above fair value, she would in effect be borrowing money from the marketplace at less than 8.5% to pay down the balance of her loan. Conversely, she would be adding to her borrowing needs if her trade purchase amounts cost more than she received from the sales. If her purchases are below fair value, she is in effect lending to the marketplace at a rate better (higher) than her rate of 8.5%.

Scenario 2. The Trader Is Already Investing Heavily at 7%

If a trader has a large number of reversals, is net short options value, or has a futures margin variation credit, then he has a huge total equity credit balance and needs to invest (loan) money. Until such time as the futures move against him, generating a draw-down of cash, he buy stocks back, or his trades accumulate a total equity debit balance, he should set his interest rate to the lending rate (7%). When he spends money by buying something on subsequent trades at fair value, he will be reducing the balance of his investment at the bank, and will instead be lending to the market place at 7%. This reduction in the investment balance also reduces his exposure to interest rates. If the buys are

---

[11] **Scratch**

A break-even trade.

better than (below) fair value, he will in effect be lending money to the marketplace at more than 7% and reducing the credit balance at his bank. He may be adding to his credit by selling more items, but if his sales are made above fair value he is in effect borrowing more from the marketplace at a rate better (lower) than his bank is paying (7%).

Scenario 3. The Trader Currently Has a Neutral Cash Position

A trader sets his or her interest rate to the average between 7% and 8.5%, namely 7.75%, until he or she generates a sizable debit or credit. If he or she then trades beating the sheets (buying below and/or selling above), and maintains a neutral total equity balance, it is synonymous to borrowing below and lending above 7.75%.

EQUITY CONVERSION/ REVERSAL (WITH DIVIDEND)

The fair value equation is as follows: $k + c = u + p + i - d$

where $i =$ (cash flow x days left x interest rate)/365,
and $d =$ dividend

The only new twist for traders with a reversal (or any position that is short stock on the date of record) is that in addition to receiving interest, they are also subject to paying a dividend. Remember when someone shorts shares,[12] although he or she is borrowing from someone who is long them, new shares are created for the new buyer. Where does the dividend payment come from? The corporation pays that new shareholder but the stock loaner gets reimbursed through the stock lending and clearing function with funds charged to the short seller. The converter, on the other hand, pays the interest expense, and receives the dividend.

Here is an example of 1000*70 reversals with a dividend with 60 days to go at 6.5% interest (the short stock rebate is $.75 which is 70 x 60/365 x 6.5%) with a $1.00 quarterly dividend. The dividend to be paid is in 30 days (Exhibit 8–2). Notice the break after 30 days, in the profit and loss graph when just after the dividend is paid the whole value of the reversal shifts, no longer including the dividend.

---

[12] **Shorting Stock**

Shorting stock is difficult in most cases and impossible in others, owing to restrictions in some countries. The restrictions can include forfeiture of the carry rebate or mandatory buyback provisions within certain time frames.

E X H I B I T   8 – 2

Equity Reversal with $1.00 Quarterly Dividend payable in 30 Days
(+1000*70C/-1000*70P/-1000ooU) Binomial Model.

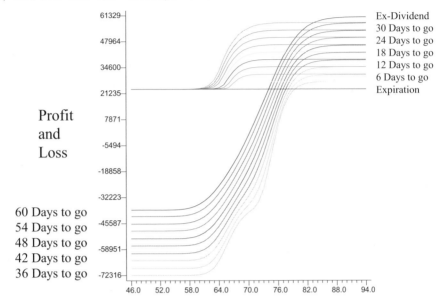

Profit
and
Loss

60 Days to go
54 Days to go
48 Days to go
42 Days to go
36 Days to go

Ex-Dividend
30 Days to go
24 Days to go
18 Days to go
12 Days to go
6 Days to go
Expiration

Underlying Price

Price:	46.0	52.0	58.0	64.0	70.0	76.0	82.0	88.0	94.0
P&L	-38671	-38664	-37637	-26180	0	34832	55756	60153	60555
Delta	0	7	590	3147	4996	5159	1666	192	10
Gamma	2222	1968	2032	1810	1222	-143	-437	-79	-5
Theta	-629	-630	-707	-975	-993	-519	-420	-586	-614
Vega	0	9	364	989	-54	-1910	-1411	-252	-22

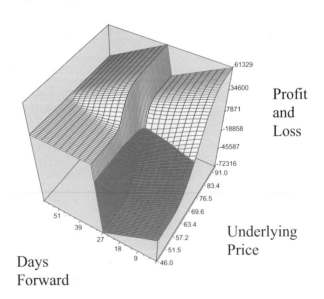

Profit
and
Loss

Underlying
Price

Days
Forward

JELLY ROLL: EQUITIES

A jelly roll is merely a conversion in one expiration and a reversal in another, where the stock is eliminated by canceling out the short and long stock. If the strikes are different, it is sometimes called a time box. The safest way to handle this inventory is to remember that each part of it must be treated separately, as if they were a conversion and a reversal.

The more dynamic a position is, the more dynamic the hedge it requires. Take, for example, an options position that has long-dated options and short-dated options. The overall cash position may be flat, but there is considerable interest rate exposure (rho risk).

If a trader has a jelly roll with short combos on a stock expiring in two years compared with long combos in the current expiration, he or she would have a total equity balance of close to zero. Dissecting the position to view it as conversions in the far term and reversals in the near term would enable the trader to identify the rho exposure along the yield curve. The ideal way to hedge $1 million is almost impossible, but it is possible to get close. A reasonable hedge would be a strip of Eurodollar futures—$1 million every 90 days for eight quarters ($8 million). The ideal hedge would be to sell a strip instrument starting with one day, two days, and three days up to 730 days. This is preferable because the synthetic long stock is based on overnight financing, one day at a time. If two-year money rates were to increase by 2%, it would cost roughly $40,000 for the period. A 2% fall in rates would send the Eurodollars up 2.00; at $2,500 per contract per point, eight contracts would be needed [$40,000 / ($2,500 x 2 points)] for the complete hedge.

OEX CONVERSION/REVERSAL

The OEX conversion/reversal uses one CBOE S&P 100 option combo against one CME E-Mini S&P 500 future. Although it is called a conversion/reversal, it is not a true conversion/reversal. The "cash spread", as it is called, has many different variables that affect its value, such as dividend streams, interest rates, multiplier changes between the two underlying indexes, exercise, and supply and demand nuances. Before one considers dabbling in the cash spread one should be comfortable and experienced with its price history. It has fluctuated considerably in recent times, much greater than that of other common intermarket spreads—such as Swiss Francs versus Deutsche Marks, T-Notes versus T-Bonds (The NOB), T-Bills versus EuroDollars (TED Spread) or GM versus Ford. Traders use some pricing nuances of the cash spread and the C/R to signal a good buy or sell, but these still do not guarantee a profit. A trade may be good when executed, but favorable prices do not ensure that the price relationship will not go against the trader, causing a severe loss.

OEX SYNTHETIC FUTURES AND THEORETICAL VALUES

One thing worth mentioning about trying to price OEX options is that the underlying instrument is a basket of 100 stocks that is usually traded only by heavily capitalized traders doing the arb. There is no OEX future that can be used to lock in the trade prices, as there is with most of the other options traded on exchanges. This is why many traders base OEX options prices on the combos at each strike rather than on the S&P 500 future. Combos are essentially OEX synthetic futures. The S&P 500 consists of the same 100 stocks and another 400.

It is surprising that professional OEX traders use the cash price of the index as the underlying price from which to generate theoretical values of options. The bid-ask spread on the underlying index should prohibit this because it is so wide (about $1.50 wide) for the whole basket of stocks. The combo is usually one-eighth ($0.125) wide except in volatile markets, where it can easily widen to 1.00.

Although sophisticated models have been built to account for the probability of the OEX options being exercised, it is easy to get a close estimation provided that one makes a few mental adjustments. A futures model with the interest rate set to zero could be used. This is not a very scientific method but it is effective in preventing boxes and combos from being valued at their present values. It will price boxes at their nominal value and combos to the intrinsic value of the in-the-money amount ($5.00 boxes are worth at least $5.00, and combos are worth at least parity with the synthetic futures). The in-the-money amount is based on the forward value, which is the cash price of the index plus a premium or discount based on dividends versus interest and supply and demand pressures. Pricing in this fashion is particularly desirable because most boxes trade between .03 and .25 over their basic value. The absolute value of each combo also trades at a surplus to its forward value. This nuance exists because of the benefits from controlling the exercise by being long the deeper in-the-money options.

The combo (synthetic future) price at each underlying price increment should be used in place of an underlying price. The three closest-to-the-money options should be displayed to provide other possibilities in case of liquidity problems. Most people use a futures model but fail to account for the forward value of the index. The forward value is simply the interest less the dividends. Suppose that the value implies that an at-the-money combo, when added to the strike, should trade at a premium of $4.00 over the cash (e.g., OEX cash at 580.00

would make the 580 combo equal to $4.00 plus combo). This is the synthetic underlying futures price. At least one could then say that the OEX synthetic future is trading at 584.00 (the strike combo is liquid most of the time) and can act as a substitute for the underlying futures contract when the trader needs to generate the theoretical values of other options for relative pricing purposes. By using this pricing method, one avoids the distortion of calls being overvalued and puts being cheap, as would be perceived if you tried to calculate implied volatilities using the cash price, which in this case is $4.00 lower. Traders will also benefit from seeing an accurate skew with which to do their analyses. When setting the interest rate to zero for OEX options, one must realize that with certain programs the global setting will change and will therefore affect the other contract and basket valuations. *Note that this zero setting should be used only for* American-style cash settled index options.

THE OEX EARLY EXERCISE

An exercise usually takes place from just after the cash market closes (3:00 P.M. Chicago time) until the futures and options close (3:15 P.M. Chicago time) when the OEX combos or the S&P futures at the CME make a significant move in either direction. If there is a large move in the market, traders take the opportunity to buy/sell the S&Ps and exercise the OEX calls/puts that are far enough in the money. Traders have until 3:20pm, or five minutes after the options market close to exercise, and public customers have a little bit more time. "Far enough in the money" means that they could either buy the same strike puts, for example in the case of a break (market decline), for significantly less than the combo's discount to cash (dividends on the basket minus the implied carry) and still be in the conversion (inter-market spread), or buy the same strike puts a lot cheaper than they have recently been trading for. Conversely, if there is an after-cash-market rally, traders will sell the S&Ps and exercise their puts. Of course, the corresponding calls must be trading cheaper than the premium to cash (implied interest minus dividends) and still put the trader into the reversal at a favorable price.

An experienced OEX options trader, Shelly, recalls a story that helps to identify an exercise nuance in the OEX and the additional risks inherent in being short cash settled American-style options.

Story: Uh-OEX: In the days before the Iraqi invasion of Kuwait in August 1990, a customer of a major New York investment firm entered the OEX options market as a size (i.e. huge) buyer of out-of-the-money puts. Over the course of several hours, the customer accumulated several thousand put options. The customer single-handedly inflated the value of that particular put from approximately 2 5/8 to nearly 3

1/2, with little movement in the underlying price. In the process, due to his demand pressures, he forced OEX implied volatility a lot higher. Within a week, Iraq initiated its invasion of Kuwait, sending tremors through the international oil, gold, and equity markets. The U.S. markets fell in response to both higher oil prices and the uncertainty of turmoil in the Middle East.

Within days, the market suffered a decline in excess of 10 percent. The puts purchased for around 2 5/8 to 3 1/2 were now trading over 14. The intrinsic value of these puts was just over 13, thus they still had about a dollar in time premium. Then the customer did the unthinkable; he exercised his puts early. To the OEX crowd, it appeared to be a gigantic blunder. Why would someone exercise these puts while they had time value remaining? With hindsight, it wasn't such a bad ploy. By exercising, the customer liquidated his position immediately by effectively selling his puts at parity. In view of his purchase price and exercise price, he realized an incredible profit on his investment. He may have been able to get better prices. However, by entering the markets during the trading day, his actions would certainly have affected the underlying price of the market, effectively diminishing the value of his put position. (By selling a large quantity of in-the-money puts, traders on the other side of the order, that are buying them, are forced to hedge by buying S&P futures or stocks, which forces the market higher and causes put values to fall).

Those traders and individuals who were assigned on their short put positions, initially believed that a mistake had been made. However, it was soon evident that the quantity assigned was significant. By the time the markets opened the following morning, the crowd asa a whole had a large short delta position in the OEX market (by being assigned on short puts, one is effectively forced to buy them back at parity). Assuming that the customer bought and then exercised over 10,000 contracts, the assignments represented nearly 2,000 short S&P 500 futures contracts (one S&P future is usually offset by five OEX combos). On the opening, the value of the puts that had been assigned decreased by about $4.00 (the market makers were no longer short them) because the short market positions were covered. Over the long term, the impact of this sort of position on the markets is negligible. The short-term impact on the neutral trader is quite dramatic (traders lost $8,000,000 collectively). **End**

The important lesson to be learned from this example is that with cash-settled products, deltas disappear upon exercise (the holder has the control) and assignment (the trader who is short may find that he or she has more or less deltas than anticipated). Each party is subject to the payment and receipt of the cash value as opposed to the delivery of an instrument (stock or futures contract) that replaces the lost deltas. In the OEX, the assigned loses approximately 1.00 for each assigned short put, or −1.00 for each assigned call. As I mentioned earlier, when exercising an option one must buy the corresponding same strike OTM option in order to maintain one's exposure. As of July 23rd 2001, the CBOE launched a new S&P 100 index with European-style exercise, XEO. XEO options are cash settled and may only be exercised at expiration.

BOXES

The box is also considered a flat position and a way to get flat for a market maker who trades many strikes. It involves two strikes and can be perceived as a long combo at one strike and a short combo at another. It can be perceived as conversion at one strike and a reversal at another, with the underlying canceling out. It can also be perceived as a bull spread in the calls against a bear spread in the puts, or vice versa. Exhibit 8–3 shows three perceptions of a long box. Each pair of ovals represents a different perception.

E X H I B I T   8 – 3

Compositions of a Box

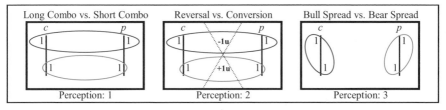

Long Combo vs. Short Combo	Reversal vs. Conversion	Bull Spread vs. Bear Spread
Perception: 1	Perception: 2	Perception: 3

As shown in Chapter 2, a box is a useful tool in dissection for perceiving a position in different ways. Boxes help traders to uncover aspects of their risk of which they may be unaware. Normally a box is an interest rate sensitive strategy used for financing positions and hedging interest rate exposure. Long boxes can be used to capitalize on early exercise situations.

EUROPEAN-STYLE BOXES

European-style options, such as in the SPX (S&P 500 options on the CBOE) cannot be assigned, so locks will be priced with regard to interest rates, using the Black-Scholes model. These boxes are priced around the present value of the difference between the strikes. For example, the present value of 5.00 is equal to 5.00 minus the cost of carry for 5.00. At 5% for 146 days, the cost of carry is .10, making each box worth 4.90.

To illustrate the concept of present value, observe Exhibit 8–4. The curved shape represents the present value, while the square represents the expiration maturity value (or expiration). As time goes by, the curved area will expand to completely fill in the square. The .10 represents the P&L from trading exchange-traded products (this is how it is registered on traders' 1099 forms for the purpose of filing income tax returns).

The box market will most likely be 4.85–4.95. If the crowd has predominately total equity credit balances, they need to invest them by making the box 4.90–5.00. This is, in effect, advertising their need to invest and eliminate their rho risk at fair value. Conversely, if the crowd is borrowing funds, they would be more aggressive on the offer and be 4.80–4.90. This would promote an opportunity to raise funds at fair value and remove rho exposure.

E X H I B I T 8 – 4

Box at Present Value and Maturity Value (Expiration)

Present value = 4.90　　　　Interest = .10　　　　Maturity value = 5.00

IMPLIED INTEREST RATE ON A BOX TRADE

The implied interest rate calculation on a box trade is very similar to that of the conversion/reversal. Take the discount on the box and divide it by the cost of the box, multiply the result times 365 days a year, and divide it by the numbers of days left to go.

$$\frac{\text{Box Discount}}{\text{Box Price}} \times \frac{365}{\text{Days left}} = \text{Implied interest rate}$$

If the box in the last example had had a market of 4.85–4.95 the trades would yield the implied interest rates as shown below.

Long Box:

$$\frac{0.15}{4.85} \times \frac{365}{146} =$$

Lending to the market place:
7.73%

Short Box:

$$\frac{0.05}{4.95} \times \frac{365}{146} =$$

Borrowing from the market place:
2.53%

Obviously, this is a very wide market relative to the risk. The markets on boxes at the CBOE on the SPX (S&P 500) contract are very tight. A market on the $5.00 box with 30 days to go could be 4.97– 4.99. See the effective rates below.

Long Box:

$$\frac{0.03}{4.97} \times \frac{365}{30} =$$

Lending to the market place:
7.34%

Short Box:

$$\frac{0.01}{4.99} \times \frac{365}{30} =$$

Borrowing from the market place:
2.44%

Implied interest rates are posted along with market quotes on the boxes. It is done this way because the SPX is a European-style exercise, which makes it attractive to use for financing the rest of the products traded on the CBOE without the fear of or benefit of the early exercise.

THE EQUITY BOX

Equity boxes that do not have dividends expand when the underlying market trades lower and there is an opportunity to save or collect interest by exercising. A box in an equity will expand to the upside because a trader can receive or avoid paying a dividend. Again, the Black-Scholes model is very useful if there is no exercise. However the valuation skyrockets (see Exhibit 8–5) at a stock price of about 67.00 because the upper strike conversion will collapse when the out-of-the-money call trades less than the cost of carry.

E X H I B I T   8 – 5

Equity Box Priced with the Black-Scholes Model (without dividend)

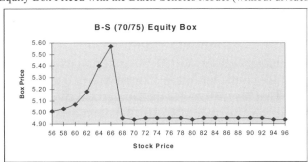

It is better to use the binomial model as discussed in the conversion/reversal section of this chapter, because it smoothes out the prices more gradually. Although it is less accurate, if there is no exercise opportunity, it does price in the possibility of an early exercise by discounting the conversion/reversal.

EXERCISING AND THE MONEY

Story: Profit by Exercising: My friend Joe once went into the soybean pit and asked for the market on a 50-cent box (each cent is worth $50). He was given a quote of 49.25–49.50. He bought a bunch at 49.50, and asked, "Now where?" He got a market of 49.25–49.75, and bought some more at 49.75, then some more at 50 cents, then 50.25, then 50.50, then 50.75, then 51 cents. He exercised his long calls and covered his short puts, which left him with a conversion with a $250,000 edge. **End**

To explain where the potential profit comes from, let us use some stock options prices in Exhibit 8-6 so that we can relate to the concept. Although the box is worth 10.24, some traders still price a box using their calculators and determine that if there are 74 days to go, at 7.25% the box is worth 9.86 (10–(10.00 x 7.25% x 74/365). The crowd then quotes something like 9.80–9.92.

E X H I B I T   8 – 6

Option and Spread Values

Calls	@ 100.00	Puts	Carry	Box	
2.13	125	26.11	1.84	125/135	10.24
1.09	135	35.31	0.78	Binomial Model	

Joe may buy some at 9.90, 9.95, 10.00, and 10.05, then finally at 10.10. Say Joe's average cost is 10.05, the stock is trading at 100, and his position is carded up along with the transaction price averages as shown in Exhibit 8–6.

Summary of this example

Joe has bought 2000*125/135 boxes for an average price of 10.05. The number 1.05 on the far left in Exhibit 8–7 is the call vertical spread at fair value. That leaves 9.05 for the put vertical spread price (on the far right), showing the box trade at 10.10. When traders trade a spread such as a box in the pit or over the phone they must establish the prices of the individual "legs." They can use any prices as long as the prices were within the daily range[13].

---

[13] **Within Daily Range**

Some exchanges have relaxed this rule and allow traders to simply report the spread price and not the individual legs of it. The trade has to be labeled as a spread for clearing purposes; otherwise the computer used for settlements would reject the trade as being outside the daily range.

If Joe were to do nothing and wait until expiration, they would lose $10,000 (.05 x 2000 x $100). Suppose that Joe buys back the 135 calls for 1.10, then exercises the 135 puts. This leaves him with the 125 reversal at a 1.20 debit (see explanation of price below) when it is worth 1.84 (cost of carry from Exhibit 8–6). On 2000 spreads, that is a potential profit of $128,000 (2000 x .64 x 100) and is the reason Joe would be willing to pay more than 10.00 for the 10-point box.

E X H I B I T   8 – 7

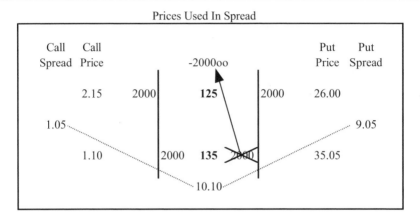

Prices Used In Spread

Explanation of Residual Price

When Joe exercises the 135 puts, he has the right to sell the stock at 135, but he loses the 35.00 premium, which means that the stock was in effect executed at 100 for the reversal calculation. The 135 calls were a scratch (breakeven), which leaves him with the 125 reversal, with prices of 2.15 for the 125 calls, 26.00 for the 125 puts, and 100 for the stock. Plug these prices into the equation $(k + c) – (u + p)$ to see where he transacted the resulted reversal:

Buy   Sell
$(2.15+125.00) – (100+26.00) –.05* = 1.20$ debit.
*Factor in loss of premium over parity of 135 put (35.05–35.00)

When Joe bought back the 135 calls, he could have used the opportunity to scalp before exercising, as conveyed in the 'rent a call' example earlier in this chapter.

STOCKS INVOLVED IN TENDER OFFERS

Normally a short put and a buy-write[14] (in a reversal) will offset each other to a large degree if absolutely nothing unusual happens to the stock. However, during stock takeover rumors and tender offers, instruments take on different characteristics. Even locks (reversals, conversions, boxes and jelly rolls) act differently and can cause profits and losses to fluctuate as if the position were naked.

If a takeover is being attempted, a tender offer will be made by the management, of the bidding company, to the stockholders of the target firm for their shares. A partial tender offer is an offer to buy a fixed amount of the company's outstanding shares (usually in an attempt to get 51% ownership). The Chiron deal was for 49% for cash and shares. Options become very difficult to price when a stock is involved in a partial tender offer. Even the most sophisticated players take it on the chin occasionally and are confounded until after all of the smoke has cleared. Traditionally, when stockholders tender their shares to the buyer they receive a certain amount in cash for each share and will be issued new shares of the same company and / or another company. There are a few unknown factors that cause the options to trade very far from their theoretical value.

The traditional models cannot value options properly when unknown factors exist. These include (1) when the deal will take place, (2) the pro rata factor and (3) the difficulty of borrowing stock to short before and after the deal date. Until these factors are actually known there is considerable speculation and the risks are enormous. Even when the details are announced, they are understood only by an elite group. This elite group, though well capitalized, is constrained by position limit problems, which means that the price relationships stretch beyond their ability to put them back into line. Other traders avoid the situation due to a lack of understanding, fear of risk, or both. When price relationships stretch, there is still opportunity to utilize certain nuances and trade at more favorable prices. When it seems like free money, traders will hesitate; experienced traders may be too disciplined to jump in for more at better prices when the prices of their earlier trades were not as good. "Never add to a loser" and "never try to be bigger than the market" are common adages. Examine the unknown factors mentioned above:

1. Deal Date

It is possible to guess when the deal will actually happen. Under the Hart-Scott-Rodino Act, any deal that brings a shareholder to above a 5% stake in the

---

[14] **Buy-Write**

A buy-write is the opposite of a covered write; that is, long call/short stock.

company must be approved by the Federal Trade Commission. Once approved, the tender date will be set for 20 days later. This may affect the options if the expiration date happens to be after the deal date. If it is known that expiration will occur before the deal date, the options should behave as they do in a normal market although the stock price may fluctuate wildly. When there is uncertainty, the options will trade at compromised values somewhere between the values based on today's break-even price and normal expiration values. Each order that comes into the market will be scrutinized by the crowd for a hint of where the price of the deal might be done.

2. The Pro Rata Factor

The pro rata factor is the percentage division of each shareholder's stock that will be exchanged for either cash or new shares. The amount that this factor changes during the period of uncertainty is not as significant to investors as it is to arbitrageurs. The pro rata factor is an estimate used in determining where the stock should trade. Professional arbitrageurs try to guess what percentage of shares outstanding will in fact be tendered to the company. Shareholders sometimes forget to tender their shares or prefer not to do so for tax purposes. This can be a big mistake, especially where the cash per share is much higher than the price at which the stock is likely to be trading after the deal is struck. Since the buyer is getting a fixed number of shares, for every share not tendered there is an increase in the percentage of each shareholder's stock that is eligible for the cash portion.

Suppose for example, that LIL Corp. had 100 million shares outstanding of which a trader is long 1,000 shares. LIL was trading at $50 when it was announced that BIG Corp. was approved to buy 40 million shares at $120 per share. The remaining shares of LIL will be exchanged for new shares of LIL each valued at the going $50 value that they were trading at before the announcement of the deal.

This would never happen, but if only 40 million shares are tendered (the trader's 1000 along with them) then those lucky few (the trader included) would receive a full $120 while the remaining shareholders would receive new shares valued at $50.

This never happens either, but if 100 percent are tendered, then the trader will get to sell 400 shares at $120. The remaining shares will be valued at $50, so the break-even value for the stock would be priced at $78 [(400 shares x $120) + (600 shares x $50)], 1,000 total number of shares]. If he paid less than $78 then he would have been a winner because his break-even cost is $78.

Suppose that 3 million shares of the stock were held by an absentminded waiter who forgot where he put his stock certificates, and when he finally found them, he forgot to mail them to the company. In this case, only 97% of the shares would have been tendered, which means that when the trader tendered his shares he would have received $120 for 412.3711 shares (40 million bought / 97 million tendered = 41.24%) and 587.6289 new shares valued at $50. The break-even value per share for the stock is $78.87. [(412.3711 x $120) + (587.6289 x $50)] / 1000.

The .87 difference between the two previous calculations is a result of the pro-rata factor going from 40% to 41.24%. Certain arbitrageurs play for this, anticipating an increase in the pro rata factor. 0.87 seems like nothing to an investor with 100 to 1000, shares but to the professional who has the equivalent of hundreds of thousands of shares this it is a huge amount.

3. Borrowing Shares

The difficulty or impossibility of borrowing shares to sell short is another minor issue but one that can become a big problem for the arbitrageurs following the tender. This is dangerous for the trader who is short the stock and is called upon to return the shares to the party lending them.   When borrowed stock is threatened with being called in, or is actually being called in, the shorts have to go out and buy the stock in the open market. This creates upward demand pressure on the stock versus the options. Combos (synthetic stock) trade well below the stock causing the reversal to trade at huge credits when theoretically they are worth debits. Traders have to be careful to find out whether or not there is old stock and when-issued[15] stock to trade. The when-issued shares can be borrowed, but it may not be possible to borrow the old shares and can explain why the when-issued stock is trading for $1.00 less. This does not mean that one should short the old shares just because they are trading for $1.00 higher.

THE CHIRON TENDER OFFER

Story: The Chiron Deal: On November 21, 1994 Ciba Geigy announced that it wanted to buy 11.9 million shares (37%) of Chiron's 32 million outstanding shares for $127.00 per share. This would bring their 12% ownership stake to 49% (they liked how the company was being run and so did not opt for a 51% controlling interest). A friend of mine, Scotty, decided to get involved on December 2nd, when the news wire reported that the FTC waiting period for The Hart-Scott-Rodino Act for the Ciba Geigy/Chiron deal would expire on December 28. Chiron's stock price rose from $60 per share ($60 was also where it was expected to trade after the tender) to the low $80s by mid December. On December 20 Ciba Geigy extended the tender date to January 3rd, 1995, at Chiron's request. (The shareholders probably wanted to realize their gains in 1995 because they believed that capital gains taxes would decrease.) Let us take a look at the approximate prices that Scotty was faced with on the day he got involved (see Exhibit 8–8).

Notice the conversions / reversals, boxes, and even the butterflies are very much out of line with normal model valuations.

---

[15] **When-Issued Stock**

When issued shares are the newly issued stock of the company in question. The new and old shares have to be differentiated between, because the old shares have to be re-registered.

This happens because the back-end of the deal[16] at this point assumes that the stock will trade back down to $60. Though the stock is at $80, the 80 puts are trading at $12 because it is believed that the stock will trade at a back-end price of around $60. The options pricing is based on the future stock price being between those prices.

E X H I B I T   8 – 8

12/2/94 Chiron Stock Option Prices following Ciba Geigy Tender

12/02/1994 Conversion	Chiron Reversal	Call Butterfly	Call	80.00 Strike	Put		Box	Put Butterfly
2.00	-2.00		25.00	55	2.00			
						55/60	6.00	
3.00	-3.00	0.00	20.00	60	3.00			0.25
						60/65	6.25	
4.25	-4.25	0.00	15.00	65	4.25			0.5
						65/70	6.75	
6.00	-6.00	0.00	10.00	70	6.00			0.75
						70/75	7.50	
8.50	-8.50	1.00	5.00	75	8.50			1
						75/80	7.50	
11.00	-11.00	3.25	1.00	80	12.00			1
						80/85	5.25	
11.25	-11.25		0.25	85	16.50			

On December 29th the FTC stated that Ciba was free to buy the stock and that the tender period would definitely expire on January 3rd. The puts exploded in value. Exhibit 8–9 is a snapshot of the prices after this news came out.

Scotty overlooked the distinction between the old shares and the when-issued shares, and shorted 40,000 shares of the old before his clearing firm told him to stop. He was lucky that the shares were not called, because he would have had to buy them at potentially astronomical prices.

E X H I B I T   8 – 9

12/29/94 Chiron Stock Option Prices after News Release

12/29/1994 Conversion	Chiron Reversal	Call Butterfly	Call	80.00 Strike	Put		Box	Put Butterfly
2.00	-2.00		25.00	55	2.00			
						55/60	7.00	
4.00	-4.00	0.00	20.00	60	4.00			2
						60/65	9.00	
8.00	-8.00	0.00	15.00	65	8.00			1
						65/70	10.00	
13.00	-13.00	0.00	10.00	70	13.00			0
						70/75	10.00	
18.00	-18.00	0.00	5.00	75	18.00			0
						75/80	10.00	
23.00	-23.00	5.00	0.00	80	23.00			0
						80/85	5.00	
23.00	-23.00		0.00	85	28.00			

[16] **Back End Deal**

Back end of the deal refers to the price at which the stock will be trading after the payout.

On January 4th Ciba took 38.25% of the 31,005,871 Chiron shares tendered. That was 1.25% more than the original 37% bid, which means that for every 1,000 shares, the shareholders received an additional $.7125 per share—12.5 shares (1000 x 1.25%) x $57 ($117-$60) / 1000 shares originally held. Pricing returned to normal (Exhibit 8–10) after the deal.

E X H I B I T   8 – 1 0

1/4/95 Chiron Stock Option Prices after Completion of Tender

01/04/1995 Conversion	Chiron Reversal	Call Butterfly	Call	60.00 Strike	Put		Box	Put Butterfly
0.50	-0.50		5.00	55	0.50			
						55/60	5.00	
0.50	-0.50	1.50	2.00	60	2.50			1.5
						60/65	5.00	
0.50	-0.50	1.00	0.50	65	6.00			1
						65/70	5.00	
0.50	-0.50	0.00	0.00	70	10.50			0.5
						70/75	5.00	
0.50	-0.50	0.00	0.00	75	15.50			0
						75/80	5.00	
0.50	-0.50	0.00	0.00	80	20.50			0
						80/85	5.00	
0.50	-0.50		0.00	85	25.50			

Chiron's price history for the period is displayed in the Exhibit 8–11.

Consider locks one last time. Should either a partial tender offer or a tender offer that is not a 100% cash offer occur, a trader would be better off with conversions as opposed to reversals. Such situations occur more than they once did. In a normal stock split, the share amount that each option represents is adjusted (e.g., in a 2-for-1 split each option that represented 100 shares will represent 200 shares). Exchange rules require that the quantity of options does not change because open interest figures would be distorted. In partial tender offers (e.g., Chiron and Paramount Communications), there is no adjustment. If we compare an at-the-money covered-write to an at-the-money short put, we can see that they are not equal because the stock holder participates in the cash portion of the tender and keeps the premium from the short call, while the put writer has to endure the pain of an at-the-money put which trades as if it were deep in-the-money because the back end of the deal put Chiron much lower.

Experience is the pricing model for this market nuance. Scotty said that he learned more about trading during a 20-minute period, when one of the masters of the game came into the pit, than at any other time in his career. Many other market makers dislike such competition but the liquidity that a great trader brings can be an advantage, quite apart from having the privilege of witnessing the trader's art. **End**

E X H I B I T   8 – 1 1

Chiron

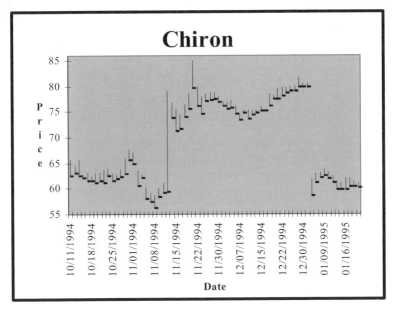

OTHER TID-BITS

The following information on implied interest rates is useful for pricing options. It becomes extremely important in three situations, namely, when tax games, interdepartmental games, and bad creditor borrowing games are being played.

TAX GAMES

In the past, options strategies in the United States were used to defer or reclassify income and expenses where there was a difference between tax rates for different types of income and expenses. The strategies involved many different types of trades. For example, traders used to defer their income by liquidating only the losing combo of a box; that is, those options would be recognized as a loss for income tax purposes. This strategy was virtually without risk, because when one combo was liquidated, a new one was initiated, thereby forming another different box. The market makers in Superior Oil had very profitable years because everyone gave up a tick on thousands of boxes at a time. The stock of Superior Oil was extremely volatile in those days, and was therefore attractive for this type of trade. The combo prices had to have changed a great amount between the time that the box was first put on and the year-end, which was the last day that the loss could be realized.

The tax authorities dealt with this by creating the mark-to-market rule for year-end income and loss determination.

Other tax games involve disparities between dividend tax treatment for nationals and foreigners, special treatment for long-term and short-term capital gains, and interest income and expenses. Details are country-specific and the regulation of such nuances changes from time to time.

INTERDEPARTMENTAL GAMES

In some banks, traders take advantage of certain loopholes in bank rules. For example, some institutions do not have interdepartmental charges for capital (due to an oversight). In other words, if department A needs 100 million, it borrows it from department B at no cost. The bonus pool to department A is based upon A's performance. A takes advantage of the situation and borrows from B to use for trading. A then purchases boxes or trades similar locks and profits .10 for each box bought, having no risk. At fair value, the trade of a 5 point box, at 4.90 normally would be a "wash," meaning that there is no profit or loss. That is what fair value is supposed to mean. In this case, however, it is not a wash because there is no cost to carry. The borrower never receives a bill. Department A gets a nice bonus and continues to do so until department B wakes up.

BAD CREDITOR BORROWING GAMES

Story: Thanks for the Loan Dude: A student of mine in a bank had been trading over-the-counter options in the foreign exchange market for five years. He could not understand why a certain customer was willing to trade $30 million worth of deep in-the-money conversion for a 50-pip[17] edge to the trader. He thought it was like stealing.

It seemed to me that the customer was selling the deep call options on the conversion and collecting cash at an unattractive implied interest rate, so I asked, "What does this customer do and how is his credit rating?" The student said, "He has a company that is strapped to the gills with debt and he cannot borrow anymore from our bank. What has that got to do with a no-risk European-style conversion?" My reply was, "There is your answer. The bank will not lend him another penny at even three times your rate, but you just lent him 30 million at a half of a percent over your rate." The student was flabbergasted. This

---

[17] **Pip**

A *pip* is a tick in the foreign exchange market representing 1/100th of a basis point.

cannot happen on a regulated exchange, but it often occurs in the OTC market.

A market maker wears many hats. One of those hats comes with a three-piece suit and gold watch and chain. An options trader is a banker who borrows and lends. The premium trader, the directional trader, the skew trader, and the risk manager are other hats that the market maker wears from time to time. **End**

CONCLUSION

How does one really know what is cheap and what is rich? The answer is known only after the fact and a model is not very helpful in predicting anything. This does not mean that the models are useless. Some traders use a different model for pricing than the model used for risk analysis. Risk analysis may be done using a combination of models and by referencing past experience of price relationships.

Understanding Greeks well enables us to see the similarities between call and put contracts. We find that in-the-money options are synthetically out of the money. Changes in implied volatility change the values of options and Greeks, just as the effects of time do. The following peculiarity may reinforce some of the concepts presented in the chapter:

When I started trading Eurodollar options in 1985, I hired a programmer to modify my software. There was very little time to prepare. The Euros are an inverted contract; that is, when they are trading at 93.00 it is like trading an underlying that is really priced at 7.00 (100.00 - 93.00). A price change from 93.00 to 92.50 will have the same effect on the 93.00 puts as it will have on the 7.00 calls with an underlying move from 7.00 to 7.50. The programmer knew very little about options but was able to make the changes in one day. I told him to leave the formulae as they were, only to rename the puts to calls and calls to puts, change the math signs (+ and -) from negative deltas to positive and positive to negative, and to express the underlying as a number subtracted from 100.00. That worked perfectly. In an inverted market the put deltas are greater than the call deltas when equidistant from the underlying. The opposite is the case for a non-inverted market.

CHAPTER

9

HYBRID HEDGING

There is a new hedge in town that is rapidly gaining in popularity. What other hedge can you put on for a credit (putting money into your account / time on your side) and still participate if a wild bull market ensues? The ever-popular collar (long stock, long protective put and short a higher strike call to pay for the put) cannot do it, it has limited upside potential (acts like a bull vertical spread). A covered write can't do it (acts like a naked short put). There is not much upside and it is not even a hedge. A married put (acts like a naked long call) gives you the upside but fails in the credit department because it costs money. I would like to introduce to you a hedging strategy called the SlingshotHedge™, from a theoretical and practical point of view.

For whom is the slingshot engineered?

It can be appropriate if you own stock that you do not really want to sell (for tax reasons or otherwise), and you are sick of collaring (selling a covered call to finance a put purchase against your stock), and you continue to lose on the way down (albeit less than if you had no hedge). What if your lousy stock finally does decide to take off? Your upside potential would be capped off with a collar because of the short call(s) component. That's ok for short-term speculation but what about doing that with some of your core holdings?

I first designed this strategy for a guy who called me and said that he wanted to collar 30,000 shares of Cisco (CSCO). I don't know what price he paid for it originally but he owned it while the stock peaked at $82 a share in March of 2000. At that time Cisco had a market capitalization close to the other two biggest companies in the world, GE and Microsoft. He rode that puppy from $82 all the way down to 8 and change by March of 2002, then CSCO hung around 12.50 and 15 for a while and this fellow called me he wanted a traditional zero-cost-collar such as buying 300 of the 12.5 puts and selling 300 of the 15 calls to finance the purchase of the puts. I did not want to see the guy merely cap-off his upside to 15 and suggested what later became known as the SlingshotHedge™. Unlike a collar which shorts the calls to have proceeds to pay for the puts, the SlingshotHedge instead shorts twice the amount of call vertical credit spreads, to pay for the puts, while leaving unlimited gain potential for the stock.

Many investors longed for the return of the market of the late 90s but find it difficult to hang in there because not all stocks participate in the rally. Whether a stock comes back or not, we all want to participate and not just with a limited gain bull spread that collared stock emulates. We would all love to have the protective quality of puts to minimize our downside. The SlingshotHedge is a versatile strategy that can be employed using a myriad of ratios along with embedded calendar spreads to further enhance strategy selection. Depending on the slingshot ratio, you will not profit in a market rally as much as you would with naked long stock, but you will still participate in the corresponding up-move. If the underlying stock doubled, naked stock would make 100% profit from its current trading level. By comparison, the slingshot, on the same move will generate approximately 50% to 75% depending on the position configuration. That's not bad considering that your stock could get clobbered on the downside while the slingshot limits the loss to a tiny fraction, comparatively.

SUITABILITY ISSUES

Is the Slingshot suitable for you?

The slingshot hedge strategy is clearly **NOT** for everyone and is most helpful if you have an advanced understanding of synthetics and other relationships of option strategies. It's also **NOT** for you if you don't have the other necessary resources: time and money. You need a bit of time to analyze/monitor the position to make adjustments required or desired, perhaps as often as two to three times a week or more. Some investors don't spend or want to spend a lot of time managing their investments to this extent. I find that a great many new clients are sophisticated investors, who had been beaten to death by the markets, and want to take control of what is left of their liquid assets. Managing a slingshot is relatively simple and the position is not very convoluted, providing that the ratio is small. The steeper the ratio, the more time and energy you must devote to the endeavor.

TIME REQUIREMENTS

Once an initial SlingshotHedge™ is 'put on' an investor can wait until the end of the cycle to roll the whole position to the next expiration or skip to the next expiration month. It can even be done with LEAPS. In the meantime you may wish to take advantage of market created opportunities and make trades that adjust the delta by rolling positions between strikes (vertical spreads and butterflies) or months (calendar spreads) or by using gamma scalping techniques to adjust deltas from time to time.

CAPITAL ALLOCATION

What size account can enjoy the slingshot?

Even with an existing portfolio of stocks it is recommended that additional capital equal to 40% of the portfolio be on hand for margin, eventual margin, repair strategies and for further adjustments desired (keep cash reserves of 40% deploying these strategies). Certainly having a portfolio of stocks enjoys the benefit of option buying power up to 50% of the stocks net liquidating value. For example, to hedge 1oo shares of Microsoft (if currently priced at 50.00), you will have $2500 in option buying power but it would be nicer to have the extra $2000 (40% of $5000) besides the 1oo shares. The same play can be made with $5000 buying stock on margin (including the 40% reserve).

Keep in mind that without stock and a protective put, a long call may be used instead (strike where the put would be bought for protection). This will require only about $2220, $220 for the options involved and the extra $2000 for all the reasons mentioned above.

ACTUAL STRUCTURE

For every 1oo shares of stock, buy one put just out-of-the-money to button up the risk to the downside. Next: sell two out-of-the-money call vertical spreads and depending on how much time there is to go and implied volatility levels you should generate enough of a credit to pay for the put you just bought. With the sale of 2 verticals the risk is pretty straightforward and easy to manage, you can even ignore the position for quite a while (barring any major moves in either direction). Generally speaking, you will not be assigned on your short call(s) until expiration unless there is a dividend being paid and even then the stock has to be in-the-money enough for the put of the same strike to be bought for less than the dividend amount.

You may consider carrying extra short or long deltas according to your short-term market opinion by increasing or decreasing the quantity of short vertical spreads. To the downside, potential loss is tightly defined. To the upside the bear spreads, whether one spread per 1oo shares or five, eventually stop losing while the stock has a chance to go on to victory. There will be plenty of rolling opportunities to capture more favorable risk/reward relationships for profit enhancement or to minimize loss. The worst place for the stock to be by expiration, assuming absolutely no adjustments during the cycle, is at the long strike of the short call verticals (top strike of the whole package).

WINGSPREAD DISSECTION

As described in Chapter 6, wingspread dissection involves making a pretend sale or purchase of a butterfly to the position and doing the opposite in a basket called the 'butterfly basket'. The reason that the dissecting buys one and sells one is because you are not really making a trade, and therefore the net effect is zero. It is like debiting a trade in one account and crediting it to another.

Dissecting out butterflies by hand can be very messy, so it is important to be methodical. Following in Exhibit 9–1 is a simple method that can be performed manually. It is assumed that you have had exposure to the position format and simple position dissection using the SynTool ς and BoxTool □.

Trying to understand this concept can be difficult at first, but once it has been grasped it can become second nature. The conversions have been removed by pretending to trade the 50 reversal, 10 times (+10C/-10ooU/-10P).

E X H I B I T   9 – 1

Slingshot Dissection #1 (Manual) – Removing 10 Conversions using the SynTool

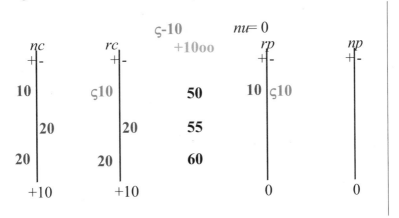

In Exhibit 9–2, The WingTool ω is used to denote the extraction of individual butterflies from the position. Before continuing, please orient yourself to the format layout with appropriate column labels

using the following legend starting with column G with the strike prices:

Column

E: Strike Prices

F: Raw (actual) put position left of the vertical line with a SynTool dissection to the right of the vertical line.

G: Net put position with a result of no puts left to consider.

D: Raw (actual) call position (the 20 lot bear spread) with a SynTool dissection to the left of the line at the 50 strike.

C: Net call position along with the first butterfly dissection using the WingTool to extract 10 long 50/**55**/60 butterflies.

B: Net call position after all dissections.

A: Butterfly basket showing the inventory of butterflies after all dissections.

The removal of the 10 long butterflies is performed in Column C, i.e. the sale of 10***50/55/60** butterflies to the position, denoted by the following: -10 ω +20 ω -10 ω

Simultaneously, this butterfly sale is offset by a purchase to the basket on the far left under column heading A. The butterfly basket is where the opposite transaction shows up so that we can monitor, separately, our inventory of butterflies. The purchase is listed as +10: 50/**55**/60.

On this ratio, short 20 vertical call spreads for each 10 units long (meaning 10oo shares and 10 married puts as protection), the position is still delta long with fairly neutral time decay. The position behaves like, and is synthetically equivalent to 10 long 50/**55**/60 butterfly spreads plus 10 long 60 calls. The position works best if the market sky-rockets but will definitely like the market to grind its way to 55 allowing the 10 long 50/**55**/60 butterflies to max-out at $5.00. The trade is employed, in this example, for a 75 cent credit, selling 2 call vertical spreads (each for a 1.00 credit, totaling 2.00 credit) for each 1 put purchased (1.25 debit) and assumes that the stock is already long.

It should be noted that the whole package is valued at a synthetic or equivalent debit of 2.00 ($2000 for all 10 spreads). This value is derived by first establishing a synthetic call price of 4.00 (the in-the-money amount of 2.50 plus the extrinsic value of the put being 1.25 plus 25 cents, the cost of carrying a $50 for 42 days at 4%. Take this 4.00 call price and subtract 2.00 that is the credit for 2 call verticals each sold for 1.00 each and you have the amount that will be lost (provided no other adjusting trades) if the stock is trading below $50 by expiration.

E X H I B I T   9 – 2

Slingshot Dissection #2 (Manual) – Removing 10 Long 50/**55**/60 Butterflies

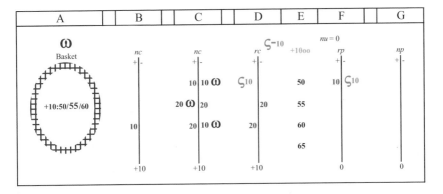

Exhibit 9–3 shows the profit and loss profile for every two weeks.

E X H I B I T   9 – 3

Slingshot P&L Profile: (2 Verticals to 1 Put) with 42, 28, 14 and 0 Days to Go

Delta = 377, Theta = +2.

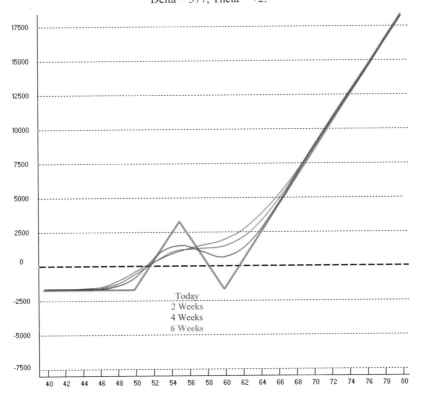

EXAMPLE PRE-TRADE CONFIRMATION

Exhibit 9–4 shows an example of a pre-trade confirmation for a .75 credit. Perhaps the middle values were .85 or .90 so often it becomes necessary to motivate the market makers to take the other side of the trade by discounting the credit you are willing to receive. In the previous exhibits the put was 1.25 and the two call verticals were 1.00. These were fill-able prices, worse than the "middles", the averages between all the bids and ask prices of the options involved. This represents a place where customer to customer trades may meet but the market makers come to work to get a positive edge, a potential for profit and in the following Exhibit we are offering the market maker the discounted .75 credit, i.e. paid 1.25 and received two times 1.00. The .75 credit is below implies that the risk from this point forward will be 1.75 down from the original 52.50 that was the risk 'on the table' when owning the shares outright.

E X H I B I T   9 – 4

SlingshotHedge™ Variation with Single Put and Double Call Credit Vertical

Stock Position before Trade:

Max Gain: Unlimited

Max Loss: $52,500   Fill Prices:

Break Even Stock Price: 52.50

U = 52.50		
Nearer Month		
50 OTM P		1.25
1.25 OTM C1 55		
.25 OTM C2 60		

After Variation 1P2CV Fill for .75 credit per spread

(paid 1.25, received 1.00 twice)

Total Value: 51,750

(10ooU + 10 P – 20*(C1–C2))

(52,500 + 1,250 –   2,000   )

Max Gain: Unlimited

Max Loss: $1750

Break Even Stock Prices:

51.75, 58.25, 61.75

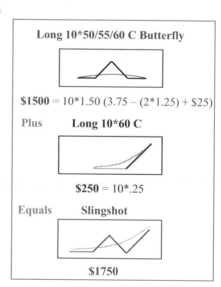

Long 10*50/55/60 C Butterfly

$1500 = 10*1.50 (3.75 – (2*1.25) + $25)

Plus   **Long 10*60 C**

$250 = 10*.25

Equals   **Slingshot**

$1750

CLOSER TO DELTA NEUTRAL ANYONE?

This next ratio is a bit more complicated and therefore requires a bit more management. In a nutshell, it is selling 30 verticals instead of 20, as in the previous example. It provides for a bigger credit (less of a synthetic debit), leaving you less long (in this case). In Exhibit 9–5, the SynTool is used again but noting column E this time showing 30 verticals and the same long butterfly dissected out:

Column

D: Net call position showing a **–10 by +20** call back spread at the 55/60 strikes.

C: Net call position along with the second butterfly dissection using the WingTool to extract 10 short 55/60/65 butterflies.

The removal of the 10 long butterflies is performed in Column C, i.e. the purchase of 10*50/55/60 butterflies to the position, denoted by the following: -10 ω +20 ω -10 ω

Column

B: Net call position after all dissections.

A: Butterfly basket showing the inventory of butterflies (long and short) after all dissections.

Simultaneously, this butterfly trades are offset by the opposite trades to the basket on the far left under column heading A. The butterfly basket is where the opposite transaction shows up so that we can monitor our inventory of butterflies. The purchase is listed as +10: 50/**55**/60. Using the same process –10: 55/60/65 is then removed and placed into the basket.

E X H I B I T   9 – 5

Slingshot Dissection #3 (Manual) – Removing 10 Long 50/**55**/60 Butterflies and 10 Short 55/**60**/65 Butterflies

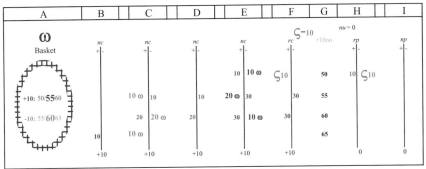

On this ratio, short 30 vertical call spreads for each 10 unit long the position is close to delta neutral with positive time decay and therefore currently has a market bias desiring a small trading range. The position works best if the market sky-rockets but will definitely like the market to grind its way to the 10 long 50/**55**/60 butterflies allowing them to max-out at 5.00 while leaving the 10 short 55/**60**/65 butterflies in the dust (worthless).

Exhibit 9–6 is an expiration shaped risk profile of this slingshot and you can pretty much see where the long and short butterflies as well as the long 65 calls come into play.

E X H I B I T   9 – 6

Slingshot (3 verticals to 1) Today (44 Days to Go) as Depicted in the thinkorswim Analyzer: Delta = 0, Theta = +7.

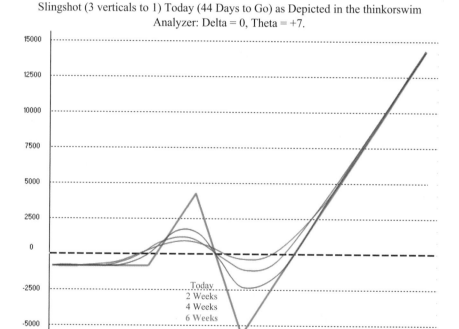

Obviously the underlying price of 60 is the price that the position most needs to stay away from. This particular ratio is done for a 1.75 credit, selling 3 call vertical spreads (each for a 1.00 credit, totaling 3.00 credit) for each 1 put purchased (1.25 debit). Assume the stock is already long and this individual is applying the options to complete the SlingshotHedge™. This ratio requires creative rolling and more active management over time and price change.

HOW ABOUT A PLAY IN EITHER DIRECTION?

Simply buy twice as many puts 20 instead of 10 when you sell twice as many (20) short verticals (Exhibit 9–7). It acts like 10 long 50/55/60 and long 10 * 50 put / 60 call strangles.

E X H I B I T   9 – 7

Double Slingshot as Depicted in the thinkorswim Analyzer

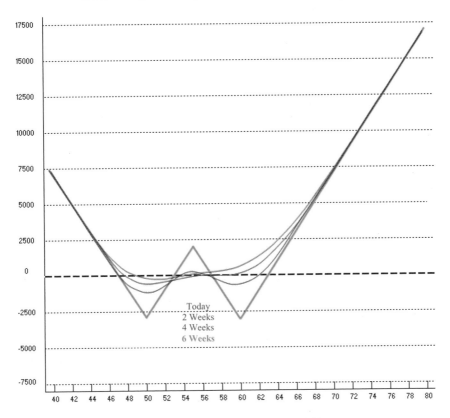

COMPARISON OF RATIOS

Exhibit 9–8 is a summary comparison of various ratios of the short verticals to the long units (10 units equals +10oo shares and +10*50 puts). The ratio will be determined based upon the individual's level of conservatism and bullish versus bearish opinion at any given time. Certainly, it will be extremely conservative and quite bullish to slingshot using a ratio of long 10 units to short only 10 verticals. An aggressive / bearish approach would be to use short 50 verticals against 10 units long. Keep in mind that depending on time to go and implied volatility levels a steep ratio may be delta neutral at the time of position entry but change quite quickly as the market begins to move. Generally speaking, I usually look for opportunities with a ratio of 3 to 1 and roll the position to the next month out when the ratio required for delta neutrality becomes anything steeper.

E X H I B I T   9 – 8

Slingshot Dissection Summary of Various Ratios of Short Call Verticals for Each Underlying Unit and Protective Put

Ratio of 10 units (10u means long 10oo shares and long 10 of the 50 puts) to short verticals (-30v means short 30 of the 55/60 call verticals)

Butterfly Strikes	Calls Strike	10u:-10v		10u:-15v		10u:-20v		10u:-25v		10u:-30v		10u:-35v		10u:-40v		10u:-45v		10u:-50v	
		Bflys	Calls	Bflys	Calls	Bflys	Calls	Bflys	Calls	Bflys	Calls	Bflys	Calls	Bflys	Calls	Bflys	Calls	Bflys	Calls
50/55/60	55	10	10	10	5	10		10		10		10		10		10		10	
55/60/65	60				5		10	(5)	5	(10)		(15)		(20)		(25)		(30)	
60/65/70	65								5		10	(5)	5	(10)		(15)		(20)	
65/70/75	70												5		10	(5)	5	(10)	
	75																5		10

CONCLUSION

A slingshot acts like a butterfly with extra long calls as in Exhibit 9–1 and 9–7 and can be put on without the use of stock; first long calls and then short twice as many short call spreads above. Or you may enter a short call credit spread and subsequently purchase half as many calls at the next strike down.

For a downside bias, a slingshot can take on the form of a butterfly with extra puts that would be a mirror image of Exhibit 9–1 (mirror on either side, not top or bottom). You purchase a put and also sell a put credit spread below. Don't forget that you can opt for your long options to be in a deferred month to add the attributes of imbedded long calendar spreads increased theta (positive time decay) in the position.

CHAPTER

10

YOU CAN LIVE WITH OR WITHOUT SKEW

This chapter defines skew and discusses graphs that show its general shapes in different markets. There also is an explanation of beliefs held by various traders about skew, and a brief presentation of different approaches to skew from a modeling standpoint. Following that, I will recall the circumstances under which I first noticed skew. The remaining information is the most important feature of this chapter. There is a library of two-dimensional graphs showing the effects of skew on the P&L and Greeks. The most common positions are presented with each of three basic skew shapes and are compared to a market with no skew or a flat skew. Pay attention to the irregularities. Knowledge of these may at least help you to identify and steer clear of danger when faced with the skew. They should serve as a guide to spreading in various markets based on the opportunities that the skew presents. The positions presented in this chapter with their respective exhibit numbers are as follows:

Reversal	(10-9)	Long Box	(10-10)
Long ATM Call	(10-11)	Long OTM Put	(10-12)
Long ATM Straddle	(10-13)	Short ATM Strangle	(10-14)
Bull Spread	(10-15)	Bear Spread	(10-16)
ATM Butterfly	(10-17)	Stretched-Out Condor	(10-18)
1x2 Call Ratio Spread	(10-19)	1x2 Put Ratio Spread	(10-20)
1.5x1 Call Back Spread	(10-21)	1.5x1 Put Back Spread	(10-22)
Risk Conversion	(10-23)	Risk Reversal	(10-24)
Short SemiFuture	(10-25)	Call Batwing	(10-26)
Put Batwing	(10-27)	Batman Spread	(10-28)

WHERE DOES THE SKEW COME FROM?

There are many different beliefs about why the implied volatility skew (also referred to as "the smile") exists. I believe that in most cases it is caused simply by supply and demand. There are more scientific reasons in the cash bonds and futures markets that can be explained by nuances of the Treasury bond basis.[1] Certain bonds can become more attractive (cheapest) to deliver, which creates an embedded option or options spread that can then be arbed against. Embedded options have an implied volatility that can be locked in using bond options.

A trader with an alternative view, who also shares the beliefs of some other market participants with us, had this to say:

> I would think that what causes the supply and demand is what causes the skew. Put another way, supply and demand is the expression of the root cause; it is not the root itself. There are many other factors to consider, including product history, product nature, the current market situation, and open interest, not to mention the involuntary mental skew invariably arising from one's own position. Yes, you can live with or without it, but you can ignore it only at your peril.
>
> One acquaintance of mine was obsessed with the skew, and often changed them (in the pricing sheets) repeatedly during a given trading session. She also tends to believe that certain skew fundamentals can be transferred from one product to another without reference to product idiosyncrasies.
>
> Another view is that the more you monkey with skews, the more lost you get, and the less you know how you got to your current position.
>
> But the best analogy that I have heard came from someone who likens skews to adjusting your position while throwing darts. "If you know that when you throw your dart a gust of wind is going to blow across its flight path, and if you have reasonable cause to anticipate specific different wind speeds coming from certain directions, you can adjust your stance even if you don't know from which direction the wind will come." It is better to show you this in person. You would see that as the wind blows one way, I have to lean into the wind a little bit in order to compensate.

Another reason that the skew may exist could be that an illiquid situation driving prices deviates far enough from the fair value to attract a counterparty for the trade. In some countries where it is difficult or impossible to short stock, deep in-the-money options with very high deltas play a surrogate role and thereby affect the deep option's supply-and-demand properties. This in turn affects the implied volatilities and skews at those strikes. Why a given skew exists is one thing, dealing with it is another.

SKEW SHAPES

Skew is a verb that means to turn aside sharply from a straight course. Most traders talk about it as if it were a noun. The skew should not be

---

[1] *The Treasury Bond Basis* by Galen D. Burghardt and Terrence M. Belton, published by McGraw-Hill. The nuances of the T-bond basis are the spread between the cash and futures prices.

ignored. It should be studied and monitored not only for its shape but also to see how naked options, locked positions, and all the other spread strategies are affected by it. Before traders commit themselves to skew exposure, they should seek to understand how it can bite them in the assets. Make a study of how it changes P&L, the Greeks, and spread prices over time with underlying price fluctuations. You will find that this unusual ambiguity is usually present.

Arbitrage is based on the idea that one thing is similar to another. Skew does strange things to even the safest of arbitrage locks (see Exhibits 10–9, 10–10, and 10–11). The market does not have to move at all, but changes in the skew can greatly affect the P&L.

A crash-type skew is depicted in Exhibit 10–1. This shape has a high chance of occurring when the market makes a fast, extended move. What happens is that traders bid higher than normal prices for both the out-of-the-money call and put sides. The market is saying, "If one wants to play, then one has to pay"; that is, if one wants to buy cheap, one has to pay an extra premium when the market has made a large and sudden move.

E X H I B I T   1 0 – 1

Crash-Shaped Skew (Not Necessarily Symmetrical)

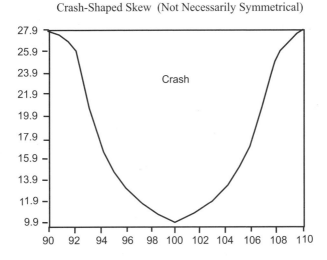

Recall the crash of 1987 when the market was in a tailspin. Obviously, the puts were trading at prices that were on the moon. Bottom pickers, hoping for a rebound, thought it safer to purchase limited-risk calls rather than stocks or futures. Those who were short or getting short wanted some upside protection, or some 'bullets' pointing to the upside, in case of a sharp rebound. That type of demand causes successively further out-of-the-money options to be pumped up in value. Traders who wanted to cover shorts found it was worth spending a few bucks to buy cheap calls. This type of buyer does not care about implied volatility levels, but is just happy that the price is relatively low on the risk-reward scale. Market makers who sold the calls did so in anticipation of buying them back at some point, therefore creating even more demand.

Following Black Monday, the bond market responded with a flight-to-quality move to the upside, creating demand for calls as traders covered their short positions or tried to get on the bandwagon. The demand for puts also increased as traders attempted to pick the top or hedge in case the rally turned out to be a blow-off spike-up.

Exhibit 10–2 shows two general shapes for skews: a stock or index skew, a grain or demand-products skew, a foreign (to the dollar) currency skew, and a bond or interest rate products skew.

E X H I B I T   1 0 – 2

General Skew Shapes for Various Markets

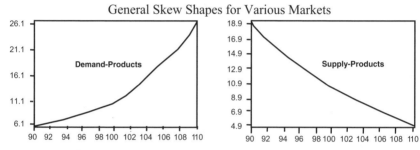

Remember that a skew is the result of supply and demand, and therefore can go up or down like any other market. As far as risk is concerned, the skew looks and acts somewhat like a yield curve.

The stock or index skew (upper right in Exhibit 10–2) slopes downward from the low strikes to the high strikes. Many investors will be long stocks and will modify their exposure by selling out-of-the-money calls (a covered write is synthetically short puts), buying out-of-the-money puts (synthetically long calls), or both (turning it into a bull spread). The demand for puts and the supply of calls creates this shape.

The grain or demand-products skew (upper right) is prevalent in products where supply could dry up suddenly, such as the grain market in a drought or a flood.

The bond or interest rate products skew (lower right) is the result of the investment world being long bonds and therefore requiring hedges.

MODELING THE SKEW

I had the honor of being invited to a research seminar sponsored by the Chicago Board of Trade. Several famous mathematicians, who are responsible for creating some of the most widely used models in the options world, were on the panel. It was attended mostly by members of the academic community. One of the professors stated that in an ideal world it should be possible to model the skew with one particular shape. The idea that I presented to him, that supply and demand rule the skew, had no meaning to him. My explanation, that the skew was caused by need and greed and oftentimes by pain, seemed to him to be like saying, "It is, because it is." I tried an analogy with IBM stock. Once it was trading at $160, then went down to $140, which may have seemed cheap after a price of $160. It dropped to $120, then to below $100. As you know, it later fell to $80, then to $60 and even lower than $50 before it eventually climbed back to $100. I asked, "Where does IBM belong?" I did not expect an answer because, if there was an answer, you could also attempt to answer the question, "Where does skew belong?" The professor did not like the IBM analogy because he believed that IBM does belong at a specific price. There is certainly no exact science to the skew; therefore, it would be almost impossible (unless there are embedded options to arb against) to try to model where it belongs. Market forces cannot be modeled.

Many market maker groups and individuals have tweaked existing models so that they more accurately reflect the nuances of the live trading environment. Each modification is based on the individual trader's market opinion and trading experience. Methods used by Option Vantage™ software, that generated the P&L graphs, are proprietary. Software such as MicroHedge™ is available to the public. MicroHedge™ allows the user to set different implied volatilities at each strike. Exhibit 10–3 displays the feature that change implied volatilities

E X H I B I T   1 0 – 3

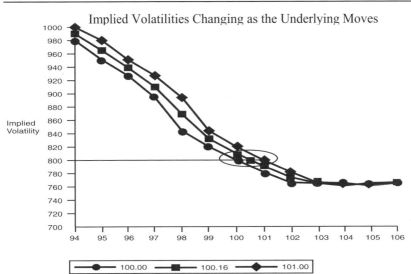

as the underlying price changes. Suppose that the 99 strike in the first of three matrices (denoted by the circle ● in) is set to an implied volatility level of 8.20%, which is .20% higher than the implied volatility (8.00%) of the 100 strike. MicroHedge™ will indicate that as the underlying price rallies one point in the third matrix (denoted by the triangle ▲) the 100 strike will take on the characteristics that the 99 strike had. There will be a new implied volatility calculation with each tick change in the underlying price. If the underlying had moved by only 16/32nds, that is, 50% of the distance to the next strike (the middle matrix denoted by the square ■), the implied volatility would change to 8.10%.

The way that the model in Exhibit 10–4 is tweaked, the options' implied volatility climb up the skew as the underlying drops. Think of a speedboat with a kite tied to its back. A movement similar to that shown in Exhibit 10–4 occurs. As the boat moves to the right, the kite flies higher. If the boat reverses, the kite will drop toward the water.

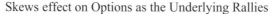

E X H I B I T   1 0 – 4

Skews effect on Options as the Underlying Rallies

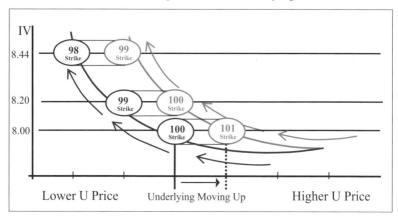

As the underlying price rallies one point from 100 to 101, the implied volatility of the 100 strike, which was formerly set at 8.00%, climbs to 8.20% (see Exhibit 10–4).

Some traders also tweak the model to adjust the Greeks, so that the new volatility levels are taken into account. Often what the deltas are indicating is apparently overlooked in the P&L scenario. Traders will therefore add or subtract an amount from their delta, which should protect them from the effect of skew on the P&L. They are mentally factoring in the newest derivative, which the author suggests be denoted by the Greek letter 'I' or "**iota**" (this stands for what I ought to do to protect myself against the skew). Some traders not only have built in features such as Iota (referred to as dollar delta or vega delta), but also have programmed a feature that allows the whole skew to shift up or down automatically. For example, if the market goes up and volatility goes down, as in bonds and index products, then traders set their model to reflect this by making all of the implied volatilities on their sheets and analyzer drop as well. Many programs allow for a skew shift setting of between 0% and 200%. In our last example, when the 100s climbed up by .20%, a 100% setting would mean that the whole skew would have also dropped by .20%. A 50% setting would cause a .10% shift lower. Remember that such features are based on the experience of the traders who use them. The past does not always reflect the future. This painful lesson was taught to many bond option traders recently when implied volatility started to go up on the upside and down on the downside.

THE DAY SKEW WAS BORN (FOR THE AUTHOR)

It took place in June 1984, in the U.S. T-bond options pit (the second year of bond options trading on the CBOT). Bonds were at about 59.00. My position is shown in Exhibit 10–5. Most traders in the pit had a similar position.

E X H I B I T   1 0 – 5

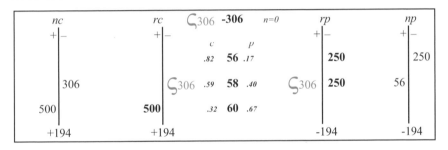

Position Prior to Skew This is a risk reversal of sorts (short low strikes and long high strikes). Traders used to make their living selling options 1 tick over theoretical value and buying them 1 tick cheaper than theoretical value (not necessarily in that that order). If they bought them 1 tick better, then there was good reason to get out at theoretical value. This particular week, no one was able to get out with a profit. Another week went by and traders could not even get out theoretical value. The low strikes were in demand. They started to trade consistently at a tick over the sheets on the bid. Normally, I would not have had more than about 200 spreads, but this time I had accumulated 500. I was getting tired of this position and decided to get out of it before the money supply number came out on Thursday night. A broker, Bob asked for a 56/58/60 call Christmas tree with a ratio of 1:1:2, 300 times. 300x300x600 was just what I needed. Of course, I also would have to trade the delta amount of futures against it (see Exhibit 10–6). I gave Bob a two-sided market along with the crowd and calculated how many futures per 100 spreads I would have to trade if I got hit. I needed to sell 77 futures for 100 spreads {100*[.82 + .59 + (-2*.32)]}

E X H I B I T   1 0 – 6

Dissection after the Trade with Bob the Broker

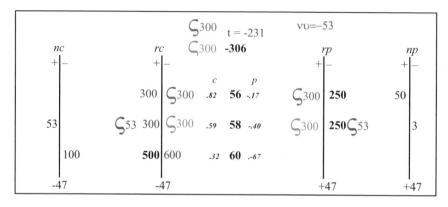

The bonds were 58.20–58.21 at the time. I decided that if I bought the spread at the broker's offer and sold the futures at the bid of 58.20, I would lose just under $4,000 from where I put it on. That was the best price relationship that I had seen for over a week. I screamed to Bob, "Done!" This was at the same moment that Bob had gotten permission from his customer to hit the market maker price. Bob gave them all to me at my price because I was first. As I made the trade the bonds went to 58.21 bid, giving me another 231 bond ticks ($31.25) for a total profit on the trade, of just over $8,500. In addition, I had over-liquidated and reversed myself into a risk conversion.

That was my last chance to get out. The money supply report that night was not so good for bonds. The following day they were limit down. Implied volatility exploded 2% (about $300 per at-the-money option) and the implied volatility increment between strikes, which had bulged to 1 tick (.10% vol.) the day before, skewed out to about 6 ticks (.60% vol.) and stayed like that for years. Trading the spread 300 times, reversing my position from 250 risk reversals to 50 risk conversions, was a $70,000 swing. Many traders had on thousands of spreads in all months. It was like a giant bowling bowl had come rolling through the bond options pit, knocking over half of the traders. The skew was born, and since that day the overvalued/undervalued situation between strikes has fluctuated between 2 and 20 ticks, but stays mostly between 2 and 4 ticks. The amount of fluctuation depends on the embedded option factor.

Another more esoteric nuance is the effect that the skew has on pricing. A good strategy is one that has more ways (as opposed to actual money) to win than to lose.

In the summer of 1992, I found a spread in soybeans to put on. Beans were at $6.40 per bushel and there was a lot of talk about a drought. If this came about, it would send beans into the teens.[4] The skew was very steep, implying the same thing. Guess where the market had priced the 5.75 / 6.00 call vertical? Most traders guessed about .21 of the maximum value of .25, which leaves just under .04 for the put vertical.[5] The price that I paid for the spread was .14. You could have bought all you wanted at that price while the futures were at $6.40. The lower strikes had implied volatilities in the high teens while the higher strikes were traveling in the high 30s. I figured I was going to profit on the play if I sat still, went higher, or went lower, but not if I went below $5.89 (my break-even price), or if the skew calmed down a bit. The only way to lose was if the market collapsed. It did, down to $5.34. I had thought about buying the 5.75 puts for .03 before I went out of town. That is what you get when you leave town with a position and do not monitor it. The complete strategy, including the puts, makes so much sense. Why be greedy when you are getting the call spread for so little in the first place? The total price for the strategy would have been .17 with a maximum profit of .08 on the upside. As it turned out, the three-way spread went to over .31 when soybeans collapsed to $5.34.

The next grid of numbers (see Exhibit 10–7) shows values taken from the U.S. Treasury note market during the spring of 1995 and transposed into decimal numbers to avoid confusion over the 64ths.

Look at the prices in Exhibit 10–7 and the graph in Exhibit 10–8. Compare the butterfly values that are equidistant from strike 101, that is, the 100 to the 102, the 99 to the 103, and so on. Since the skew is sloping downwards to the right, the butterflies are priced higher at the higher strikes (to the right of 101) than they are at the lower strikes (to the left of 101) because all butterflies vary inversely with implied volatility when there is a reasonable amount of time until expiration.

E X H I B I T   1 0 – 7

Prices of Butterflies with 11 Days and 43 Days to Go

Butterfly Middle Strike	94	95	96	97	98	99	100	101	102	103	104	105	106	107
11 Day Call Prices	700	600	500	400	303	211	130	67	28	9	3	1	0	0
11 Day Butterflies		**0**	**1**	**3**	**5**	**11**	**19**	**23**	**20**	**13**	**4**	**1**	**0**	
11 Day Put Prices	0	0	1	3	11	30	67	.128	209	303	401	500	600	700
43 Day Call Prices	701	603	506	413	323	241	167	108	64	34	16	6	3	1
43 Day Butterflies		**1**	**3**	**5**	**6**	**9**	**14**	**16**	**14**	**11**	**9**	**6**	**1**	
43 Day Put Prices	1	3	6	13	23	41	67	108	164	234	316	406	502	600

They are cheap when implied volatilities are high and rich when volatilities are low. This is also always the case for at-the-money butterflies throughout the cycle. Away-from-the-money butterflies, with

11 days to go, are more evenly priced because the vega at each strike is dwindling and has less of an effect on price. At the very end of the cycle, near expiration, the prices of out-of-the-money butterflies vary directly with implied volatility.

E X H I B I T   1 0 – 8

Butterfly Prices from Exhibit 10–7 in a Graphic Display

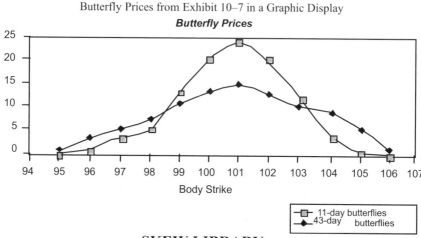

SKEW LIBRARY

There are four graphs for each position. In Exhibit 10–9, four views of a long box position are shown for 100 of the 100 strike calls with 90 days to go and an interest rate of 6.5%. The Whaley-Adesi model for futures is used with the implied volatility for the 100 strike set at 10%. Exhibit 10-9A demonstrates how the box graph should theoretically perform when there is no skew. See the tabular readout for a detailed account of the Greek values. Exhibit 10-9B shows the effect of a crash-shaped skew. The two remaining graphs display the characteristics of the supply and demand skews. The implied volatility used is not representative of implied volatilities for these products. In each case, the implied volatility for the 100 strike is set at 10% and the values are skewed from there.

Exhibits 10–10 through 10–28 show additional common spreads. See the list at the beginning of the chapter. Other spread strategies not listed here are variations and derivations of the spreads in this library. The examples are designed to be used as a handy reference when opportunities present themselves in the market. To follow up on this study, it is suggested that each trader obtain actual implied volatility levels for the markets in which he or she trades and stress test the types of positions that he or she intends to carry (from 1 day through 365 days), so that the trader understands implicitly what to expect as the market unfolds. When viewing the graphs, remember that the areas depicting the black line is the expiration day (90 days away) while the smoothest line generally is the current day.

REVERSAL

In Exhibit 10–9, the crash skew makes the reversal act like a European-style reversal because the skew staves off an early exercise. The bond and index skew have the loss potential stretched out to the upside. Notice that the right side of the graph looks very much like the European model because it is assuming that the puts will trade at higher and higher implied volatilities as the market rallies. This will prevent them from trading lower than the call's cost of carry and therefore early exercise is unlikely. The left side looks like a smaller version of the unskewed model because it assumes that the calls will be trading at very low implied volatilities. This will encourage exercise to take place sooner than normal.

Flat or No Skew

Price:	85.00	88.00	91.00	94.00	97.00	100.00	103.00	106.00	109.00	112.00	115.00
P&L	70	745	4687	5799	3469	0	-3478	-5985	-5999	-2023	-394
Delta	6	54	143	-39	-105	-121	-106	-53	68	104	23
Gamma	5	35	-95	-35	-12	0	10	26	58	-49	-12
Theta	-5	-37	-113	-70	-36	0	36	70	109	85	23
Vega	115	791	1512	307	30	0	-28	-264	-1145	-1744	-491

Crash Skew

Price:	85.00	88.00	91.00	94.00	97.00	100.00	103.00	106.00	109.00	112.00	115.00
P&L	16363	13244	10070	6863	3547	0	-3391	-3368	-7	0	0
Delta	-82	-87	-92	-101	-113	-121	-97	112	1	0	0
Gamma	-7	-7	-7	-8	-6	0	17	114	-1	0	0
Theta	-176	-141	-106	-71	-36	0	36	75	1	0	0
Vega	93	80	65	40	10	0	-57	-1486	-30	0	0

Supply-Products Skew

Price:	85.00	88.00	91.00	94.00	97.00	100.00	103.00	106.00	109.00	112.00	115.00
P&L	0	0	24	3739	3398	0	-3526	-6696	-9603	-12328	-14943
Delta	0	0	3	96	-97	-121	-111	-93	-77	-65	-55
Gamma	0	0	5	-111	-18	0	7	10	11	10	10
Theta	0	0	-2	-73	-36	0	36	71	106	141	175
Vega	0	0	76	1199	53	0	-15	-74	-144	-213	-275

Demand-Products Skew

Price:	85.00	88.00	91.00	94.00	97.00	100.00	103.00	106.00	109.00	112.00	115.00
P&L	15942	13201	10221	6910	3532	0	-3539	-6962	-10355	-13450	-16354
Delta	-72	-85	-98	-103	-111	-121	-112	-106	-104	-95	-85
Gamma	-8	-7	-6	-7	-7	0	6	5	4	4	5
Theta	-176	-141	-107	-71	-36	0	36	72	107	142	177
Vega	131	85	47	33	14	0	-12	-27	-35	-68	-109

EXHIBIT 10-9A (comment and profiles on page 247)

Flat or No Skew

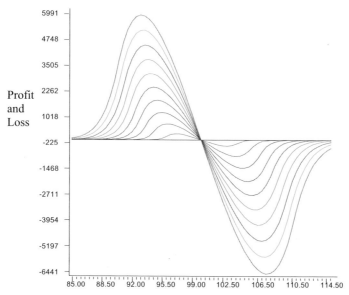

EXHIBIT 10-9B

Crash Skew

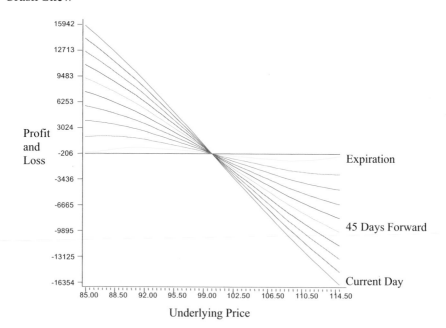

EXHIBIT 10-9C

Supply Product Skew

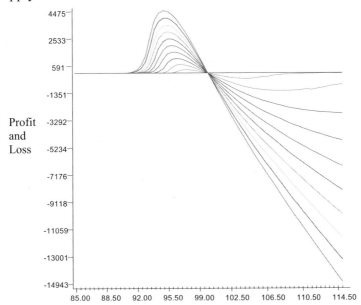

EXHIBIT 10-9D

Demand-Products Skew

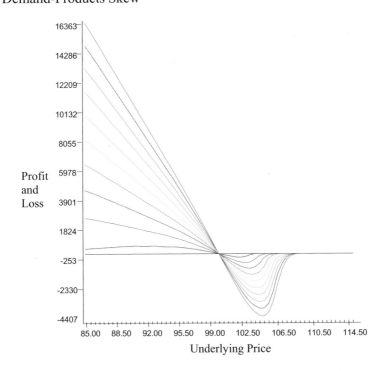

EXHIBIT 10-10A (comment and profiles of page 252)
Flat or no skew

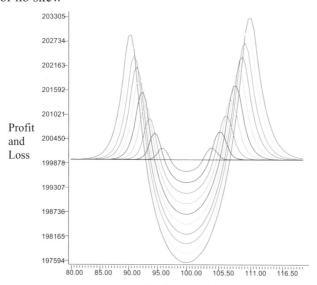

EXHIBIT 10-10B

Crash Skew

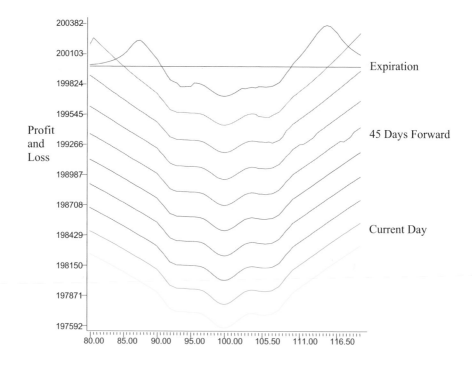

EXHIBIT 10-10C
Supply-Products Skew

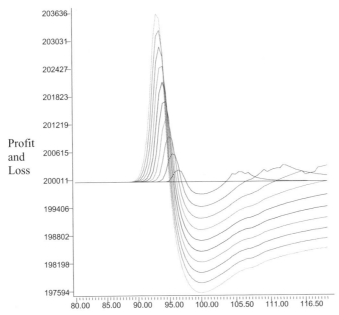

EXHIBIT 10-10D
Demand-Products Skew

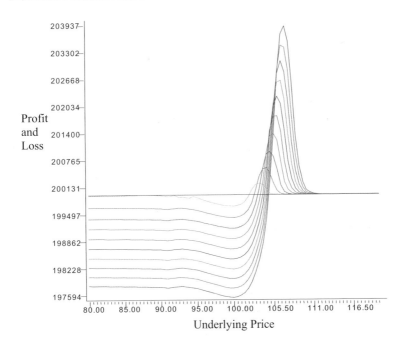

Underlying Price

LONG BOX

In the bond and index skews (see Exhibit 10–10), the zone of discounted value for a box is wider on the upside because the out-of-the-money puts climb to higher and higher implied volatility levels, preventing them from trading lower than the carry cost of their corresponding in-the-money call. The opposite holds true for the currency and demand-products skews, where the calls seldom trade lower than the cost to carry of the put. The crash skew postpones either side from being an exercise situation situation[2].

Flat or No Skew

Price:	80.00	84.00	88.00	92.00	96.00	100.00	104.00	108.00	112.00	116.00	120.00
P&L	200001	200046	200978	201069	198198	197594	198164	200543	202469	200325	200031
Delta	0	4	64	-128	-34	0	31	98	-114	-18	-2
Gamma	0	3	37	41	12	7	10	26	46	9	1
Theta	0	-3	-39	30	23	24	23	27	-80	-17	-2
Vega	3	73	783	-902	-127	-2	-119	-739	1553	361	54

Crash Skew

Price:	80.00	84.00	88.00	92.00	96.00	100.00	104.00	108.00	112.00	116.00	120.00
P&L	198275	198146	198002	197772	197734	197592	197729	197761	198007	198186	198353
Delta	-6	-6	-6	-3	-6	0	6	3	7	7	7
Gamma	0	0	0	-1	0	6	0	0	0	0	0
Theta	23	23	23	24	24	24	24	24	23	23	23
Vega	-25	-24	-21	-7	-13	-2	-13	-8	-24	-32	-37

Supply-Products Skew

Price:	80.00	84.00	88.00	92.00	96.00	100.00	104.00	108.00	112.00	116.00	120.00
P&L	200000	200000	200001	201743	198802	197594	197856	198129	198341	198470	198558
Delta	0	0	0	153	-75	0	13	11	10	8	7
Gamma	0	0	0	118	35	7	3	0	0	0	0
Theta	0	0	0	-66	23	24	23	23	23	23	23
Vega	0	0	2	1891	-358	-2	-37	-51	-56	-52	-47

Demand- Products Skew

Price:	80.00	84.00	88.00	92.00	96.00	100.00	104.00	108.00	112.00	116.00	120.00
P&L	197874	197863	197848	197843	197760	197594	198859	202622	200004	200000	200000
Delta	0	-1	-2	-4	-8	1	77	-180	0	0	0
Gamma	-1	-1	-1	-1	1	7	34	-142	1	0	0
Theta	23	23	23	23	24	24	23	-88	0	0	0
Vega	0	-2	-5	-13	-18	-2	-392	2055	14	0	0

---

[2] The call spread plus the put spread should add up to the present value of the difference between the two strikes plus any early exercise value.

LONG AT-THE-MONEY CALL

With the currency and demand-products skews, the losses diminish as the market falls because the calls climb up the skew as they lose value (see Exhibit 10–11). The bond and index skews lose even more than the currency and demand-products skews when the market falls because the calls slide to lower and lower implied volatilities.

Flat or No Skew

Price:	95.00	96.00	97.00	98.00	99.00	100.00	101.00	102.00	103.00	104.00	105.00
P&L	-158199	-140055	-115910	-84904	-46391	0	54322	116329	185500	261121	342357
Delta	1547	2100	2746	3469	4243	5039	5824	6571	7254	7858	8376
Gamma	503	602	688	754	790	796	770	718	645	561	474
Theta	-617	-752	-876	-976	-1040	-1061	-1038	-974	-877	-756	-623
Vega	11467	13886	16098	17889	19081	19556	19279	18299	16734	14745	12510

Crash Skew

Price:	95.00	96.00	97.00	98.00	99.00	100.00	101.00	102.00	103.00	104.00	105.00
P&L	-60146	-68426	-68496	-52970	-31774	0	70580	148986	237391	338002	449185
Delta	2825	2969	3239	3712	4306	5039	5772	6366	6809	7091	7246
Gamma	419	491	577	655	736	796	712	623	531	445	371
Theta	-1479	-1321	-1210	-1174	-1122	-1061	-1130	-1176	-1237	-1352	-1531
Vega	15978	16500	17273	18284	19131	19556	19333	18690	17942	17374	17078

Supply-Products Skew

Price:	95.00	96.00	97.00	98.00	99.00	100.00	101.00	102.00	103.00	104.00	105.00
P&L	-182334	-166822	-141040	-105208	-58382	0	67516	142175	222052	307429	395842
Delta	838	1503	2351	3266	4184	5039	5781	6403	6916	7324	7654
Gamma	439	621	759	832	841	796	723	640	561	487	423
Theta	-297	-480	-677	-844	-972	-1061	-1113	-1135	-1134	-1131	-1121
Vega	7583	11376	14909	17503	19029	19556	19324	18623	17677	16674	15686

Demand-Products Skew

Price:	95.00	96.00	97.00	98.00	99.00	100.00	101.00	102.00	103.00	104.00	105.00
P&L	-61367	-55529	-48034	-41140	-24872	0	39409	92846	153651	225763	312334
Delta	2815	3073	3395	3786	4334	5039	5882	6774	7711	8612	9240
Gamma	420	473	538	625	713	796	806	832	736	601	444
Theta	-1470	-1412	-1345	-1245	-1161	-1061	-954	-823	-625	-395	-223
Vega	15953	16743	17576	18389	19151	19556	19215	17854	15181	11143	7196

EXHIBIT 10-11A (comment and profiles page 253)
Flat or No Skew

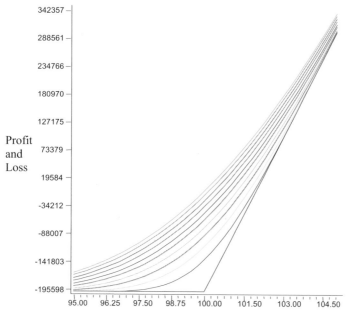

EXHIBIT 10-11B
Crash Skew

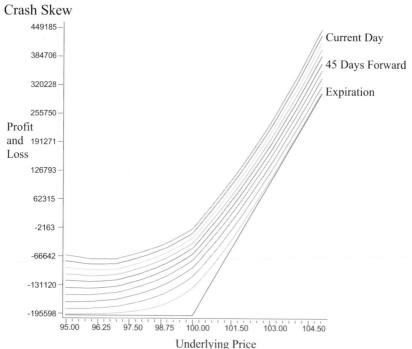

EXHIBIT 10-11C
Supply-Products Skew

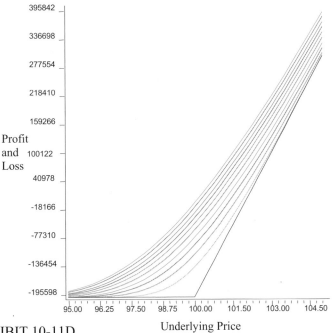

Underlying Price

EXHIBIT 10-11D
Demand-Products Skew

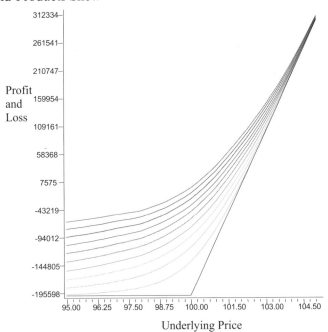

Underlying Price

EXHIBIT 10-12A (comment and profiles page 258)

Flat or No Skew

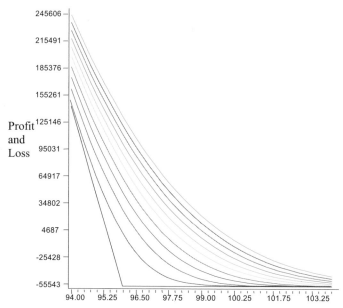

EXHIBIT 10-12B

Crash Skew

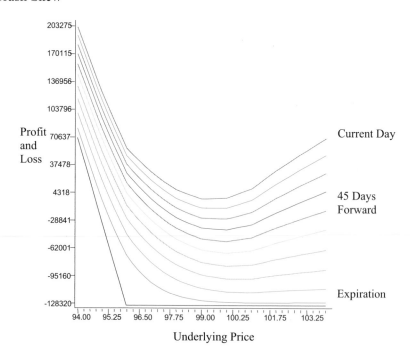

EXHIBIT 10-12C
Supply-Products Skew

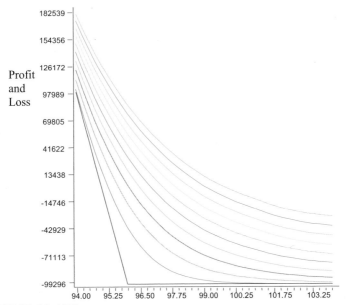

Underlying Price

EXHIBIT 10-12D
Demand-Products Skew

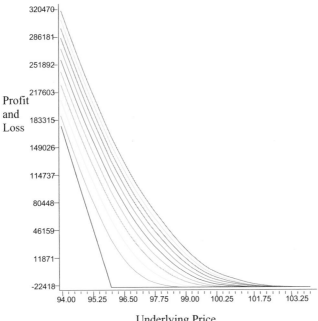

Underlying Price

LONG OUT-OF-THE-MONEY PUT

Compared to the bond and index skews, the currency and demand-products skews provide a better opportunity for the puts to win as the market drops (see Exhibit 10–12). Do not forget that overall implied volatility tends to explode on the downside in the stock and bond markets, which shifts the whole skew up. The shift upward usually more than compensates for the slide down the skew when the market drops like a stone.

Flat or No Skew

Price:	94.00	95.00	96.00	97.00	98.00	99.00	100.00	101.00	102.00	103.00	104.00
P&L	245606	184803	132231	87918	51556	22528	0	-16991	-29442	-38307	-44442
Delta	-6481	-5671	-4840	-4024	-3256	-2561	-1958	-1455	-1050	-736	-502
Gamma	788	826	829	797	735	650	553	453	357	271	199
Theta	-906	-984	-1019	-1007	-953	-864	-752	-630	-507	-394	-295
Vega	17041	18282	18773	18482	17470	15876	13886	11704	9518	7476	5677

Crash Skew

Price:	94.00	95.00	96.00	97.00	98.00	99.00	100.00	101.00	102.00	103.00	104.00
P&L	203275	126032	59455	30729	9977	-909	0	11029	32667	52215	71097
Delta	-6227	-5605	-4840	-4079	-3466	-3013	-2728	-2572	-2512	-2452	-2398
Gamma	685	769	829	738	640	541	450	374	312	268	235
Theta	-1097	-1063	-1019	-1095	-1147	-1212	-1329	-1508	-1763	-2002	-2235
Vega	17454	18334	18773	18539	17872	17103	16523	16222	16189	16147	16118

Supply-Products Skew

Price:	94.00	95.00	96.00	97.00	98.00	99.00	100.00	101.00	102.00	103.00	104.00
P&L	182539	129563	88478	56815	32489	13505	0	-10467	-19642	-25520	-28502
Delta	-6692	-5732	-4840	-4069	-3428	-2904	-2492	-2162	-1886	-1678	-1527
Gamma	870	879	829	748	658	570	490	421	364	315	275
Theta	-779	-919	-1019	-1079	-1107	-1113	-1115	-1111	-1094	-1091	-1107
Vega	16638	18228	18773	18529	17803	16832	15814	14822	13855	13044	12420

Demand-Products Skew

Price:	94.00	95.00	96.00	97.00	98.00	99.00	100.00	101.00	102.00	103.00	104.00
P&L	320470	238548	165356	106750	62288	25537	0	-11991	-19282	-21652	-22335
Delta	-6150	-5577	-4840	-3965	-3048	-2104	-1232	-670	-254	-76	-11
Gamma	654	745	829	861	822	730	562	371	184	69	13
Theta	-1166	-1101	-1019	-926	-807	-621	-404	-249	-105	-35	-5
Vega	17564	18355	18773	18416	17015	14317	10400	6848	3283	1232	231

LONG AT-THE-MONEY STRADDLE

Notice the effect of the index skew on the straddle (see Exhibit 10–13). It profits on a rally because the 100 strike climbs up the left side of the skew. The opposite happens with the demand-products skew. Remember that the overall implied volatility level could go up or down as well, which means that if implied volatility declined on the upside in the index, the P&L would be overstated.

Flat or No Skew

Price:	95.00	96.00	97.00	98.00	99.00	100.00	101.00	102.00	103.00	104.00	105.00
P&L	178352	115443	64712	27820	6014	0	9847	35031	74479	126720	190046
Delta	-6836	-5710	-4404	-2949	-1395	198	1768	3256	4614	5810	6829
Gamma	1030	1221	1388	1514	1584	1592	1537	1429	1280	1108	928
Theta	-1174	-1457	-1717	-1927	-2067	-2123	-2089	-1973	-1789	-1559	-1305
Vega	22773	27696	32166	35770	38160	39111	38559	36606	33496	29560	25162

Crash Skew

Price:	95.00	96.00	97.00	98.00	99.00	100.00	101.00	102.00	103.00	104.00	105.00
P&L	373922	258488	159476	91675	35248	0	42363	100358	178321	280679	404181
Delta	-4245	-3955	-3410	-2460	-1268	198	1664	2849	3731	4291	4598
Gamma	845	989	1161	1315	1476	1592	1241	1057	883	736
Theta	-2899	-2595	-2384	-2323	-2232	-2123	-2272	-2376	-2509	-2752	-3122
Vega	31928	32978	34533	36563	38261	39111	38667	37385	35896	34769	34181

Supply-Products Skew

Price:	95.00	96.00	97.00	98.00	99.00	100.00	101.00	102.00	103.00	104.00	105.00
P&L	130856	62175	14521	-12775	-17967	0	36236	86733	147630	219485	297369
Delta	-8312	-6926	-5201	-3356	-1513	198	1682	2923	3944	4753	5407
Gamma	936	1275	1536	1674	1686	1592	1442	1276	1115	965	837
Theta	-535	-913	-1319	-1665	-1931	-2123	-2238	-2293	-2305	-2310	-2301
Vega	14705	22582	29766	34995	38058	39111	38649	37252	35369	33378	31422

Demand-Products Skew

Price:	95.00	96.00	97.00	98.00	99.00	100.00	101.00	102.00	103.00	104.00	105.00
P&L	366217	279701	196664	112912	47727	0	-18517	-8663	16777	64995	140799
Delta	-4447	-3910	-3241	-2425	-1281	191	1946	3789	5696	7477	8656
Gamma	869	981	1118	1301	1487	1658	1727	1655	1480	1160	801
Theta	-2961	-2865	-2748	-2563	-2408	-2216	-2001	-1728	-1312	-829	-481
Vega	30186	31807	33522	35196	36767	37594	36870	34047	28593	20597	13160

EXHIBIT 10-13A (comment and profile page 259)

Flat or No Skew

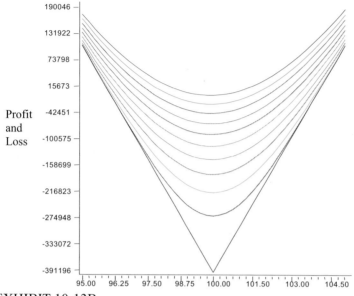

Underlying Price

EXHIBIT 10-13B

Crash Skew

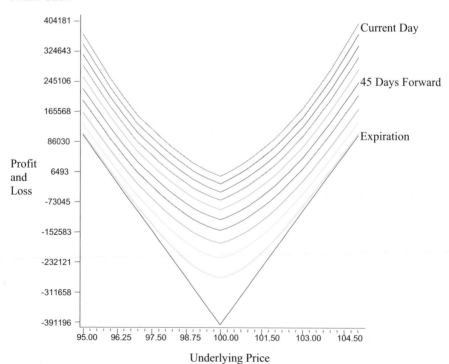

Underlying Price

EXHIBIT 10-13C
Supply-Products Skew

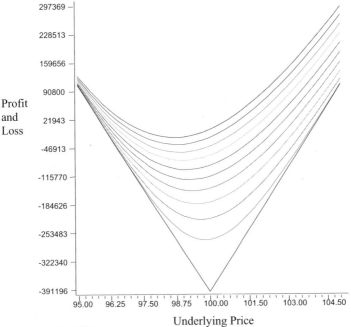

Profit and Loss

Underlying Price

EXHIBIT 10-13D
Demand-Products Skew

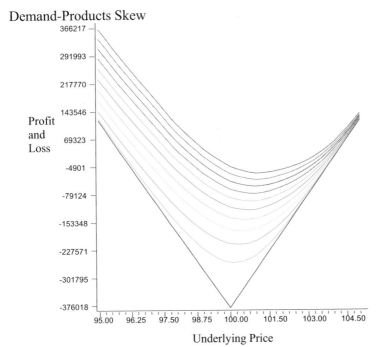

Profit and Loss

Underlying Price

EXHIBIT 10-14A (comment and profile page 264)

Flat or No Skew

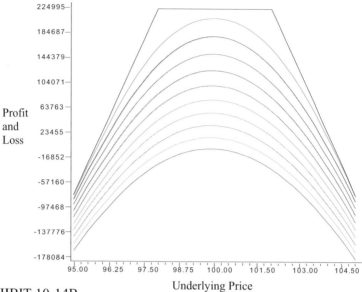

EXHIBIT 10-14B

Crash Skew

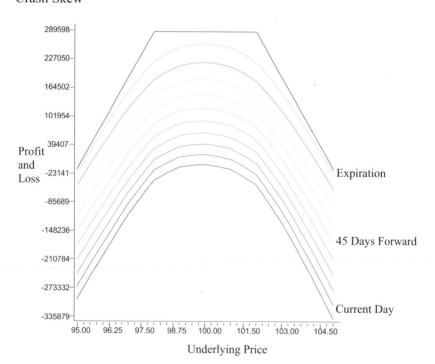

EXHIBIT 10-14C
Supply-Products Skew

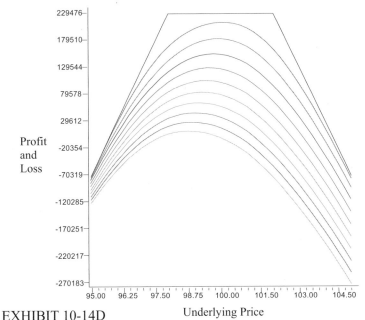

EXHIBIT 10-14D
Demand-Products Skew

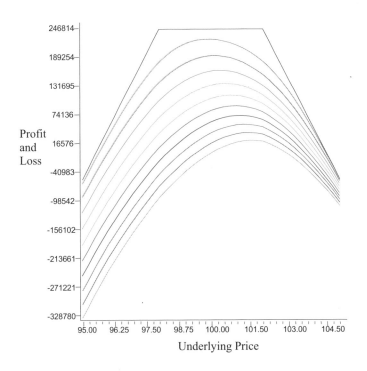

SHORT AT-THE-MONEY STRANGLE

Examine the index skew in Exhibit 10–14. It looks as though traders would suffer a greater loss if the market rallied than if it broke, because the short options all climb up the skew against them. Remember that overall implied volatility usually declines as the market rallies, which would overshadow the effect of skew. The reverse is true for the demand-products skew.

Flat or No Skew

Price:	95.00	96.00	97.00	98.00	99.00	100.00	101.00	102.00	103.00	104.00	105.00
P&L	-164530	-105836	-58897	-25044	-5238	0	-9358	-32868	-69657	-118535	-178084
Delta	6405	5304	4057	2693	1254	-212	-1657	-3035	-4308	-5448	-6440
Gamma	-1020	-1179	-1312	-1409	-1461	-1464	-1418	-1330	-1210	-1067	-914
Theta	1198	1436	1649	1818	1929	1974	1950	1860	1716	1530	1319
Vega	-22879	-26980	-30622	-33516	-35422	-36196	-35799	-34298	-31856	-28701	-25092

Crash Skew

Price:	95.00	96.00	97.00	98.00	99.00	100.00	101.00	102.00	103.00	104.00	105.00
P&L	-294310	-199953	-109892	-34193	-5213	0	-10325	-43195	-125703	-226844	-335879
Delta	3962	3410	2723	1833	820	-246	-1275	-2274	-3148	-3792	-4288
Gamma	-911	-1031	-1167	-1296	-1291	-1272	-1256	-1225	-1069	-921	-789
Theta	3026	2831	2607	2396	2359	2374	2388	2447	2703	3014	3324
Vega	-32546	-33921	-35153	-36101	-36636	-36979	-37057	-36906	-36394	-35732	-34958

Supply-Products Skew

Price:	95.00	96.00	97.00	98.00	99.00	100.00	101.00	102.00	103.00	104.00	105.00
P&L	-120638	-60918	-17347	7216	12190	0	-28300	-73493	-130702	-196198	-270183
Delta	7464	6247	4833	3288	1689	156	-1262	-2507	-3562	-4447	-5160
Gamma	-899	-1120	-1308	-1434	-1485	-1465	-1387	-1264	-1126	-991	-867
Theta	679	961	1254	1541	1800	1998	2134	2230	2281	2292	2294
Vega	-16232	-21564	-26656	-31015	-34293	-36144	-36692	-36207	-35001	-33356	-31621

Demand-Products Skew

Price:	95.00	96.00	97.00	98.00	99.00	100.00	101.00	102.00	103.00	104.00	105.00
P&L	-328780	-235983	-158178	-90215	-38434	0	21522	23372	-3082	-48230	-105707
Delta	4011	3475	2705	1730	556	-729	-2199	-3760	-5156	-6464	-7581
Gamma	-887	-1013	-1145	-1278	-1373	-1423	-1424	-1346	-1197	-988	-805
Theta	2932	2760	2636	2489	2323	2100	1826	1505	1240	959	686
Vega	-32265	-33645	-35148	-36340	-36814	-36240	-34327	-30819	-26891	-21869	-17041

BULL SPREAD

The demand-products and currency skews lose less on the downside and profit more on the upside, simply because the skew makes the bull spreads extra cheap to begin with (see Exhibit 10–15). Consider the soybean example in this chapter.

The crash skew causes the bull spread to react in a way similar to the demand-products and currency skews on a rally, but it loses more than they do on a break.

These profiles suggest that bear spreads will be more profitable with the bond and index skews than with the other types of skew (see Exhibit 10–16).

Flat or No Skew

Price:	95.00	96.00	97.00	98.00	99.00	100.00	101.00	102.00	103.00	104.00	105.00
P&L	-67907	-57362	-44928	-30901	-15734	0	15688	30748	44685	57152	67965
Delta	955	1153	1330	1469	1555	1581	1546	1457	1324	1165	996
Gamma	201	190	161	114	57	-5	-64	-114	-149	-167	-169
Theta	-245	-234	-199	-141	-64	23	109	185	243	279	293
Vega	4367	4171	3561	2562	1262	-200	-1661	-2966	-3996	-4686	-5031

Crash Skew

Price:	95.00	96.00	97.00	98.00	99.00	100.00	101.00	102.00	103.00	104.00	105.00
P&L	-123980	-111561	-87374	-65791	-49355	0	46658	64241	86145	108482	129525
Delta	181	376	711	1042	1314	1466	1340	1060	755	471	252
Gamma	134	166	174	171	155	-10	-160	-170	-170	-154	-129
Theta	380	305	178	115	136	15	-91	-80	-145	-259	-395
Vega	450	860	1359	1446	870	-195	-1267	-1803	-1739	-1296	-767

Supply-Products Skew

Price:	95.00	96.00	97.00	98.00	99.00	100.00	101.00	102.00	103.00	104.00	105.00
P&L	-99340	-82565	-62890	-42441	-20362	0	16067	28327	39003	47548	51874
Delta	1084	1468	1722	1802	1756	1596	1378	1159	953	775	650
Gamma	362	320	217	94	-22	-104	-142	-151	-145	-132	-113
Theta	-315	-361	-344	-274	-196	-119	-50	4	32	45	67
Vega	6817	6876	5678	3692	1644	-104	-1334	-2061	-2378	-2434	-2419

Demand-Products Skew

Price:	95.00	96.00	97.00	98.00	99.00	100.00	101.00	102.00	103.00	104.00	105.00
P&L	-55381	-52291	-50923	-41853	-23498	0	28982	50924	70243	96667	117965
Delta	427	542	681	916	1240	1550	1751	1859	1878	1574	1241
Gamma	103	126	161	187	185	134	24	-86	-199	-291	-285
Theta	150	162	199	212	208	229	259	349	448	421	358
Vega	1080	1191	1225	1165	766	-335	-2109	-4465	-7165	-8448	-9168

EXHIBIT 10-15A (comment and profile page 265)
Flat or No Skew

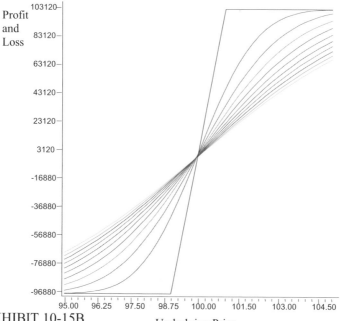

EXHIBIT 10-15B
Crash Skew

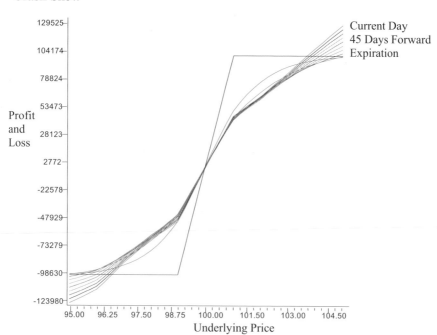

EXHIBIT 10-15C
Supply-Products Skew

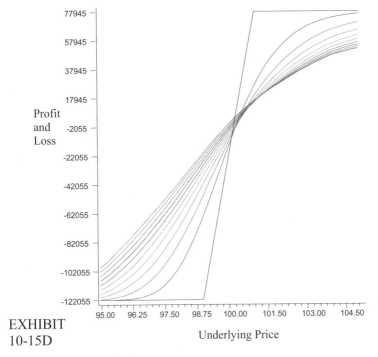

Underlying Price

EXHIBIT
10-15D
Demand-Products Skew

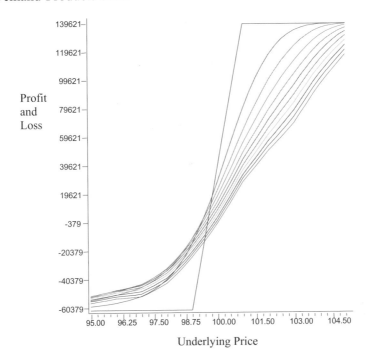

Underlying Price

EXHIBIT 10-16A (comment and profile page 270)
Flat or No Skew

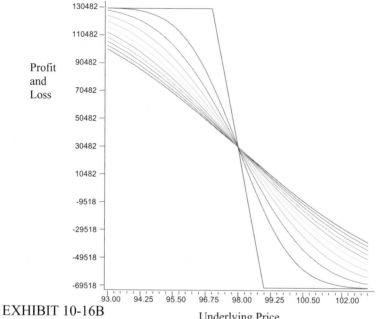

EXHIBIT 10-16B
Crash Skew

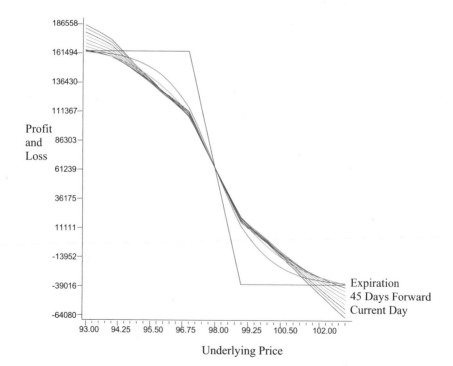

EXHIBIT 10-16C
Supply-Products Skew

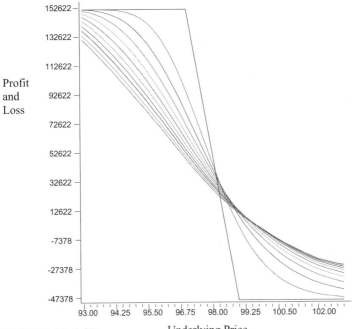

Profit and Loss

Underlying Price

EXHIBIT 10-16D
Demand-Products Skew

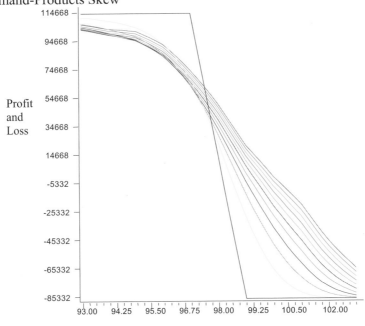

Profit and Loss

Underlying Price

BEAR SPREAD

The bond and index skews lose less on the upside and profit more on the downside simply because the skew makes the bear spreads extra cheap to begin with (see Exhibit 10–16).

The crash skew causes the beaar spread to react in a way similar to the bond and index skews on a rally, but it loses more than they do on a break.

The graphs suggest that demand products and currency skews work more favorably with bull spreads, as shown in Exhibit 10–15.

Underlying Price

Flat or No Skew

Price:	93.00	94.00	95.00	96.00	97.00	98.00	99.00	100.00	101.00	102.00	103.00
P&L	101116	90111	77258	62829	47276	31194	15229	0	-13965	-26295	-36785
Delta	-1005	-1196	-1371	-1508	-1592	-1613	-1569	-1467	-1319	-1143	-954
Gamma	-192	-186	-159	-113	-53	12	75	128	165	186	189
Theta	267	259	225	167	89	1	-86	-164	-222	-258	-270
Vega	-4596	-4333	-3676	-2636	-1298	198	1680	2983	3980	4600	4832

Crash Skew

Price:	93.00	94.00	95.00	96.00	97.00	98.00	99.00	100.00	101.00	102.00	103.00
P&L	186558	174423	150694	129300	112732	63807	17567	0	-21614	-43518	-64080
Delta	-188	-388	-731	-1070	-1345	-1495	-1361	-1071	-759	-471	-251
Gamma	-137	-170	-177	-173	-154	16	170	179	176	157	131
Theta	-344	-270	-146	-84	-107	9	110	97	160	272	405
Vega	-468	-890	-1402	-1488	-896	193	1282	1819	1748	1299	767

Supply-Products Skew

Price:	93.00	94.00	95.00	96.00	97.00	98.00	99.00	100.00	101.00	102.00	103.00
P&L	131585	113449	92969	71893	49368	28684	12390	0	-10692	-19190	-23496
Delta	-1230	-1551	-1782	-1852	-1798	-1629	-1399	-1171	-956	-772	-642
Gamma	-292	-295	-209	-90	28	113	152	160	154	139	119
Theta	334	381	367	298	219	141	69	14	-15	-28	-50
Vega	-7743	-7275	-5887	-3802	-1691	100	1350	2078	2385	2427	2394

Demand-Products Skew

Price:	93.00	94.00	95.00	96.00	97.00	98.00	99.00	100.00	101.00	102.00	103.00
P&L	106996	103813	102257	93092	74709	51123	22085	0	-19228	-44764	-63961
Delta	-441	-559	-701	-940	-1270	-1580	-1776	-1864	-1843	-1481	-1036
Gamma	-105	-128	-164	-189	-185	-129	-11	109	239	346	378
Theta	-118	-130	-167	-180	-178	-201	-234	-325	-424	-394	-322
Vega	-1117	-1230	-1263	-1200	-789	335	2132	4468	7018	7947	7673

AT-THE-MONEY BUTTERFLY

Notice that as the market rallies, the butterfly holds its value with the demand-products skew because, as all the options in the butterfly slide down the skew to loweer implied volatilities, the value of the whole butterfly is increasing (see Exhibit 10–17). When a butterfly is near to the money, it increases in value as implied volatility declines.

Flat or No Skew

Price:	90.00	92.00	94.00	96.00	98.00	100.00	102.00	104.00	106.00	108.00	110.00
P&L	-7128	-6062	-4387	-2393	-716	0	-481	-1863	-3531	-4917	-5847
Delta	38	69	96	98	64	5	-51	-82	-80	-56	-92
Gamma	14	16	9	-8	-25	-31	-23	-7	8	16	-152
Theta	-15	-18	-10	11	34	44	35	13	-7	-17	-44
Vega	274	314	163	-192	-578	-752	-608	-266	47	164	297

Crash Skew

Price:	90.00	92.00	94.00	96.00	98.00	100.00	102.00	104.00	106.00	108.00	110.00
P&L	-104808	-124294	-90291	-58428	-57482	0	-57061	-53725	-93253	-146815	-108295
Delta	-17	-139	124	537	622	52	-567	-496	-98	157	13
Gamma	13	37	57	-15	-315	-14	37	55	39	148	
Theta	100	239	-36	-213	-49	-227	-47	-239	-11	404	148
Vega	-113	-408	303	926	-467	-2137	-495	956	248	-639	-222

Supply-Products Skew

Price:	90.00	92.00	94.00	96.00	98.00	100.00	102.00	104.00	106.00	108.00	110.00
P&L	-35714	-31996	-18388	-700	5582	0	-13092	-22950	-24608	-29183	-35871
Delta	23	294	728	636	59	-349	-404	-293	-231	-146	-49
Gamma	26	181	149	-133	-231	-121	-8	28	27	23	16
Theta	-11	-110	-179	-25	148	149	87	41	-22	-28	25
Vega	382	2874	3164	-1175	-3992	-2972	-1072	-69	459	495	141

Demand-Products Skew

Price:	90.00	92.00	94.00	96.00	98.00	100.00	102.00	104.00	106.00	108.00	110.00
P&L	-54148	-37833	-41876	-48215	-25149	0	-10796	-4097	-31528	-52405	-53261
Delta	15	181	212	263	577	540	151	-633	-1056	-228	0
Gamma	17	21	32	62	29	-160	-231	-93	-34	320	0
Theta	10	-124	-55	41	1	47	188	-94	-311	-63	0
Vega	45	534	439	165	-438	-2884	-5102	-1998	6780	2839	0

EXHIBIT 10-17A (comment and profile page 271)

Flat or No Skew

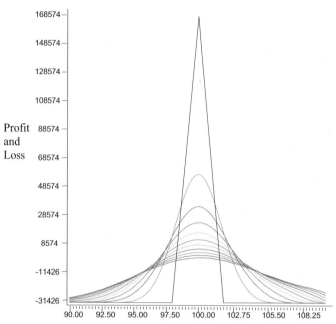

EXHIBIT 10-17B

Crash Skew

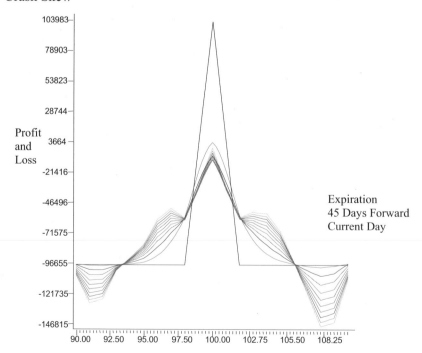

Underlying Price

EXHIBIT 10-17C
Supply-Products Skew

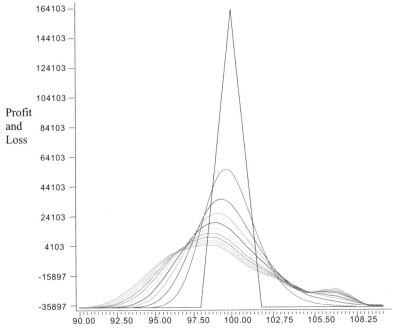

EXHIBIT 10-17D
Demand-Products Skew

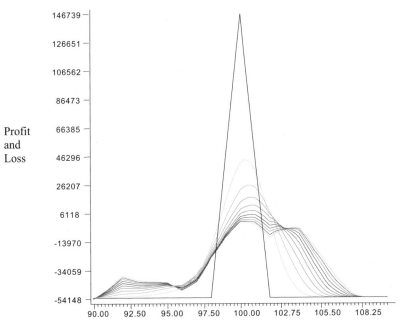

Underlying Price

EXHIBIT 10-18A (comment and profile page 276)

Flat or No Skew

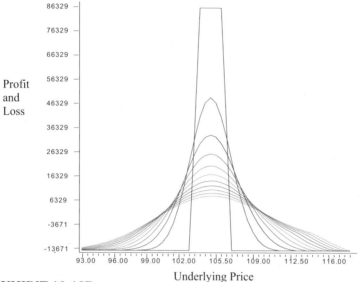

EXHIBIT 10-18B

Crash Skew

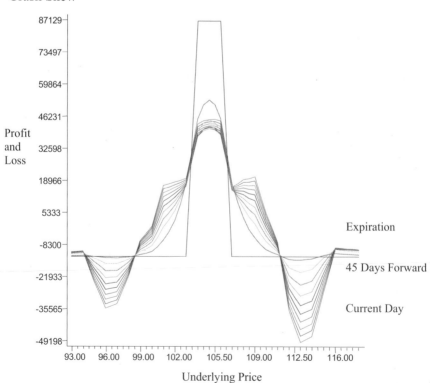

EXHIBIT 10-18C

Supply-Products Skew

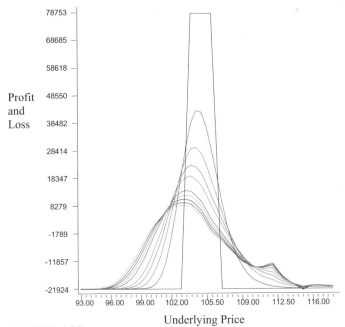

EXHIBIT 10-18D

Demand-Products Skew

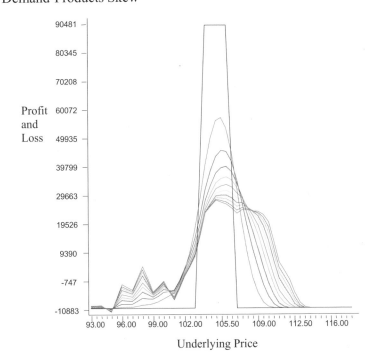

STRETCHED-OUT CONDOR

The stretched-out condor's profits more on a break with the bond and index skews if very little time passes because the lower strike spreads are cheaper (see Exhibit 10–18). They are cheap because implied volatilities are higher for the lower strikes. With a significant amount of time to go (89 days in this case), high implied volatility levels make butterflies and multi-strike butterflies cheaper because high implied volatility suggests that there is going to be a move away from the current range.

The crash skew causes the far away-from-the-money options to be priced at much higher implied volatilities than the close ones. This makes the at-the-money stretched-out condor more expensive to begin with. As the underlying moves away from the middle range, it has more to lose than if the skew were flat.

Flat or No Skew

Price:	93.00	95.50	98.00	100.50	103.00	105.50	108.00	110.50	113.00	115.50	118.00
P&L	-12503	-10024	-5189	1335	6932	8712	5974	693	-4302	-8813	-13508
Delta	60	144	239	264	162	-25	-180	-223	-164	-240	-72
Gamma	25	40	30	-14	-65	-76	-42	6	37	42	166
Theta	-30	-49	-38	22	97	121	73	0	-42	-113	-34
Vega	556	864	637	-402	-1650	-2059	-1322	-190	400	2245	1390

Crash Skew

Price:	93.00	95.50	98.00	100.50	103.00	105.50	108.00	110.50	113.00	115.50	118.00
P&L	-10975	-29052	-21295	8436	20408	45468	19898	-621	-49198	-18513	-10108
Delta	35	-65	-9	295	464	-105	-401	-147	98	-4	-28
Gamma	4	15	33	37	-20	-155	7	37	27	5	2
Theta	-1	146	69	-123	-69	-119	-128	-75	284	81	10
Vega	73	-224	-35	558	-310	-1349	298	372	-417	-110	26

Supply-Products Skew

Price:	93.00	95.50	98.00	100.50	103.00	105.50	108.00	110.50	113.00	115.50	118.00
P&L	-21245	-20642	-12714	2497	8887	1957	-7885	-13487	-16888	-20993	-20467
Delta	0	59	425	467	12	-273	-254	-166	-98	-36	-28
Gamma	1	51	140	-67	-153	-55	10	20	16	10	6
Theta	0	-26	-132	-38	108	98	39	2	-11	15	4
Vega	9	833	2797	-423	-2926	-1774	-333	216	305	114	119

Demand-Products Skew

Price:	93.00	95.50	98.00	100.50	103.00	105.50	108.00	110.50	113.00	115.50	118.00
P&L	-8643	-6095	5114	-3357	8694	27839	25010	13725	-7815	-9519	-9519
Delta	15	46	170	183	389	329	-198	-751	-321	0	0
Gamma	7	13	16	35	23	-120	-140	-156	328	0	0
Theta	-7	-27	-103	2	17	62	44	-208	-94	0	0
Vega	49	143	451	197	-388	-2536	-2726	3347	3893	0	0

CALL RATIO SPREAD

Call ratio spreads theoretically perform better to the upside with the currency and demand-products skews, providing overall implied volatility levels do not increase as well (see Exhibit 10–19). However, implied volatility usually does increase as these markets rally. The reward is theoretically better than it is with other skews because the spread is initiated for better than flat skew prices, and traders have the two options sliding down the skew in their favor instead of only one long option hurting them. It makes sense that if someone is willing to take on the risk of a call ratio spread in one of these markets, that the reward should be proportionately greater than that with a flat skew. Call ratio spreaders who were trading the Japanese yen during the first half of 1995 are probably now working in the back office.

Flat or No Skew

Price:	90.00	92.50	95.00	97.50	100.00	102.50	105.00	107.50	110.00	112.50	115.00
P&L	-22640	-18989	-11538	-2381	0	-16991	-62762	-137982	-235710	-349365	-474147
Delta	85	219	366	309	-208	-1219	-2447	-3521	-4233	-4895	-5000
Gamma	39	65	37	-102	-315	-474	-482	-363	-207	-261	0
Theta	-43	-76	-43	137	436	686	729	571	345	47	0
Vega	806	1308	581	-2682	-7905	-12274	-13255	-10939	-7476	-1949	0

Crash Skew

Price:	93.00	95.50	98.00	100.50	103.00	105.50	108.00	110.50	113.00	115.50	118.00
P&L	-88646	-82725	-30673	19582	52323	-1075	-129104	-333560	-450514	-559162	-671248
Delta	-1218	-1240	-799	-598	-1828	-3113	-3484	-3398	-3606	-3808	-3968
Gamma	-72	-53	-70	-268	-517	-379	-226	-139	-114	-96	-81
Theta	1430	1292	861	664	493	332	492	1229	1321	1303	1280
Vega	-7304	-7591	-7121	-9202	-11654	-10057	-9254	-9895	-9475	-8877	-8310

Supply-Product Skew

Price:	93.00	95.50	98.00	100.50	103.00	105.50	108.00	110.50	113.00	115.50	118.00
P&L	-54151	-39762	-10803	-769	-38516	-115546	-212843	-325761	-447037	-569058	-692431
Delta	113	776	938	-208	-1734	-2843	-3531	-3901	-4094	-4228	-4321
Gamma	96	261	-100	-482	-503	-378	-265	-187	-138	-107	-85
Theta	-48	-233	-93	310	569	636	604	591	624	645	670
Vega	1487	4969	-272	-8703	-11905	-11231	-9525	-8160	-7361	-6732	-6276

Demand-Product Skew

Price:	93.00	95.50	98.00	100.50	103.00	105.50	108.00	110.50	113.00	115.50	118.00
P&L	-42880	-23865	-20554	7474	34450	17537	-58282	-181999	-306999	-431999	-556999
Delta	-1051	-930	-880	-647	-1088	-2646	-4658	-5000	-5000	-5000	-5000
Gamma	-76	-82	-74	-164	-490	-638	-480	0	0	0	0
Theta	1189	975	928	834	836	666	95	0	0	0	0
Vega	-6774	-6742	-7374	-9296	-14240	-15859	-4259	0	0	0	0

EXHIBIT 10-19A (comment and profile page 277)
Flat or No Skew

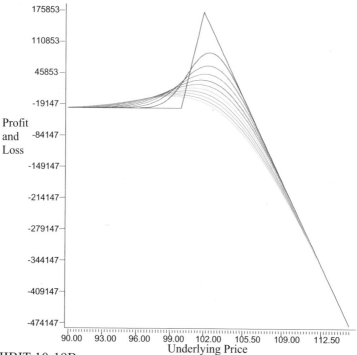

EXHIBIT 10-19B
Crash Skew

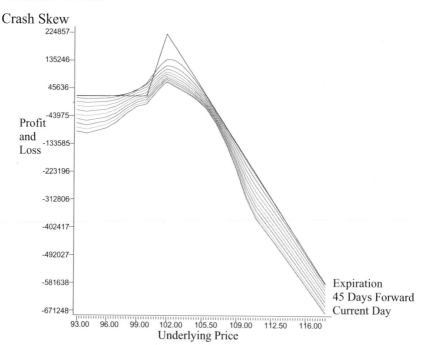

EXHIBIT 10-19C
Supply-Products Skew

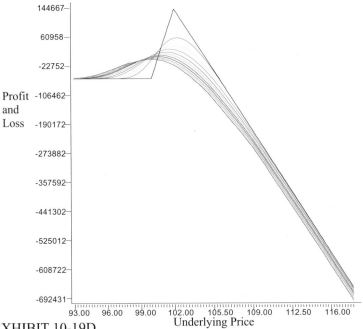

EXHIBIT 10-19D
Demand-Products Skew

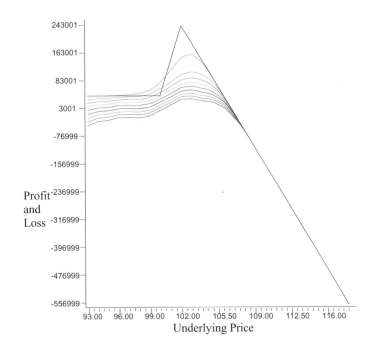

EXHIBIT 10-20A (comment and profile page 282)
Flat or No Skew

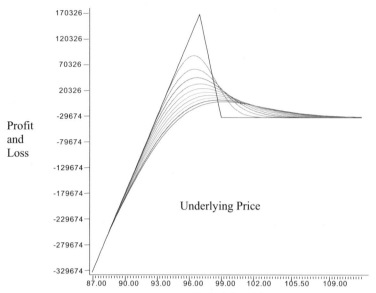

EXHIBIT 10-20B
Crash Skew

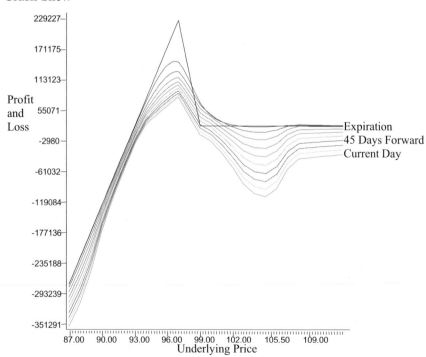

EXHIBIT 10-20C
Supply-Products Skew

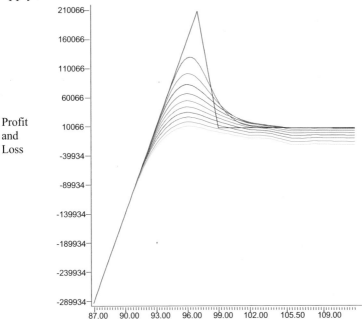

Underlying Price

EXHIBIT 10-20D
Demand-Products Skew

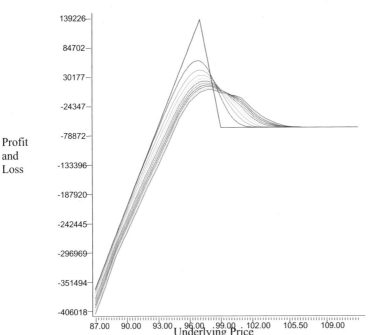

Underlying Price

PUT RATIO SPREAD

Put ratio spreads theoretically perform better to the downside with the bond and index skews, providing that the overall implied volatility level does not increase as well (see Exhibit 10–20). Implied volatility usually does increase as these markets break though. The reward is theoretically better than that for the other skews because the spread was initiated for better than flat skew prices, and traders have the two short options sliding down the skew in their favor instead of only one long option hurting them. If someone is willing to take on the risk of a put ratio spread in one of these markets, the reward should be proportionately greater than it would be with a flat skew. Put ratio spreads destroyed a lot of European bond option traders in 1994 when the bonds fell out of bed.

Flat or No Skew

Price:	87.00	89.50	92.00	94.50	97.00	99.50	102.00	104.50	107.00	109.50	112.00
P&L	-329674	-211404	-114349	-44367	-7745	615	-6310	-16423	-23733	-27498	-29009
Delta	5000	4262	3413	2137	828	-67	-403	-367	-216	-95	-34
Gamma	0	-234	-442	-551	-463	-242	-41	52	59	36	15
Theta	0	268	514	678	604	335	63	-76	-92	-58	-26
Vega	0	-6060	-9822	-12251	-10782	-6112	-1371	1183	1606	1086	524

Crash Skew

Price:	87.00	89.50	92.00	94.50	97.00	99.50	102.00	104.50	107.00	109.50	112.00
P&L	-351291	-209736	-56511	40416	82708	5846	-49750	-102261	-52800	-30166	-25546
Delta	3568	3509	3460	2683	1075	407	824	1068	772	612	537
Gamma	-161	-210	-322	-494	-564	-114	-29	-39	-63	-57	-48
Theta	920	659	320	355	408	698	1036	1518	1227	1068	1039
Vega	-7330	-7617	-7919	-9744	-10380	-7233	-6923	-7664	-6686	-5946	-5515

Supply-Products Skew

Price:	87.00	89.50	92.00	94.50	97.00	99.50	102.00	104.50	107.00	109.50	112.00
P&L	-289934	-164934	-50894	3856	11947	1370	-7190	-11075	-18790	-17959	-19058
Delta	5000	5000	3837	1894	622	302	320	349	413	378	361
Gamma	0	0	-735	-677	-382	-145	-71	-54	-48	-44	-39
Theta	0	0	318	733	734	602	536	523	604	611	644
Vega	0	0	-9637	-14511	-11175	-7003	-5099	-4413	-4479	-4221	-4106

Demand-Products Skew

Price:	87.00	89.50	92.00	94.50	97.00	99.50	102.00	104.50	107.00	109.50	112.00
P&L	-406018	-278143	-171666	-67525	4402	2800	-25651	-54274	-60658	-60774	-60774
Delta	3843	3706	3260	2554	1150	-540	-1136	-428	-14	0	0
Gamma	-172	-227	-308	-445	-595	-346	158	236	16	0	0
Theta	595	488	526	464	337	84	-265	-165	-7	0	0
Vega	-6463	-7076	-8495	-9929	-10274	-4772	4416	4560	303	1	0

CALL BACK SPREAD

Notice the properties of the cash and demand-products skews on a move to the downside (see Exhibit 10–21). They do much better than the bond, index, and flat skews because all of the options in the spread swim to higher and higher levels of implied volatility. Since there are more long than short options in a back spread, these two skews provide a better performance in the downward direction than do the others because of the skews' steep incline. The incline causes all of the options in the spread to climb to higher implied volatility levels very quickly.

Flat or No Skew

Price:	90.00	92.50	95.00	97.50	100.00	102.50	105.00	107.50	110.00	112.50	115.00
P&L	-18681	-20139	-22061	-19555	0	54600	158534	314001	511217	735994	981970
Delta	-36	-80	-44	331	1362	3110	5221	7148	8529	9455	10000
Gamma	-16	-13	60	265	567	808	842	674	430	396	0
Theta	17	15	-75	-345	-775	-1154	-1249	-1022	-642	-250	0
Vega	-304	-142	1677	6652	14245	20928	22871	19440	13291	6789	0

Crash Skew

Price:	90.00	92.50	95.00	97.50	100.00	102.50	105.00	107.50	110.00	112.50	115.00
P&L	43520	65330	111809	69480	0	-38859	64313	261804	580984	895938	1112996
Delta	1897	2177	2652	2578	2266	3264	5587	6922	7113	7228	7634
Gamma	180	202	206	235	397	831	772	509	313	226	191
Theta	-2224	-2310	-2517	-1991	-1376	-1091	-1061	-1063	-1816	-2573	-2543
Vega	12367	13738	15532	15812	16495	20766	21020	18496	18371	18534	17386

Supply-Products Skew

Price:	90.00	92.50	95.00	97.50	100.00	102.50	105.00	107.50	110.00	112.50	115.00
P&L	22327	22238	17778	13	0	62407	205347	399305	611990	854926	1098442
Delta	0	-12	-322	-662	643	3175	5427	6853	7767	8172	8458
Gamma	0	-14	-183	19	662	923	765	548	390	283	217
Theta	0	6	121	111	-436	-968	-1199	-1239	-1146	-1224	-1266
Vega	-1	-221	-3112	-707	11959	20772	21586	19178	16173	14591	13303

Demand-Products Skew

Price:	90.00	92.50	95.00	97.50	100.00	102.50	105.00	107.50	110.00	112.50	115.00
P&L	53836	40170	8152	-2913	0	-22413	26695	143895	362735	612735	862735
Delta	2203	2262	2192	2295	2543	3043	4866	7753	10000	10000	10000
Gamma	173	194	230	278	343	648	973	1051	0	0	0
Theta	-2655	-2384	-1954	-1726	-1613	-1395	-1303	-667	0	0	0
Vega	13389	13955	14156	15128	17066	21142	25597	19809	0	0	0

EXHIBIT 10-21A   (comment and profile page 283)
Flat or No Skew

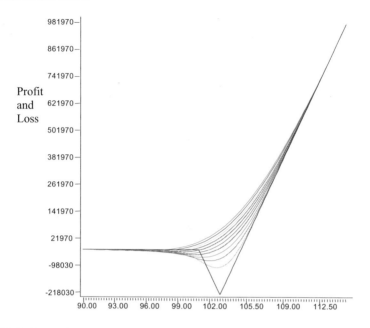

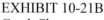

Underlying Price

EXHIBIT 10-21B
Crash Skew

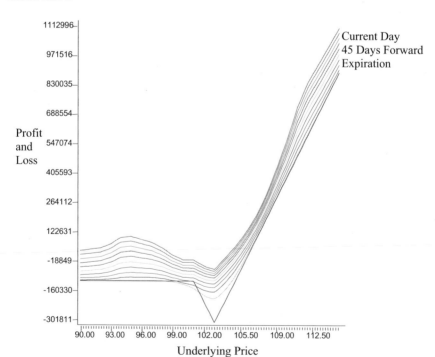

Underlying Price

EXHIBIT 10-21C

Supply-Products Skew

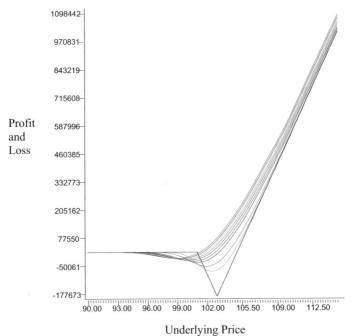

Underlying Price

EXHIBIT 10-21D
Demand-Products Skew

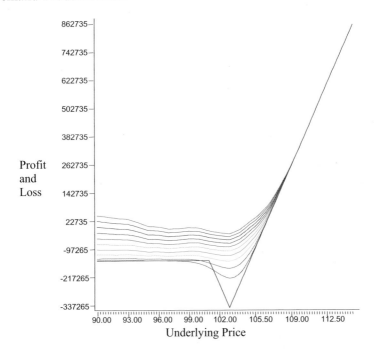

Underlying Price

EXHIBIT 10-22A (comment and profile page 288)
Flat or No Skew

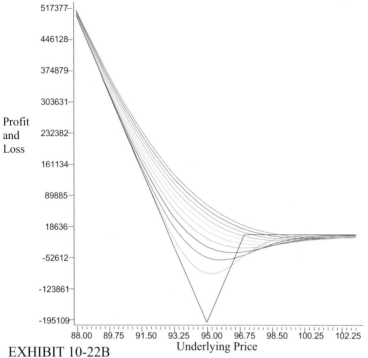

EXHIBIT 10-22B
Crash Skew

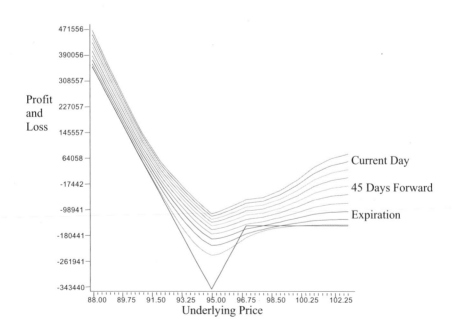

EXHIBIT 10-22C
Supply-Products Skew

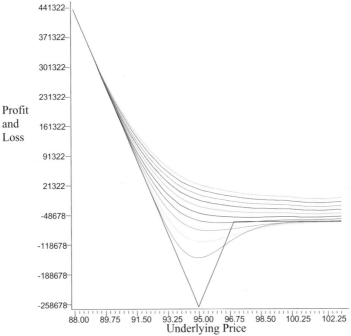

EXHIBIT 10-22D
Demand-Products Skew

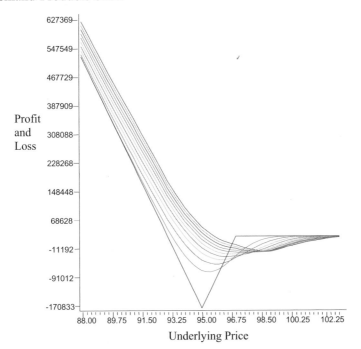

PUT BACK SPREAD

The demand-products and currency skews perform best as the market breaks for two reasons (see Exhibit 10–22). First, the spreads are discounted. The options bought are skewed cheaper relative to the ones that are sold. Second, as options go into-the-money, all of the spread's options climb up the right side of the skew. Since the back spread has more longs than shorts, the results of demand-products and currency skews are better than those of other skew shapes.

Flat or No Skew

Price:	88.00	89.50	91.00	92.50	94.00	95.50	97.00	98.50	100.00	101.50	103.00
P&L	517377	390225	277525	183387	110360	58598	25774	7806	0	-1882	-998
Delta	-8857	-8044	-6933	-5587	-4145	-2780	-1641	-807	-281	-5	102
Gamma	442	644	832	948	954	848	662	449	258	118	33
Theta	-406	-657	-907	-1088	-1143	-1055	-853	-599	-357	-169	-50
Vega	9054	13192	17232	20057	20766	19101	15552	11115	6837	3448	1212

Crash Skew

Price:	88.00	89.50	91.00	92.50	94.00	95.50	97.00	98.50	100.00	101.50	103.00
P&L	471556	302807	146057	29206	-55740	-96955	-60901	-43010	0	54691	83012
Delta	-7253	-7143	-6837	-5943	-4523	-2953	-2065	-1917	-2074	-2258	-2226
Gamma	402	503	657	829	956	865	470	310	216	174	161
Theta	-1316	-1043	-854	-897	-975	-1005	-1239	-1373	-1748	-2274	-2619
Vega	14331	14854	15854	17918	19654	18936	16363	14725	14686	15303	15379

Supply-Products Skew

Price:	88.00	89.50	91.00	92.50	94.00	95.50	97.00	98.50	100.00	101.50	103.00
P&L	441322	296286	181367	100343	48013	23583	10991	3165	0	-5394	-2763
Delta	-10000	-9138	-7343	-5505	-3860	-2676	-1988	-1590	-1358	-1169	-1099
Gamma	0	822	949	1120	987	723	506	368	279	226	187
Theta	0	-225	-709	-1063	-1207	-1220	-1159	-1092	-1059	-1016	-1058
Vega	0	7853	17676	21920	21892	19286	16224	13798	12137	10868	10278

Demand-Products Skew

Price:	88.00	89.50	91.00	92.50	94.00	95.50	97.00	98.50	100.00	101.50	103.00
P&L	627369	490193	359655	226988	110262	36541	5817	-12631	0	16012	25985
Delta	-7430	-7037	-6471	-5752	-4626	-2953	-1221	268	824	672	247
Gamma	421	502	607	760	948	1026	836	470	6	-242	-166
Theta	-1188	-1176	-1163	-1053	-917	-788	-564	-124	148	212	100
Vega	13862	15199	16768	18210	19382	18850	14634	6431	-1278	-4846	-3017

RISK CONVERSION

This risk conversion spread, common for Market Makers in Demand-Products, has the elements of a put back spread and a call ratio spread, so its properties will be consistent with merging those two (see Exhibit 10–23). It does not even matter that the delta is short at the starting point of 100 for the crash, currency, and demand-products skews. The short options are sliding down the skew as the market rallies, and they yield a profit for a small move upward. In this example, it is possible to see that the deltas at the beginning have to be overridden by another Greek, such as iota.

Flat or No Skew

Price:	90.00	92.00	94.00	96.00	98.00	100.00	102.00	104.00	106.00	108.00	110.00
P&L	171808	99806	46055	13911	1368	0	-2352	-16826	-49775	-101950	-170270
Delta	-3968	-3185	-2157	-1071	-254	12	-344	-1158	-2143	-3048	-3748
Gamma	325	460	552	504	287	-28	-315	-475	-489	-406	-294
Theta	-215	-439	-608	-601	-362	36	430	665	690	554	351
Vega	5026	8951	11559	11005	6503	-664	-7736	-12181	-13052	-11063	-7655

Crash Skew

Price:	90.00	92.00	94.00	96.00	98.00	100.00	102.00	104.00	106.00	108.00	110.00
P&L	103453	18759	-33129	-43442	-21352	0	-251	-34047	-84268	-153046	-229075
Delta	-4600	-3824	-2228	-466	420	61	-992	-2061	-2910	-3442	-3791
Gamma	0	490	783	752	291	-181	-398	-388	-307	-224	-164
Theta	0	-212	-607	-867	-766	-419	-126	36	12	-31	-100
Vega	0	6424	14056	16484	10477	1454	-4577	-6640	-6109	-5040	-3930

Supply-Products Skew

Price:	90.00	92.00	94.00	96.00	98.00	100.00	102.00	104.00	106.00	108.00	110.00
P&L	151572	26389	-87947	-123710	-86496	0	84281	131947	95458	-31461	-185934
Delta	-3979	-4065	-3924	-2942	-1573	-920	-1519	-2823	-3672	-3801	-3676
Gamma	128	204	337	446	320	-26	-343	-426	-308	-182	-105
Theta	511	838	1076	833	434	28	-372	-865	-1099	-765	-216
Vega	1551	1189	1343	2595	2097	-596	-3284	-3559	-2473	-2538	-3327

Demand-Products Skew

Price:	90.00	92.00	94.00	96.00	98.00	100.00	102.00	104.00	106.00	108.00	110.00
P&L	207862	134144	70796	13433	-13647	0	47689	82484	77138	28591	-54050
Delta	-4326	-4028	-3513	-2706	-1450	-168	356	-539	-2247	-3774	-4600
Gamma	147	203	284	406	441	202	-317	-737	-725	-451	0
Theta	911	783	633	569	596	762	939	947	655	248	0
Vega	494	1316	2407	3205	2000	-3660	-12685	-18500	-15851	-7896	0

EXHIBIT 10-23 (comment and profile page 289)
Flat or No Skew

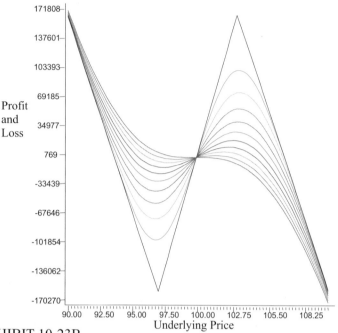

EXHIBIT 10-23B

Crash Skew

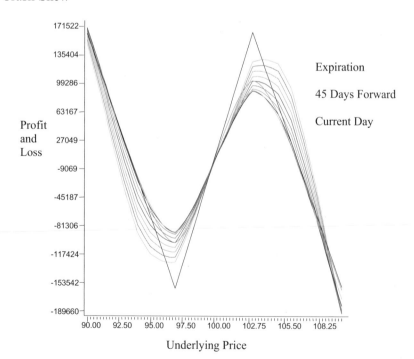

EXHIBIT 10-23C

Supply-Products Skew

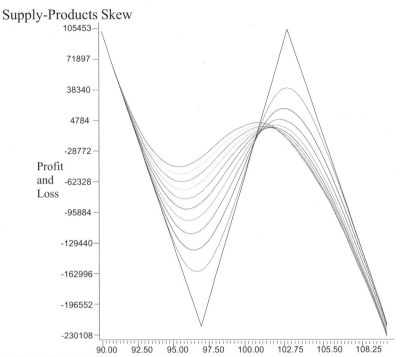

Underlying Price

EXHIBIT 10-23D

Demand-Products Skew

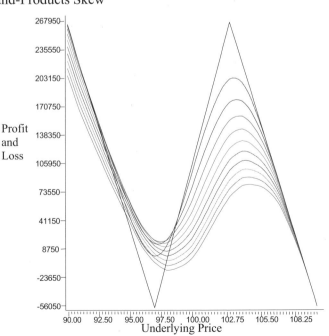

Underlying Price

EXHIBIT 10-24A (comment and profile page 295)
Flat or No Skew

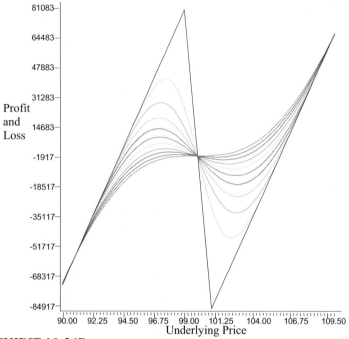

EXHIBIT 10-24B
Crash Skew

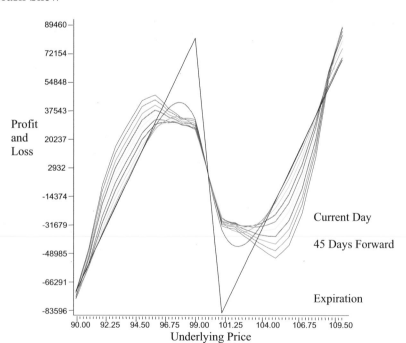

EXHIBIT 10-24C
Supply-Products Skew

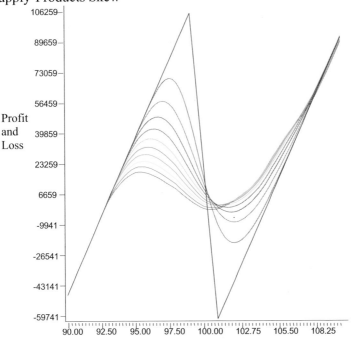

EXHIBIT 10-24D
Demand-Products Skew

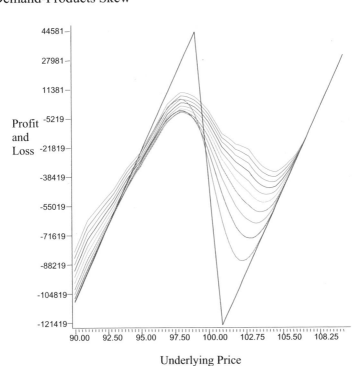

Underlying Price

RISK REVERSAL

This risk reversal spread, common for Market Makers in Supply-Products, has the elements of a call back spread and a put ratio spread, so its properties will be consistent with merging those two (see Exhibit 10–24).

Flat or No Skew

Price:	90.00	92.00	94.00	96.00	98.00	100.00	102.00	104.00	106.00	108.00	110.00
P&L	-70676	-40938	-19112	-5970	-693	0	980	6734	19785	40477	67879
Delta	1671	1297	877	443	112	-1	138	459	848	1212	1519
Gamma	-183	-197	-221	-202	-118	9	124	187	194	168	141
Theta	-21	86	174	199	129	-11	-149	-220	-206	-131	-32
Vega	-200	-2536	-4024	-4140	-2561	199	2937	4540	4612	3449	1539

Crash Skew

Price:	90.00	92.00	94.00	96.00	98.00	100.00	102.00	104.00	106.00	108.00	110.00
P&L	-70159	-6145	31825	48295	34199	0	-32575	-45086	-42591	10587	89356
Delta	1356	1518	1493	1213	538	115	528	1122	1436	1396	1261
Gamma	-40	-66	-109	-173	-174	13	176	160	105	56	30
Theta	-157	-422	-455	-341	-127	-3	116	319	533	391	22
Vega	-688	-183	-237	-846	-1445	194	1790	1271	485	674	1307

Supply-Products Skew

Price:	90.00	92.00	94.00	96.00	98.00	100.00	102.00	104.00	106.00	108.00	110.00
P&L	-46741	-12714	14305	19162	10847	0	3352	15978	38963	59043	90820
Delta	1700	1704	1002	135	-221	-16	430	826	1079	1311	1385
Gamma	0	5	-385	-338	-98	107	158	141	107	81	59
Theta	0	-2	175	325	262	131	32	14	13	102	104
Vega	1	86	-5157	-6822	-3690	103	2045	2383	2164	1438	1214

Demand-Products Skew

Price:	90.00	92.00	94.00	96.00	98.00	100.00	102.00	104.00	106.00	108.00	110.00
P&L	-80095	-53172	-32633	-10962	10259	0	-19108	-31833	-28995	-2425	31581
Delta	1568	1481	1293	1045	665	32	-256	117	1010	1701	1700
Gamma	-52	-70	-95	-131	-189	-130	103	348	367	-1	0
Theta	-395	-335	-241	-198	-224	-217	-313	-362	-189	1	0
Vega	-59	-324	-807	-1180	-1165	333	4406	7918	5941	-26	0

SHORT SEMI-FUTURE

When observing Exhibit 10–25, notice that the range is between 97.50 and 102.50. This is necessary to display the subtle differences between the skews. For example, when comparing the demand-products skew to the index skew, we can see that the demand-products skew causes less of a loss on a rally than the index skew and profits more on a break.

Flat or No Skew

Price:	98.00	98.40	98.80	99.20	99.60	100.00	100.40	100.80	101.20	101.60	102.00
P&L	200031	159758	119667	79710	39837	0	-39853	-79771	-119801	-159988	-200375
Delta	-10095	-10044	-10004	-9977	-9962	-9959	-9969	-9992	-10026	-10070	-10125
Gamma	141	113	84	53	21	-10	-41	-71	-99	-125	-149
Theta	-154	-125	-93	-59	-23	13	49	85	119	150	179
Vega	3073	2485	1847	1173	473	-239	-949	-1645	-2313	-2943	-3524

Crash Skew

Price:	98.00	98.40	98.80	99.20	99.60	100.00	100.40	100.80	101.20	101.60	102.00
P&L	158161	118124	78753	47220	23433	0	-24822	-49891	-81742	-120585	-160110
Delta	-10606	-10476	-10345	-10217	-10132	-10098	-10125	-10198	-10322	-10460	-10593
Gamma	209	203	193	147	67	-15	-91	-164	-203	-210	-212
Theta	152	153	159	130	66	4	-51	-108	-136	-135	-139
Vega	1734	1532	1234	824	319	-233	-788	-1293	-1694	-1970	-2148

Supply-Products Skew

Price:	98.00	98.40	98.80	99.20	99.60	100.00	100.40	100.80	101.20	101.60	102.00
P&L	186183	149552	112681	75542	38029	0	-39273	-79146	-119815	-161255	-203223
Delta	-9695	-9696	-9724	-9778	-9852	-9941	-10045	-10153	-10263	-10371	-10476
Gamma	118	56	0	-50	-93	-128	-152	-170	-181	-187	-189
Theta	-314	-284	-252	-219	-187	-158	-127	-101	-77	-56	-38
Vega	4429	3431	2448	1510	646	-124	-793	-1353	-1810	-2173	-2454

Demand-Products Skew

Price:	98.00	98.40	98.80	99.20	99.60	100.00	100.40	100.80	101.20	101.60	102.00
P&L	186889	147687	109258	71869	35511	0	-34000	-67359	-102580	-139666	-176271
Delta	-10758	-10608	-10449	-10291	-10141	-9998	-9885	-9797	-9731	-9679	-9653
Gamma	227	229	226	213	189	156	108	50	-7	-62	-124
Theta	269	258	252	250	253	260	267	277	301	339	376
Vega	1397	1283	1070	725	234	-400	-1164	-2042	-3030	-4126	-5287

EXHIBIT 10-25A (comment and profile page 295)

Flat or No Skew

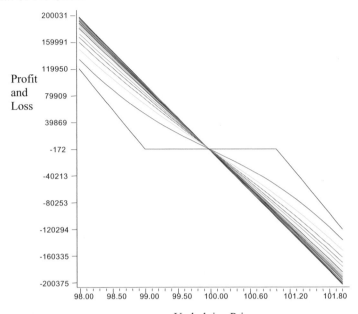

EXHIBIT 10-25B

Crash Skew

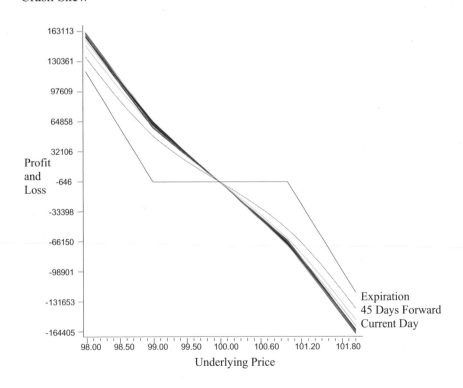

EXHIBIT 10-25C
Supply-Products Skew

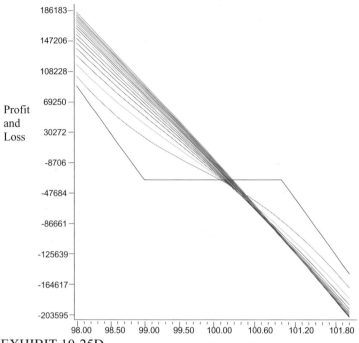

EXHIBIT 10-25D
Demand-Products Skew

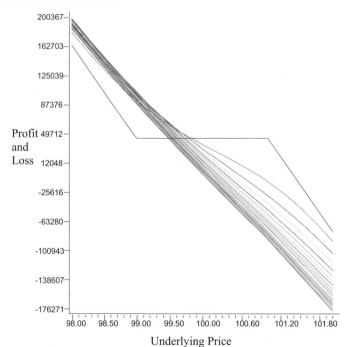

EXHIBIT 10-26A (comment and profile page 300)
Flat or No Skew

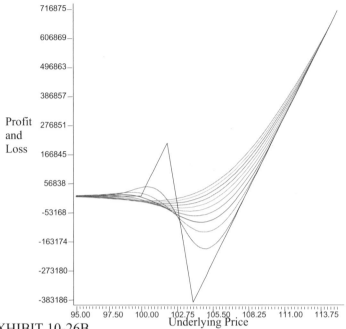

EXHIBIT 10-26B
Crash Skew

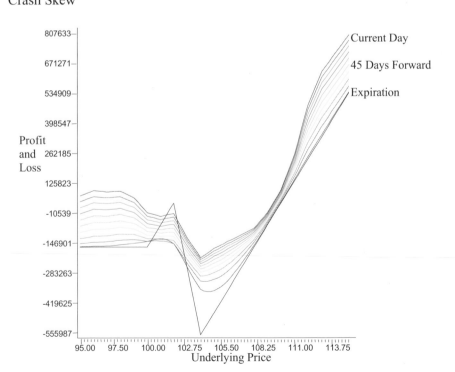

EXHIBIT 10-26C
Supply-Products Skew

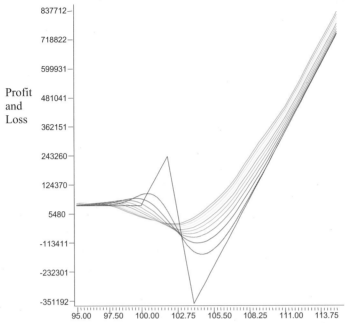

Profit
and
Loss

Underlying Price

EXHIBIT 10-26D
Demand-Products Skew

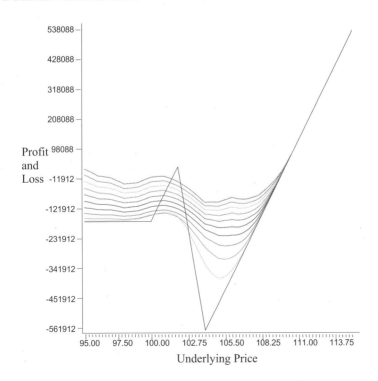

Profit
and
Loss

Underlying Price

CALL BATWINGS

Exhibit 10-26. Call Batwings and slingshots are a nice way to play the skew in Beans because, on balance, you have a lot of beefy options smimming down the skew.

Flat or No Skew

Price:	95.00	97.00	99.00	101.00	103.00	105.00	107.00	109.00	111.00	113.00	115.00
P&L	14496	9469	2599	-558	10401	47624	119947	229376	371193	532828	716875
Delta	-175	-322	-319	94	1110	2692	4560	6345	7723	8421	9918
Gamma	-75	-56	82	350	665	893	942	819	433	868	665
Theta	92	71	-112	-492	-968	-1346	-1465	-1303	-988	-731	-37
Vega	-1546	-887	2579	9295	17534	24104	26420	24082	18787	18357	3106

Crash Skew

Price:	95.00	97.00	99.00	101.00	103.00	105.00	107.00	109.00	111.00	113.00	115.00
P&L	76569	94305	67838	-17215	-115972	-163411	-101874	-340	265052	641118	807633
Delta	2506	2838	2838	1713	1115	3113	5521	6906	7041	6735	7138
Gamma	185	180	95	58	570	863	605	387	260	227	
Theta	-2905	-2869	-2409	-1628	-1297	-1171	-927	-490	-1130	-2689	-2690
Vega	15117	16240	15778	13719	18722	24123	22094	18774	18630	20338	19425

Supply-Products Skew

Price:	95.00	97.00	99.00	101.00	103.00	105.00	107.00	109.00	111.00	113.00	115.00
P&L	56508	52438	19954	-12817	-24895	38124	144849	304042	449982	645875	837712
Delta	320	-571	-1699	-1263	713	3134	5103	6297	7371	7774	8106
Gamma	13	-535	-352	396	964	996	827	623	477	360	283
Theta	-76	321	489	-21	-641	-1105	-1233	-1371	-1129	-1249	-1285
Vega	718	-8977	-8531	4896	18103	23738	23447	21733	18146	16753	15365

Demand-Products Skew

Price:	95.00	97.00	99.00	101.00	103.00	105.00	107.00	109.00	111.00	113.00	115.00
P&L	31041	-2514	-20199	3364	-49621	-92217	-81329	-22486	138088	338088	538088
Delta	2333	2208	2214	2319	1693	1971	3716	6609	10000	10000	10000
Gamma	176	199	230	116	213	737	1094	1812	0	0	0
Theta	-2541	-2124	-1862	-1852	-1565	-1617	-1703	-1027	0	0	0
Vega	14481	14299	14507	14695	16503	24684	33754	32524	0	0	0

PUT BATWINGS

Exhibit 10-27. Put Batwings and slingshots are a nice way to play the skew in Bonds because, on balance, you have a lot of beefy options smimming down the skew.

Flat or No Skew

Price:	85.00	87.00	89.00	91.00	93.00	95.00	97.00	99.00	101.00	103.00	105.00
P&L	725005	525381	351374	204593	93711	26544	-1621	-3870	5091	14940	21401
Delta	-10000	-9729	-7885	-6577	-4456	-2298	-631	279	530	421	227
Gamma	0	989	400	964	1117	993	650	269	8	-94	-90
Theta	0	-93	-760	-1068	-1315	-1231	-845	-368	-15	134	135
Vega	0	4104	15730	19920	23681	21947	15274	7057	819	-2049	-2318

Crash Skew

Price:	85.00	87.00	89.00	91.00	93.00	95.00	97.00	99.00	101.00	103.00	105.00
P&L	708870	535241	230686	27115	-126575	-167692	-112540	-18956	58571	140494	72176
Delta	-7320	-6881	-7311	-6918	-5655	-2750	-607	-1251	-2210	-2445	-1844
Gamma	310	355	490	694	1015	1129	518	12	73	120	154
Theta	-1789	-1832	-767	-588	-686	-1097	-1208	-1484	-2206	-3081	-2751
Vega	13825	15276	14265	15671	18819	21962	16485	11795	14106	15889	14259

Supply-Products Skew

Price:	85.00	87.00	89.00	91.00	93.00	95.00	97.00	99.00	101.00	103.00	105.00
P&L	651079	451079	251079	78431	4865	-19425	-3055	-2554	2800	-4462	17755
Delta	-10000	-10000	-10000	-6999	-3795	-1681	-972	-974	-992	-865	-1034
Gamma	0	0	0	1950	1204	873	322	192	155	145	124
Theta	0	0	0	-812	-1516	-1432	-1199	-1005	-1001	-953	-1221
Vega	0	0	0	24776	29104	22454	14459	10650	9561	8750	9569

Demand-Products Skew

Price:	85.00	87.00	89.00	91.00	93.00	95.00	97.00	99.00	101.00	103.00	105.00
P&L	857998	651458	462314	297150	132670	-18140	-34561	-3685	42504	75971	74475
Delta	-7766	-7603	-7190	-6351	-5181	-3284	-106	1967	1914	341	-405
Gamma	322	396	502	648	864	1195	1065	257	-584	-526	89
Theta	-1265	-1085	-1041	-1120	-1020	-708	-513	153	600	261	-123
Vega	12382	13189	14748	17263	19579	20774	16218	1155	-12508	-8941	2184

EXHIBIT 10-27A (comment and profile page 301)
Flat or No Skew

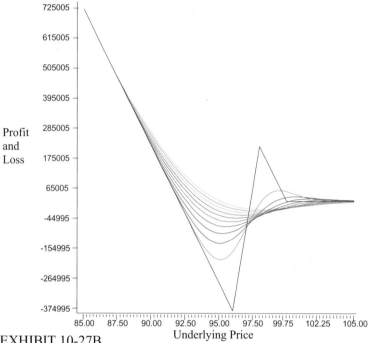

EXHIBIT 10-27B
Crash Skew

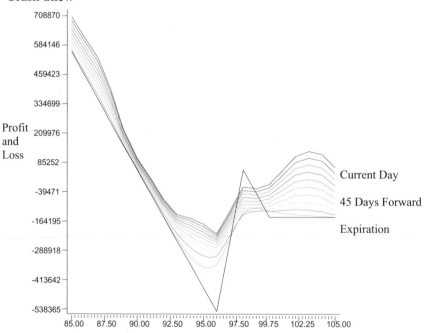

EXHIBIT 10-27C
Supply-Products Skew

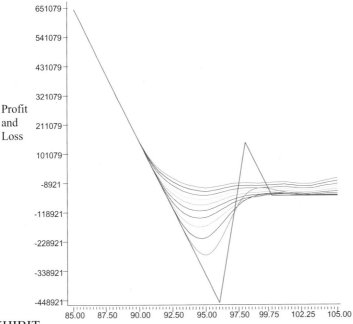

EXHIBIT
10-27D
Demand-Products Skew

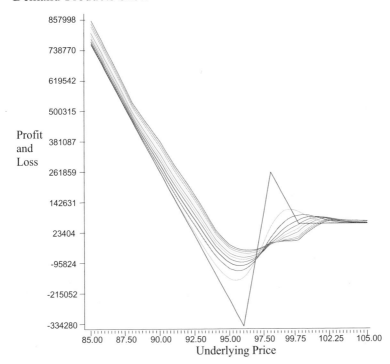

EXHIBIT 10-28A (comment and profile page 306)
Flat or No Skew

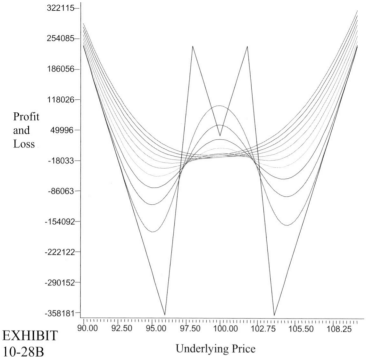

EXHIBIT
10-28B
Crash Skew

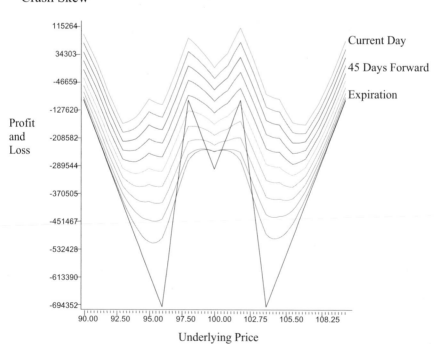

Current Day

45 Days Forward

Expiration

EXHIBIT 10-28C
Supply-Products Skew

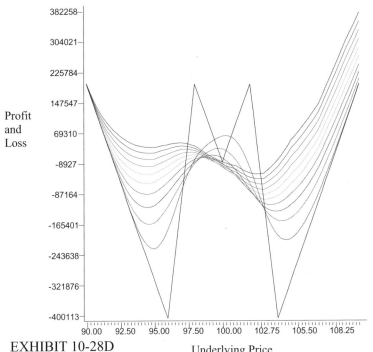

Profit and Loss

Underlying Price

EXHIBIT 10-28D
Demand-Products Skew

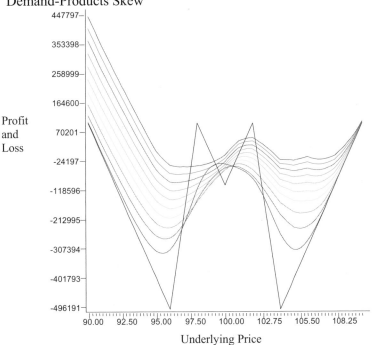

Profit and Loss

Underlying Price

BATMAN SPREADS

Flat or No Skew   (Batman spreads are really cool in 3-D)

Price:	90.00	92.00	94.00	96.00	98.00	100.00	102.00	104.00	106.00	108.00	110.00
P&L	291932	160858	70597	20637	1024	0	12679	43711	102346	195189	322115
Delta	-7384	-5576	-3452	-1631	-434	290	1023	2166	3759	5526	7116
Gamma	579	1046	1029	762	447	320	449	698	871	865	706
Theta	-892	-1197	-1244	-969	-598	-448	-646	-1035	-1334	-1361	-1131
Vega	16835	21786	22245	17580	11527	9129	12385	18817	23916	24714	21259

Crash Skew

Price:	90.00	92.00	94.00	96.00	98.00	100.00	102.00	104.00	106.00	108.00	110.00
P&L	95907	-80812	-144131	-108022	86352	0	115264	-76888	-158453	-102828	78056
Delta	-5542	-4718	-2238	1251	2330	484	-1244	-315	2990	5206	5937
Gamma	734	1020	1288	1308	106	210	120	1200	1127	865	589
Theta	-2842	-2799	-3351	-3869	-4349	-3511	-4546	-4049	-3169	-2565	-2636
Vega	26240	29156	34621	36012	29639	26776	30938	37661	36355	31625	29463

Supply-Products

Price:	90.00	92.00	94.00	96.00	98.00	100.00	102.00	104.00	106.00	108.00	110.00
P&L	202053	81559	40686	44167	40710	0	-28869	4739	98789	228697	382258
Delta	-9223	-5073	-2307	-1146	-2151	-2742	-1329	1013	3255	4949	6118
Gamma	1440	1200	1343	272	-333	177	895	1160	1042	821	638
Theta	-196	-1335	-1627	-1218	-630	-676	-1294	-1984	-2397	-2488	-2484
Vega	8465	31280	28568	14039	1587	7089	21248	30984	33247	31187	28234

Demand-Products

Price:	90.00	92.00	94.00	96.00	98.00	100.00	102.00	104.00	106.00	108.00	110.00
P&L	447797	264930	95137	-32186	-34493	0	56567	-15500	-5376	-1436	108461
Delta	-4518	-3554	-2020	523	3184	4940	2938	1542	2150	4965	8938
Gamma	715	901	1213	1418	896	-14	-635	332	1179	1146	1292
Theta	-4287	-4001	-3627	-2917	-2185	-1281	-1273	-1438	-1951	-1485	-300
Vega	29662	32354	35018	34098	23954	6181	2405	17285	33527	37405	13035

CONCLUSION

Keeping the customer order flow and the amount of open interest in mind can influence one's strategic approach to the skew. In other words, if customers are long and buying certain strikes, market makers are short those strikes. This increases open interest and tends to drive up implied volatility at those strikes. It makes sense that if market makers are all short certain strikes, their prices will tend to be inflated. If market makers have to accumulate more and more shorts at given strikes, these simply require more premium as an incentive to take on the additional exposure. To reduce their inventory, market makers are continually bidding premium to high levels until they can cover their shorts. If implied volatility is low at particular strikes, it is because customers have sold large quantities of those options and market makers carrying them in inventory already have too many of them. Until the market makers can liquidate this excess long inventory, demand is reduced and premium levels will remain low.

CHAPTER

11

OPTION DIALOGUE

If you are reading this Chapter first, before the rest of the book, then I advise that you read it straight through without skipping back to the references identified (intended for the trader to revise with). Do this to get oriented to options jargon witness the depth at which this book wishes to take you in your options career. If you have completed at least one read though CWS Meets OPD, then you may proceed and follow references to readings within the book.

Mentoring has been an interesting part of my trading career. I had a few mentors, starting in 1981 when I was an apprentice on the CBOE floor. They all had different styles of trading and different ways of explaining the nuances of the trade. Mostly, I learned by doing. I obtained financial backing from one of my mentors and went over to the CBOT in 1983. Within a year I established a trading group. Some of the traders had experience others did not. I gave classes at my clearing firm and got a seat on the CME to expand my operation in 1985. While interacting with experienced and inexperienced traders, I found that I had a knack for interpreting complicated ideas from my veteran traders and explaining them to my novices. In late 1989, I set out to create the curriculum for the International Trading Institute, Ltd. and traveled extensively working with and training traders. Since my first book was published, I have continued to work with traders in person, over the telephone, via email and interactive forums.

Email was my favorite medium back in the 90s, because they are easy to save, edit and illustrate when necessary. Email is particularly good because my pupils can save them, study them and revise from them. The forum at RiskIllustrated.com is even better because more people can share in the discussion. The following dialogue, between a an ex-floor trader and myself, covers the first couple of months of trading after he migrated from the floor to the screen and had finished reading Options: Perception and Deception. I chose this trader's emails because at that particular time period the market was not trending in an obvious manner. Both the Dow and the NASDAQ Composite were in tight trading ranges, 9000 and 2200 respectively. It was not a particularly easy time to trade, unlike the period in late 1999 / early 2000 when almost any call went into the money or later in 2000 almost any put went into the money. In the nonvolatile environment of 2001 having either bullish or bearish strategies failed while butterflies and time spreads prospered. The dialogue is presented in two different font colors (for color versions). The red font represents emails from the trader to myself. These are also left justified. The black font represents emails from myself to the trader, and each paragraph is indented and right hand justified.

Getting Started

Trader:
December 31, 1998
What do I do?

I've been studying the material for some time now. As usual, I understand some of it, but haven't digested all of it yet. One question, or issue, is looming ever larger as my first day of trading draws near. What will my first trade be? What strategy or strategies should I employ? I was thinking to use mostly verticals.

I think that I would like to trade some of the following stocks: Compaq, Microsoft, America Online, Yahoo, Amazon, Cisco, Dell, etc. It seems to me that I should start out slowly and probably with only one stock, mastering one or two strategies. I want to keep this as simple and as painless as possible in the beginning.

I have dozens of questions floating through my mind so rather than try to discuss them all now, which will probably lead to more questions, is there a way to devise a sort of recipe or set of instructions for the total beginner to follow? Can you provide me with a short list of basic strategies to learn and master, a secondary list of intermediate strategies and then some more advanced plays. I feel the simpler we can keep this in the beginning the faster my learning curve and confidence level will be.

What do you think? Would you rather I propose a list or set of guidelines?

Ri$kDoctor:
January 4, 1999
Re: What do I do?

"Thinking to use mostly verticals" gives you a lot of versatility and allows you to profit from being correct in your market opinion by being able to employ a wide variety strategies for almost any market scenario (bullish, bearish, tight range, big move either way, not to mention vega and theta control -- volatility long versus short versus neutral, etc. Now, if verticals were to become your bread and butter spread, you should also read, Chapter 5's: "Adjusting Speculative Trades Using Verticals".

All trades start with a directional opinion and/or a volatility assumption. Where has the stock and implied volatility been and where might they be going?

Take it slowly. Walk before you run.

An analogy to playing a hole in golf:
Remember that if you take a triple bogie on a hole, there are still a lot more left to birdie. Don't get discouraged and upset your inner game.

1. Line up your shot and take your stance (get a hunch).

2. Drive the ball (Put on your play or spread).

3. Go to where you hit the ball in order to plan your next shot (after some time or a market move, assess the situation).

4. Hit it again (adjust, exit or stay with it).

There is no need to wonder anything until you get to the ball. (Until you get to know your trading self, learn. Don't worry about the strategy until your time horizon expires or your price targets or exit points have been met). Each time, assess your lie and your view to the pin.

You are going to slice, hook and fall into traps so keep your exposure low until you can rely on your own experience and abilities (not the golf book or video) to get you back on course.

I think it would also be helpful to review some sections in the book. Please re-read "Rule the Beast" in Chapter 2.

Trader:
January 4, 1999
Understood

OK, I got it. Thanks for the reply. I will follow those words to the Tee. Here's the update for today, my first day trading:

1. I have put $50,000 in my account to start with.

2. My only expenses will be commissions, and interest currently calculated at 5.75%. I will receive 4% on credit balances over 25,000. There is no monthly charge for my Internet real-time data.

3. I intend to take my time by starting out small (10 to 20 contracts). I do not need any added pressure to make money.

4. My trading software looks pretty thorough and sophisticated. It uses the Binomial model and can provide me with all my analysis.

I think that's all, for now anyway.

Trader:
January 7, 1999
Quick Update

Just wanted to let you know that everything is going well and that I don't really have any major news yet. I've been spending the past few days setting up and getting familiar with my software. I'm actually very pleased and impressed with all of its capabilities. I'm going to use the rest of the week to finish customizing my screens and get into the market's rhythm as it relates to options. On Monday I'll make my opening move, perhaps in AOL (American Online) or MSFT (Microsoft). Once I have a position I'll email you with daily updates. Let me know if there is any information that you want specifically. "Options Metamorphosis" in Chapter 1 is a beautiful thing. I am making it my goal to completely master it, both in theory and in execution. Life is great!

Trader:
January 8, 1999
Cox Ross Model

Have you heard of the Cox Ross and the Cox Rubenstein model? If so, does it yield significantly different values for equity options than the Binomial model?

> Ri$kDoctor:
> **January 10, 1999**
> **Re: Cox Ross Model**
>
> The Cox Ross, Cox Rubenstein and the Cox Ross Rubenstein models are all the same. It is the binomial model (discussed in Chapter 8) that discounts conversions/reversals and pumps up boxes by factoring in a probability of early exercise. I have also heard it called the Cox Ross Rubenstein model.
>
> Become an expert in the pricing of the markets that you intend to trade. Get to know your skews and how they affect different positions (Chapter 9). It is not imperative that you understand conversion/reversal (C/R) values, so much because market makers keep them in line. C/Rs will help you understand your risk better by using them in the dissection process explained in Chapters 1 and 2. Apply these understandings to by concentrating on only AOL and MSFT for now.

Trader:
January 11, 1999
The Basics

Thanks for your last response. I already have the MSFT and AOL price histories. I will do exactly as you say. I thought I'd send you an email just to let you know my intentions. I've been reading the pages that you mentioned earlier and it all makes very good sense. I especially like the "Managing the Beast" section. I plan to follow that very carefully. The flow charts are also an excellent tool. I intend to review them daily, quizzing myself, until they become second nature. Here is a rough outline of what I plan to do, based on the fact that I'm a beginner:

1. Stick with one stock in the beginning. This will allow me to focus on one position and the necessary adjustments. I will also have less to worry about as I

figure out the best way to get filled on my option orders. (My stock orders shouldn't pose any problems.)

2. I think that it is best, initially, to try to focus on two quadrants of the "Options Metamorphosis" at the end of Chapter 2 and each dissection in the Appendix. Since I am bullish for the near term and believe volatility will stay at current levels or possibly increase, I think that I should try to stick with the adjustments in the long call quadrant and the long straddle quadrant in the early days to keep things simple. What do you think of this?

3. Since everything will be new to me (i.e., pricing, placing orders), I am trying to figure out what the best initial trade would be. I know I can get quick easy fills on stock, but perhaps a better idea is to go with a relatively price insensitive strategy such as a vertical. If you have any thoughts on this let me know, otherwise I'll play it by ear and market opinion.

4. Am I right in assuming that I should be concerned with deltas? My concerns will also be with pricing, premium (especially vega and theta), P&L, and market opinion.

5. I am planning to trade with a maximum delta of 6oo to start with.

If you agree with everything I've stated here then you really don't need to give me much of a response. I'm feeling very happy, comfortable and confident these days. I'll give you an update tomorrow when I get home.

Ri$kDoctor:
January 11, 1999
Re: The Basics

I agree with everything. Quadrants IV is the most practical of the Options Metamorphosis are the appropriate quadrants for you right now. Remember that the price and delta of a vertical spread are relatively small when compared to a naked option. With 20 spreads you will generally have between 2oo and 5oo deltas, well within your self-imposed parameter of 6oo deltas. The important thing is to predetermine where you are going to get out if you are wrong. If you do think about liquidating, remember that there are other options (alternatives). You can leave the position as is, instead of spreading your existing position off. It may be wiser, as another alternative, to trade the adjacent vertical and leave yourself with a long butterfly that may come back and reward you with profits at a later date.

Trader:
January 11, 1999
The Basics 2

A quick question: you said that it is not necessary to liquidate the bull spread, but that I could trade the adjacent bear spread against it. This in turn will produce a short butterfly, will it not (short referring to the wings of the butterfly)?

Ri$kDoctor:
January 11, 1999
Re: The Basics 2

Selling the vertical above produces long wings, hence a long butterfly. Say for example that you have the 170/175 bull spread on. If you trade into the 175/180 bear spread you will end up long the 170/175/180 butterfly. To spread it off into a short butterfly you would have to trade into a bear spread using lower strikes. For example, trading into the 165/170 bear spread leaves you short the 165/170/175 butterfly. Long is not necessarily better or worse than short but you would have to desire the position.

Trader:
January 12, 1999
1/11/99

Thanks for the clarification on the vertical / butterfly. Who would have thought that you could sell the vertical above (at higher strikes than what I have on)? Wow, I like it! Unfortunately I don't have any news regarding trading today. I was still tying up some loose ends and missed the opportunity to jump into MSFT. Incidentally, I'm trying to get into the February options. They still have some time to go, aren't too sensitive to volatility, and have quite a bit of premium. I also think this rally will play itself out before February expiration. April seems a little far out to me. Am I looking at this the right way? Sorry I still don't have a vertical for you.

Ri$kDoctor:
January 12, 1999
Re: 1/11/99

Your assessment is correct.

PULLING THE TRIGGER

The following chart of Microsoft starts 10 months prior to the next series of trades and covers the period (within rectangle) involving the positions.

Microsoft Corp (MSFT)

Trader:
January 12, 1999
MSFT FEB 145/150 Vertical
Actual Position Before Open: None
Basic Position: Flat

I have made some trades. Here is what I did:
I sold 20 FEB 150 calls for 6.25 with MSFT trading at 143.38.
An hour later I bought 20 FEB 145 calls for 7.88 with MSFT trading at 142.13.

MSFT closed on the day's low of 142.06. My call vertical (I paid 1.62 for the FEB 145/150) is worth about 2.00 at that stock price. The FEB 150/155 call vertical closed around 1.56 (5.75–6.00 and 4.25–4.38 respectively). So tomorrow I'll have to make a decision about whether to adjust or not. Intel's earnings were good, but maybe not good enough to rally the tech sector. My market opinion may be changing. My only question to you is how do you feel about me having legged into the spread? MSFT followed the S&P futures, trading with them almost tick for tick, all day. That is how I chose my entry points. I was very systematic. It worked, but I know there was also some luck on my side. Had I traded it as a spread I would have probably paid 2.13 or 2.25. I chose the 145/150 because at the time the 150/155 would have cost about 1.75 or 1.88. Let me know what you think.

Actual Position at Close: +20*FEB 145 Calls / -20*FEB 150 Calls
Basic Position: 20 FEB 145 / 150 Bull Spread.   Stock at 142.06

Ri$kDoctor:
January 12, 1999
Re: 1/12/99
Basic Position: 20 FEB 145 / 150 Bull Spread
Stock at 142.06

Legging Verticals

The following will apply to when you will be getting out of this particular vertical. Most likely, at that point, you will no longer be feeling bullish (you may even be feeling bearish). Perhaps you may have subsequently adjusted into a 145/150/155 butterfly by selling the 150/155. Later you will want to leg out of butterfly; vertical to vertical:

1. I would prefer that when you leg a vertical spread you start with the buy side. Obviously that will prevent you from getting stuck with a *naked* short option growing exponentially if the market explodes.

2. You are probably saying to yourself, "but I was *bearish* at the time, wanting to leg out of the 145/150 bull vertical - if I buy the 150 calls first, then I would temporarily have the opposite of what I want – bullish instead of bearish". That is true, but you could buy the 150 puts first and then sell the 145 puts later, and you would end up with the same spread synthetically. Why? Because you are boxing off the

145/150 call bull spread (see Chapter 5's discussion on Legging).

3. Your educated mind is probably thinking that the total play does not seem to be the same. It is not the same with regard to the deltas on the individual legs. It will, however, end up the same once the spread is completed. For example, you could be faced with a choice of selling a 5o delta option on the 145 calls or buying a minus 70 delta with the 150 put.

4. I suggested that you could start with a 20 lot-spread which on a 30 delta vertical would be a *limited risk exposure* of 6oo deltas total. That means that when you leg into a spread, the trading leg can be no more than 6oo deltas. Using the example deltas in point number three above, if you were to leg with a naked 50 delta option you would have to limit the trade to 12 contracts. With a 70 delta option, 9 contracts would put you slightly over, at 630 deltas (which is reasonably close).

Trader:
January 13, 1999
1/13/99
Actual Position before Open: +20*FEB 145 Calls / -20*FEB 150 Calls
Basic Position: 20 FEB 145 / 150 Bull Spread
Stock at 138

The S&Ps were down 27.00 (over 2%) on Globex trading before New York opened. MSFT was trading around 138.00, prior to New York's open. Something was happening in Brazil. It looked as though it was time to change my market opinion, but I sat tight and observed. The market was very jittery today but the tech sector rebounded almost all the way to the previous day's close. I made no adjustments to my bull spread, and am still bullish after today's rebound. I have some questions developing and will soon email them.

Ri$kDoctor:
January 13, 1999
Re: 1/13/99
Basic Position: 20 FEB 145 / 150 Bull Spread

I admire your patience. Some times it is wise to just sit back and observe all the panic. It is nice to have a vertical on when the market is bowling everybody over, especially when your size is manageable. The beautiful thing about it is that when the market totally goes against you:

1. You can afford the maximum loss (debit of $1.62 x 20 contracts = $3240.00 represents about 6.5% of your $50,000 trading account).
2. All the losses can come back another day.

Trader:
1/14/99
Verticals
Basic Position: 20 FEB 145 / 150 Bull Spread
Stock at 138

I would like to run by you what I've been doing and see if I'm on the right track. Also, I want to see if I'm looking for the right verticals (pricing), what kind of profits to shoot for in percentage terms, how many trades per day or week I should be thinking about, and what other things / areas I'll be getting into later.

Ri$kDoctor:
1/18/99
Re: Verticals

One method of measuring *consistency* is to trade equal sizes on all trades. This is for the simple reason that your profits, say of $30,000 in a month for example, can consist of three hundred trades yielding an average of $100 profit per trade or one 100 lot trade profiting $4.00 ($40,000) offset by $10,000 worth of many losing trades. The importance of consistency is so that you can learn about a very important factor in the market: YOU! Get to know your trading-self as an Internet based trader. YOU will be your greatest asset. Performance data can be cluttered with sporadic sizes. For now, based on your risk threshold, why don't you maintain a maximum trade size of 600 deltas per trade, for example, until you are able to get an idea of what works for you. Keep up the good work.

Trader:
January 19, 1999
Condor
Basic Position: 20 FEB 145 / 150 Bull Spread
Stock at 151

Good Morning!
MSFT opened up 1.00 (after the previous day's 12.00 rally) and traded around 151.00. The high so far has been 153.50. MSFT was trading around 153.00 when I sold the 155/160 call spread (selling the 155 calls and buying the 160 calls), 20 times, for 2.00. I put the offer in (MSFT was around 152.00) when the crowd was 1.88–2.38, so it was a mediocre fill. At the time, I might have been able to get around 3 or 3.13 for my long 145/150 call spread (long the 145s and short the 150s). So, I now own the 145/150/155/160 condor 20 times for a .38 credit (I love fee money don't you?). Now the stock is trading around 151.50–152 with the 145/150 call spread trading around 2.38–3.13 while the 155/160 is around 1.75–2.25. My market opinion is neutral to a little bearish, at this moment. We didn't rally as strong as I expected, and now we're slowly selling off. MSFT has earnings today after the bell.
Actual Position at Close:
+20*FEB 145 Calls / -20*FEB 150 Calls / -20*FEB 155 Calls / +20*160 Calls
Basic Position: Long 20 MSFT FEB 145/150/155/160 Condor

Ri$kDoctor:
January 19, 1999
Re: Condor
Basic Position: Long 20 MSFT FEB 145/150/155/160 Condor

Well done! Yes, I love buying wingspreads for less than free. As far as your market opinion is concerned, if you feel strongly about a sideways to down market, there is a slightly aggressive strategy that you may wish to consider at sometime in the future: Ratioed Verticals (or unbalanced butterflies discussed in Chapter 6 but not depicted in the Options Metamorphosis). A lopsided wingspread if you will. It simply involves trading more of one vertical versus the other. It has the effect of a ratio spread without the open-ended risk. For example, you could sell 20 additional 155/160 call spreads against the existing condor (leaving you with 20*145/150 bull spreads against 40*155/160 bear spreads). It would be aggressive, but it is not uncommon for a trader to have one lower vertical against two or upper verticals or vice versa. The best experience to be had with no risk would be to paper trade it for actual pricing and monitor it with pricing analysis over time.

Trader:
January 19, 1999
MSFT Earnings
Basic Position: Long 20*145/150/155/160 Condor

That ratioed vertical strategy sounds interesting, but I am glad that I did not try it. MSFT rallied 6.00 points in anticipation of earnings today. They beat the street's numbers by 0.14 (.59 vs. .73), which is considered to be BIG. After the announcement the stock was trading around 160.00 (up another 5.00 from the close). At 160.00 I have my 145/150 worth about 3.56. The 155/160 should be about 2.88. That puts the condor at .69. There is now a lot of bullish talk, especially in the tech sector. I will make a point of looking into studying ratioed verticals further for the future.

That's all for now.

Ri$kDoctor:
January 19, 1999
Re: MSFT Earnings
Basic Position: Long 20 MSFT FEB 145/150/155/160 Condor

Oops! Well its nice to know that when you are wrong that you don't lose too much or anything at all. I hope that you are cognizant of the fact, that by selling the 155/160 spread (bear spread), you were in effect getting out of your bullish play (145/150 bull spread) and simultaneously initiating a new trade that desired market stability (the 145/150/155/160 condor). OK, the condor is taking it on the chin a little bit but there is a lot of time until expiration and there is bound to be some correction by then. I would hang on to it and regard the old bullish trade as water over the dam with a completely new trade in progress. Owing to the nature of the spread's risk, I would put this spread out of your mind right now. Look for a new opportunity to play the direction again while ignoring the condor. It can take care of itself for a while. You will find that it is easier to generate trading decisions when you have something on. A condor is about the best spread to have on for that.

Trader:
January 21, 1999
1/21/1999
Basic Position: Long 20 MSFT FEB 145/150/155/160 Condor

Today MSFT traded as high as 166.00–167.00. In the final hour, after looking strong all day, the tech sector sold off big to end almost unchanged (the NASDAQ was up over 50 points, i.e. 2%, earlier in the day). MSFT closed at 162.63 below it's opening price of 163.00–164.00. My condor was trading at about .94 because the short call vertical (155/160) was trading at 3.06 (the market was 2.63–3.50) while my long 145/150 call vertical was trading at 4.00 (the market was 3.50–4.50). I made no adjustments during the day. Tomorrow (Thursday) I am looking for continued selling, maybe after an up opening. I think that I may sell the 155/160 synthetically, 20 more times (to go into the ratioed condor for a while), by legging into the 155/160 put vertical (buying the 160 puts then selling the 155 puts). If we start going up after I have bought the first leg (160 puts) I can buy stock and turn the puts into calls and hopefully sell them out for even, or a small profit. What do you think? I am still basically bullish, but today's rally was very narrow and I think tomorrow might be my opportunity to undo my short vertical.

> Ri$kDoctor:
> **January 21, 1999**
> **1/21/1999**
>
> Your thinking is correct. There is nothing wrong with the proposed series of trades.

Trader:
January 21, 1999
New Idea
Basic Position: Long 20 MSFT FEB 145/150/155/160 Condor

What do you think of this idea?
I like SunMicro (SUNW) a lot.
Today they will announce earnings. I'm expecting them to be good. The historical implied volatility in the options is around

45. Today they are trading with implied volatility of 70% - 75%. I would like to do a ratio-write. I would like to buy 10oo shares of stock at around 100.00 and sell 15 FEB 115 calls for about 4.00 each, leaving me 1 by 1.5. The stock rallied the other day to 115.13. Now it is trading around 100.00. Last week during the Brazil scare it went as low as 88.00. This would be a volatility play for maybe a week or so. I realize it has *unlimited risk* in both directions, but it seems reasonably safe. If you don't like it, do you have another idea? What about a vertical spread?

> Ri$kDoctor:
> **January 21, 1999**
> **Re: New Idea**
>
> You are correct about the unlimited risk aspects. You are wrong in mentioning that it is only a "volatility play" by itself. I believe that you realize that it is bullish because you are "expecting good earnings". Specifically the strategy is no different to a ratioed straddle, i.e. short 5*115 calls and short 10*115 puts. Obviously it is not market neutral because there would be half the amount of short out-of-the-money (OTM) calls against the deep in-the-money (ITM) puts. A much safer set of strategies would involve either ratioed vertical spreads or a vertical at-the-money (ATM) against one further away. Both involve four strikes. Perhaps sell an out-of-the-money vertical on each side but make the call spread further away from the money. It would probably be safer to do a bigger size of these strategies than do something with unlimited risk that can ruin you. Simply stated, and for the record; if you are bullish on the market and, at the same time, bearish on implied volatility, sell an OTM put vertical (same as buying the ITM call vertical). I believe that your proposed strategy is too risky for you at this stage of your development and capital structure.

Trader:
January 21, 1999
JAN 21, '99
Basic Position: Long 20 MSFT FEB 145/150/155/160 Condor

Here's the recap: the market was wild today. It looked lousy almost all day, then rallied before selling off in the final 20 minutes. I was trying to get into a long call vertical in SUNW most of the day. I missed two great opportunities when the stock was at or near it's low of the day (~97.00). I was trying to get into the 100/105 for ~1.88 or 2.00. I did not get filled, and at the end SUNW closed off it's low at 98.25. Earnings came in 0.02 above the street's estimate, and I'm pretty glad I did not try to pay up for my spread! MSFT closed at 158.06. Tomorrow it will probably sell off some more, and I may have to adjust.

Trader:
January 22, 1999
JAN 22, Opening
Basic Position: Long 20 MSFT FEB 145/150/155/160 Condor

It looks as if MSFT is going to open at around 155.00, down 2.00–3.00 points. Right in my sweet spot. If you have any strong ideas let me know.

> Ri$kDoctor:
> **January 22, 1999**
> **Re: JAN 22 Opening**
> Basic Position: Long 20 MSFT FEB 145/150/155/160 Condor
>
> I would sit tight with the condor - it needs time. Find a new bull or bear leg in SUNW or MSFT and act on it.

Trader:
January 22, 1999
JAN. 22, 1999
Basic Position: Long 20 MSFT FEB 145/150/155/160 Condor

GREAT NEWS!!!
Last night I finally got my pricing software to provide me with decent theoretical values - I'm more on track. Now here's the good news. Shortly after the open I bought 20 MSFT FEB 155 puts for 5.13. I was bearish when the stock was trading around 158.00. Soon afterwards I picked up some buy signals (from my pocket oscillator) and bought 20oo shares at 157.88, turning the puts into calls. I sold and bought stock all day, between a range of 157.75 and 159.75, for a total of $5,900. In the final hour of trading I sold my 20 puts for 5.25. Total gross profits for the day, ~$6,100. My position over the weekend is the same trusty old condor. I'm earning decay, and my deltas are flat. MSFT will close around 156.00 (we have a few minutes to go) and the puts are now trading around 6.00–6.25. Also volatility came up several points. That's all for now. YOU are a GENIUS! I had a great time today. Have a great weekend.

Ri$kDoctor:
January 22, 1999
Re: JAN 22, 1999
Basic Position: Long 20 MSFT FEB 145/150/155/160 Condor

Good work! Have a great weekend and come down to earth with a soft landing on Monday. Start out cautious like in your first week. Never lose that healthy fear. If you can maintain that cautionary fear throughout your career you will become extraordinarily profitable.

Trader:
January 24, 1999
Some Thoughts and Ideas
Actual Position Before Open:
+20*FEB 145 Calls / –20*FEB 150 Calls / –20*FEB 155 Calls / +20*160 Calls
Basic Position: Long 20 MSFT FEB 145/150/155/160 Condor

I'm having a great weekend, but I'm also eager to get back to trading. I love it when that happens! Here are some thoughts about the days ahead:

1. I know my condor needs time, and there still are some 26 days before expiration. Are there any basic guidelines to unwinding it? When do I start thinking about this? Does it make any sense to roll it (or part of it) into the next month?

2. In the next few trading days I see a possibility of MSFT trading below 150.00. Is there a "best" (or most appropriate) defensive strategy to protecting the currently long, in-the-money, 145/150 call vertical?

3. On Monday, I can imagine that, we will be trading in my "sweet spot", between 150.00 and 155.00. Is this not a good time to make adjustments to the Big Bird?

That's all for now.

Ri$kDoctor:
January 24, 1999
Re: Some Thoughts and Ideas
Actual Position Before Open:
+20*FEB 145 Calls / −20*FEB 150 Calls / −20*FEB 155 Calls /
+20*160 Calls
Basic Position: Long 20 MSFT FEB 145/150/155/160 Condor

To see a similar predicament, you might want to read "The Ugly
Butterfly" from chapter 5. In this situation, you must ask
yourself a series of questions:
What is the condor worth?

Is that price cheap or expensive (not to theoretical values but to
whether you would buy it or sell it at that price)? Say, for
example, it is worth .625 (twenty times so $1,250 is the amount
of your money that is still on the table). That seems like a cheap
shot, and so you would probably have a tendency to want to buy
it at .63. If you think it is cheap, you will naturally stay long the
spread for a little while, waiting to see what develops. It is not
worth hedging because there is not much value left to protect.

On the other hand, say for example that the condor is valued at
1.75 (which adds up to $3,500 that would be left on the table).
This price is rather high with 26 days to go. In this case you
might be a little bit worried about how much you have left on the
table. At this point you have to ask yourself how you can I
protect your $3,500 with very little money? You could buy
some strangles or straddles if the price was right. This
adjustment would protect it and change the position into a
Batman spread of sorts. You would then have to ask yourself
whether you would initiate the Batman spread at all the available
prices (forget about your original costs -- those are old P&L
trades i.e. history). You might find that, in this case, it is not
worth protecting and therefore it is desirable to liquidate the
condor. I would then, according to my market opinions, use the
remaining components of the position to unwind as the market
unfolds.

Since you see MSFT going below 150.00 take your profits now
on the long 145/150 call spread, and then when you think that
MSFT is bottoming, cover the 155/160 call spread. Keep in
mind that taking profits on the 145/150 call spread leaves you
short the 155/160 call spread. The question is, if you had no

position, would you short the 155/160 call spread at the current market values? If you would, then go ahead and sell out the 145/150 and stay short the 155/160. If you would not, then you have a much shorter term leg and must look to cover the 155/160 at some point soon.
I hope this helps.

Trader:
January 25, 1999
Thanks

Thanks for the helpful explanation! MSFT just announced a two for one stock split. Prior to this morning's open it was trading about 4.00 higher than Friday's close (156.00). I guess we may be going higher now but what exactly happens to my positions, strikes and costs?

Ri$kDoctor:
January 25, 1999
Re: Thanks
Actual Position Before Open:
+20*FEB 145 Calls / −20*FEB 150 Calls / −20*FEB 155 Calls / +20*160 Calls
Basic Position: Long 20 MSFT FEB 145/150/155/160 Condor

Your position will change in a two for one stock split on the ex-date. At that time your statement will reflect a position of twice as many options, still each representing 1oos. Your current position would, for example, be:
Actual Position in the Event of a 2 for 1 Stock Split:
+40*FEB 72.50 Calls / −40*FEB 75 Calls / −40*FEB 77.50 Calls / +40*80 Calls
Basic Position in the Event of a 2 for 1 Stock Split:
Long 40 MSFT FEB 72.50 / 75 / 77.50 / 80 Condor
The other difference will be that everything will be carried at half the price it used to be. The stock will be valued at half the previous market close plus or minus the new day's net change. The strikes will all be halved along with the closing prices and costs of the transactions. What will change for the worse are the commissions. It may cost twice the amount to get out of the trades, depending on your cost structure.

Trader:
January 26, 1999
JAN 25, '1999
Actual Position Before Open:
+20*FEB 145 Calls / –20*FEB 150 Calls / –20*FEB 155 Calls / +20*160 Calls
Basic Position: Long 20 MSFT FEB 145/150/155/160 Condor

Apparently I played with my pocket oscillator too much this weekend. It wasn't working very well today and I ended up trading for a loss of $950 (plus ~$350 in commissions). I was trying to do what I did on Friday but MSFT wasn't following the S&Ps due to the stock split news. I should have known this, and should have played it differently. Anyway, it was a good learning experience. For Tuesday, I think, MSFT may go higher. I keep thinking that I should adjust one of my verticals. Obviously, if I am bullish, that would mean covering the short 155/160 call vertical. If I am still bullish at the open, and we haven't gapped up, I should consider covering (buying in my shorts) the 155 calls (either real or synthetically) on a leg for a scalp - hopefully at a higher price. Is this what you were telling me to do in your last response dated the 24th? Perhaps even buy a greater amount (say 40 of the 155 calls) and sell the same amount of 160 calls against them after a move up. This would leave me with two separate bull spreads (the 145/150 spread 20 times, and the 155/160 spread 20 times). Then I can sell the 160/165 vertical, or perhaps the 165/170, against the higher vertical and have a new butterfly or condor. I would of course still have the deep in-the-money vertical, (the 145/150, now worth 4.13) which is the same as short the put vertical at about .88. Am I being realistic, or reaching for the stars? I do see the possibility of MSFT testing last week's high of 166.00. Plenty of money keeps flowing into this market.
Proposed Position for Tomorrow (never executed):
+20*FEB 145 Calls / –20*FEB 150 Calls / +20*FEB 155 Calls / –20*160 Calls
Basic Position: Long 2 sets of 20 Bull Spreads 145/150 and the 155/160

Ri$kDoctor:
January 26, 1999
Re: JAN. 25, '1999

Affirmative to all your thoughts except one: buying 40 of the 155 calls (each having a delta of about 7o) would be buying 28oo deltas. Don't you think that size of a trade is a little too big for someone with your level of experience? Perhaps it isn't, but we talked about 10oo last week. You need a steady performance before you can ramp up your size. Granted a $1,300 loss versus a $6,100 gain the day before is nice work but is it a pattern that you can hold on to? It does not take many $1,300 losses to deplete the $6,100 in profits. Steady as she goes skipper. Let's not dock this ship on the reef. Now as far as delta size goes, what is going to be your limit intraday and interday? Keep to it until you establish a recognizable track record (not just a couple of lucky sessions). The jury is still out about whether your recent trading was luck or skill. If I had to vote now, I would say skill but I have been wrong before. Repeat: do not get overly confident. Remember that 20oo deltas can go against you for 5.00 points very quickly in a stock like MSFT. That is $10,000. Can you imagine what a hit like that can do to one's confidence? How long will it take for you to shake that off? Not all sluggers bat 350 year after year. Grind out the money in little chips and someday you may have a big pile. May the force be with you.

Trader:
January 26, 1999
Follow Up
Actual Position Before Open:
+20*FEB 145 Calls / –20*FEB 150 Calls / –20*FEB 155 Calls / +20*160 Calls
Basic Position: Long 20 MSFT FEB 145/150/155/160 Condor

ROGER, ROGER.
I HAVE A GOOD COPY ON ALL OF THAT.
You are right, I wasn't even thinking of deltas. I don't intend to play with more than 20oo at a time. As for overnight, so far I've enjoyed being relatively flat. I didn't mean to sound over confident.

Ri$kDoctor:
January 26, 1999
Re: Follow Up
Actual Position Before Open:
+20*FEB 145 Calls / –20*FEB 150 Calls / –20*FEB 155 Calls /
+20*160 Calls
Basic Position: Long 20 MSFT FEB 145/150/155/160 Condor

What will your deltas be until further notice? I will help you decide when to start increasing them and how to decrease them when in rusty slumps. Please reply, and get into the habit of including delta information in your updates. It will sharpen your perception of what is happening to your deltas as you adjust.

One thing to consider is your eventual "half" size delta so that you can add to your position at better prices if the first trade goes against you a bit. In other words, you fade the market as it keeps coming. You let them have some and then give them some more. Some would argue that this method is dangerous because you would be adding to a loser. The difference is that you are pre-determining how many 'bullets' you have and conserving them while the market is volatile. For now you shouldn't be adding to a position unless it is a winner. Eventually you will be able to add, if the position is against you. In the distant future you will perhaps vary your size according to opportunity. A grade 'A' trade, for example, might be 100oo deltas (in a certain stock), a grade 'B' trade might be 50oo (in the same stock), a grade "C" trade would be 30oo, "D" 20oo and "E" 10oo. So MSFT down at 158.00 might be a grade C for getting long, but down at 153.00 you could add 20oo upping it to a B trade. If it comes down to 148.00 you may want to be all out long with 100oo deltas. You are not ready for anything like this until you know your trading-self better and have made enough to be able to afford big losses when they come. It will be something for us to discuss when a solid track record is cemented into place.

Trader:
January 26, 1999
Deltas
Actual Position Before Open:
+20*FEB 145 Calls / –20*FEB 150 Calls / –20*FEB 155 Calls /
+20*160 Calls
Basic Position: Long 20 MSFT FEB 145/150/155/160 Condor

I seem to be OK with about 15oo deltas. In other words, on Friday I bought 20 of the 155 puts each with a delta of about 30 to 35 each. I then bought 20oo shares, which made me long about 13oo to 14oo deltas as we were moving up. I liquidated both before the close, first the stock then the puts. So far today I haven't done anything. I missed the move after the open, (we had already gapped up 4.00+ points). Now I'm looking for an end of the day play.

Actual Position at Close:

+20*FEB 145 Calls / −20*FEB 150 Calls / −20*FEB 155 Calls / +20*160 Calls

Basic Position: Long 20 MSFT FEB 145/150/155/160 Condor

> Ri$kDoctor:
> **January 26, 1999**
> **Re: Deltas**
>
> OK then, for the record, your maximum intraday delta will be 30oo and 15oo for interday (overnight).

Trader:
January 26, 1999
JAN 26, '99

Well the stock was up ALL day. I think it closed up about 9.69 at 171.56. Essentially all that I have to show for the day is buying 20 of the FEB 175 puts for 8.63, when the stock was trading 171.00. Tomorrow if we open here, where we closed, they will be worth 8.25. I bought stock against 5 of them (5oo shares at 171.50) and am going home short 6oo deltas (although I currently have a 171.50 bid in for 6oo more in the after hours trading session). It was not a good day. I am learning some valuable lessons though. Hopefully they won't cost too much. Following is the position, carded-up, using the formatting discussed on page 11 of Chapter 1.

Actual Position at Close:

+20*FEB 145 Calls / −20*FEB 150 Calls / −20*FEB 155 Calls / +20*160 Calls

Plus: +20*175 Puts / +5oo MSFT

·Basic Position: Long 20 MSFT FEB 145/150/155/160 Condor

Plus: Ratioed 175 Straddle (+5c by +15p)

	nc	rc	ς -5 MSFT $nu=0$ +5oo	rp	np
			140		
	20	20	145		
	20	20	150		
	20	20	155		
	20	20	160		
			165		
			170		
	5	ς 5	175	20 ς 5	15
			180		
	+5	+5		+15	+15

Ri$kDoctor:
January 27, 1999
Re: JAN 26, '99

Suppose you get filled on your 6oo shares, what then? I understand that sometimes you want to have a flat delta but how do you feel about having on the (+11 calls versus +9 puts) ratioed straddle?

Trader:
January 27, 1999
More Thoughts

I got filled on my 6oo shares and felt comfortable with the ratioed straddle for overnight. I was just ending my bearish stance. I have been thinking, after trying for the last two days to replicate Fridays success, that I have come to realize that it probably had more to do with luck than anything else (don't tell anyone). I'm throwing away the "pocket oscillator", at least for now. Each day I've gone home thinking of what I want to do for the next day. Then in the morning something minor, like a gap opening, has distracted me from sticking with my game plan. So I try some concocted way of "legging" into a vertical that will also leave me a way out should things go against me. It sounds fine, but is actually rather difficult to execute. By the end of the day I'm wondering why I didn't simply stick with my original plan. Right now the market looks very bullish. The tech sector is very hot and MSFT is leading the way. After today's close, the S&Ps continued rallying above 1260 by some 3.00 to 4.00 points. I think that they could go towards their high of about 1280 in the next few days. Tomorrow I would like to keep it simple (like you've been trying to get me to do!) and try to get into the 175/180 bull vertical. It may cost me extra because of today's debacle, but when we're trading above 175.00 it will probably look like a winner. If it goes against me, and starts looking ugly, I will spread it off into a butterfly by selling the vertical above. End of story. Since I already own 20 of the 175 puts (sold out my 11oo shares–too early), I'll probably do the spread only 20 times. Next time I'll do it 50 times.

Basic Position: Long 20 MSFT FEB 145/150/155/160 Condor
Plus: +20*175 Puts

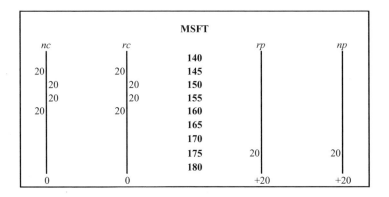

Ri$kDoctor:
January 27, 1999
Re: More Thoughts

What is this pocket oscillator? Do you mean that you trade from the seat of your pants or are you using something real that has potential only if fine-tuned? You should perhaps have positions on before the gap (perhaps overnight). If you are in fact bullish, then there is no need to go home with short deltas. It would be better to pay-up on 12oo and go home long 6oo. Be consistent by having positions that confirm your beliefs, unless of course your market opinion is always wrong. In that case if you are bullish go home short as you did. Some people do better doing the opposite of what they think (on every trade). This is all part of getting to know your trading-self.

Trader:
January 27, 1999
JAN 27, 1999

I have good news and bad news. First the good news: I did not do what I said I would do. Now the bad news: I did what I said I wouldn't do. When I came in this morning the market was up but not looking very strong. MSFT was up most of the day but it looked/felt like it was near a top. The S&Ps never looked good. So I did not put my bull spread on. Instead I got sucked in to the "day trading" game again (that's my "pocket oscillator"). In the end we were way down, closing around 168.63. My 20*175 puts kicked in around 170.00 on the stock and erased most of my losses. For the day I traded for a $500 loss, commissions were probably about another $500. My position now consists of the condor, nothing else. I'm short about 7o deltas. I am frustrated. It seems difficult, when beginning, to figure out what to do, what not to do, and when to do it, especially if the market is difficult (I think it is a jittery market right now). So many things seem to conflict. It's hard to know if you are doing the right thing but the timing is wrong, or whether you are actually doing the wrong thing. I know you know all this. I'm just complaining.

Basic Position at Close: Long 20 MSFT FEB 145/150/155/160 Condor

> Ri$kDoctor:
> **January 27, 1999**
> **Re: JAN. 27, 1999**
>
> It is always bad news when you do not carry out your plan, even if you save money, because you are losing control of yourself. You may have saved money for today but what about what may be on the heels of that trade over the next few days? It is twice as bad when you do the opposite of what you have planned because you can really get into trouble and lose your confidence. It might be a good time to do a post mortem on your experiences. You are up money and have on a decent spread:
>
> What are you good at?
> What are you not so good at?
> What have you done right?
> What have you done wrong?
> What works?
> What doesn't?
>
> Revise your set of trading rules and follow them to a tee. Be a machine.
>
> Have no emotion, no frustration. It is hard to do that but it is a goal to attain for long term trading success.

Trader:
January 27, 1999
That makes sense

That makes sense. I've actually been thinking of the machine approach.
I'm thinking I might not do anything tomorrow, regroup mentally, and make a move when it feels right.
Thanks.

Trader:
January 28, 1999
JAN 28, 1999
Basic Position: Long 20 MSFT FEB 145/150/155/160 Condor

Are you ready for this story?
I sat out the whole day watching what MSFT was going to do. It was up 4.00 by mid-day, where it hovered for some time. I decided that the S&Ps, and MSFT, were going to either rally further or sell off in the final hour. I bought 20 of the 175 puts when the stock was trading 173.00. My plan was to have the 170/175 bear spread on by the end of the day. I got a good fill on the puts and the stock started looking heavy, with only one hour to go. MSFT fluttered around 173.00 but I thought it was leaning toward the down side, and I was ready to buy 20oo shares in case we rallied. Finally, we were trading around 172.38 with fifteen minutes to go. It still wasn't clear what was going to happen, when all of a sudden I noticed that they were buying IBM. Moments later, sure enough, the S&Ps and MSFT started to rally along with IBM. MSFT was around 172.50, with the stock looking ready to rocket upward, I was ready to buy my stock. What happened? I SOLD 20oo shares at 172.75 by mistake with a keypunch error. I was certain that I had it set up to BUY but in fact it was set, inadvertently, to SELL. I have recognized, and was warned by others, that professional electronic traders as well as Internet traders can very easily do the opposite of what you intend to actually do. With my past stock executions I realized the need to be very careful and double-check my order before I send it. This is what I need to be extremely thorough about, and is where I made the mistake.

In the end, I bought my 30oo (the 20oo that I was short on the error and an additional 10oo to spread off the 20*175 Puts) shares at 174.00 and am now neutral. So I essentially have the

175 straddle on 10 times, delta neutral. This fiasco cost me about $5,000 today. My Internet trading system is fast and efficient, but requires a lot of dexterity with the mouse and is very difficult to change/cancel orders, etc. Well the good news is that I planned my entry points and predicted accurately what the stock was going to do. I am a machine, and tomorrow is another day!

Actual Position at Close:
+20*FEB 145 Calls / –20*FEB 150 Calls / –20*FEB 155 Calls / +20*160 Calls
Plus: +20FEB 175 Puts / +10oo MSFT
Basic Position: Long 20 MSFT FEB 145/150/155/160 Condor
Plus: +10 FEB 175 Straddles

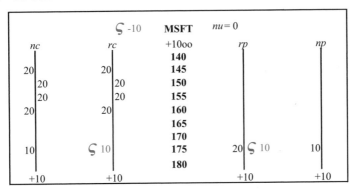

Ri$kDoctor:
January 29, 1999
Re: JAN 28, 1999

Regarding the keypunch error, perhaps it would be wise to speak out loud when executing, so that you can HEAR what you are clicking in addition to SEEING what you click.

You had a good plan with very sound reasoning. I like what you did save the execution error.

Trader:
January 29, 1999
JAN 28, 1999 Too

Good idea about speaking while I click. I will try that for a while and see if I don't drive myself nuts.

The total loss was $4,300. I'm glad to hear you approve of my reasoning. It would have been good for about $3,000-$4,000. Well, I'm ready to try again today.
Trader:
January 30, 1999
JAN 29, 1999

I'll try to keep this one short.

My 20 FEB 175 puts were marked yesterday at 6.75. On today's open I sold the 10oo shares at 174.50. During the day I traded the stock back and forth for a total net profit of $4,625 (including commissions). Just before the close I was long 20oo shares of stock, long 20*175 puts, and then I sold the 170 calls, 20 times, for 8.63 while the stock was trading around 175. The vertical has a delta of about 12, so with my condor being short about **7o** deltas, I should be short about **31o** deltas ((12o x 2) + 7o). Vega and theta should both be close to neutral. That's all. The day went well and I'm feeling as though I'm getting a little better at this.

 Actual Position at Close:
+20*FEB 145 Calls / –20*FEB 150 Calls / –20*FEB 155 Calls / +20*160 Calls
Plus: +20*FEB 175 Puts / +20oo MSFT / –20 FEB 170 Calls
Basic Position: Long 20 MSFT FEB 145/150/155/160 Condor
Plus: 20 FEB 170/175 Bear Spreads

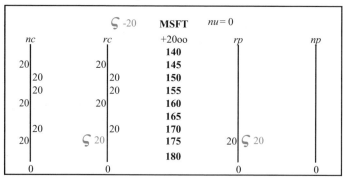

Ri$kDoctor:
January 30, 1999
Re: JAN. 29, 1999

That was a beautiful display of resiliency. You were not phased by the previous day's debacle - a great sign. The only comment

I have is minor as everything else demonstrates correct thinking: 12 x 2o (12 deltas x 20 spreads) = the 24o. More accurately: –12 x 2o = –24o plus –7o = –31o.
Have a good weekend.

Trader:
January 30, 1999
Minus signs

I guess I was just thinking positively!

Trader:
FEB 1, 1999
Scalp

I sold the 2o0o shares of stock at 174.88 at the beginning of the late
session sell off during the final hour (I missed the early morning sell off). I bought them back in at the close for a net profit of about $3,500. So for tomorrow I'm going in SHORT just over 3oo deltas with my 170/175 call bear spread 20 times.

That's all for today.

> Ri$kDoctor:
> **February 2, 1999**
> **Re: Scalp**

> Sounds good.

Trader:
February 3, 1999
FEB 2, 1999

Today I missed the 5-point downward move (I wanted to sell my 20s on the way down) and instead got caught negative scalping stock for a $2,000 loss. But my bear spread is now dong well, and if we stay around here tomorrow, and volatility comes in a bit, it should be trading for around 1.50 or maybe even less. Let me know when I should consider closing any of my FEB positions.

Ri$kDoctor:
February 3, 1999
Re: FEB 2, 1999
Position Coming In:
Basic Position: Long 20 MSFT FEB 145/150/155/160 Condor
Plus: 20 FEB 170/175 Bear Spreads

We have a problem. The problem has to do with perception and violation of one's rules. Let's start with rules:

One of YOUR self-imposed rules are that you are going to trade with limited risk, always. If this rule has changed, I need to know. One of my tasks is to help you enforce your rules by letting you know that you have violated one. Here is where perception and the options metamorphosis come in: although you had actual stock in your position you synthetically had no stock position. The stock that you had was a vital component of your bear spread. Without the stock you have a semi-future or off strike-combo (naked application). There was no way to get short with your existing position (by liquidating something) in a limited risk fashion. You chose to liquidate your stock but were negligent according to your rules that you are trading under. Again, I am here to make sure that you adhere to your rules. Breaking them from time to time is going to put you on the edge. Some people would argue that it is not as exciting to be playing with spreads as it is with stock. Stock gives immediate results. You want to make a career out of what you are trying to do, not make a quick buck to satisfy your ego. Am I right? You are in a development phase, one in which you are learning about yourself. Do you know your trading-self well enough to move on to the next step? I believe that you are still in uncharted territory. Why? You still don't know enough about your trading-self:

1. Error capacity–your reverse stock order.

2. Lifting the wrong leg, like in yesterday's trade that left you naked short calls.

3. Knowing where to get in or out. (You just asked me in this email). You, the trader, have to know that.

4. Making yourself get short (long) when you want to:

Half of your emails tell me that you wanted to do something but didn't (not 'couldn't'). MSFT was down about 7.00 for a while and it was still down around 3.50 for a longer while–I would say that you had plenty of chances to take a nice piece of the remaining 3.50 at some point or another. Remember that you, personally, are playing for 5.00 to 10.00 point moves in the stock.

Since you are playing for 5.00 and 10.00 point moves (based on your market analysis and opinion), when the market yields a profit, take it (just like when the dog barks, you have to feed him). At a minimum, adjust to take a lot off the table. Missing a trading point by a couple of points should not be a deterrent from you entering or exiting the market. You would have liked to get short yesterday at 175.00 because you thought–what? You probably thought that it was going into the mid-160s. So you missed an opportunity at 175.00 but there were a few chances around 171.00 weren't there? MSFT opened in the 172.00 area– it traded down to 170.00 and back up to 171.50 and then established a down-trend to the 167.00 area. But when is the right time to pull the trigger? You will know the answer to that question after a healthy amount of experience and analysis of where you will buy and sell in the market.
Bottom line: Before you take your trading to the next level you need more experience. Your trading has to become more instinctive. That next level does not only pertain to the size of your delta but the nature of the beasts that you manage.

Please give me an official answer to the next question: Are you or are you not going to trade with limited risk applications, even between legs? I need to know this in order to let you know if you are making mistakes. In order to abide by the limited risk trading rule, the only trade for you was to buy some 170 puts and later either sell them out (for a profit) or sell the 175 puts against them to synthetically liquidate your spread. The latter would have left you with the 170 conversion 20 times (–20*170 Calls / +20*170 Puts / +20oo Stock). Eventually you may wish to become a day trader of stock. You need the staying power to get there. Staying power includes conservation of capital and accumulation of trading experiences to establish YOUR ultimate rules. The plan is to have you trade in a fashion that will keep you safe until you become a fully established trader. You will know that when, all of a sudden, you have no more questions and only answers that you will probably be unwilling to share.

Trader:
February 3, 1999
Limited Risk
Basic Position: Long 20 MSFT FEB 145/150/155/160 Condor
Plus: 20 FEB 170/175 Bear Spreads

I have read your last email and I get the feeling you want me to trade with only limited risk strategies–so yes, I intend to trade with only limited risk strategies.   Yesterday I didn't.   I understand about buying the 170 puts to leg out of my exposure. I could also have bought the 175 calls and then sold stock against them when we turned down, Couldn't I?   Then I could have either sold the 170 puts to spread off my synthetic long 175 puts, or I could have sold the 175 calls and bought back the stock.   Is that correct?   I am unclear about whether I can scalp stock or not. Do you want me to not scalp it at all, or to just do it when it is part of a long (premium) option strategy?   You also say that I may become a stock day trader.   I have been plugging along thinking that I will try every day to make a little money trading stock.   When I have an actual market opinion I will implement an option strategy to capitalize on my opinion.   I feel more comfortable with the idea of having a spread on 100 times (or 1000   times!),   being   right   with   opinion,   and   profiting handsomely.   This to me is much more prudent than scalping stock day after day.   I am still not comfortable increasing my spread size since I'm not yet confident in my market opinions. On the other hand, scalping seems to offer a way to make money on small intraday moves that occur almost everyday.   I have been approaching this thinking that I need to learn both, long-term spread strategies and daily stock scalping techniques.   That is where I thought that I was going.   Is this right?   What is the next level?   Where am I going?   I hope I am not sounding defensive.   I only wish to convey to you my thoughts and understanding of your lessons.

    Ri$kDoctor:
    February 3, 1999
    Re: Limited Risk
    Basic Position: Long 20 MSFT FEB 145/150/155/160 Condor
    Plus: 20 FEB 170/175 Bear Spreads

    You are mistaken about the idea of buying the 175 calls first and then selling stock because you start off with a LONG DELTA and it is your aim to get short in the first place.   But, of course, if you did do the opposite, subsequently, you would have been liquidating it. However, once long the 175 calls and short stock, you could not sell the 175 calls first and buy back the stock. Selling the calls first would leave you with unprotected NAKED short stock in the interim.

You can scalp stock against long options, i.e. buy stock against long puts to turn it all into synthetic long calls. You may then, if you wish, take the stock off and be in just puts.

All I meant about becoming a stock day trader is that there are immediate results (good or bad) in trading the underlying. With options spreads, you tend to have positions on for a longer time horizon than a scalp.

Where are you going? Your goal is to make money and accumulate the necessary experience to graduate your size and develop your strategies whether they are limited risk strategies, naked stock or options strategies.

Trader:
February 4, 1999
FEB 4, 1999
Basic Position: Long 20 MSFT FEB 145/150/155/160 Condor
Plus: 20 FEB 170/175 Bear Spreads

I fully understand your drift. You have my permission to shoot me if I violate that rule again, and thank you in advance.

Early in the morning I thought that we had hit the bottom, when the stock was trading around 166.00. I covered my short 20*170 calls for 3.88 thinking that we were going up. Well, as you may know we went down another 6.00–7.00 points. I tried to sell and buy the stock when it seemed appropriate, but in the end I only made about $400 on my stock trades and totally liquidated my stock position. Finally, in the final half hour, when it was obvious they were taking the S&Ps to their support of about 1252, I tried to buy the 160 puts (I wanted to roll out of my 175 puts). By the time I had bought them, I had to pay 6.00 for 20 of them. I sold the 175 puts for 16.75. Each put trade was made when the stock was trading around 159.00. I'm not sure that I like my put roll. Of course, if we continue to sell off tomorrow I'll like it, but I now own a fair amount of premium at 160. I also own 20 of the 160 calls (from my condor), that is the 160 straddle 20 times, with about $200 in time decay (negative theta) per day and some 200 vegas after a 6 percentage point increase in implied volatility. My deltas should be close to neutral. What do you think?

Closing Position:

Basic Position: Long 20 MSFT FEB 145/150/155/160 Condor

Ri$kDoctor:
February 5, 1999
Re: FEB 4, 1999

To me it doesn't sound like you did so bad. Maybe I am still in the dark but I think that you are still quite short.

Your position was synthetically long the put spread or short the call spread 20 times. When you covered the 170 calls that left you long cheap little 175 calls on a shot (synthetically). You cannot lose much with that, even if you were wrong. When MSFT went down another 6.00–7.00 points you were not losing much on the long 170 calls. The stock trades made about $400 and you ended up with no stock, which then turned the 175 calls into 175 puts. That beats losing 6.00 or 7.00 points, which the stock had dropped (you saved $12,000 to $14,000). Your long deep in-the-money 175 puts went further in-the-money, more so the longer you waited as the stock was dropping. It was a good idea to roll the 175 puts into the 160 puts. Long out-of-the-money 160 puts are a lot less risky than the long in-the-money 175 puts. By the way, you said that you will be happy with the 160 puts on a continued drop. For your information the 175 puts will do a lot better because they are almost like short stock when going down. The purpose of your rolling the 175s into the 160s was to take money off the table. You did that to the tune of $21,000 (20 x 10.50 x which is 16.50–6.00). It might have been easier to enter the order as a vertical spread, i.e. to sell 20*160/175 put spreads.

As far as owning 20 of the 160 calls goes, part of the condor, it is not wise to combine a cheap condor with a naked put play and add up all your deltas. Your condor loved what happened today and will love it even more when the gas comes out (when implied volatility decreases). I would just try to concentrate on the 160 puts alone.

I think that, other than getting the best prices of the day, you did great.

I would have done it a little differently. After buying the 170 calls,   I would have left the 175 synthetic calls alone (don't mess with deeps versus stock unless you have to). What were the calls trading for at the time? About 1.75? I would have then played the market with options closer to the money versus stock.

On Friday try not to let your condor inventory cloud your mind and confuse you. You seem to be getting wrapped up in the components. Think synthetically. If you happen to trade a vertical, which involves parts of your position, trade it or keep it as that vertical until that new trade is over. If you decide at the end of the day that it has you half way liquidated, then assume the balance of the position as your new position. You will need to decide whether you want to leave it, liquidate it (in its simplest form), add to it or spread it off a new way. Keep it simple. Your condor can take care of itself as it is. You take care of those 160 puts. If those are still versus stock, then train yourself to think of the package as simply long the 160 calls–nothing more. You are doing well.

Trader:
February 5, 1999
Clarification

I incorrectly stated that I was going home delta neutral. In fact, I'm SHORT roughly 10oo deltas from the 20*160 puts. I wasn't sure if I was happy about being short 10oo deltas and long all that premium (right after the close the S&Ps rallied 5.00–7.00 points, and MSFT was trading around 159.50–159.75) but three hours later the S&Ps were DOWN 3.50 from where they closed. My hunch is that the selling may continue on Friday. I'll focus on the 160 puts and be sure to not disturb the bird. She may lay a golden egg.

Ri$kDoctor:
February 5, 1999
Re: Clarification

You are also a tad short with the condor that desires MSFT to be between 150.00 and 155.00.

Over the past few sessions you have had positions involving

many strikes. You will most likely have to break the position down over and over in order to keep it straight. During slow times and especially after fills, which do not require a quick second leg, dissect to check to see if you are where you intended to be. Don't forget to check your units and ensure that both sides be either positive or flat (zero) after each trade. It should be a good exercise. If you have trouble or get confused, decrease your leg sizes until you get comfortable again. Do it all by hand until you are proficient at it.

In addition to taking profits on the 160 puts, I would consider buying back the 155/160 spread (in the condor), if MSFT gets down close to 155.00 or if the spread gets cheap enough not to be short it. By then, the stock will have been down about 10% from its highs at that point.

Trader:
February 5, 1999
Friday AM Update

I am looking at my position as the long 145/150 call vertical against the short 155/160 call vertical, both 20 times. I also own 20 of the 160 puts with no stock. Today I'll work the 160 puts with 20oo shares of stock for instant gratification. I imagine, by the end of the day, I will have either liquidated the puts and stock, or spread off the puts into either a bull or bear spread.

In your last email you told me to perhaps buy back "the 155/160 spread" from the condor, should we trade near the 155.00 level. I'll do that should we trade in that range, otherwise I'll leave the condor alone and focus on my 20*160 puts. Thanks for all the help.

Ri$kDoctor:
February 5, 1999
Re: Friday AM update & Chart Update

If you buy the 20oo stock then all you will be left with is long 20*160 calls. You might want to cover at least half of the 155/60 call spreads here, if you haven't already.

Trader:
February 6, 1999
FEB 5, 1999 (sorry for the delay)

I don't know how dynamic your market data is over there, but after we hung up MSFT rallied another 3.00 points. Before I knew what was happening the stock was trading 160.75! When I first clicked on my transaction screen we were trading around 155.50. So I was short some 10oo deltas for over 5.00 miserable points! The bounce happened so fast that I couldn't find my footing in the market. I had lost touch with my indicators and the flow. Something was wrong, I couldn't tell what, and MSFT was soaring. I was caught off balance, confused, and in disbelief. It turns out that the S&Ps only rallied a few points, which normally wouldn't spike MSFT up 5.00 points. I was furious that I had again missed the big move of the day! Now instead of a reasonable profit I was looking at a nasty loss. I could tell that I was about to lose it completely. Adrenaline was pumping, not from market excitement, but sheer rage. Like someone caught in a burning building, I was now looking for an exit strategy. I just wanted out. However, I couldn't bear the thought of going home with a $5,000 loss (that's what my software was telling me anyway), on a Friday, and my birthday. No way! I took a deep breath. I thought, "I'll be darned if MSFT doesn't sell off at least a little." I was short. I sat tight. With only about 20 minutes to go, the S&Ps started selling off towards the day's low of 1238.00 But MSFT was barely moving. Finally, MSFT gave way and started trading around 159.00, and then in the 158.00 range. Oh, she fluttered back and forth like a rabid bat! The S&Ps were now hovering at a new intraday low of 1236.00, INTC, IBM, the NASDAQ Comp., etc. were all down, but off their lows of the day. I couldn't tell if we were about to collapse (those S&Ps still haven't tested their 50 day moving average of 1228.00) or if it was just another fake sell off. I didn't want to just "throw the dice" and try to buy stock around 158.50 in case we were about to tank. So I watched for clues. There were only some five minutes to my nightmare left. I knew that she was almost ready to reveal her secret. Finally, I decided it was time to buy the stock - and got filled at 159.00. We rallied further. So I tried to hit the $5 bid for the 160 puts - and actually got filled. At the closing bell MSFT was trading 160.00. I sold my 20oo shares, prior to opening in New York, for 160.13. The puts were marked at 5.00 (closing market was 4.75–5.13). I lost 1.13 ($2,250) on them and traded stock all day for a $250 loss.

All in all it was a lousy day but I feel as though I was given a second chance at life.
Lessons learned:

1. Don't get caught chatting on the phone during a 5.00 point move. (By the way, you were absolutely right about covering in the 155.00 area. It was time to buy in my short call spread!)

2. Recognize when you are about to lose it and get neutral. Take your losses before you make them worse. (I came within an inch of throwing it all in for a heavy, reckless loss.)

3. Be very grateful if you ever, are lucky enough to, come out of a near meltdown with your losses cut in half. (I am. Believe me!)

I can imagine that these numbers aren't that much to most other traders. I know they're not. But I really hate giving away any money. Not losing money (well, actually...) but giving it away! I'm satisfied that I was able to recover some of it. My position now consists of nothing but my condor. Short 155 deltas, short 21 vegas, and earning $42/day over the weekend. That's all to my miserable tale. I'm actually happy because I know how close it came to a mild disaster. I'm going to eat sushi, drink saki and beer, and see my girlfriend.

Have a good weekend.

> Ri$kDoctor:
> **February 7, 1999**
> **FEB 5, 1999 (sorry for the delay)**
>
> One major lesson that you are not seeing is that your original position was right for 5 lousy points!!! That's nothing to sneeze at. Most short sellers would take their profits and run.
>
> Important: This is one of those important things that you need to take note of. Remember what I told you about learning about your trading-self (page 24, 40% down the page, the paragraph beginning: "Until traders'... What have you learned about your trading-self here? I will suggest for you what I hope you will learn:

1. You are able to lose your "footing in the market".
2. You are able to lose "touch with your indicators and the flow". These are signs that perhaps your reasons for being long or short are no longer valid. Get flat until the market corresponds with your indicators otherwise you may get shell-shocked and freeze. I'll reiterate reasons for exiting a trade: a) enough profits b) enough of a loss c) you lose your reasons for being bullish, bearish or thinking that the market is moving sideways (i.e. trading in a small range). What do you do? Get flat...now! Shoot first, and ask questions later. When you are no longer confused, you can look for a new entry point. You said that the S&Ps rallied only a few points (.025%) while MSFT rallied 5.00 points (over 3%). There is nothing 'normal' in this business. With this type of trading you must keep your finger on the trigger at all times. My daughter would not normally run out into the street but I hold her hand just the same.
3. **Important!** You are able to become "furious".
    Anger can work for very few successful traders when they learn how to channel that negative energy to work for them in the markets. If you become one of them it will take an enormous amount of work on your part to get in touch with how to benefit from that. For most traders, however, anger is their worst enemy. Anger can cause stubbornness and rash decision making which can be devastating. Until you learn how to control (use) your anger, do not use anger as a trading tool or strategy! It will most likely destroy you. When angry, get flat!
4. You are able to "again miss the big moves and you are not going to miss all of the big moves. It is going to be somewhere in between. It is just another day. Don't dwell on it. Until you become a master at integrating your disappointment, depression and anger into your trading, as stated above, it can serve you harmfully.
5. If you understand what I have been talking about (above) it will help you to react instinctively faster in the future and avoid becoming enraged.

The market does not know that you are down $5,000 but it does have a way of knowing that you are short. Of course you have to be cognizant of the fact that it could cruise to 177.00 in a heartbeat, in spite of all your indicators.

You did a good job on your eventual cover point. Violating your trading rule about trading stock by itself, however, was not good.

You did undo the rule violation quickly though.

Have you thought about what would you have done if the price had broken to 158.00, prior to the opening in New York?

You are doing fine. Don't look a gift horse in the mouth. There will be days on the horizon that will be boring with small moves. You will be praying for one and two strike moves in a single session. This time you got in the way on the down move, but had you not, you probably would have flattened at 155.00 because the move was big and the profits large enough.

It was not a lousy day at all. There were some shining moments in a day that ended in a loss. The day before you had the same kind of a day and you made a good profit. You are a businessman operating in a business that trades physically and emotionally. It is important to know this aspect of your trading-self: trading is very dramatic for you, which is not a problem as long as you recognize consists of managing profits and losses. You actually manage these and accept it.

If you are chatting on the telephone while trading, learn to hang up on people when you have to go. Say, "I've got to go" and just hang up. Whoever it is will learn to call you back after the close or sooner. Do not be afraid to hang up on your mother or me. Don't be polite and ask whether you can call the person back or wait for a reply. Let each person know in advance that you may have to go without warning.

As far as being right about pricing or market opinions in general goes, it is up to the trader to sift through all the information available, i.e. what their mentor says/thinks, what the trader next to him says/thinks, what the phone-order person says/thinks, what the indicators say or what you think they are saying, and form an opinion from this.

Pay no attention to what you hear about the profits and losses of other traders in chat sessions, because it is mostly hearsay.

You say that you hate give away money. Days like the one that you have described can teach you a great deal and can make you more careful in the future.

By the way, your condor position is fine.

CONCLUSION

A lot can happen over the life of an option and the life of an options trader. As the trader, featured in this chapter, got more and more comfortable with trading, he began to trade more stock outright and he believes that dabbling in options helped with that a lot. Stock trading provides one with immediate results, whereas options are more desirable for longer time horizons on bigger sizes. It is very easy to get discouraged by the markets, but he developed a system of pulling in the reins when things get tough. As he found his footing, he gradually increased his size as profitability became more consistent.

Established your own set of rules to trade by and trading options will become more second nature to you.

E P I L O G U E

"Tell me and I will forget.
Show me and I will remember.
Involve me and I will understand."
Aristotle

The best way for options knowledge to be absorbed is through experience, which can be costly in the options business. Learn from the triumphs and the mishaps that are passed on throughout this book and the live interactive Webinars (Web Based Seminars) hosted at www.RiskDoctor.com. These experiences are supported by graphic illustrations and commentary in the Forums at www.RiskIllustrated.com.

Seminars/Webinars

RD1 is a four-hour course that starts beyond the basics. Get started with pre-requisite basics at www.cme.com/edu/options/ and a fresh perspective on the basics at www.chartbenders.com/learnoptions.aspx. There is a pretty decent animated tutorial that was created by the Options Institute available at http://www.888options.com/strategy/default.jsp.

RD2 is an intermediate twelve-hour course using this book as the main text and considering current market nuances.

RD3 is an advanced Webinar series that will bring the intermediate trader to the next level (RD2 is recommended first, but can also be taken simultaneously to RD3). This series addresses the pros and cons of current stock, future or index options scenarios submitted by members. Hybrid Hedge strategies based on stocks such as in Warren Buffet's portfolio are discussed. New portfolio components are added frequently. The presentations/discussions include position dissection examples and market forecasting methods using Diamonetrics™. We debate different methods of getting long, short or market neutral, capturing time decay (all with limited risk exposure) and the Art of Position Adjustment over the life of the options.

RD4U – is an individual one on one consultation with The Ri$k Doctor, cutting to the chase with post mortems and individual trading issues. An extensive questionnaire needs to be filled out prior to doing this.

Position Dissection is now being taken to an intermediate market maker level, stretching the retail investor's consciousness in order to enable more swift and appropriate dissections with retail customer type positions. The three-hour course includes a manual and the Excel version of Position Dissector Software that can help with trading and risk management.

Diamonetrics™

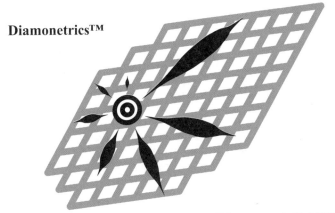

DiamonetricGrid™

Diamonetrics™ has been my proprietary technical analysis tool. I have never really shared because it was rather difficult to explain how to build a proper Diamonetric Grid™. But now the essential Diamonetric Grid comes pre-built, ready to copy and paste, to simply stretch, scrunch and swivel into place capturing the market's essence. Diamonetrics is a very efficient tool used to determine profit opportunities based on the forecasting of probable trading ranges at particular options expiration dates.

I know of nothing better available for speculating with limited risk, high probability short premium (time on your side) plays (butterflies, condors, calendar spreads, iron calendars, etc.) and hedges for stocks, equity indexes, financial futures, currencies, commodities and other underlying securities.

Based on pattern recognition, the symmetrical diamond shaped grid (Diamonetric Grid™) is overlaid on a chart to highlight symmetrical trend channels and project them out to expiration day. The slopes are sometimes different to traditional trend lines due to the width of the WickZones™ (where the wicks of the candle sticks dip or spike) and to the placement of the grid accentuating up-trends and down-trends.

The course includes three-hours of recorded (audio/visual) instruction: Diamonetrics.avi, the Diamonetrics.pdf Manual and the Diamonetrics Grid.xls (with pre-drawn objects to overlay charts).

APPENDIX

DISSECTIONS FOR OPTIONS METAMORPHOSIS

This Appendix is to be used in conjunction with Chapter 2's Options Metamorphosis in exhibits 2-11 and 2-12, to get a close-up view of each transformed position and the proofs of their dissections.

The diagrams are color-coded to match the 4 quadrants in Exhibit 2-11 and follow clockwise (1-8) around the quadrant. Each diagram is numbered with the quadrant number and the position number (e.g., I-6) and follows the order listed in Exhibit 2-12.

In each dissection proof, various font styles are used to aid the reader in understanding how the actions progress. The original position of **+10ooU** is presented within a red imploding square. The first adjustment is typed in bold and color matched to the background color in the centre of the quadrant it represents. The second adjustment (where appropriate) is shown in blue italics. The SynTool is depicted with a red ς to the immediate left while the BoxTool is also in red surrounded by a red box □. The resulting positions are matched in both color and shape to Exhibit 2-11. (E.g., Green Octagon for position 'II', Green Circle for position 'II-2').

I) LONG STRADDLE: by BUYING twice the number of PUTS

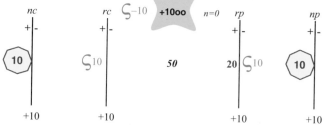

I-1) SHORT BUTTERFLY with a 4 strike value range: by SELLING a STRANGLE two strikes out.

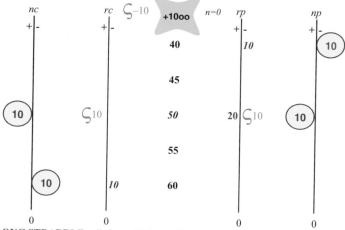

I-2) LONG STRADDLE rolled to a higher strike: by TRADING twice the amount of BEAR SPREADS with the sale strike = to the original hedge strike.

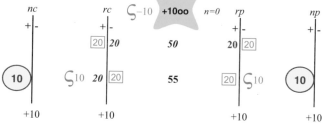

I-3) PUT (LongMore) BACK SPREAD: by SELLING a higher strike CALL.

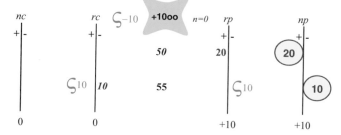

I-4 LONG STRANGLE: by TRADING a BEAR SPREAD with the sale strike = to the original hedge strike.

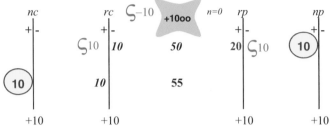

I-5 SHORT BUTTERFLY with a 2 strike value range: by SELLING a surrounding STRANGLE.

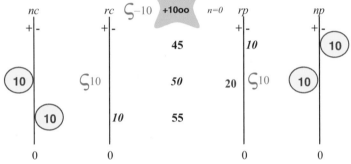

I-6 LONG STRANGLE: by TRADING a BULL SPREAD with the sale strike = to the original hedge strike.

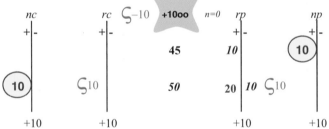

I-7 CALL (LongMore) BACKSPREAD: by SELLING a lower strike PUT.

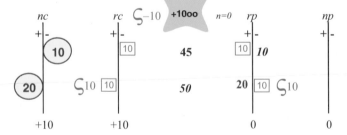

I-8 LONG STRADDLE rolled to a lower strike: by TRADING twice the amount of BULL SPREADS with the sale strike = to the original hedge strike.

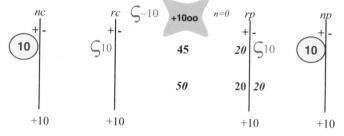

II SHORT PUT (Covered Write): by SELLING a CALL.

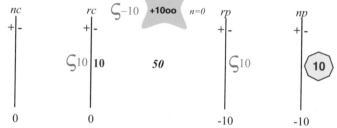

II-1 PUT (LongMore) BACKSPREAD: by BUYING twice the number of lower strike PUTS.

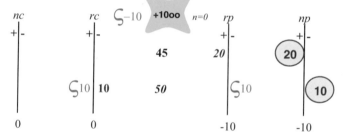

II-2 LONG SEMI-STOCK: by BUYING a higher strike CALL.

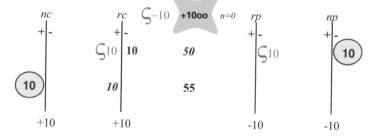

II–3) CONVERSION (Flat): by BUYING a same strike PUT.

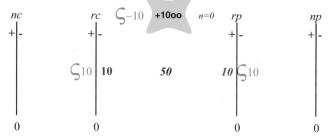

II–4a) SHORT PUT rolled to a deeper strike: by TRADING a BULL SPREAD with the purchased strike = to the original hedge strike.

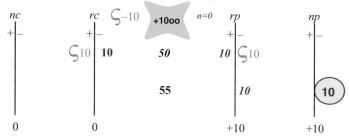

II–4b) SHORT PUT rolled to a cheaper strike: by TRADING a BEAR SPREAD with the purchased strike = to the original hedge strike.

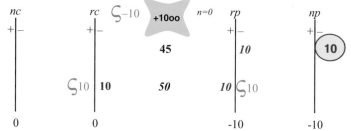

II–5) PUT (ShortMore) RATIO SPREAD: by BUYING half the amount of higher strike PUTS.

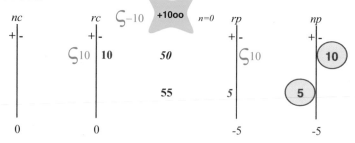

II–6 BEAR SPREAD: by BUYING a higher strike PUT.

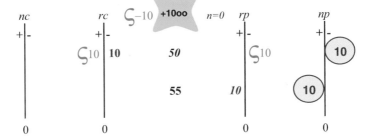

II–7 SHORT STRANGLE: by SELLING a different strike CALL.

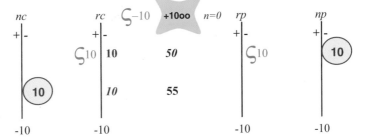

II–8 BULL SPREAD: by BUYING a lower strike PUT.

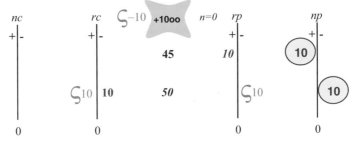

III SHORT STRADDLE: by SELLING twice the number of CALLS.

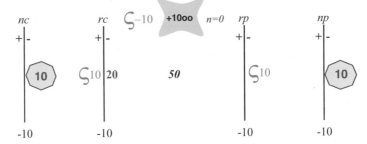

III–1 LONG BUTTERFLY with a 2 strike value range: by BUYING a surrounding STRANGLE.

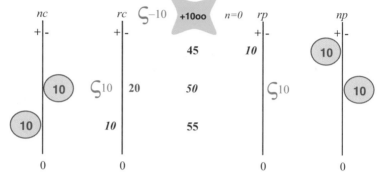

III–2 SHORT STRANGLE: by TRADING a BULL SPREAD with the purchase strike = to the original hedge strike.

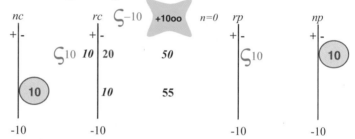

III–3 PUT (ShortMore) RATIO SPREAD: by BUYING a higher strike CALL.

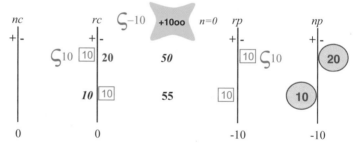

III–4 SHORT STRADDLE rolled to a higher strike: by TRADING twice the amount of BULL SPREADS with the purchase strike = to the original hedge strike.

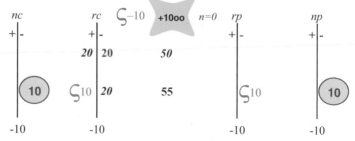

III–5 LONG BUTTERFLY with a 4 strike value range: by BUYING a STRANGLE two strikes out.

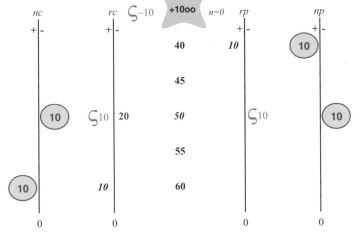

III–6 SHORT STRADDLE rolled to a lower strike: by TRADING twice the amount of BEAR SPREADS with the purchase strike = to the original hedge strike.

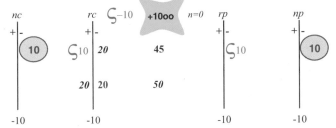

III–7 CALL (ShortMore) RATIO SPREAD: by BUYING a lower strike PUT.

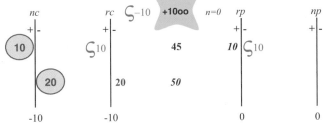

III–8 SHORT STRANGLE: by TRADING a BEAR SPREAD with the purchase strike = to the original hedge strike.

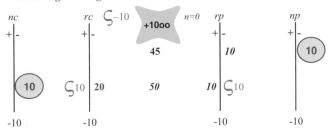

IV LONG CALL: by BUYING a PUT.

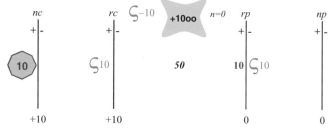

IV–1 CALL (LongMore) BACK SPREAD: by SELLING half the number of lower strike CALLS.

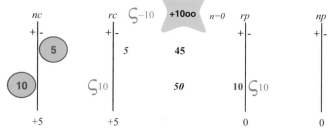

IV–2 BEAR SPREAD: by SELLING a lower strike CALL.

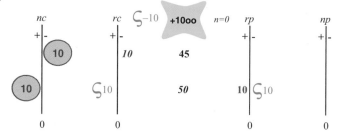

IV–3 LONG STRANGLE: by BUYING a different strike PUT.

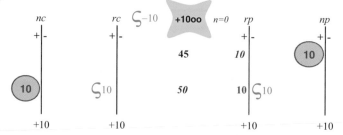

IV-4 BULL SPREAD: by SELLING a higher strike CALL.

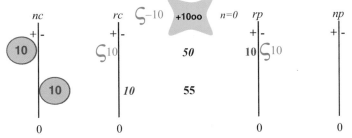

IV-5 CALL (ShortMore) RATIO SPREAD: by SELLING twice the amount of higher strike CALLS.

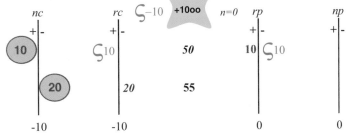

IV-6a LONG CALL rolled to a deeper strike: by TRADING a BULL SPREAD with the sale strike = to the original hedge strike.

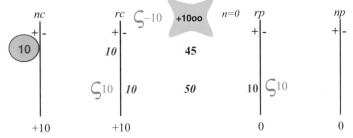

IV-6b LONG CALL rolled to a cheaper strike: by TRADING a BEAR SPREAD with the sale strike = to the original hedge strike.

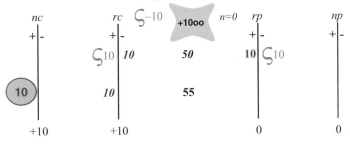

IV–7 CONVERSION (Flat): by SELLING a same strike CALL.

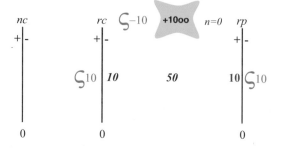

IV–8 LONG SEMI-STOCK: by SELLING a lower strike PUT.

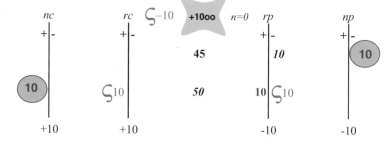

G L O S S A R Y

ABANDON: The act of not exercising or selling an option before its expiration.

ACCRUED INTEREST: The interest due on a bond since the last interest payment was made, up to, but not including the settlement date. Anyone wishing to buy the bond pays the market price of the bond plus any accrued interest. Conversely, anyone selling a bond will have the proceeds increased by the amount of accrued interest.

ACQUISITION: The 'A' in M&A (Mergers and Acquisitions) is when one company buys enough stock of another company to take control of that company. When a take-over attempt is "unfriendly", the buying company may offer a price for the other company's stock that is well above current market value. The management of the company that is being bought might ask for a better stock price or try to join with a third company to counter the take-over attempt.

ADJUSTED OPTION: An option resulting after an event such as a stock split (2 for 1 stock split), stock dividend, merger, or spin-off. An adjusted option may represent some amount other than the one hundred shares that is standard in the U.S. For example, after a 2 for 1 stock split, the adjusted option will represent 200 shares. For certain adjusted options, the multiplier of the option may be something other than the $100 that is standard in the U.S.

AFFIDAVIT OF DOMICILE: A notarized affidavit executed by the legal representative of an estate reciting the residence of the decedent at the time of death. This document would be required when transferring ownership of a security from a deceased person's name.

ALL-OR-NONE ORDER (AON): An order that must be filled completely when the order is executed or not filled at all. In other words, partial fills are not allowed on this type of order.

AMERICAN DEPOSITORY RECEIPT (ADR): Foreign company equities traded on a U.S. exchange. The ADR is issued by a U.S. bank in place of the foreign company's shares, which are held in trust by the bank. ADRs facilitate the trading of foreign stocks in U.S. markets. ADRs have exposure to currency fluctuations.

AMERICAN STOCK EXCHANGE (AMEX): One of the major stock and option exchanges in the U.S. It is located in the financial district of New York City.

AMERICAN-STYLE OPTION: An option contract that can be exercised at any time from the time the option is purchased to the expiration date of the option.

ARBITRAGE: The simultaneous purchase and sale of identical or equivalent financial instruments in order to benefit from a discrepancy in their price relationship. More generally, it refers to an opportunity to make risk-free returns that are greater than the risk-free rate of return.

ASK or OFFER: The price of a stock or option at which a seller is offering to sell a security, that is, the price that investor may purchase a stock or option.

ASSIGNED: To have received notification of an assignment on short options by The Options Clearing Corporation through a broker.

ASSIGNMENT: When the seller (writer) of an option receives an exercise notice that obligates him to sell (in the case of a call) or purchase (in the case of a put) the underlying stock at the option's strike price.

AT-THE-MONEY (ATM): An option is at-the-money when the price of the stock is at or near the strike price.

AUTOMATED ORDER ENTRY SYSTEM: Some exchanges have computerized systems designed to route stock and option orders directly to the trading pit. They are intended to speed the execution of orders. These systems generally have limits on the size of orders. Examples of these systems are: RAES, AUTO EX, and SUPERDOT.

AUTOMATED EXECUTION SYSTEM (AUTO EX): The automated order routing system on the American Stock Exchange.

AUTOMATIC EXERCISE: The Options Clearing Corporation (OCC) uses this procedure to exercise in-the-money options at expiration. Doing so protects the owner of the option from losing the intrinsic value of the option because of the owner's failure to exercise. Unless instructed not to do so by the owner of the option (through the owner's broker), The Options Clearing Corporation will exercise all expiring equity options that are held in customer accounts if they are in-the-money by 75 cents

(3/4 of a point) or more. The OCC will automatically exercise an option position if it is 75 cents (3/4 of a point) or greater in-the-money at expiration unless the owner of the option instructs otherwise.

BACK MONTHS: A rather arbitrary term that refers to the classes of options with the expiration months that are further dated the option class with the nearest expiration month.

BACKSPREAD: An option position composed of either all calls or all puts, with long options and short options at two different strike prices. The options are all on the same stock and usually of the same expiration, with more options purchase than sold. A backspread is the sale of an option(s) and the purchase of a greater number of the same type of options that are out-of-the-money with respect to the one(s) purchased. For example, an 80/90 put 1-by-3 backspread is long 3*80 puts and short 1*90 put.

BANK GUARANTEE LETTER: The document supplied by a bank certifying that a person has a specific amount of funds on deposit with the bank.

BASIS: Generally referring to the futures markets, it is the difference between the cash price of the underlying commodity and the price of a futures contract based on that underlying commodity. Cash price minus futures price equals basis.

BASIS POINT: A .01% tick on a 1.00% scale used to describe the yields of interest rates or interest rate products. For example, when the U.S. Fed raises the discount rate 25 basis points, the discount rate goes from 5.00% to 5.25%.

BASIS RISK: The risk of the basis between the cash price and the future price widening or narrowing between the time a hedge position is implemented and liquidated.

BEAR: A person who believes that the price of a particular security or the market as a whole will go lower.

BEARISH: The outlook of a person anticipating lower prices in a particular security or the market as a whole.

BEAR MARKET: Any market in which prices are trending lower.

BEAR SPREAD: Generally speaking, it is any spread that theoretically profits when the market moves down. Specifically it refers to a vertical spread.

BETA: A measure of the return (in percentage terms) on a stock relative to the return (in percentage terms) of an index. For example a stock with a beta of .80 should have a percentage net change equal to 80% of the percentage net change of the index. Therefore if the index is down 2% the stock in question should be down 1.6% (.80x2%).

BID: The price of a stock or option at which a buyer is willing to purchase a security; the price at which a customer may sell a security.

BID/ASK (OFFER) SPREAD: The difference between the bid and ask prices for a particular stock or option.

BINOMIAL MODEL: A mathematical model used to price options. Generally used for American-style options, the model creates a binomial lattice to price an option, based on the stock price, strike price, days until expiration, interest rate, dividends, and the estimated volatility of the stock. One of the main differences from the Black Scholes Model is that it factors in the possibility of early exercise of the options.

BLACK SCHOLES MODEL: A mathematical model used to price options. Generally used for European-style options, the model prices options using a probability-weighted sum of stock and a bond. Black-Scholes uses the stock price, strike price, days until expiration, interest rate, dividends, and the estimated volatility of the stock as variables in the model.

BLOCK or BLOCK TRADE: A large position or transaction of stock, generally at least 10,000 shares or more.

BLUE SKY LAWS: The popular name for laws enacted by various states to protect the public against securities fraud. The term is believed to have been coined by a judge who stated that some brokers were selling everything including the "blue sky" to investors.

BOND: A debt instrument or promissory note of a corporation, municipality, or the U.S. Government. A bond represents debt on which the issuer of the debt usually promises to pay the owner of the bond a specific amount of interest for a defined amount of time and to repay the loan on the maturity date. Bonds are distinct from stock (equity), which represents ownership.

BOX SPREAD: An option position composed of a long call and short put at one strike, and a short call and long put at a different strike. For example, a long 50/60 box spread would be long the 50 call, short the 50 put, short the 60 call and long the 60 put. Considered largely immune to changes in the price of the underlying stock, in most cases, a box spread is an interest rate trade. For all intents and purposes, the buyer of the box is lending money to the options market, and the seller of the box is borrowing money from the options market.

BREAK-EVEN POINT(S): The stock price(s) at which an option position generates neither a profit nor a loss. An option position's break-even point(s) are generally calculated for the options' expiration date. Option pricing models can be used to calculate a position's break-even point before the options' expiration date.

BROKER: A broker is an individual or firm that charges a fee or commission for executing, either on the floor of an exchange or electronically, buy, sell, or spread orders submitted by a customer or firm.

BROKER LOAN RATE: This is the interest rate that banks charge brokerage firms to finance their (the brokerage firms) customers' stock and option positions.

BROKER-DEALER: Generally, a broker-dealer is a person or firm who facilitates trades between buyers and sellers and receives a commission or fee for his services. When a broker acts in the capacity of a dealer, he may buy and sell stocks and options for his own account, which can generate profits or losses.

BULL: A person who believes that the price of a particular security or the market as a whole will go higher.

BULLISH: The outlook of a person anticipating higher prices in a particular security or the market as a whole.

BULL MARKET: Any market in which prices are trending higher.

BULL SPREAD: Generally speaking, it is any spread that theoretically profits when the market moves up. Specifically it refers to a vertical spread.

BUTTERFLY SPREAD: An option position composed of either all calls or all puts (with the exception of an iron butterfly), with long options and short options at three different strikes. The options are all on the same stock and of the same expiration, with the quantity of long options and the quantity of short options netting to zero. The strikes are equidistant from each other. For example, a long 50/60/70 put butterfly is long 1*50 put, short 2*60 puts, and long 1*70 put.

BUY ON CLOSE: To buy at the end of a trading session at a price within the closing range.

BUY ON OPENING: To buy at the beginning of a trading session at a price within the opening range.

BUYING POWER: The amount of money available in an account to buy stocks or options. Buying power is determined by the sum of the cash held in the brokerage account and the loan value of any marginable securities in the account without depositing additional equity.

BUY-TO-COVER: A buy order that closes or offsets a short position in stock or options.

BUY-WRITE: Synonymous to a covered call or covered write, this is a position of long stock and short a number of calls representing the same amount of shares as the long stock position. This position may be entered into as a spread order with both sides (buying stock and selling calls) being executed simultaneously. For example, a buy-write is buying 500 shares of stock and writing 5*50 strike calls.

CABINET OR "CAB" TRADE: An option trade at a "cabinet price", which is equal to one dollar. Generally, cabinet trades only occur at very far out-of-the-money options. Cabinet trades are not always available depending on who you clear.

CALENDAR SPREAD (TIME SPREAD): An option position composed of either only calls or only puts, with the purchase or sale of an option with a nearby expiration offset by the purchase or sale of an option with the same strike price, but a more distant expiration. The options are on the same stock and have the same strike price. The quantity of long options and the quantity of short options net to zero. For example, long the AUG/NOV 65 call calendar spread is short 1 August 65 call and long 1 November 65 call.

CALL OPTION: A call option gives the buyer of the call the right, but not the obligation, to buy the underlying stock at the option's strike price. The seller of the call is obligated to deliver (sell) the underlying stock at the option's strike price to the buyer of the call when the buyer exercises his right.

CALLED AWAY: The term used when the seller of a call option is obligated to deliver the underlying stock to the buyer of the call at the strike price of the call option.

CALL WRITER: An investor who receives a premium and takes on, for a specified time period, the obligation to sell the underlying security at a specified price at the call buyer's discretion.

CANCELED ORDER: An order to buy or sell stock or options that is canceled before it has been executed. Generally, it is easier to cancel a limit order than a market order. A limit order can be canceled at any time as long as it has not been executed. Market orders can get executed so quickly that it is usually impossible to cancel them.

CAPITAL GAIN OR CAPITAL LOSS: Profit or loss generated from transactions in stocks, options, bonds, real estate, or other property.

CARRY/CARRYING CHARGE: Interest is charged on any money borrowed to finance a position of stocks or options. The interest cost of financing the position is known as the carry.

CASH ACCOUNT: An account in which all positions must be paid for in full. No short positions in stocks or options are allowed in a cash account.

CASH MARKET: Generally referred to regarding futures markets, the cash market is where transactions are made in the commodity or instrument underlying the future. For example, there are cash markets in physical commodities such as grains and livestock, metals, and crude oil, financial instruments such as U.S. Treasury Bonds and Eurodollars, as well as foreign currencies such as the Japanese yen and the Canadian dollar. As it relates to futures on stock indices, the cash market is the aggregate market value of the stocks making up the stock index.

CASH SETTLED OPTION: An option that delivers a cash amount, as opposed to the underlying stock or futures contracts such as with options on stocks or futures, when exercised. The amount of cash delivered is determined by the difference between the option strike price and the value of the underlying index or security. In the U.S., stock index options like the OEX and SPX are cash settled options.

CHICAGO BOARD OF TRADE (CBOT): Founded in 1848 with 82 original members, today the CBOT is the one of the largest futures and options exchanges in the world. It is known for its grain and U.S. Treasury Bond futures. Futures and futures options are traded at the CBOT.

CHICAGO BOARD OPTIONS EXCHANGE (CBOE): The Chicago Board Options Exchange is currently (2000) the largest option exchange in the U.S. Formed in 1973, the CBOE pioneered "listed options" with standardized contracts. Equity and index options are traded at the CBOE.

CHICAGO MERCANTILE EXCHANGE (CME): Originally formed in 1874 as the Chicago Produce Exchange, where products such as butter, eggs, and poultry were traded, the CME is now one of the biggest futures and options exchanges in the world. The CME trades futures on stock indices, foreign currencies, livestock, and Eurodollars. Futures and futures options are traded at the CME.

CLASS OF OPTIONS (OPTIONS CLASS): Options of the same type either all calls or all puts on the same underlying security.

CLEAR/CLEARING: The process by which orders are accounted for and matched, and funds transferred.

CLEARING BROKER-DEALER: A broker-dealer that clears its own trades as well as those of introducing brokers.

CLEARING HOUSE: An agency connected with an exchange through which all stock and option transactions are reconciled, settled, guaranteed, and later either offset or fulfilled through delivery of the stock and through which payments are made. It may be a separate corporation, rather than a division of the exchange itself.

CLEARING MEMBER: Clearing members of U.S. exchanges accept responsibility for all trades cleared through them, and share secondary responsibility for the liquidity of the exchanges' clearing operation. Clearing members earn commissions for clearing their customers' trades. Clearing members must meet minimum capital requirements.

CLOSE (C), THE: The time at which trading on a stock or option ends for the day. In reference to the O,H,L,C "C" represents the closing price of the session.

CLOSING PRICE: The price of a stock or option at the last transaction of the day.

CLOSING PURCHASE: A transaction in which a person who had initially sold short a stock or option exits or closes his short position by buying back the stock or option.

CLOSING RANGE: The range of high and low prices, or bid and ask prices, recorded during the close (the final closing minutes of the trading day).

CLOSING TRANSACTION: A transaction in which a person who had initially bought or sold stock, futures or options exits or closes (liquidates) his position by selling his long stock, futures or options or buying back his short stock, futures or options.

COMBO: Often another term for synthetic stock, a combo is an option position composed of calls and puts on the same stock, same expiration, and typically the same strike price. The quantity of long options and the quantity of short options nets to zero. Buying a combo is buying synthetic stock; selling a combo is selling synthetic stock. For example, a long 60 combo is long 1*60 call and short 1*60 put. Sometimes, combo is used to describe options at two different strikes, in which case it would not be synthetic stock.

COMMINGLING: The combining by a brokerage firm of customer securities with firm securities and pledging them as joint collateral for a bank loan; this practice is prohibited unless authorized by customers.(NASD)

COMMISSION: The one time fee charged by a broker to a customer when the customer executes a stock or option trade through the brokerage firm.

CONDOR SPREAD: An option position composed of either all calls or all puts (with the exception of an iron condor), with long options and short options at four different strikes. The options are all on the same stock and of the same expiration, with the quantity of long options and the quantity of short options netting to zero. Generally, the strikes are equidistant from each other, but if the strikes are not equidistant, the spread is called a pterodactyl. For example, a long 50/55/60/65 call condor is long 1*50 call, short 1*55 call, short 1*60 call, and long 1*65 call. In a long (short) condor the highest and lowest stikes are both long (short) while the two middle strikes are both short (long).

CONFIRMATION STATEMENT: After a stock or options transaction has taken place, the brokerage firm must issue a statement to the customer. The statement contains the name of the underlying stock, the number of shares or options bought or sold and the prices at which the transactions occurred.

CONSOLIDATED TAPE: The ticker reporting transactions of NYSE listed stocks that take place on the NYSE or any of the other regional stock exchanges. Similarly, transactions of AMEX listed securities, and certain other securities listed on regional stock exchanges, are reported on a separate tape.

CONTINGENCY ORDER: When you place a stock or options order you can choose to place contingencies on that order, meaning that the order will be filled only when a specific event has occurred. For example, a contingency order might be, "Buy 10 XYZ 80 calls at the market if XYZ stock trades above 75".

CONTRACT: The basic unit of trading for options. An option, whether it's a put or a call, is an agreement between two parties (the buyer and the seller) to abide by the terms of the option contract as defined by an exchange.

CONTRACT MONTH: Generally used to describe the month in which an option contract expires.

CONTRACT SIZE: The number of shares of the underlying stock that an options contract would deliver if exercised. Contract sizes for equity options in the U.S. are generally 100 shares, unless the contract size has been adjusted for a split, merger, or spin-off. For example, if you are long 1 XYZ 50 call with a contract size of 100 and you exercise that call, you will get 100 shares of XYZ for a price of $50 per share. If you are long 1 ABC 90 call with a contract size of 250 and you exercise that call, you will get 250 shares of ABC for a price of $90 per share. Most software incorporates the contract size in the calculation of your delta and gamma.

CONVERSION: A position of long stock, short a call, and long a put (with the call and put having the same strike price, expiration date, and underlying stock). The short call and long put acts very much like short stock, thus acting as a hedge to the long stock. So, a conversion has a very small delta. A conversion is a way to exploit mispricings in carrying costs.

CORRECTION: A temporary reversal of direction of the overall trend of a particular stock or the market in general.

COST BASIS: The original price paid for a stock or option, plus any commissions or fees. It is used to determine capital gains or losses when the stock or option is sold.

COVER: Frequently used to describe the purchase of an option or stock to exit or close an existing short position.

COVERED WRITE OR COVERED CALL OR PUT/COVERD CALL OR PUT WRITING (SELLING): An option strategy composed of a short call option and long stock, or a short put option and short stock. For example, selling (writing) 2 XYZ 50 calls while owning 200 shares of XYZ stock is a covered call position.

COVERED WRITER (SELLER): Someone who sells or "writes" an option is considered to have a "covered" position when the seller of the option holds a position in the underlying stock that offsets the risk of the short option. For example, a short put option is covered by a short position in the underlying stock, and a short call option is covered by a long position in the underlying stock.

CREDIT: An increase in the cash balance of an account resulting from either a deposit or a transaction. As it relates to option orders, a credit is how much the premium collected from selling options exceeds the premium paid for buying options.

CREDIT BALANCE (CR): This is the money the broker owes the customer after all commitments have been paid for in full. The money could come after a sale of securities, or simply be cash in the customer's account.

CREDIT SPREAD: Any option spread where you collect a credit when you execute the spread.

CROSSED MARKET: A situation that occurs on multiple-listed stock and options, where the highest bid price for a stock or option on one exchange is higher than the lowest ask price for that same stock or option on another exchange.

CROSSING ORDERS: The practice of using one customer's orders to fill a second customer's order for the same security on the opposite side of the market. For this to occur each order must be first offered on the exchange floor; if there are no takers, the broker may cross the orders usually at a price somewhere in between the existing bid and ask prices.

CURRENT MARKET VALUE (CMV): The current worth of the securities in an account. The market value of listed securities is based on the closing prices on the previous business day. Syn. long market value (LMV). (NASD)

CUSTOMER: Any person or entity that opens a trading account with a broker-dealer. The customer may be classified in terms of account ownership, payment methods, trading authorization or types of securities traded.

CUSTOMER AGREEMENT: The document a customer signs when opening a margin account with a broker-
dealer; this document allows the firm to liquidate a portion or all of the customer's account if the customer fails to meet margin requirements set by the firm or Exchange.
CUSTOMER STATEMENT: This document displays a customer's trading activity, positions and account balance. The SEC requires the statement be sent quarterly, however, Many firms' customer statements will be sent daily via email or may be accessed on line at anytime day or night.

DATE OF RECORD (RECORD DATE): Date on which you must own shares of a stock to be entitled to the dividend payment on that stock. The day after the record date and until the day the dividend is actually paid, the stock trades ex-dividend.

DAY ORDER: A day order is an order that is "good for the day" and is automatically cancelled if it cannot be executed the day it was placed. Compare to good-til-cancelled (GTC) orders.

DAY TRADE: A stock or option position that is purchased and sold on the same day.

DAY TRADING: Buying and selling the same stock or option position in one day's trading session, thus ending the day with no position.

DEALER: A firm or individual engaged in the business of buying or selling securities for its own account.

DEBIT BALANCE (DR): In a customer's margin account, that portion of the value of stocks that is covered by credit extended by the broker to the margin customer. In other words, the amount of money a customer owes the brokerage firm. (NASD)

DEBIT SPREAD: Any option spread where you pay money for the spread. The debit occurs when the amount of premium paid for the option purchased exceeds the premium received for the option sold.

DECK: The stack of stock or option orders that are to be filled by a broker on the floor of an exchange.

DECLARATION DATE: The date a company announces the payment date, record date and amount of an upcoming dividend.

DEFERRED: Refers to "back month" options or futures.

DELAYED OPENING: Exchange officials can postpone the start of trading on a stock beyond the normal opening of a day's trading session. Reasons for the delay might be an influx of large buy or sell orders, an imbalance of buyers and sellers, or pending important corporate news that requires time to be disseminated.

DELAYED QUOTES: Stock or option price quotes that are delayed by the exchanges 15 or 20 minutes from real-time.

DELIVERY: When referring to stock options, delivery is the process of delivering stock after an option is exercised. If a trader is long a call, and he exercises that call, the person who is short that call must deliver the underlying stock to the trader who is long the call. If a trader is long a put, and he exercises that put, the trader will deliver the underlying stock to the person who is short that put. Actually, the delivery of the stock takes place through clearing firms under very specific terms and procedures established by the exchange where the option is traded. See assignment and exercise.

DELTA: An approximation of the change in the price of an option relative to a change in the price of the underlying stock when all other factors are held constant. For example, if a call has a price of $1.5 and a delta of .33, if the underlying stock moves up $1, the option price would be $1.83 ($1.5 + (.33 x $1.00)). Generated by a mathematical model, delta depends on the stock price, strike price, volatility, interest rates, dividends, and time to expiration. Delta also changes as the underlying stock fluctuates. See gamma.

DERIVATIVE SECURITY: A security whose value is derived from the value and characteristics of another security, called the underlying security. Calls and puts are derivative securities on underlying stocks.

DESIGNATED ORDER TURNAROUND (DOT): NYSE's automated order entry system.

DIALGONAL SPREAD: Long a call (put) in one month and a short call (put) in another month with different strikes

DOUBLE DIAGONAL: Two diagonal spreads, one is in the calls and the other is in the puts. AKA Straddle Strangle Swap or Calendarized Iron Wing Spread. Usually configured as short closer dated straddle or strangle protected by wider strike further dated strangle.

DISCOUNT RATE: The rate that the Federal Reserve Bank charges on short term loans it makes to other banks and financial institutions.

DISCRETIONARY ACCOUNT: An account in which the customer has given the registered representative authority to enter transactions at the rep's discretion.

DIVIDEND: A payment made by a company to its existing shareholders. Dividends are usually cash payments made on a quarterly basis. Dividends can also be in the form of additional shares of stock or property.

DIVIDEND FREQUENCY: Indicates how many times per year (quarterly, semi-annually) a particular stock pays a dividend.

DIVIDEND YIELD: The annual percentage of return that received from dividend payments on stock. The yield is based on the amount of the dividend divided by the price of the stock and of course fluctuates with the stock price.

DON'T KNOW (DK) NOTICE: A term used when brokers or traders compare confirmations on a transaction. If one party receives a confirmation on a trade that it does not recognize, that party would send the other party a D.K. notice.

DOWN-TICK: A term used to describe a trade made at a price lower than the preceding trade. A short sale may not be executed on a down or minus tick.(NASD)

DOWNTREND: Successive downward price movements in a security over time.

DUAL/MULTIPLE LISTED: When the same stock or option is listed on two or more different exchanges. For example, IBM options are traded on the CBOE, PHLX and AMEX.

DUPLICATE CONFIRMATION: SRO regulations require a duplicate confirmation (of a customer's confirmations) be sent to an employing broker-dealer, if the customer is an employee of another broker dealer. Also, this duplicate confirmation may be sent to a customer's attorney if the request is put in writing. (NASD)

EARLY EXERCISE: A feature of American-style options that allows the buyer to exercise a call or put at any time prior to its expiration date.

EQUITY: Equity can have several meanings, including 1) stock, as it represents ownership in a corporation, or 2) in a margin account, equity represents a customer's ownership in his account; it is the amount the trader would keep after all his positions have been closed and all margin loans paid off.

EQUITY OPTIONS: See Stock options.

EUROPEAN-STYLE OPTIONS: An option contract that can only be exercised upon its expiration date. Compare to American-style options.

EXCESS EQUITY: The value of cash or securities held in a margin account that exceeds the federal requirement. (NASD)

EXCHANGE: An association of persons (members) who participate in buying and selling securities. It also refers to the physical location where the buying and selling takes place.

EXCHANGE-LISTED SECURITY: Securities that have met certain requirements and have been admitted for full trading privileges on an exchange such as the NYSE or AMEX. These securities will have a three letter designation (IBM) rather than a four letter designation (MSFT) for over-the-counter securities.

EX-DIVIDEND: Describes a stock whose buyer does not receive the most recently declared dividend. Dividends are payable only to shareholders recorded on the books of the company as of a specific date of record (the "record date"). If you buy the stock any time after the record date for a particular dividend, you won't receive that dividend.

EX-DIVIDEND DATE: The day on and after which the buyer of a stock does not receive a particular dividend. This date is sometimes referred to simply as the "ex-date," and can apply to other situations beyond cash dividends, such as stock splits and stock dividends. On the ex-dividend date, the opening price for the stock will have been reduced by the amount of the dividend, but may open at any price due to market forces.

EXECUTION: The actual completion of an order to buy or sell stock or options.

EXERCISE: If the buyer of a stock option wants to buy (in the case of a call) or sell (in the case of a put) the underlying stock at the strike price or, in the case of a cash-settled option, to receive the index price and the strike price settlement amount, the option must be exercised. To exercise an option, a person who is long an option must give his broker instructions to exercise a particular option (or if the option is ¾ of a point in-the-money at expiration it will be automatically exercised for a customer) Someone with short option positions must be aware of the possibility of being assigned if his short options in-the-money, and he must make sure he has adequate buying power available in his account to cover any such potential assignment.

EXERCISE PRICE (STRIKE PRICE): The cost per share at which the holder of an option may buy or sell the underlying security. (NASD/Options)

EXPIRATION CYCLE: The expiration cycle has to do with the dates on which options on a particular underlying security expire. A stock option, other than LEAPS, will be in one of three cycles, the January cycle (with options listed in January, April, July or October), the February cycle (with options listed in the February, May, August or November) or the March cycle (with options listed in March, June, September or December). At any given time, an option will have contracts with four expiration dates outstanding.

EXPIRATION (EXPIRATION DATE): On the expiration date, an option and the right to exercise it cease to exist. Every option contract becomes null and void after its expiration date. For stock options, this date is the Saturday following the third Friday of the expiration month.

EXTRINSIC VALUE (TIME VALUE): The difference between the entire price of an option and its intrinsic value. For example, if a call option with a strike price of $50 has a price of $2.75, with the stock price at $52, the extrinsic value is $.75. The price of an out-of-the-money (OTM) option is made up entirely of extrinsic value.

FAST MARKET: The exchange declares trading in stocks or options to be in a "fast market" when transactions in the pit occur in such volume and with such rapidity that price reporters are behind in entering quotes. During this time, executing brokers are not held to any fills if a price is traded through on a limit order.

FED FUNDS (FEDERAL FUNDS): The money a bank borrows from another night to meet its overnight reserve requirements.

FED FUNDS RATE: Set by the Federal Reserve Board, the Fed Funds Rate is the rate banks charge each other on overnight loans held the Federal Reserve Bank.

FEDERAL OPEN MARKET COMMITTEE (FOMC): A committee of the Federal Reserve Board which operates by buying and selling government securities in the open market. This buying and selling is how the Federal Reserve Board controls the U.S. money supply. The FOMC decides whether to change the discount rate or not.

FEDERAL RESERVE BOARD (FRB): A seven-member board of governors of the Federal Reserve System, appointed by the U.S. President and confirmed by the Senate, that is responsible for monetary policy within the United States. It controls the supply of money and credit to try to control inflation and create a stable, growing economy.

FENCE: An option and stock position consisting of long stock, long an out-of-the-money put and short an out-of-the-money call, which emulates a bull spread. Alternatively, a reverse fence can be long stock, long in-the-money put and short in-the-money call which emulates a bear spread. All the options have the same expiration date.

FILL: The result of executing an order.

FILL OR KILL (FOK): A type of order that is canceled unless it is executed completely within a designated time period, generally as soon as it is announced by the floor broker to the traders in the pit. Compare to all-or-none (AON).

FLAT: Used to describe an account that has no open positions in stocks or options. Flat can also be regarding a position with little or no delta or gamma.

FLOAT: Number of shares of stock of a corporation that available for public trading.

FLOOR: Physical location of an exchange where the buying and selling of stocks or options takes place.

FLOOR BROKER: A member of an exchange who executes orders on the exchange floor for clearing members or their customers.

FLOOR TRADER: A member of an exchange who trades only for his own or proprietary account. On the CBOE, they are known as "market makers".

FREE CREDIT BALANCE: The amount of cash in a customers account. Broker-Dealers are required to notify customers of their free credit balances at least quarterly..

FROZEN ACCOUNT: An account which requiring cash in advance for a buy order to be executed or securities in hand before a sell order is executed. In most cases customers whose accounts are frozen will be restricted to closing transactions only. (NASD)

FULL POWER OF ATTORNEY: A written authorization for someone other than the beneficial owner of an account to execute trades, make deposits or withdrawals in a customer account. (NASD)

FULL TRADING AUTHORIZATION: An authorization, usually provided by a full power of attorney, which gives someone other than the customer full trading privileges in the account. (NASD)

FUNDAMENTAL RESEARCH: Analysis of companies based on such factors as revenues, expenses, assets, debt level, earnings, products, management, and various financial ratios. As is relates to the economy, fundamental research includes analysis of gross national product, interest rates, unemployment, savings, etc.

FUNDAMENTALS: Factors that are used to analyze a company and its potential for success, such as earnings, revenues, cash flow, debt level, financial ratios, etc.

FUNGIBILITY: Interchangeability resulting from identical characteristics or value. Options on a stock with the same expiration date, type (call or put) and strike price as standardized by the Options Clearing Corporation (OCC) are fungible. Therefore, dual-listed options traded on the CBOE can be liquidated or closed on the AMEX.

FUTURE(S) CONTRACT: A forward contract for the future delivery of a financial instrument (ex. Treasury bond) or physical commodities (corn), traded on a futures exchange (ex. CBOT, CME).

GAMMA: An approximation of the change in the delta of an option relative to a change in the price of the underlying stock when all other factors are held constant. Gamma is accurate for small changes in the price of the underlying stock, but is expressed in terms of a change in delta for a 1 point move in the stock. For example, if a call has a delta of .49 and a gamma of .03, if the stock moves down 1 point, the call delta would be .46 (.49 + (.03 x -$1.00)). Generated by a mathematical model, delta depends on the stock price, strike price, volatility, interest rates, dividends, and time to expiration.

GOOD-TIL-CANCELED (GTC): A type of limit order that is active until it is filled or canceled. As opposed to a day order, a GTC order can remain active for an indefinite number of trading sessions.

GREEKS: Regarding options, it's a colloquial term for the analytic measurements such as delta, gamma, theta, vega and rho, etc.

HANDLE: The whole-dollar part of the bid or offer price. For example, if the bid and offer prices for an option are 3 1/8 bid, offer 3/1/2, the handle is 3.

HEDGE: A position in stock or options that is established to offset the risk of another position in stock or options.

HIGH (H): In reference to the O,H,L,C, "H" represents the high price of the session.

HISTORICAL VOLATILITY: The annualized standard deviation of percent changes in the price of a stock over a specific period. Compare to implied volatility.

HOLDER: Someone who has bought an option or owns a security.

HYPOTHECATION: The act of pledging of securities as collateral, as might be done in a margin account.

IMMEDIATE OR CANCEL (IOC): A type of order that must be filled immediately or be canceled. IOC orders allow partial fills, with the balance of the order canceled.

IMPLIED VOLATILITY: An estimate of the volatility of the underlying stock that is derived from the market value of an option. Implied volatility is the volatility number that, if plugged into a theoretical pricing model along with all the other inputs, would yield a theoretical value of an option equal to the market price of the same option. Compare to historical volatility.

INDEX: A proxy for the overall stock market or segments of the stock market. An index is typically made up of a group of stocks that are selected to represent all stocks in the stock market or market segment (such as technology stocks or big capitalization stocks). The performance of the index gives an idea of how individual stocks might be performing. The S&P 500 (Standard & Poor's 500) and Dow Jones Industrial Average are two well-known indices.

INDEX OPTION: An option that has a stock index as the underlying security. The value of an index option is based on the value of the index. Typically, index options are cash settled options.

INITIAL MARGIN REQUIREMENT: The amount of equity a customer must deposit when making a new purchase in a margin account. For retail customers the SEC 's Regulation T requirement for equity securities currently stands at 50% of the purchase price. In addition, the NASD and NYSE initial margin requirement is a deposit of $2,000 but not more than 100% of the purchase price. Purchases of options must be paid for in full while the sale of naked options is subject to house requirements. Also, the amount of money required to be in an account with a brokerage firm to carry a new position into the next trading day.

INITIAL PUBLIC OFFERING (IPO): A corporation's first sale of stock to the public.

INSTITUTIONAL INVESTORS: Organizations such as mutual funds, pension funds, endowment funds, and insurance companies that typically have very large sums of money to invest.

INTEREST: Money paid when borrowing money or money earned when lending money.

INTEREST RATE: A percentage that is charged when borrowing money, or that is earned when lending money.

INTEREST RATE RISK: Risk that a change in interest rates will cause a position to change in value.

IN-THE-MONEY (ITM): A call option is in-the-money when the price of the underlying stock is greater than the call's strike price. . Conversely, a put option is in-the-money when the price of the underlying stock is lower than the put's strike price. At expiration, options that are ¾ of a point ITM are automatically exercised.

INTRINSIC VALUE: Any positive value resulting from the stock price minus the strike price (for calls) or strike price minus the stock price (for puts). Only in-the-money options have intrinsic value, and intrinsic value can never be zero or less. For example, if a call option with a strike price of $50 has a price of $2.75, with the stock price at $52, the intrinsic value is $2.00. If a put option with a strike price of $15 has a price of $1.50, with the stock price at $14, the intrinsic value is $1.00. Compare to extrinsic value.

INVESTOR: Someone who purchases a stock with the intent of holding it for some amount of time and profiting from the transaction. Compare to day trading.

IRON BUTTERFLY SPREAD: An option spread composed of calls and puts, with long options and short options at three different strikes. The options are all on the same stock and of the same expiration, with the quantity of long options and the quantity of short options netting to zero. The strikes are equidistant from each other. An iron butterfly can be seen as a straddle at the middle strike and a strangle at the outer strikes. For example, a long 50/60/70 iron butterfly is long 1*50 put, short 1*60 call, short 1*60 put, and long 1*70 call. It's important to understand that you buy an iron butterfly for a credit, that is, you take money in when you buy it.

IRON CONDOR SPREAD: An option spread composed of calls and puts, with long options and short options at four different strikes. The options are all on the same stock and of the same expiration, with the quantity of long options and the quantity of short options netting to zero. Generally, the strikes are equidistant from each other, but if the strikes are not equidistant, the spread is called an iron pterodactyl. An iron condor can be seen as a strangle at the middle strike and a strangle at the outer strikes. For example, a long 50/55/60/65 iron condor is long 1*50 put, short 1*55 put, short 1*60 call, and long 1*65 call. It's important to understand that you buy an iron condor for a credit, that is, you take money in when you buy it.

ISSUE: As a verb, when a company offers shares of stock to the public; as a noun, the stock that has been offered by the company.

ISSUER: (1) An entity that offers or proposes to offer its securities for sale. (2) The creator of an option; the issuer of a listed option is the OCC.

JOINT ACCOUNT: An account that has two or more owners who possess some form of control over the account and these individuals may transact business in the account. See also joint tenants.

JOINT TENANTS (JT): A type of account with two owners. There are two types of joint tenant accounts: 1) Joint Tenants With Rights of Survivorship - in the event of the death of one party, the survivor receives total ownership of the account and 2) Joint Tenants in Common - in the event of the death of one party, the survivor receives a fractional interest of the account, the remaining fractional interest goes to the deceased party's estate.

JUNK BOND (HIGH-YIELD BOND): A bond with a credit rating of BB or lower, carrying higher risk of default than investment grade bonds.

KEOGH PLAN: Qualified retirement plan designed for employees of unincorporated businesses or persons who are self-employed, either full-time or part-time.

KNOW YOUR CUSTOMER: The industry rule that requires that each member organization exercise due diligence to learn the more essential facts about every customer.

LAST (PRICE): The price of the last transaction of a stock or option for a trading session.

LAST TRADING DAY: The last business day prior to the option's expiration date during which options can be traded. For equity options, this is generally the third Friday of the expiration month. Note: If the third Friday of the month is an exchange holiday, the last trading day will be the Thursday immediately preceding the third Friday.

LEAPS: An acronym for Long-term Equity AnticiPation Securities. LEAPS are call or put options with expiration dates set as far as two years into the future. They function exactly like other, shorter-term exchange-traded options.

LEG(S) LEGGING: A term describing one option of a spread position. When someone "legs" into a call vertical, for example, he might do the long call trade first and does the short call trade later, hoping for a favorable price movement so the short side can be executed at a better price. Legging is a higher-risk method of establishing a spread position, and RiskDoctor STRONGLY suggests that if you decide to leg into a spread, you should, for margin and risk purposes, do the long trades FIRST.

LEVERAGE: The ability to control of a larger amount of money or assets with a smaller amount of money or assets, typically done by borrowing money or using options. If prices move favorably for a leveraged position, the profits can be larger than on an unleveraged position. However, if prices move against a leveraged position, the losses can also be larger than on an unleveraged position, but not necessarily with an options position. Buying stock on margin is using leverage. A long option position is leveraged because it "controls" a large number of shares with less money than it would take to maintain a position with the same number of shares.

LIMIT MOVE: Relating to futures markets, a limit move is an increase or decrease of a futures price by the maximum amount allowed by the exchange for any one trading session. Price limits are established by the exchanges, and approved by the Commodity Futures Trading Commission (CFTC). Limit moves vary depending on the futures contract.

LIMIT (PRICE) ORDER: An order that has a limit on either price or time of execution, or both. Compare to a market order that requires the order be filled at the most favorable price as soon as possible. Limit orders to buy are usually placed below the current ask price. Limit orders to sell are usually placed above the current bid price. It is wise to use limit orders when trading spreads. In markets with low liquidity or in fast markets, some traders use limits to ensure getting filled by putting in a limit order to buy at or above the ask price or a limit order to sell at or below the bid price.

LIMITED POWER OF ATTORNEY: An authorization giving someone other than the beneficial owner of an account the authority to make certain investment decisions regarding transactions in the customers account.

LIMITED TRADING AUTHORIZATION: This authorization, usually provided by a limited power of attorney, grants someone other than the customer to have trading privileges in an account. These privileges are limited to purchases and sales; withdrawals of assets is not authorized.

LIQUIDATION: A transaction or transactions that offsets or closes out a stock or options position.

LIQUIDITY: The ease with which a transaction in stock or options can take place without substantially affecting their price.

LIQUIDITY RISK: The potential that an investor might not be able to buy or sell a security when desired.

LISTED OPTIONS: An exchange-approved call or put traded on an options exchange with standardized terms. Listed options are fully fungible. In contrast, over-the-counter (OTC) options usually have non-standard or negotiated terms.

LISTED STOCK: The stock of a corporation that is traded on a securities exchange.

LOAN CONSENT AGREEMENT: The agreement between a brokerage firm and its margin customer permitting the brokerage firm to lend the margined securities to other brokers; this contract is part of the margin agreement.

LOAN VALUE: The maximum amount of money that can be borrowed in a margin account at a brokerage firm using eligible securities as collateral.

LOCAL: A term for a trader at the CBOT or CME who trades for his own account. They compete with each other to provide the best bid and ask prices for futures. Locals are basically the same type of traders that market makers are at the CBOE.

LOCKED LIMIT: Refers to a futures market that has moved its daily maximum amount and, if the move is up, no one is willing to sell. Conversely, if the move is down, no one is willing to buy. Hence, the market is "locked" at the limit price with no trading.

LONG: As a noun, it refers to people who have bought stock or options. As an adjective, it refers to a position of long stock or options. Compare to short.

LONG HEDGE: The strategy of buying puts as protection against the decline in the value of long securities.

LONG MARKET VALUE (LMV): See Current Market Value.

LOT: Contract

LOW (L): In reference to the O,H,L,C, "L" represents the low price of the session.

MAINTENANCE MARGIN: An amount of cash or margin-eligible securities that must be maintained on deposit in a customer's account to maintain a particular position. If a customer's equity in his account drops to, or under, the maintenance margin level, the account may be frozen or liquidated until the customer deposits more money or margin-eligible securities in the account to bring the equity above the maintenance margin level.

MARGIN: The amount of equity contributed by a customer (in the form of cash or margin-eligible securities) as a percentage of the current market value of the stocks or option positions held in the customer's margin account.

MARGIN ACCOUNT: An account that allows a customer to borrow money from a brokerage firm against cash and margin-eligible securities held in the customer's margin account at that brokerage firm.

MARGIN BALANCE: The amount a customer has borrowed, using cash or margin-eligible securities as collateral, in his margin account.

MARGIN CALL: A brokerage firm's demand of a customer for additional equity in order to bring margin deposits up to a required minimum level. If the customer fails to deliver more equity in the account, the customer's positions may be liquidated.

MARGIN-ELIGIBLE SECURITIES: Securities, such as stocks or bonds, that can be used as collateral in a margin account. Options are not margin-eligible securities.

MARGIN REQUIREMENT: The minimum equity required in an account to initiate or maintain a position in stock or options.

MARKET: 1) A quote, that is a bid and ask price for a stock or option, ex. the market on the XYZ Dec 75 calls is 2 ½ - 3, or 2) a term for all stocks as a whole, ex. the market is going up means stocks in general are rising, or 3) a place to trade.

MARKET ARBITRAGE: The simultaneous purchase and sale of the same security in different markets to take advantage of price disparity between the two markets. For example, purchasing a call or put on the CBOE subsequently selling the contract at the PHLX at a higher price.

MARKET IF TOUCHED (MIT): A type of stock order that becomes a market order when a particular price on a stock is reached. A buy MIT order is placed below the market; a sell MIT order is placed above the market.

MARKET MAKER: A term for a trader at the CBOE or PCX who trades for his own account. They compete with each other to provide the best bid and ask prices for options to the public.

MARKET ON CLOSE (MOC): An order to buy or sell stock or options at the end of the trading session at a price within the closing range of prices. MOC orders must be placed 45 minutes before the close of trading.

MARKET (PRICE) ORDER: An order to buy or sell stock or options that is to be executed as soon as possible at the best possible price. Compare to a limit order or stop order, which specifies requirements for price or time of execution.

MARK-TO-MARKET: The daily updating of the value of stocks and options to reflect profits and losses in a margin account.

MARRIED PUT: The purchase of a put option and the underlying stock on the same day. Special tax rules may apply to this position.

MERGER: The act of combining two or more corporations into one corporate entity. Options on stocks involved in mergers can be difficult to evaluate.

MINIMUM PRICE FLUCTUATION: The smallest possible increment of price movement for a stock or option. It is often referred to as a "tick".

MODEL: Any one of the various option pricing models used to value options and calculate the "Greeks". Models typically use six factors in their calculations: the underlying stock price, the strike price, the time until expiration, dividends, interest rates, and the volatility of the stock. RiskDoctor uses the Black-Scholes model for European-style options, and the Binomial model for American-style options.

MONEY MARKET FUND: A special type of mutual fund that invests only in short-term, low-risk fixed-income securities, such as bankers' acceptances, commercial paper, repurchase agreements and Treasury bills. The money market fund manager tries to maintain a share price of $1.00. Money market funds are not federally insured, even though the money market fund's portfolio may consist of guaranteed securities.

MULTIPLE LISTED: When the same stock or option is listed on two or more different exchanges. For example, IBM options are traded on the CBOE, PHLX and AMEX.

MULTIPLIER: Refers to the number, typically $100, used to calculate aggregate strike prices and premiums for options. The multiplier affects profit/loss calculations on options positions.

NAKED CALL OR PUT: Refers to a short option position that doesn't have an offsetting stock position. For example, a customer has a naked call if he sells a call without being long the quantity of stock represented by his short call or a long another call spread against it. He has a naked put if he sells a put without being short the quantity of stock represented by his short put or long another put spread against it. Compare to covered call or put.

NATIONAL ASSOCIATION OF SECURITIES DEALERS (NASD): Is an association of brokers and dealers in the over-the-counter (OTC) stock business.

NATIONAL ASSOCIATION OF SECURITIES DEALERS AUTOMATIC QUOTATION SYSTEM (NASDAQ): An electronic information network that provides price quotations to brokers and dealers for the more actively traded common stock issues in the OTC market. There are three levels to the NASDAQ. Level I shows highest bid and lowest ask prices in the system for an OTC stock. Level II shows individual OTC stock market maker's quotes for an OTC stock. Level III is used by OTC stock market makers to enter their quotes into the NASDAQ system.

NET CHANGE: The change in the price of a stock or option from the closing price of the previous day.

NET POSITION: The difference between a customer's open long and open short positions in any one stock or option.

NEW YORK STOCK EXCHANGE (NYSE): Founded in 1792, it is the oldest and largest stock exchange in the United States. Options are not traded on the NYSE.

NOMINAL OWNER: The role of a brokerage firm when customer securities are held in street name.

NON-MARGIN SECURITY: Security that must be paid for in full. Call and put option contracts are examples of this type of security.

NOT HELD ORDER (NH): An order that gives the floor broker discretion on time and price in getting the best possible fill for a customer. When entering a not held order, a customer agrees to not hold the broker responsible if the best price is in not obtained.

NUMBERED ACCOUNT: This account is titled with something other than the account holder's name (for example-symbols or numbers). To open this type of account the customer usually must sign a form designating ownership of the account.

ODD LOT: The purchase or sale of stock in less than the round lot increment of 100 shares.

OEX: OEX is the symbol for the Standard & Poor's 100 cash Index. It is a capitalization-weighted index of 100 stocks from a broad range of industries. Cash-settled, American-style options on the OEX are traded at the CBOE.

OFFER: Another name for the ask price. The price of a stock or option at which a seller is offering to sell.

ONE CANCELS OTHER (OCO): Two orders submitted simultaneously by one customer, where if one order is filled, the other is canceled immediately. A type of order which treats two or more option orders as a package, whereby the execution of any one of the orders causes all the orders to be reduced by the same amount. For example, the investor would enter an OCO order if he/she wished to buy 10 May 60 calls or 10 June 60 calls or any combination of the two which when summed equaled 10 contracts. An OCO order may be either a day order or a GTC order.

OPEN (O), THE: The beginning of the trading session. In reference to the O,H,L,C, "O" represents the opening price of the session.

OPEN EQUITY. The value of all open positions in stock and options, less the margin requirements of those positions.

OPEN INTEREST: The number of outstanding option contracts in a particular class or series. Each opening transaction (as opposed to a closing transaction) has a buyer and a seller, but for the calculation of open interest, only one side of the transaction is counted.

OPEN (PRICE) ORDER: An order that is active until it is either executed or canceled.

OPEN OUTCRY: A public auction, using verbal bids and offers, for stocks or options on the floor of an exchange.

OPEN POSITION: A long or short position in stock or options.

OPENING PRICE/RANGE: The range of the first bid and offer prices made or the prices of the first transactions.

OPENING ROTATION: Process by which options are systematically priced after the opening of the underlying stock.

OPENING TRADE/TRANSACTION: An opening purchase transaction adds long stock or options to a position, and an opening sale transaction adds short stock or options to a position.

OPTION: A call or a put, an option is a contract that entitles the buyer to buy (in the case of a call) or sell (in the case of a put) a number of shares of stock at a predetermined price (strike price) on or before a fixed expiration date.

OPTION CHAIN: A list of all options on a particular stock.

OPTION CLASS: See CLASS OF OPTIONS

OPTION PRICING MODEL: Any one of the various models used to value options and calculate the "Greeks". Models typically use six factors in their calculations: the underlying stock price, the strike price, the time until expiration, dividends, interest rates, and the volatility of the stock. RiskDoctor uses the Black-Scholes model for European-style options, and the Binomial model for American-style options.

OPTIONS CLEARING CORPORATION, THE (OCC): The issuer and registered clearing facility of all options contracts traded on the AMEX, CBOE, PCX, and PHLX. It supervises the listing of options and guarantees performance on option contracts.

OPTIONS DISCLOSURE DOCUMENT: This document is published by The Options Clearing Corporation (OCC) and must be distributed to all customers intending to open an option account.. The document itself outlines the risks and rewards of investing in options. The document is also called the OCC Risk Disclosure Document.

ORDER: An instruction to purchase or sell stock or options.

ORDER BOOK OFFICIAL (OBO): Employees of the exchanges, OBOs manage customers' limit orders on the floor of the exchange.

ORDER FLOW: The orders to buy and sell stock or options that brokers send to market makers.

ORDER ROUTING SYSTEM (ORS): The system utilized by the Chicago Board Options Exchange (CBOE) to collect, store, route and execute orders for customers of the exchange. The ORS system automatically routes option market and limit orders to the various execution vehicles at the CBOE including the RAES system.

OTC OPTION: Options traded in the OTC market. OTC options are not listed on or guaranteed an options exchange and do not have standardized terms, such as standard strike prices or expiration dates. (see Fungibility).

OUT-OF-THE-MONEY (OTM): A call is out-of-the-money when the price of the underlying stock is lower than the call's strike price. A put is out-of-the-money when the price of the underlying stock is higher than the put's strike price. Out-of-the-money options have zero intrinsic value.

OUT-TRADE(S): A situation that results when there is some error on a trade. Differences between the buyer and seller regarding option price, option strike price or expiration month, or underlying stock are some of the reasons an out-trade might occur. Other costly errors occur when there was a buy versus a buy or a sell versus a sell.

OVER-THE-COUNTER (OTC) MARKET: A securities market made up of dealers who may or may not be members of a securities exchange. In the OTC market, there is no exchange floor, such as the NYSE or CBOE.

PACIFIC EXCHANGE (PCX): Located in San Francisco, the PCX is one of four U.S. exchanges that trade equity options.

PARITY: A term used to describe an in-the-money option when the option's total premium is equal to its intrinsic value. Such an option moves 1 point for every 1 point move in the underlying stock, and is said to be "worth parity" or "trading for parity".

PARTIAL FILL: A limit order that is only partially executed because the total specified number of shares of stock or options could not be bought or sold at the limit price.

PAYABLE DATE: Date on which the dividend on a stock is actually paid to shareholders of record. Compare to ex-dividend date and record date.

PHILADELPHIA STOCK EXCHANGE (PHLX): Located in Philadelphia, the PHLX is one of four U.S. exchanges that trade equity options.

PIN RISK: The risk to a trader who is short an option that, at expiration, the underlying stock price is equal to (or "pinned to") the short option's strike price. If this happens, he will not know whether he will be assigned on his short option. The risk is that the trader doesn't know if he will have no stock position, a short stock position (if he was short a call), or a long stock position (if he was short a put) on the Monday following expiration and thus be subject to an adverse price move in the stock.

PLUS TICK or UP TICK: A term used to describe a trade made at a price higher than the preceding trade.

PLUS TICK RULE: SEC regulation governing the market price at which a short sale may be made. Meaning, no short sale may be executed at a price below the price of the last sale. See also down tick or minus tick.

POINT: The minimum change in the handle of a stock or option price. For stock or options in the U.S., a point means $1. If the price of an option goes from $2.00 to $7.00, it has risen 5 points.

POSITION: Long or short stock or options in an account.

POSITION LIMIT: For a single trader, customer, or firm, the maximum number of allowable open option contracts on the same underlying stock. The limits are established by the exchanges.

POSITION TRADING: Establishing a position in stocks or options and holding it for an extended period of time. Compare to day trading.

PREFERRED STOCK: A class of stock (as distinguished from common stock) with a claim on a company's earnings before dividends may be made on the common stock. Preferred stock usually has priority over common stock if the company is liquidated.

PREMIUM: The price of an option.

PRIME RATE: The lowest interest rate commercial banks charge their largest and most credit-worthy corporate customers.

PUT OPTION: A put option gives the buyer of the put the right, but not the obligation, to sell the underlying stock at the option's strike price. The seller of the put is obligated to take delivery of (buy) the underlying stock at the option's strike price to the buyer of the put when the buyer exercises his right.

QUOTE: The bid to buy and the offer to sell a particular stock or option at a given time. If you see a "quote" for an option on the screen "3 ½ - 3 $^7/_8$", it means that the bid price is $3.50 and the ask price is $3.875. This means that at the time the quote was disseminated, $3.50 was the highest price any buyer wanted to pay, and $3.875 was the lowest price any seller would take.

RALLY: A rise in the price of a stock or the market as a whole. Compare to reaction.

RANGE: The high and low prices of a stock or option recorded during a specified time.

RATIO SPREAD: An option position composed of either all calls or all puts, with long options and short options at two different strike prices. The options are all on the same stock and usually of the same expiration, with more options sold than purchased. A ratio spread is the purchase of an option(s) and the sale of a greater number of the same type of options that are out-of-the-money with respect to the one(s) purchased. For example, a 50/60 call 1-by-2 ratio spread is long 1*50 call and short 2*60 calls.

REACTION: A decline in price of a stock or the market as a whole following a rise. Compare to rally.

REALIZED GAINS OR LOSSES: The profit or loss incurred in an account when a closing trade on a stock or option is made and matched with an open position in the same stock or option.

RECORD DATE (DATE OF RECORD): The date by which someone must be registered as a shareholder of a company in order to receive a declared dividend. Compare to ex-dividend date and payment date.

REGISTERED OPTIONS PRINCIPAL: An employee of a brokerage firm who has passed the NASD Series 4 exam, which provides in-depth knowledge related to options. The registered options principal is an officer or partner in a brokerage firm who approves customer accounts in writing.

REGISTERED REPRESENTATIVE: An employee of a brokerage firm who has passed the NASD Series 7 and Series 63 exam.

REGULATION T (REG T): The regulation, established by the Federal Reserve Board, governing the amount of credit that brokers and dealers may give to customers to purchase securities. It determines the initial margin requirements and defines eligible, ineligible, and exempt securities.

REHYPOTHECATION: The practice of pledging a customer's securities as collateral for a bank loan. A brokerage firm may rehypothecate up to 140% of the value of their customers' securities to finance margin loans to customers.

REJECTED ORDER: An order that is not executed because it is invalid or unacceptable in some way.

RESTRICTED ACCOUNT: A margin account in which the equity is less than the REG-T initial requirement. A restricted account will be restricted to closing transactions only.

RETAIL AUTOMATIC EXECUTION SYSTEM (RAES): The system utilized by the CBOE to execute option market and executable limit orders for retail customers received by the exchange's ORS. Retail option orders executed via the RAES system are filled instantaneously at the prevailing market quote and are confirmed almost immediately to the originating firm.

REVERSAL (MARKET REVERSAL): When a stock's direction of price movement stops and heads in the opposite direction.

REVERSAL (REVERSE CONVERSION): A position of short stock, long a call, and short a put (with the call and put having the same strike price, expiration date, and underlying stock). The long call and short put acts very much like long stock, thus acting as a hedge to the short stock. So, a reversal has a very small delta. A reversal is a way to exploit mispricings in carrying costs.

REVERSE SPLIT: An action taken by a corporation in which the number of outstanding shares is reduced and the price per share increases. For example, if a trader were long 100 shares of stock of a company with a price of $80, and that company instituted a 1-for-4 reverse split, the trader would see his position become long 25 shares of stock with a price of $320. The value of the trader's position does not change (unless the price of the stock subsequently changes) and his proportionate ownership in the company remains the same. Compare to stock split.

RHO: An approximation of the change in the price of an option relative to a change in interest rates when all other factors are held constant. This is typically expressed for a one-percent (100 basis point) change in interest rates. For example, if a call has a price of $4.00 and a rho of 0.2, if interest rates rise 1%, the call would have a price of $3.8 ($4.00 – (.2 x 1.00)). Generated by a mathematical model, rho depends on the stock price, strike price, volatility, interest rates, dividends, and time to expiration.

ROLL, THE: An option spread position composed of both calls and puts. The options are all on the same stock and strike price, but on two expirations. The roll is long synthetic stock (long call, short put) at one expiration and short synthetic stock (short call, long put) at another expiration. The quantity of long options and the quantity of short options net to zero. For example, short the SEP/DEC 70 roll is long 1 September 70 call, short 1 September 70 put, short 1 December 70 call, and long 1 December 70 put. The roll is usually executed when someone wishes to roll from a hedge in an expiring month to a hedge in a deferred month for added time.

ROLL, TO: Adjusting or changing a position by closing out an existing option position and substituting it with an option on the same stock but with a different strike price or expiration date.

ROUND LOT: A standard quantity of trading. For example, in U.S. equities, a round lot is 100 shares of stock.

SCALP: A quick entry and exit on a position.

SCALPER/SCALPING: Someone who enters and exits stock or options positions quickly, with small profits or losses, holding a position only for a short time during a trading session.

SEAT: A name for a membership on an exchange.

SECONDARY MARKET: Markets in which securities are bought and sold subsequent to their being sold to the public for the first time.

SECURITIES AND EXCHANGE COMMISSION (SEC): A government agency established by Congress to help protect investors. The SEC regulates the stock, stock options, and bond markets.

SECURITIES INVESTOR PROTECTION CORPORATION (SIPC): This is a nonprofit corporation created by an act of congress to protect clients of a brokerage firms that are forced into bankruptcy. SIPC provides customers of these firms up to $500,000 coverage for cash and securities held by the firms, however, of that $500,000 only $100,000 in cash is covered.

SECURITY: A generic term for investment or trading vehicles. Securities can be stock, bonds, or derivative securities such as options or futures.

SEGREGATION: The holding of customer-owned securities separate from securities owned by other customers and securities by the brokerage firm.

SELF REGULATORY ORGANIZATION (SRO): Organizations accountable to the SEC for the enforcement of federal securities laws and the supervision of securities practices within their assigned fields of jurisdiction. Examples of these organizations are: NASD, NYSE and the CBOE.

SERIES: All option contracts of the same class that also have the same exercise price and expiration date.

SETTLEMENT: The conclusion of a stock or options trade through the transfer of the security (from the seller) or cash (from the buyer).

SETTLEMENT DATE: Date on which a transaction must be settled. Buyers pay for securities with cash and sellers deliver securities.

SETTLEMENT PRICE: The closing price of a stock or option used for account statements and to calculate gains and losses in an account.
SHARES: Stock.

SHORT: As a noun, it refers to people who have sold stock or options without owning them first. As an adjective, it refers to a position of short stock or options. Compare to long.

SHORT COVERING: Buying stock or options to close out a short position.

SHORT HEDGE: The selling of options as protection against a decrease in value of a long securities position.

SHORT INTEREST: The number of shares of stock that have been sold short is known as a stock's short interest.

SHORT SELLER: Someone who sells stock or options without owning them first. The short seller looks to profit from buying the stock or options back later at a price lower than where he sold it.

SHORT SQUEEZE: When traders who have sold a stock short start to lose profits or incur losses as the stock begins to rise, sometimes dramatically. The short sellers are forced to buy back their short stock positions in order to limit their losses.

SINGLE ACCOUNT: An account type in which only one individual has control over the investments and may transact business.

SKEW: See volatility skew.

SKIP-STRIKE-FLY: Butterfly configuration with a skipped strike. The result is a convoluted butterfly with many baby butterflies embedded within.

SLINGSHOT, SLINGSHOTHEDGE™: Position that behaves like a butterfly and an extra call and/or extra put. It can be performed with options only or with the underlying included.

SLIPPAGE: The difference between the price someone might expect to get filled at on an order, and the actual, executed price of the order.

SPECIAL MEMORANDUM ACCOUNT (SMA): A line of credit in a customer's margin account, it's a limit on the amount of money a customer can borrow against collateral in the account.

SPECIALIST: Members of the NYSE, PHLX, and AMEX whose function is to maintain a fair and orderly market by managing the limit order book and making bids and offers in a particular stock or class of options.

SPECULATOR: Someone who buys or sells stocks or options hoping to profit from favorable moves in their price or volatility. Generally, a speculator does not hedge his positions.

SPIN-OFF: When a corporation divides its assets into two companies, one the original company and the other a new, independent company. Shares of stock in the new company are issued to stockholders of the original corporation.

SPLIT: An action taken by a corporation in which the number of outstanding shares is increased and the price per share decreases. For example, if a trader were long 100 shares of stock of a company with a price of $120, and that company instituted a 3-for-1 split, the trader would see his position become long 300 shares of stock with a price of $40. The value of the trader's position does not change (unless the price of the stock subsequently changes) and his proportionate ownership in the company remains the same. Compare to reverse split.

SPREAD: 1) a position or order involving two or more different options or stock and options (see leg), or 2) the difference between the bid and offer prices of a stock or option.

SPREAD ORDER: A type of order specifying two different option contracts on the same underlying security.

SPX: SPX is the symbol for the Standard & Poor's 500 cash index. It is a capitalization-weighted index of 500 stocks from a broad range of industries. Cash-settled, European-style options on the SPX are traded at the CBOE.

"SPYDERS" (SPDR): Standard & Poor's Depository Receipts are pooled investments that trade like a stock, and are designed to provide investment results that generally correspond to one of the Standard and Poor's indices.

STATEMENT: A summary of a brokerage account's activity and balances.

STOCK: Another name for equity, it is a security that represents ownership in a corporation.

STOCK OPTIONS: Calls or puts with the right to buy or sell individual stocks.

STOP LIMIT (PRICE) ORDER: A type of order that turns into a limit order to buy or sell stock or options when and if a specified price is reached. Stop limit orders to buy stock or options specify prices that are above their current market prices. Stop limit orders to sell stock or options specify prices that are below their current market prices.

STOP (STOP LOSS) ORDER: A type of order that turns into a market order to buy or sell stock or options when and if a specified "stop" price is reached. Stop orders to buy stock or options specify prices that are above their current market prices. Stop orders to sell stock or options specify prices that are below their current market prices.

STRADDLE: An option position composed of calls and puts, with both calls and puts at the same strike. The options are on the same stock and of the same expiration, and either both long or both short with the quantity of calls equal to the quantity of puts (with the exception of a ratioed straddle). For example, a long 50 straddle is long 1*50 call and long 1*50 put. A long straddle requires a large move in the stock price, an increase in implied volatility or both for profitability, while a short straddle performs well when the stock is in during a tight trading range, decreased implied volatility or both.

STRADDLE STRANGLE SWAP: AKA Double Diagonal or Calendarized Iron WingSpread. Usually configured as short closer dated straddle or strangle protected by wider strike further dated strangle.

STRANGLE: An option position composed of calls and puts, with both out-of-the-money calls and out-of-the-money puts at two different strikes. The options are on the same stock and of the same expiration, and either both long or both short with the quantity of calls equal to the quantity of puts (with the exception of a ratioed strangle). For example, a short 50/70 strangle is short 1*50 put and short 1*70 call. A long strangle requires a large move, an increase in implied volatility or both for profitability, while a short strangle performs well during a tight trading range, decreased implied volatility or both.

STREET NAME: Securities held in the name of a brokerage firm on behalf of a customer. This is required for margin accounts, and facilitates delivery for stock transactions.

STRIKE PRICE: The pre-determined price at which underlying stock is purchased (in the case of a call) or sold (in the case of a put) when an option is exercised.

SYMBOLS: Every corporation whose stock is traded on the NYSE, AMEX or NASDAQ, and every option traded on the CBOE, AMEX, PHLX, or PCX is given a unique identification symbol of up to five letters. Generally, these symbols abbreviate the corporation's complete name and, in the case of options, their strike price, expiration date, and whether they are calls or puts.

SYNTHETIC: Creating a position that emulates another by combining at least two of calls, puts or stock that acts very much like a position of outright stock, calls or puts.

SYNTHETIC LONG CALL: An option position composed of long puts and long stock. The quantity of long puts equals the number of round lots of stock. For example, long 5 synthetic 70 calls at can be created by being long 5*70 puts and long 500 shares of stock.

SYNTHETIC LONG PUT: An option position composed of long calls and short stock. The quantity of long calls equals the number of round lots of stock. For example, long 8 synthetic 80 puts at can be created by being long 8*80 calls and short 800 shares of stock.

SYNTHETIC LONG STOCK: An option position composed of long calls and short puts on the same stock, strike price and expiration. The quantity of long options and the quantity of short options nets to zero. For example, long 500 shares of synthetic stock can be created by being long 5*70 calls and short 5*70 puts. See combo.

SYNTHETIC SHORT CALL: An option position composed of short puts and short stock. The quantity of short puts equals the number of round lots of stock. For example, short 3 synthetic 60 calls at can be created by being short 3*60 puts and short 300 shares of stock.

SYNTHETIC SHORT PUT: An option position composed of short calls and long stock. The quantity of short calls equals the number of round lots of stock. For example, short 4 synthetic 70 calls at can be created by being short 4*70 calls and long 400 shares of stock.

SYNTHETIC SHORT STOCK: An option position composed of short calls and long puts on the same stock, strike price and expiration. The quantity of long puts and the quantity of short calls nets to zero. For example, short 400 shares of synthetic stock can be created by being short 4*70 calls and long 4*70 puts. See combo.

SYSTEMATIC RISK: The broad macroeconomic factors that affect all companies in a stock market. It is also known as market risk. Theoretically, it's the risk in a portfolio that cannot be reduced through diversification. Compare to unsystematic risk.

TECHNICAL ANALYSIS: Calculations that use stock price and volume data to identify patterns helping to predict future stock movements. Some technical analysis tool include moving averages, oscillators, and trendlines.

TENDER OFFER: An offer from one company to buy shares of stock of another company from that other company's existing stockholders. Those stockholders are asked to "tender" (surrender) their shares for a specific price (represented by cash, shares in another company, or both), which is usually higher than the current market price of the stock.

THEORETICAL VALUE: An estimated price of a call or put derived from a mathematical model, such as the Black-Scholes or binomial models.

THETA: An approximation of the decrease in the price of an option over a period of time when all other factors are held constant. Theta is generally expressed on a daily basis. For example, if a call has a price of $3.00 and a theta of 0.10, one day later, with all else unchanged, the call would have a price of $2.90 ($3.00 – (.10 x 1)). Generated by a mathematical model, theta depends on the stock price, strike price, volatility, interest rates, dividends, and time to expiration.

TICK: The smallest possible price increment for a stock or option.

TICKER: The telegraphic system which prints or displays last sale prices and volume of securities transactions on exchanges on a moving tape within a minute after each trade. Also known as the "tape".

TIME AND SALES: A record of the time, price and volume of each transaction of every stock and option.

TIME DECAY: Option price erosion over time. Another name for theta.

TIME SPREAD: Another name for calendar spread.

TIME VALUE: Another name for extrinsic value.

TRADING AUTHORIZATION: Written permission from the owner of an account authorizing another person to enter trades on behalf of the owner. Also called Power of Attorney.

TRADING FLOOR: The part of an exchange where the stocks and options are actually bought and sold.

TRADING HALT: A temporary suspension of trading in a particular stock due anticipation of a major news announcement or an imbalance of buy and sell orders.

TRADING PIT: A particular location on the trading floor of an exchange designated for the trading of a specific stock or options on a specific stock or index.

TRANSFER AGENT: Usually a division of a large bank or other financial institution that keeps records of the names of registered shareholders of a particular stock, the shareholders' addresses, the number of shares owned by each shareholder, and oversees the transfer of stock certificates from one shareholder to another.

TREASURY STOCK: Shares of stock issued by a company but later bought back by the company. These shares may be held in the company's treasury indefinitely, used for employee bonus plans, reissued to the public, or retired. Treasury stock is ineligible to vote or receive dividends.

TREND: Either an uptrend or a downtrend, successive price movements in the same direction in a security over time

TRUST: A legal relationship in which a person or entity (the trustee) acts for the benefit of someone else.

TYPE: The classification of an option as either a call or a put.

UNCHED: When the market is unchanged.

UNCOVERED CALL OR PUT: Another term for naked call or put.

UNDERLYING (STOCK OR SECURITY): The stock or other security that determines the value of a derivative security and that (with the exception of cash-settled options) would be purchased or sold if an option on that underlying stock or security was exercised. Examples of underlying securities are stocks, bonds, futures and indices.

UNSYSTEMATIC RISK: The company-specific microeconomic factors that affect an individual stock. Theoretically, it's the risk in a portfolio that can be reduced through diversification. Compare to systematic risk.

UP-TICK: A term used to describe a trade made at a price higher than the preceding trade.

UPTREND: Successive upward price movements in a security over time.

VEGA: An approximation of the change in the price of an option relative to a change in the volatility of the underlying stock when all other factors are held constant. This is typically expressed for a one-percent change in volatility. For example, if a call has a price of $2.00 and a vega of .65, if volatility rises 1%, the call would have a price of $2.65 ($2.00 + (.65 x 1.00)). Generated by a mathematical model, vega depends on the stock price, strike price, volatility, interest rates, dividends, and time to expiration.

VERTICAL: An option position composed of either all calls or all puts, with long options and short options at two different strikes. The options are all on the same stock and of the same expiration, with the quantity of long options and the quantity of short options netting to zero. A long call vertical (bull spread) is created by buying a call and selling a call with a higher strike price. A short call vertical (bear spread) is created by selling a call and buying a call with a higher strike price. A long put vertical (bear spread) is created by buying a put and selling a put with a lower strike price. A short put vertical (bull spread) is created by selling a put and buying a put with a lower strike price. For example, a short 70/80 put vertical is long 1*70 put and short 1*80 put.

VIX (VOLATILITY INDEX): Created by the CBOE, the VIX is an index of volatility calculated from the implied volatility of the OEX index options.

VOLATILITY: Generically, volatility is the size of the changes in the price of the underlying security. In practice, volatility is presented as either historical or implied.

VOLATILITY SKEW: Volatility skew, or just "skew", arises when the implied volatilities of options in one month on one stock are not equal across the different strike prices. For example, there is skew in XYZ April options when the 80 strike has an implied volatility of 45%, the 90 strike has an implied volatility of 47%, and the 100 strike has an implied volatility of 50%. If the implied volatilities of options in one month on one stock ARE equal across the different strike prices, the skew is said to be "flat". You should be aware of volatility skew because it can dramatically change the risk of your position when the price of the stock begins to move.

VOLUME: The total number of shares of stock or option contracts traded on a given day.

WARRANT: A security issued by a corporation that gives the holder the right to purchase securities at a specific price within a specified time limit (or sometimes with no time limit). Warrants are sometimes like call options, but the main differences are that warrants typically have much longer lives whereas options tend to expire relatively soon, and that warrants are issued by a company to raise money whereas options are created by the OCC.

WRITE/WRITER: An individual who sells an option short.

I N D E X

Adjustment, 1-2, 15, 29-46, 91, 110, 128, 129-132, 136, 142, 144, 146, 151, 168-170, 185, 191, 210, 222, 227-229, 312-3, 317, 321, 324-5, 350, 352

Arb, Arbitrage, Arbitrageurs, 5, 37, 89-90, 203, 210, 219-220, 238-39, 241, 364-365, 368, 388

Assignment, (Exercise), 10, 12, 53, 77-90, 115, 120, 152, 180-182, 190, 204, 211-217, 247, 364, 366, 369, 372, 375, 377, 378, 401

Automatic exercise, 10, 90, 364

Back end deal, 221

Back spreads, 35, 111, 130, 135-7, 147, 151, 186

Banking, 77, 90, 198, 200

Basis of one method, 141

Bear Collar, (see Collar)

Bear Spread, (see Vertical Spread)

Bid/Ask Spread, 115, 120, 132, 197, 366

Binomial model, 8, 50, 182, 204, 208, 215, 216, 311-312, 366, 389, 392, 402

Black-Scholes, 8, 48-50, 56-62, 66-8, 70-73, 78-9, 84, 123, 198, 202-4, 213-5, 366, 389, 392, 402

Box Spreads, BoxTool, Boxes, Box Dissection, 1, 5, 11, 13, 14, 15, 17-19, 31-36, 77, 90, 116-117, 119-120, 130, 132, 134, 152-154, 166-167 171, 174, 189, 196, 200-201, 209-210, 213-218, 220, 222-4, 229, 250-252, 316, 352, 367

Bull Collar, (see Collar)

Bull spread, (see Vertical Spread)

Butterfly, Iron Butterfly (Wingspread), 19-27, 36, 46, 98, 117, 136-138, 140, 148-179, 185-187, 190-193, 221, 222, 229-30, 233, 236, 237, 245-246, 271, 314, 316, 325, 327, 332, 353-4, 358-359, 367-368, 383, 399

Buy-write (covered write), 2-4, 15, 22, 30, 44, 46, 125, 218, 222, 355, 368, 373

Calendar risk, 184-5

Calendar spreads, 15, 27, 111, 130, 132, 170, 180-195, 227-8, 236, 351, 368, 376, 401

Call, 9, 12, 22, 38, 45-46, 47-48, 360
    P&L Graph, 22, 49

Call-Put parity, (see Parity Options)

Cap and Floor, (see Collar)

Carding trades, 11-12

Carry Cost , (see Cost of Carry)

Cash settlement, Cash settled, 53, 76, 78 (OEX), 209-212, 369, 390

Christmas Tree, 26, 243

Collar, (Fence or Tunnel or Cap and Floor), 23, 115-127, 226-227
Combo, Same Strike, 13, 15, 21, 40, 109, 113-114, 180-184, 202-205, 209-213, 223, 371, 402
Combo, Off Strike, 125-127, 338
Condor, Iron Condor, Stretched-Out Condors, 15, 24, 27, 148-154, 161, 166-168, 171, 190-194, 274-276, 319-349, 351, 371, 372, 383-384,
Conversion/Reversal, 1, 5-17, 30, 44, 46, 77, 79, 81-83, 87-88, 90, 116, 171, 174, 182, 196-222, 224, 229, 312, 339, 356, 362, 372
Cost of Carry, 7, 38, 53, 75-90, 111, 117, 119, 167, 180, 182, 186, 200-204, 207, 211, 213, 215-217, 224, 230, 247, 252, 369, 372, 396
Covered write, 2-4, 15, 22, 30, 44, 46, 125, 218, 222, 355, 368, 373
Crashes, 4, 12, 74, 95, 115, 142, 145, 146, 239, 247, 265, 270, 276, 289
Credit (Spreads traded for a credit), 7-11, 21, 23-24, 125-128, 133, 136-137
Curvature, Curve, 97, 107-108, 124, 192, 213-214

DARTS (Dynamic Adjustable Risk Transactions), 28, 238
Decay, (see Theta)
Delta, 47-60, 65, 74, 92, 100-111, 122-123, 137-139, 154-156, 160, 185-186, 204, 212, 242-243, 313, 317-318, 328-346, 375, 381
Diagonal, Double Diagonal, 27, 180, 188-195, 376, 401
Diamonetrics™, Diamonetric Grid™, 148, 170-171, 174, 350-351
Discipline, 2, 65, 85, 105,132, 135, 218
Dissection, Dissecting positions, 1-5, 9-18, 31-37, 78, 91, 106, 129, 148, 170-179, 181-193, 213,229, 229-236, 244, 350-352, 353-362
Dividend, 3, 5, 7, 38, 53-54, 74-77, 79-80, 198-199, 207-211, 224, 363, 366, 374, 375, 376, 377-378, 395
   Dividend risk, 53
   Ex-date, ex-dividend date, 53, 75, 77, 208, 374, 377-378
   International dividends, 76
   Payable date, 75, 393
   Record date, 75-76 374, 375, 378, 393, 395
Double Diagonal, (see Diagonal)
Early exercise, 9, 47, 75, 78-80, 84,102, 115, 117, 182, 186, 211-215, 247, 312, 366, 377
Edge, 6, 115, 140, 197
European-style vs. American-style, 78-79, 81, 196, 213, 215, 224, 247, 366, 377, 389, 400
Ex-dividend date, ex-date, 53, 75, 77, 208, 374, 377-378
Exercise, (Assignment), 10, 12, 53, 77-90, 115, 120, 152, 180-182, 190, 204, 211-217, 247, 364, 366, 369, 372, 375, 377, 378, 401
Extrinsic premium, 120, 201, 230, 379, 393 403,

Fair value, 6-10, 77, 111, 132-133, 163, 198, 201-203, 206-207, 214, 216, 224, 238

Fence, (see Collar)

Flat, Flatten, Flattening, 7, 9, 11, 18, 46, 54, 65. 79, 88, 100, 105-106, 142-146

Flight to Quality (Rocket to Quality), 74, 145-146, 240

Gamma, 50-52, 59-65, 91 (Grammas), 96-103, 122-124, 136-139, 156-157, 165, 186, 181, 381

Gamma scalping, 59-60, 65, 87-88, 90, 92, 95, 100-110, 116, 129-130, 228

Guts, 18-19, 22, 39, 129

Greeks, 47, 50-51-74, 91, 97, 98, 122-123, 137-139, 154-160, 179, 201, 237, 239, 242, 246, 381

Hedge, 4, 20, 28, 37, 40, 44-46, 113-114, 125-127, 136, 147, 200, 204, 209, 212, 226-236, 350, 351, 353-362, 372, 381, 387, 398, 399

Implied volatility, 16, 34-35, 47, 50-55, 58-60, 62-63, 68-69, 72-74, 92-95, 97-98, 100-101, 105-106, 106-110, 115-121, 132-133, 144, 156, 164-165, 181-187, 190-194, 211-212, 225, 228, 235, 240-247, 271, 276, 321-322, 381, 382, 400, 401, 405

Implied volatility skew, 16, 53, 97-98, 119-120, 137, 144, 186, 191, 195, 225, 237-307, 405

Intrinsic premium, 9, 92, 120, 201, 210, 212, 364, 379, 383, 393

Iron Butterfly, (see Butterfly)

Iron Calendar, (see Double Diagonal)

Iron Condor, (see Condor)

Jelly roll, 1, 5, 13, 15, 180-184, 189, 209, 218

Leg, legging, legged, 28, 43, 112-113, 131-135, 141, 216, 316-317, 321, 327, 338-340, 344, 385

Liquidity, 52, 131, 146, 197-198, 222, 385, 386

Lock, locking in, locked positions, 1, 5-7, 10-11, 13, 17-18, 37, 44, 77-78, 83-84, 113, 120, 145, 147, 190, 196, 200, 205, 222, 224, 238-239,

Locked Limit, 386

Market Maker, 6-7, 32, 37, 52, 54, 74, 92, 97, 100, 115, 131-136, 140-141, 152, 178, 196-225, 232, 240-241, 289-294, 307, 312, 350, 380, 386, 388, 389, 392

Married put, 20, 22, 226, 230, 388

Naked, 3-4, 16, 32, 79, 91, 95-96, 105, 115, 132-136, 143, 146, 179, 181, 218, 226-227, 313-317, 338, 341, 382, 389, 404
Net, net calls and puts, net contract exposure, net units, 11-13, 33, 53, 96, 107-110, 129-130, 144-146, 177, 230, 233, 402
Non-transparent, 5, 83, 111, 180
Not held, 89, 379, 390

OEX, (XEO), 53, 175, 185, 196, 209-212, 369, 390, 405
Off-strike combo, 26, 125-127, 289-297
Omega, (see Vega)
Opening Rotation, 131, 391
Options Metamorphosis, 44-47, 319-329
OO's (Options Only Strategies), 28

Parity Options, 1, 9, 12, 14, 78-82, 186, 210, 212, 393
Partial tender offer (see Tender offer)
Payable date, 75, 208, 377, 393
Pin risk, 9-10, 53, 86-87, 90, 134, 393
Position adjustments, (see adjustments)
Position dissection, (see Dissections)
Pregnant butterfly, 166, 169-170
Premium, Time Premium, 3-4, 11, 32, 36, 43, 48-52, 59-60, 65, 80-81, 92-111, 115-129, 136-138, 162, 165, 184-186, 200, 217, 222, 225, 239, 313, 314, 340-343, 351, 393, 394
Premium to Cash, 210-211
Profit-and-loss (P&L) (P/L) profile, 19-28, 44-46, 47-49, 93-94, 107-108, 116, 123, 126, 128, 130, 137, 142, 149-150, 152, 164, 167-170, 175, 177-178, 185, 188, 193-195, 208, 231-235, 248-306
Put, 9, 12, 22, 38, 45-46, 47-48, 360
    P&L Graph, 22, 48
    Married put, 20
Put-call parity, (see Parity Options)

Quote, 43, 54, 98, 115, 120, 131-133, 135, 140-141, 215-216, 375, 379, 388, 389, 394, 396

Rate of return, 3, 44, 51, 364
Ratioed straddle, 40, 92, 106-110, 322, 331, 400
Ratio Spread, 25, 30, 33, 34-36, 39, 46, 74, 131, 135-138, 140-147, 277-283, 289, 294, 356, 359, 394-395
Raw position, 1, 9, 11, 15, 17-18, 32-33, 176, 179, 230
Record date, 75-76, 207, 374, 375, 377-378, 393, 394, 395, 403
Rent-a-Call, Rent-an-option, 75, 77, 80-86, 89-90, 217
    Futures options, 80-86

Stock options, 89-90
Reversal/ Conversion, 1, 5-17, 30, 44, 46, 77, 79, 81-83, 87-88, 90, 116, 171, 174, 182, 196-222, 224, 229, 312, 339, 356, 362, 372
Renting Options, 80-89
Reverse Collar, Fence or Tunnel, (see Collar)
Rho, 50, 52, 74, 77, 200, 209, 217, 396
Risk Reversal, Risk Conversion, 26, 244, 289-294
Risk management, 33, 65, 117, 178, 181, 351
Risk reversal/conversion, 26, 289-294
Risk conversion/reversal, 26, 289-294
Risk profiles, (see Profit and Loss Profiles)
Rolling, 42, 115, 127-129, 183-184, 191-192, 228, 234, 244, 342

Scalp gammas, (see Gamma Scalping)
Semi-Stock, 26, 289-297
Settlement Date, 75-76, 363, 398
Skew, (see Implied Volatility Skew)
Skip-Strike-Fly, 172-178, 399
Slingshot (SlingshotHedge™) 27, 226-236, 399
Smile, (see Implied Volatility Skew)
Story,
        Better To Be Late For The Early Exercise, 80-89
        Covered-Write, 2-3
        Crashes, Takeovers, Shortages, and Flight to Quality, 145
        Liquidity and the Bid/Ask Spread, 197-198
        Reversal's Revenge, 204
        Mishandled Reversal, 78
        Missing The Hedge, 113-114
        Profit by Exercising, 216
        Renting Options, 80-89
        Scalping Gammas In My Sleep, 100-110
        Thanks for the Loan Dude, 224-225
        The Chiron Deal, 220-222
        The Edge as Defined by Airport Banks, 6,
        The Ugly Butterfly, 162-166
        Trading Barrage (Example), 29-32
        Uh-OEX, 211-212
Straddle, 16, 17, 22, 31, 34, 40, 45-46, 92-114, 130, 151, 154, 165, 184, 190, 193-194, 259-261, 313, 335, 342, 353-355, 357-359, 383, 400, 401
Straddle Strangle Swap,   (see Double Diagonal)
Strangle, Guts Strangle (see Guts) 22, 27, 39-40, 46, 92-114, 129-130, 154, 167, 190-195, 262-264, 353-354, 357-359, 360, 376, 383, 384, 401

Stress testing (see What-if)

Synthetic positions, 1-4, 15-17, 19-28, 37-41, 78, 80-86, 115-116, 125, 131-134, 169, 177, 190, 230, 233, 340-343, 401, 402
Synthetic Underlying, 13, 15, 21, 40, 53, 109, 113-114, 180-185, 202-205, 209-213, 223, 371, 402
SynTool, 14-17, 171, 229-233, 352-362
Tender offer, 3, 77, 92, 218-223, 402
Theta, Time Decay, 21, 47, 50-51, 65-69, 92, 95, 99, 100, 102, 115-116, 122-125, 137-139, 165, 181, 186, 189, 191, 201, 230, 234, 236, 310, 313, 323, 336, 342, 350, 381, 402-403
Theoretical values (TV), 8-9, 55, 88, 202, 218, 243, 382, 402
Time Decay, (see Theta)
Time Spreads, (see Calendar)
Top picking, 96
Tunnel, (see Collar)

Vega, 47-52, 60, 69-74, 97-102, 122-124, 137-139, 156-158, 186-190, 246, 310, 313, 404
Vertical Spread, 20, 23-24, 26, 30-31, 39, 46, 115-147, 151-152, 154, 162, 167, 175, 213, 228, 230, 237, 265, 270, 314, 320, 334, 336-341, 344, 354-61, 366, 379, 405
Volatility (see Implied Volatility)

Webinars, 96, 350, (see also www.riskdoctor.com/webinars.html)
What- if Scenario, , 9-10, 50, 54, 143-144, 195, 246
Wings, 20-24, 27, 96-98, 148-151, 153-154, 160, 167, 169, 175-176, 190-192, 314
Wingspread, (see Butterfly)

Underlying, (see Synthetic Underlying)